UGC NET

Paper - 1 (Common For All)

Latest Edition
Practice Kit

20 Tests
20 Mock Test

Based On Real Exam Pattern

✓ Thoroughly Revised and Updated

✓ Detailed Analysis of all MCQs

Title : UGC NET Paper - 1 (Common For All)
Author Name : Mr. Rohit Manglik
Published By : EduGorilla Community Pvt. Ltd.
Publishers Address : 12/651, First Floor Opp. Arvindo Park, Near Jama Masjid, Indira Nagar, Lucknow, Uttar Pradesh-226016, India

Copyright EduGorilla

ISBN : 978-93-90893-87-4
Second Edition

Disclaimer EduGorilla

Compiled and created by EduGorilla Community Pvt. Ltd

Printed By EduGorilla Community Pvt. Ltd.

ROHIT MANGLIK
CEO, EduGorilla

Editor's Note

Dear Applicants,

People say *"Success comes to those who work hard."* But I've seen people working hard for their exams day in and day out for marginal success. While others succeed in their examinations by putting in just half the work. So are they God Gifted? No! I believe that it's because they work *smart* and not just *hard*. Similarly, for your exams, you should strategize your preparation so as to increase the likelihood of success. Well with EduGorilla get ready to increase your *chances of selection* in your exam by *16x*.

EduGorilla helps you in not only working *hard* but also working in a *smart and strategic* manner. With EduGorilla's preparation package, you get a chance to make your exam preparation easy, and a fun learning path towards selection. Finding the right path to your preparations can be difficult if you don't know in which direction to head. Don't worry, we have you covered! EduGorilla will be your guide to success in your journey. With our Preparation Package, you can prepare strategically and beat the exam in just one attempt.

EduGorilla's Preparation Package includes-

- **Test Series**
- **Books**

Our preparation package is handcrafted as per the latest changes, expert opinions, and students' discretion. Thus, enabling you to get through each stage of the selection process for your exam.

Our Books are designed by the teachers and experts of the respective exam with a combined 150+ years of experience; to provide you with easy, efficient, and effective learning. Our books are smart, in the sense that not only do they give you the answers to the questions but also provide similar questions for practice.

EduGorilla's competent Test Series gives you real-time experience and confidence through which you can clear your offline or online exam in just one attempt. We currently host 83,000+ mock tests for 1,440+ competitive and academic exams.

Thus, EduGorilla misses no chance to assist you in your preparation and covers all stages of the exam, so that you don't have to look anywhere else.

We provide complete preparation packages for defense, banking, teaching, and other National & State-Level exams. Hence, it doesn't matter which exam you aspire to because you will reach your success.

ALL THE BEST !

Let EduGorilla be your Guide to Success.

Rohit Manglik,
Founder and CEO, EduGorilla

INTRODUCTION

EduGorilla focuses on guiding students to succeed in their examinations. With that in mind, our book, titled "UGC NET : Paper - 1 (Common For All)", has been drafted through the collective efforts of our distinguished experts with 150+ years of combined experience. This book consists of questions that are created following the latest changes in the syllabus and exam pattern. We compiled the book on the basis of questions that are most likely to appear in the UGC NET Paper I. Through EduGorilla's "UGC NET : Paper - 1 (Common For All)" your chances of success will increase 16x.

EduGorilla does this through our Complete Preparation Package. This package consists of well-conceptualized and structured content in the form of questions that are tailor-made according to your needs and will help you practice for exams in a smart way by pinpointing all the necessary information. It also provides hints and solutions, along with a smart answer sheet for your self-evaluation. You can assess your shortcomings and work accordingly on areas that may require more of your attention.

EduGorilla promises to help you succeed in your examination and accomplish your dream goals. We believe in our aspirants and see them at the top of the merit list. And the first step towards the top is to start preparing with us. EduGorilla's "UGC NET : Paper - 1 (Common For All)" includes the following attributes.

- Well-Researched Content
- Top-Notch Quality
- Detailed Answers and Analysis
- Smart Answer Sheet
- Exam Relevant Questions

Therefore, EduGorilla fortifies your preparation and makes it durable enough to help you stand tall and beat the examination.

UGC NET Paper I

Scan QR code for Eligibility, Exam Pattern, Syllabus and more.

Book ID: 0719

TABLE OF CONTENTS

Mock Test 01

Q.1 What should be the main objective of teaching?

A. Prepare students to pass the examination
B. To dictate good notes
C. Provide required information related to the subject
D. To develop the thinking power of students

Q.2 Asking an open-ended question for gaining feedback can be classified as a ______ question.

A. Contradictory **B.** Polemic
C. Rudimentary **D.** Rhetorical

Q.3 Flak in media communication often refers to ________.

A. Propaganda **B.** Criticism
C. Feedback **D.** Advertising

Q.4 Which of the following statements is not true?

A. Upward communication is when the teacher communicates with the head of the department.
B. Horizontal communication is when the teacher communicates with other teachers.
C. Upward communication is also called diagonal communication.
D. Horizontal communication is also called lateral communication.

Q.5 Which of these would count as 'good communication strategies'?

i. Changing your tone
ii. Giving personal examples
iii. Using pauses
iv. Eye contact
v. Vibrant clothes
vi. Using hand movements

A. i, ii, iv, v **B.** i, iii, iv, vi
C. i, iii, iv, v **D.** All of them

Q.6 Direction: Study the following information carefully and answer the given questions.
Seven person - P, Q, R, S, T, V and W are sitting in a straight line facing North but not necessarily in the same order.
(a) Q sits third to the right of T. W sits second to the right of Q.
(b) V and R are immediate neighbours of each other. V is not an immediate neighbour of T.
(c) Only one person sits between S and P.
(d) S is not an immediate neighbour of Q.
Which of the following pairs sits at the extreme corners of the line?

A. R,W **B.** S,T **C.** W,Q **D.** T,R

Q.7 Pinki lives with her husband Raju in Noida. One day, a person Anmol came to his house and said to Raju that you are my elder brother's father's son-in-law. How's Anmol related to Pinki?

A. Brother **B.** Father **C.** Uncle **D.** Cousin

Q.8 What will come in place of the question mark?

1, 1.5, 3, 7.5, 22.5, ?

A. 85.23 **B.** 78.75 **C.** 29.56 **D.** 56.36

Q.9 In an examination, the total number of students is 10. The average marks of 20% of students are 40 marks, the average marks of 30% of students are 50 and the average marks of the remaining students are 75. Find the average marks of all the students.

A. 50.5 **B.** 60.5 **C.** 65 **D.** 57.5

Q.10 Vanya gave 10% in charity from her salary, and then 20% from the remaining she gave to her friend as a loan. She is left now with 7200. What is the salary of Vanya?

A. 12000 **B.** 10000 **C.** 10200 **D.** 11000

Q.11 Which of the following is a point source of water pollution?

A. Oil spills
B. Industrial wastewater
C. Surface run-off
D. Municipal wastewater

Q.12 A perfect ecological equilibrium among the producers, decomposers & consumer groups of organisms exist among which of the following lakes?

A. Senescent lakes **B.** Oligotrophic lakes
C. Eutrophic lakes **D.** Mesotrophic lakes

Q.13 Capturing the imagination and initiative of the student is of crucial importance in:

A. The case method of teaching
B. Concept mapping
C. Peer instruction
D. Quizzes

Q.14 Which of the following statement(s) is/are true about **"Ecosystem"**?

1. It is defined as the community of living organisms in association with the non-living components and their physical interaction.
2. An ecosystem consists of various niches and ecotones.

Select the correct answer from the codes given below.

A. Statement 1 only
B. Statement 2 only
C. Both Statements 1 and 2
D. Neither of statement 1 nor 2

Q.15 Which one of the following forms of energy leads to the least environmental pollution in the process of its harnessing and utilization?

A. Nuclear energy **B.** Thermal energy
C. Solar energy **D.** Geothermal energy

Q.16 Which of the following initiatives has been taken by the government to promote research in Higher Education through ICT?

(i) E-pathshala

(ii) National Repository of Open Educational Resources (NROER)

(iii) SWAYAM

(iv) IMPRINT

(v) Operation Digital Board

A. (i), (ii) only
B. (i), (ii), (iii), (iv), (v)
C. (iv) only
D. (ii), (iii), (v) only

Q.17 What regarding the RUSA (Rashtriya Uchchatar Shiksha Abhiyan) is true?

I. RUSA is a centrally sponsored scheme which was launched in 2015.

II. The states are funded by the centre as per their higher education plans, describing their strategy.

III. The aim is to increase the Gross enrolment ratio to 35%, which currently is around 20%.

A. Both I and II **B.** Only II
C. Both I and III **D.** All of the above

Q.18 If FRIEND is coded as HTKGPF then REVEAL will be coded as?

A. TGXFCN **B.** TGXNGC
C. TXGNCG **D.** TGXGCN

Q.19 If 36 men can do a piece of work in 25 hours, in how many hours will 15 men do it?

A. 60 Hours **B.** 55 Hours
C. 65 Hours **D.** None of the above

Q.20 Educational planning is required at _______ level.

A. Central **B.** State **C.** World **D.** Rural

Ques (21-25):Direction: The following table shows the population in five major cities and the capital of India (Delhi). The population measurement was done every five years and recorded in lakhs. Study the table and answer the questions that follow.

Year	Delhi	Mumbai	Banglore	Indore	Kolkata	Gangtok
1995	12.6	18.4	10.6	15.5	16.3	4.2
2000	15.0	20.8	13.2	16.8	14.7	3.8
2005	15.3	21.3	14.9	12.2	13.8	6.8
2010	18.8	25.1	23.8	10.0	13.2	7.0
2015	24.2	27.4	32.5	13.5	15.0	8.2

Q.21 Which was the year when the population from Gangtok had maximum representation (%) in the total population from all the cities recorded?

A. 1995 **B.** 2005 **C.** 2010 **D.** 2015

Q.22 What is the mean of annual growth rates (%) of the population of Delhi?

A. 18.15% **B.** 19.04% **C.** 22.87% **D.** 16.50%

Q.23 Which city has registered an overall maximum growth rate (%) from 1995 to 2015?

A. Delhi **B.** Mumbai
C. Bangalore **D.** Gangtok

Q.24 What was the approximate percentage of the population from Kolkata in 2015?

A. 8.6% **B.** 12.4% **C.** 15% **D.** 10.8%

Q.25 Which of the following city shows population growth only once during the recorded years?

A. Bangalore **B.** Indore
C. Kolkata **D.** Gangtok

Q.26 The straight-out recommendations having the same subject and predicate terms may vary in quality and amount or in both. This differing is called ____.

A. Relational argument
B. Immediate inference
C. Opposition
D. None of the above

Q.27 Premise: All cats have short ears.

Premise: Ragdoll is a cat.

Conclusion: Therefore, Ragdoll has short ears.

Which type of reasoning is this?

A. Deductive reasoning
B. Inductive reasoning
C. Relational reasoning
D. None of the above

Q.28 If **'All Americans are spiritual'** is true, then **'Some Americans are spiritual'** is also true. This type of relationship is correctly represented by which of the following options?

A. Sub-contrary
B. Contrary
C. Contradictory
D. Sub-alternation opposition

Q.29 Match list-1 with list-2 and select the correct code for the answer.

List-1 (Fallacies)		List-2 (explanation)	
a.	Fallacies of Presupposition	i)	At the point when the premises in an argument don't give significant reason for accepting the truth of the conclusion.
b.	Fallacies of Relevance	ii)	Because they are based on unwanted assumptions.
c.	Fallacies of Denying the Antecedent	iii)	By denying the antecedent of a conditional proposition can not

			deny the consequent

A. a-i, b-ii, c-iii **B.** a-ii, b-iii, c-i
C. a-ii, b-i, c-iii **D.** a-i, b-iii, c-ii

Q.30 Which Indian educational institute occupies the first position as per QS India University Rankings 2019?

A. IIT Delhi
B. IIT Bombay
C. University of Delhi
D. Indian Institute of Science

Q.31 The use of traditional teaching methods is justified on grounds that

i. They are easy to execute

ii. They are effective when the group of learners is homogenous and large

iii. They are economic in terms of time and money

iv. They do not require to evaluate the teaching skills of teachers

V. They are examination-oriented

A. i, ii, v **B.** i, ii, iii **C.** i, ii, iv **D.** ii, iii, iv

Q.32 Which of the following strategies can be helpful for improving the teacher-student relationship?

I. Banish them

II. Give feedback

III. Delegation of responsibility

IV. Setting examples

V. Clear instructions

A. I, II, IV, V **B.** II, III, IV, V
C. II, III, V **D.** All of them

Q.33 If you see a conflict between two students in the classroom, what should be your strategy as a teacher to address the issue?

A. Complain to the administration
B. Discuss the issue within the class
C. Have a face-to-face conversation with each student
D. Barring them from your class

Q.34 Match the List 1 with List 2.

List-1		List-2	
a.	CGPA	i)	Student's average over a semester
b.	SGPA	ii)	Student's overall average performance throughout their academic program
c.	CBCS	iii)	Continuous evaluation framework
d.	CCE	iv)	System that allows to choose between different courses

A. a – i, b – iii, c – ii, d - iv
B. a – ii, b – i, c – iv, d - iii
C. a – i, b – ii, c – iii, d - iv
D. a – ii, b – iv, c – iii, d - i

Q.35 Assertion (A): Education system demand promoting 'reflective level of teaching'.

Reason (R): Memory level of teaching does not improve intelligence and increase student's ability.

A. Both A and R are true and R is the correct explanation of A
B. Both A and R are true but R is not the correct explanation of A
C. Only A is true
D. Only R is true

Q.36 Statement A: The disparity caused by individual's access or lack of access to digital technology is called internet inequality.

Statement B: The problem of access has been a major downside of emerging technologies.

A. Both statements are true
B. Only statement A is true
C. Only statement B is true
D. None of the statements is true

Q.37 An email from a well-known person or institution that tries to gather sensitive information for misuse is called ______.

A. Scam **B.** Spam **C.** Phishing **D.** Lurking

Q.38 Which of the following is the highest storage device?

A. CD-ROM **B.** Hard Drive
C. SSD **D.** DVD-ROM

Q.39 Which of the following is not a characteristic of a domain name?

A. They are separated by a dot
B. They contain underscores
C. Domain name is website name
D. Domain name is always unique

Q.40 What is EDI?

A. Electronic distant interface
B. Electronic development interface
C. Electronic data interface
D. Electronic data interchange

Ques (41-45):Direction: Read the following passage carefully and answer the question.

India has not done well in the World University Rankings 2020 conducted by Times Higher Education (THE); for the first time since 2012 none of its higher education institutions makes it to the top 300. It would be wise not to dismiss this as an inconvenient assessment by a Western agency. The Indian Institute of Science, Bangalore has dropped 50 places into the 301-350 group from its earlier position within the first 300, and although the new Indian Institute of Technology, Ropar has joined it there and seven more Indian institutions have been added to the last year's 49 in a total of 1,300, it may be worthwhile to decipher the message concealed in the rankings. Indian institutions have lost out on two criteria, although scores in the teaching environment and industrial income are good.

The IISc, Bangalore has lost its former place because of its lower citation impact score, indicating that its research is not being considered as valuable to other scholars as before. The message here is not for the IISc, Bangalore alone; it is, first and foremost, for policy-makers who also control the funds. Indian institutions lag behind in international outlook: nurturing a multicultural community among students and teachers, educating students to fit into social and political environments anywhere in the world and establishing international alliances through research and education. This failure is particularly ironic in the context of the government's plan of making India into a global destination for education by identifying 10 private institutions as institutions of excellence, free from prevalent rules of recruitment, salary and student fees. In practice, though, some of the best-known universities in different states are now going into the protectionist mode in favor of local applicants. Nothing could be worse for education than the continuous narrowing down at all levels. As long as political priorities drive education, India will keep sliding down all lists.

Q.41 India has not done well in the World University Rankings 2020 as:

A. A Western agency conducted an inconvenient assessment
B. The Indian Institute of Science, Bangalore has dropped 50 places into the 301-350 group from its earlier position within the first 300
C. India's presence in the world rankings has improved with 56 institutions being ranked instead of 49 last year
D. No higher educational institution in the country has managed to figure in the top 300

Q.42 Indian institutions have lost out on two criteria, what are those two criteria?

A. Teaching environment and industrial income
B. Research and citations
C. Citations and International outlook
D. Only one criterion, citations, is mentioned in the passage

Q.43 The IISc, Bangalore has lost its former place because:

A. Its research is not being considered as valuable to other scholars as before
B. Of its lower research productivity
C. Of policy-makers who also control the funds
D. All of the above

Q.44 According to the passage, which of the following statements is FALSE?

I. Indian institutions lag behind in the development of a multicultural community among students and staff, preparing its students for global, political and social environments, and the development of international alliances in research and education.

II. The government is focusing on attracting foreign students to improve India's position as a higher education destination.

III. 10 private institutions are declared as institutions of excellence, freed from prevalent rules of recruitment, salary and student fees.

A. Only II　**B.** Only III
C. Both II and III　**D.** Both I and II

Q.45 What will happen if the best-known universities make a clear embrace of a protectionist mode?

A. They will only favour local applicants
B. India will keep sliding down all lists
C. Political priorities will drive education
D. It will be the worst challenge for the education system

Q.46 What is the purpose of the cross-sectional study?

A. To compare the status of different variables for a short period of time.
B. To explore the status of one variable at different point of time.
C. To study the development of different groups/variables at one point in time.
D. To study the development of different groups/variables for a long period of time.

Q.47 Randomization in research means

i. Selection or non-selection of one unit has no impact on the selection of another.

ii. Each & every unit of the population stand equal chances of being selected.

iii. Picking up a unit based on chance alone method.

A. Only i　**B.** Only ii
C. i and ii　**D.** i, ii and iii

Q.48 Statement A: A null hypothesis exists when the researcher finds that there is no specified relationship between the two variables.

Statement B: In order to disapprove a null hypothesis, an alternative hypothesis is needed.

A. Both Statements A and B are true
B. Only Statement A is true
C. Only Statement B is true
D. Both Statements are false

Q.49 An analysis in research that is grounded in ethno methodology is called ________.

A. Covert research
B. Conversation analysis
C. Content analysis
D. Paradigm

Q.50 A researcher intends to find out the differences in the motivational outlook of first-degree level students in terms of their belongingness to rural/urban areas and the educational status of parents. What will be the dependent variable in this study?

A. Belongingness to rural/urban areas
B. First-degree level
C. Educational status of parents
D. Motivational outlook

// Smart Answer Sheet //

Correct Indicates percentage of students who answered questions correctly.

Skipped Indicates percentage of students who skipped questions.

Q.	Ans.	Correct	Skipped
1	D	60.13 %	7.13 %
2	D	29.17 %	7.94 %
3	B	28.66 %	10.99 %
4	C	44.8 %	10.46 %
5	B	46.24 %	13.0 %
6	B	39.02 %	16.01 %
7	A	52.33 %	12.79 %
8	B	31.57 %	15.38 %
9	B	36.88 %	16.02 %
10	B	32.62 %	16.37 %
11	B	53.4 %	13.55 %
12	B	25.16 %	15.27 %
13	A	33.36 %	15.99 %
14	C	50.56 %	13.07 %
15	C	58.87 %	15.06 %
16	C	15.85 %	15.01 %
17	B	17.22 %	15.71 %
18	D	50.87 %	17.64 %
19	A	31.25 %	16.34 %
20	A	34.73 %	11.25 %
21	B	22.7 %	16.71 %
22	A	23.7 %	16.75 %
23	C	36.23 %	18.8 %
24	B	25.37 %	15.06 %
25	C	28.71 %	19.35 %
26	C	29.11 %	18.78 %
27	A	31.51 %	17.3 %
28	D	33.41 %	13.54 %
29	C	29.86 %	19.64 %
30	B	30.35 %	15.31 %
31	B	32.23 %	18.01 %
32	B	47.74 %	17.34 %
33	C	53.76 %	16.95 %
34	B	51.49 %	15.57 %
35	B	30.86 %	18.94 %
36	C	18.79 %	18.94 %
37	C	30.86 %	16.58 %
38	C	21.92 %	18.8 %
39	B	32.25 %	18.5 %
40	D	22.89 %	18.9 %
41	D	24.51 %	21.32 %
42	C	19.01 %	19.59 %
43	A	24.5 %	22.25 %
44	B	18.48 %	21.51 %
45	D	17.04 %	22.47 %
46	C	35.12 %	17.83 %
47	D	26.83 %	20.61 %
48	A	43.47 %	19.73 %
49	B	22.51 %	20.93 %
50	D	38.8 %	20.08 %

Performance Analysis	
Avg. Score (%)	32.0%
Toppers Score (%)	100.0%
Your Score	

//Hints and Solutions//

1. Developing the thinking power of students is the main objective of teaching as thinking is a higher cognitive function that allows students to produce innovative ideas by using images, symbols, and languages.

Teaching is a process related to the effective transmission of knowledge and skills in an individual. It limits or enhances the ways the learners learn and assimilate concepts and ideas.

Hence, the correct option is (D).

2. Asking an open-ended question for gaining feedback can be classified as Rhetorical.

A rhetorical question is a type of question that is good to start with but may not help in getting a direct answer. For feedback, close-ended questions work better. So, asking an open-ended question for gaining feedback can be classified as rhetorical.

Hence, the correct option is (D).

3. Flak in media communication often refers to Criticism.

Flak is the criticism that newspapers receive from the general public in the form of letters, petitions, lawsuits, phone calls, etc. Flak is the term that is widely used in media communication meaning criticism.

Hence, the correct option is (B).

4. Upward communication occurs when the teacher communicates with the head of the department. This statement is correct.

Horizontal communication occurs when the teacher communicates with other teachers. This statement is also true.

The diagonal flow of communication involves more than three agents of communication, e.g. The head of the department told about the student.

So, upward communication is not called diagonal communication. Therefore, this statement is not true.

Horizontal communication is also called lateral communication. This is true.

Hence, the correct option is (C).

5.

- Giving personal examples should be avoided as it opens the room for taking the course of a lecture in another direction.
- Vibrant clothes can distract students.
- Changing your tone according to the situation will certainly help the teacher in the class in communicating properly.
- Using pauses, hand movements, eye contact will certainly help in communicating better.

So, only I, iii, iv, vi is correct.

Hence, the correct option is (B).

6. Q sits third to the right of T. W sits second to the right of Q. V and R are immediate neighbours of each other. V is not an immediate neighbour of T.

There will be two possibilities,

1. case

_ _ _ _ _ _ _

T R V Q W

2. case

_ _ _ _ _ _ _

T R V Q W

Only one person sits between S and P.

S is not an immediate neighbour of Q. Hence, the second case will not follow.

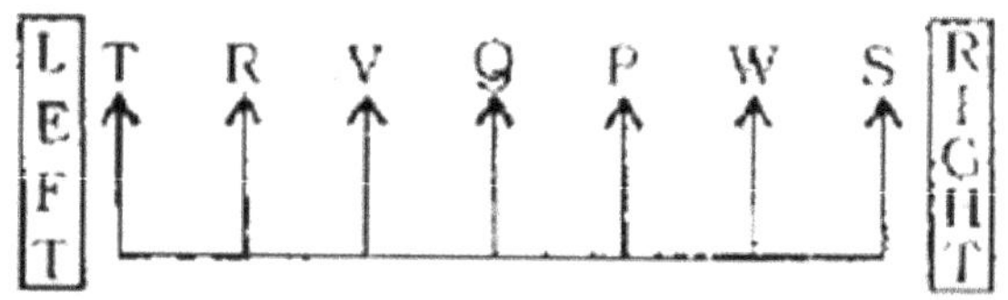

T and S sit at the extreme corners of the line

Hence, the correct option is (B).

7. From the information given in the question, we can draw the following diagram:

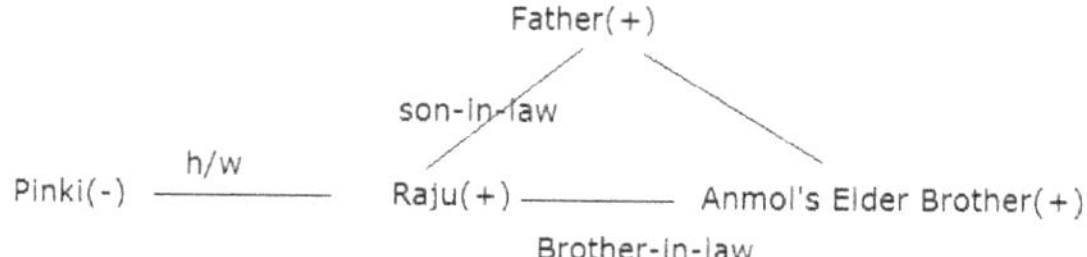

Here plus (+) is denotes male and minus(-) denotes female.

From the above figure, it's clear that Anmol is the brother of Pinki.

Hence, the correct option is (A).

8. $\Rightarrow 1 \times 1.5 = 1.5$

$\Rightarrow 1.5 \times 2 = 3 \Rightarrow 3 \times 2.5 = 7.5$

$\Rightarrow 7.5 \times 3 = 22.5$

$\Rightarrow 22.5 \times 3.5 = 78.75$

Hence, the correct option is (B).

9. It is given that the total number of students be 10.

Marks obtained by 20% of students $= \frac{20\times10}{100} \times 40 = 80$

Marks obtained by 30% of students $= \frac{30\times10}{100} \times 50 = 150$

Marks obtained by remaining 50% of students $=$ $\frac{50 \times 10}{100} \times 75 = 375$

Average marks of all the students $= \frac{(80+150+375)}{10} = \frac{605}{10} =$ 60.5

Hence, the correct option is (B).

10. Let the whole money be $= 100x$

10% of $100x = 10x$

After given to charity, Vanya had $= 100x - 10x = 90x$

The money given to her friend $= 20\%$ of $90x = 18x$

Remaining money $= 100x - (10x + 18x) = 72x$

A.T.Q

$72x = 7200$

$x = 100$

Thus, the whole money $= 100x = 100 \times 100 = 10000$

Hence, the correct option is (B).

11. Industrial wastewater is a point source of water pollution.

Industrial wastewater has organic and non-organic pollutants that not only pollute the river water but also affect human life. Oil spills, Surface run-off & Municipal wastewater are the non-point sources of water pollution.

Hence, the correct option is (B).

12. A perfect ecological equilibrium among the producers, decomposers & consumer groups of organisms exist among Oligotrophic lakes.

A perfect ecological system means that there are producers, consumers, and decomposers present in the system in such a manner that food and energy flow from one level to the other. The pollutions (nitrogen and phosphorous) disturb this equilibrium by increasing the productivity of a lake. As the productivity of a lake increases, its water quality reduces, and equilibrium is disturbed. Oligotrophic lakes have a low level of productivity so they can be considered to be a perfect ecological system.

Hence, the correct option is (B).

13. Capturing the student's imagination and initiative into the case method of teaching is crucially important.

Case Method of Teaching:

- The case method is participatory, discussion-based learning. Where students acquire skills such as critical thinking, communication and group dynamics. It is a type of problem-based learning.
- The case method is an instructional method (not hypothesis) that refers to scenarios based on situations in which students observe, imagine, analyze, record, implement, draw conclusions, or give advice.

Hence, the correct option is (A).

14.

- The ecosystem is the community of living organisms in association with the non-living components and their physical interaction. The ecosystem is mainly like Forest, Grassland, Desert, Tundra, Freshwater, Marine, etc. So, this statement is correct.
- An ecosystem consists of various niches and ecotones. An ecotone is an area between the two biomes. So, this statement is also correct.

Hence, the correct option is (C).

15. Solar energy leads to the least environmental pollution in the process of its harnessing and utilization.

In the case of nuclear energy, the major concerns of pollution are while storage and disposal of spent fuels where there is always a risk of leakage of radiation. In the case of thermal energy, an enormous amount of air pollution is produced. Even in the case of geothermal energy a little amount of pollution is produced.

Hence, the correct option is (C).

16. E-pathshala, National Repository of Open Educational Resources (NROER), SWAYAM, and Operation Digital Board initiatives have been taken by the government to provide research in schools through ICT. Only IMPRINT (Impacting Research Innovation & Technology) is the initiative taken by the government to provide research in Higher Education through ICT (Information & Communication Technology).

Hence, the correct option is (C).

17. RUSA is a CSS, centrally sponsored scheme launched in the year 2013.
It aims at providing strategic funding to eligible state higher educational institutions. The central funding is in the ratio of 65:35.
The states are funded as per the critical appraisal of their respective higher education plans.
India has reached a gross enrolment ratio (GER) of 26.3% of people going into higher education and is close to achieving a target of 30% by 2020. While the country is on the way to the massification of higher education, important questions on the quality of institutions and the employment of graduates remain, according to a report by the United States-based think tank the Brookings Institution.
Hence, the correct option is (B).

18. The pattern followed is:

F	R	I	E	N	D
(+2)	(+2)	(+2)	(+2)	(+2)	(+2)
H	T	K	G	P	F

Similarly, for REVEAL:

R	E	V	E	A	L
(+2)	(+2)	(+2)	(+2)	(+2)	(+2)
T	G	X	G	C	N

Hence, the correct option is (D).

19. If 36 men are doing work in 25 days.

36 men will do $\frac{1}{25}$, work in one day.

One man will do 25×36 work in one day.

15 men will do $\frac{1\times15}{25\times36}$ work in one day no of days 15 men will take to do a work will be $\frac{25\times36}{15}$.

$= 5 \times 12$

$= 60$ Hours

Hence, the correct option is (A).

20. Education:

- Education is the process of facilitating learning, or the acquisition of knowledge, skills, values, morals, beliefs, and habits.
- Educational methods include teaching, training, storytelling, discussion, and directed research.
- Education is beyond earning degrees it is more than bookish knowledge.
- Proper and good education is very important for all of us.
- It facilitates quality learning all through life among people of any age group, caste, creed, religion, and region.
- It is the process of achieving knowledge, values, skills, beliefs, and moral habits.

Educational planning:

- Education is the public service required by the public and provided by the government.
- For all the government efforts of such huge magnitudes like education, planning is completely necessary.
- Educational planning is among the elements of general national and socio-economic development.
- Educational planning, in its broadest generic sense, is the application of rational, systematic analysis to the process of educational development with the aim of making education more effective and efficient in responding to the needs and goals of its students and society.

Therefore, Educational planning is required at the central level.

Hence, the correct option is (A).

21. Percentage of the population from Gangtok city in the following years,

Year

$1995 : \frac{4.2}{12.6+18.4+10.6+15.5+16.3+4.2} \times 100 = \frac{4.2}{77.6} \times 100 = 5.41\%$

Year

$2005 : \frac{6.8}{15.3+21.3+14.9+12.2+13.8+6.8} \times 100 = \frac{6.8}{84.3} \times 100 = 8.06\%$

(Maximum)

Year

$2010 : \frac{7}{18.8+25.1+23.8+10+13.2+7} \times 100 = \frac{7}{97.9} \times 100 = 7.15\%$

Year

$2015 : \frac{8.2}{24.2+27.4+32.5+13.5+15+8.2} \times 100 = \frac{8.2}{120.8} \times 100 = 6.78\%$

Hence, the correct option is (B).

22. Growth of population of Delhi in the following years

Year $2000: \frac{15-12.6}{12.6} \times 100 = \frac{2.4}{12.6} \times 100 = 19.04\%$

Year $2005: \frac{15.3-15}{15} \times 100 = \frac{0.3}{15} \times 100 = 2\%$

Year $2010: \frac{18.8-15.3}{15.3} \times 100 = \frac{3.5}{15.3} \times 100 = 22.87\%$

Year $2015: \frac{24.2-18.8}{18.8} \times 100 = \frac{5.4}{18.8} \times 100 = 28.72\%$

Mean of growth rate $= \frac{19.04+2+22.87+28.72}{4} = \frac{72.63}{4} = 18.15\%$

Hence, the correct option is (A).

23. Percentage of growth rate from 1995 to 2015

Delhi: $\frac{24.2-12.6}{12.6} \times 100 = \frac{11.6}{12.6} \times 100 = 92\%$

Mumbai: $\frac{27.4-18.4}{18.4} \times 100 = \frac{9}{18.4} \times 100 = 48.91\%$

Bangalore: $\frac{32.5-10.6}{10.6} \times 100 = \frac{12.9}{10.6} \times 100 = 121.69\%$ (Maximum)

Gangtok: $\frac{8.2-4.2}{4.2} \times 100 = \frac{4}{4.2} \times 100 = 95.23\%$

Hence, the correct option is (C).

24. Percentage population of Kolkata in 2015

$= \frac{15}{24.2+27.4+32.5+13.5+15+8.2} \times 100$

$= \frac{15}{120.8} \times 100 = 12.4\%$

Hence, the correct option is (B).

25. The population of Kolkata city decreases in every record from 1995 to 2010. But it shows a growth in 2015 as compared to the previous year.

Hence, the correct option is (C).

26. The categorical propositions having the same subject and predicate terms may vary in quality and amount or in both. This differing is called Opposition.

Sub contraries: The connection between two specific recommendations having a similar subject and predicate yet contrasting in quality is subcontrary Opposition.

Immediate inference: In this, the conclusion is drawn only from one given proposition.

Relational argument: In relational arguments, both premises and their conclusions are relational propositions. There are two characteristics of a relation-relation to itself and to others.

Hence, the correct option is (C).

27. Given the premise that all cats have short ears and Ragdoll is a cat, it is logical to assume that Ragdoll has short ears.
In deductive reasoning, the conclusion is guaranteed to be true if the premises are true.
Therefore, in the deductive inference, the conclusion can not be more general than the premise(s).
Hence, the correct option is (A).

28.

- Sub-alternation opposition is the relation between two propositions having the same subject and predicate but differing in quantity only.
- If universal is true, then particular must be true. What is true about the whole population, is true about its part also.
- If universal is false, then particular may be undecided.
- The relation between 'A and I' and 'E and O' is called subalternation.

Hence, the correct option is (D).

29. Fallacies of presupposition: Some arguments are fallacies because they are based on unwanted assumptions. In these arguments, the error arises out of an implicit supposition of some other proposition whose truth is uncertain or questionable.
Fallacies of Relevance: When the premises are not relevant to the conclusion the fallacy of relevance is committed. This fallacy has many forms, appeal to force, appeal to pity, appeal to people, appeal to authority.
Fallacies of denying the antecedent: The fallacy consists in proceeding to argue by denying the antecedent of a conditional proposition.
Hence, the correct option is (C).

30. QS World University Rankings is an annual publication of university rankings by Quacquarelli Symonds Ltd. As per QS Indian University Ranking 2019, IIT Bombay occupies the first rank, followed by the Indian Institute of Science. IIT Delhi and the University of Delhi hold the 4th and 8th rank respectively.

Hence, the correct option is (B).

31. The traditional teaching method is an important teaching method because they are easy to execute, require less time and investment, are a tried and tested method of teaching when the group of learners is large.
However, traditional teaching methods suffer on certain grounds viz. they don't account for testing the effectiveness of teaching and they focus more on examinations than actual learning.
Hence, the correct option is (B).

32. The strategies that can be helpful for improving the teacher-student relationship are:
Give feedback- helps in positive reinforcement
Delegation of responsibility- develops trust
Setting examples- give inspiration
Clear instruction- important for students to know the expectations.
Hence, the correct option is (B).

33. If you see a conflict between two students in the classroom, then as a teacher the best option is to:
Have a face-to-face conversation with both students individually, which will help you to know the magnitude of the issue.
Counseling may help them to change their behavior, if not; future courses of action can be decided.
Hence, the correct option is (C).

34. CGPA: Student's overall average performance throughout their academic program. Ex. Performance of the student over 2 years in a master course.
SGPA: Student's average over a semester. Ex. If a student has 4 semesters, then performance in a particular semester only.
CBCS: System that allows choosing between different courses.
CCE: Continuous evaluation framework that covered all the aspects of the student's overall development.
Hence, the correct option is (B).

35. Memory-based teaching focuses on mugging up and cramming which is not good for developing student's capacity.
Reflective methods of teaching help students to develop higher-order skills such as critical thinking, logical reasoning, and so on.
So, memory-based teaching should be swapped out for reflective teaching.
So, both statements are true but Reason is not related to Assertion.
Hence, the correct option is (B).

36. The disparity caused by an individual's access or lack of access to digital technology is called the digital divide, not internet inequality.
It is true that the digital divide (the problem of access) has been one of the downsides of technology development.
Hence, the correct option is (C).

37. Phishing is a method of trying to gather personal information using deceptive e-mails and websites.
Phishing is a type of social engineering attack which is motivated to steal user data, like login credentials, credit card numbers, saved passwords, etc.
It is a cybercrime.

Phishing can be done not only through email but also possible through text messages etc.
Hence, the correct option is (C).

38. The correct order in terms of increasing storage capacity is:
DVD ROM and CD ROM have a memory capacity of MB's/GB.
As of now, Hard Drive has a maximum memory capacity of 16 Terabytes.
SSD (Solid State Drive) has a maximum memory capacity of 100 Terabytes.
Hence, the correct option is (C).

39. A domain name is a name or description of a location on the internet or simply a website name. This name should be unique. It is usually separated by a dot.
A domain name should be easy and short.
Domains don't contain underscores.
Hence, the correct option is (B).

40. Electronic Data Interchange (EDI) is the process of using computers to exchange business documents between companies. Previously, fax machines or traditional mail was used to exchange documents. Mailing and faxing are still used in business, but EDI is a much quicker way to do the same thing.

Hence, the correct option is (D).

41. India has not done well in the World University Rankings 2020 as **no higher educational institution in the country has managed to figure in the top 300**.

The passage states, "India has not done well in the World University Rankings 2020 conducted by Times Higher Education (THE); for the first time since 2012 none of its higher education institutions makes it to the top 300."

Hence, the correct option is (D).

42. The passage states, "Indian institutions have lost out on two criteria, although scores in the teaching environment and industrial income are good. The IISc, Bangalore has lost its former place **because of its lower citation impact score**, Indian institutions lag behind in **international outlook**."

Hence, the correct option is (C).

43. It can be deciphered from the following lines, "The IISc, Bangalore has lost its former place because of its lower citation impact score, **indicating that its research is not being considered as valuable to other scholars as before**. The message here is not for the IISc, Bangalore alone; it is, first and foremost, for policy-makers who also control the funds."

Hence, the correct option is (A).

44. It can be inferred from the following lines, "Indian institutions lag behind in international outlook: nurturing a multicultural community among students and teachers, educating students to fit into social and political environments anywhere in the world and establishing international alliances through research and education. This failure is particularly ironic in the context of the government's plan of making India into a global destination for education **by identifying 10 private institutions as institutions of excellence, free from prevalent rules of recruitment, salary and student fees**."

Hence, the correct option is (B).

45. It can be deciphered from the following lines, "In practice, though, some of the best-known universities in different states are now going into a protectionist mode in favor of local applicants. **Nothing could be worse for education than the continuous narrowing down at all levels**. As long as political priorities drive education, India will keep sliding down all lists."

Hence, the correct option is (D).

46. The purpose of a cross-sectional study is to study the development of different groups or stages at one point in time. The cross-sectional study does not provide information about the cause and effect relationship.
Hence, the correct option is (C).

47. Randomization is used in research to minimize the biases in results.
Selection or non-selection of one unit which has no impact on the selection of another is the concept of Randomisation.
Each & every unit of the population stand equal chances of being selected also defines randomization.
Picking up a unit based on chance alone method strong the method of randomization.
All the above statements about randomization are true.

A method based on chance alone by which study participants are assigned to a treatment group. Randomization minimizes the differences among groups by equally distributing people with particular characteristics among all the trial arms. The researchers do not know which treatment is better.

Hence, the correct option is (D).

48. For rejecting or disapproving a null hypothesis (H0), a new hypothesis is needed where some real effect can be offered between the two variables. This is called the alternative hypothesis (H1).
A null hypothesis (H0) exists when the researcher finds that there is no specified relationship between the two variables.
So, both statements are true.
Hence, the correct option is (A).

49. Ethno methodology is the study of how social order is produced in and through processes of social interaction. It generally seeks to provide an alternative to mainstream sociological approaches. In its most radical form, it poses a challenge to the social sciences as a whole. Its early investigations led to the founding of conversation analysis, which has found its own place as an accepted discipline within the academy. According to Psathas, it is possible to distinguish five major approaches within the ethno methodological family of disciplines.

Hence, the correct option is (B).

50. The researcher intends to find out the differences in the motivational outlook of first-degree level students in terms of their belongingness to rural/urban areas and the educational status of parents.

The motivational outlook of first-degree level students is the dependent variable here. The motivational outlook depends on the belongingness to rural/urban areas and the educational status of parents is an independent variable here.

Hence, the correct option is (D).

Mock Test 02

Q.1 Which of the following statistical tests allow determining whether there is a significant difference between means of two groups when the sample size is small?

A. z-test **B.** p-test **C.** t-test **D.** r-test

Q.2 Which of the following is not true about research ethics?

i. It relates to the accuracy of results

ii. It relates to proving one's opinion

iii. It relates to using scientific methods

iv. It relates to keeping the anonymity of the respondents

v. It relates to adhering to the propaganda of political parties

A. i, ii, iii **B.** iii, v **C.** ii, iv, v **D.** ii, v

Q.3 Direction: Answer the following question by selecting the most appropriate option.

Which of the following statement cannot be considered as a feature of 'learning'?

A. Unlearning is also a part of learning.

B. It is a process that mediates behaviour.

C. Study of behaviour is learning.

D. Learning is something that occurs as a result of certain experiences.

Q.4 Impact of a single-gender school may result in:

A. Open socialisation

B. Restricted socialisation

C. Gender sensitivity

D. Gender insensitivity

Q.5 Which of the following kinds of research doesn't require the formulation of a hypothesis?

A. Experimental Study **B.** Survey

C. Normative Study **D.** Longitudinal Study

Q.6 A lecture without feedback from the students is _____.

i. Incompetent

ii. Inconsequential

iii. Rewarding

iv. Futile

A. i, ii, iv **B.** i, iii, iv

C. i, ii, iii **D.** i, ii, iii, iv

Q.7 Which of the following is the best strategy to ensure the prominence of a teacher in the classroom?

A. Antagonist behaviour

B. Authoritative Tone

C. Confident Stance

D. Peer-Partner

Q.8 Which of the following learners' characteristics must be appreciated by the teacher?

i. Attitude of enquiry

ii. Reflection

iii. Critical thinking

iv. Submissive behaviour

v. Prior experience

vi. Motivation

A. i, ii, iv, v, vi **B.** i, ii, iii, v, vi

C. ii, iii, iv, vi **D.** ii, iii, iv, v, vi

Q.9 Match the following List 1 with List 2.

List 1	List 2
1. Choice Based Credit System	i. Learning guide and resources for Teachers
2. Continuous and Comprehensive Evaluation	ii. Evaluation based on relative performance
3. Teacher Support System	iii. A student-centred approach to learning
4. Normative Assessment	iv. The developmental process of assessment

A. 1-iii, 2-ii, 3-i, 4-iv **B.** 1-i, 2-iv, 3-iii, 4-ii

C. 1-iii, 2-iv, 3-i, 4-ii **D.** 1-iv, 2-ii, 3-i, 4-iii

Q.10 _______ environment is essential to learning among students.

A. Confrontational **B.** Exclusive

C. Obliging **D.** Progressive

Q.11 Assertion (A): Human communication involves a set of a procedure through which the information is passed among the people by means of previously agreed symbols, in order to produce the desired response'.

Reason (R): S-M-C-R Model that stands for Smarter-Message-Channel-Receiver. It is the basic communication process.

A. Both (A) and (R) are true

B. (A) is true, but (R) is false

C. Both (A) and (R) are true, but (R) is not the correct explanation of (A)

D. (A) is false, but (R) is true

Q.12 Consider the following statements about Interpersonal Communication.

1) It may be formal or informal, verbal or non-verbal.

2) It takes place anywhere by means of words, sounds, facial expression, gestures, and postures.

3) It is an effective communication situation because you can get immediate feedback.

4) It includes collective decision-making, self-expression, increasing one's effect, and elevating one's status.

Which of the following statements is/are correct?

A. Only 1 and 2 **B.** Only 2 and 3

C. 1, 2 and 3 **D.** All of the above

Q.13 Effective communication in the classroom is not important for:

A. Being understood

B. Imploring participation
C. Increasing Polarisation
D. Team Building

Q.14 The intervening element in a communication process is usually called as:

A. Interruption **B.** Noise
C. Disturbance **D.** Break

Q.15 Which of the following can be a physiological barrier to communicator?

A. Emotions of the learners
B. Gender of the learner
C. Dyslexia
D. Egocentrism

Ques (16-20):Direction: Read the following passage carefully and answer the questions.

The Draft National Education Policy, 2019 (DNEP) implements the India-centric education system, which contributes to the continuous transformation of our nation into a just and vibrant knowledge society, by providing high-quality education to all. The NITI Aayog has focused policy focus specifically on education and outcomes of education from programs. It has promoted competitive federalism among states to improve their educational indicators that are measurable by a battery of tests on students. But any serious work on 'No One Left Behind' (NOLB) can ask for a new and reformist approach. DNEP has provided some hope, but it calls for further examination of rhetoric and reality.

DNEP must be read in the context of the current economic and educational climate in order to estimate the path and speed needed to make its vision a reality. On the one hand, we are in another new era of industrial revolution or skilled age. On the other hand, at present, around one million youth enter the workforce in India each month, but most of them are just raw hands without professional technical knowledge or practical business skills. The weak relationship between education and employment poses a potential risk of turning India's demographic dividend into a demographic disaster.

In the education sector, the elusive chaos of the quantity-quality-equity triangle remains unresolved. Although the merits of education are well recognized as an invaluable public, public investment for this has been minimal. It is relevant to explore how DNEP has addressed some key areas for policy interventions in school education, namely access, which can be measured by the education system, the size and flow of students crossing over to equity, which can be seen development-deprived populations, and lack or persistence of quality, which can be understood by teaching-learning processes and developmental outcomes for children that are more easily implied by attainable scores.

Q.16 What is the aim of the Draft National Education Policy, 2019?

A. To reform and reconstruct at all levels of education from school to higher education
B. To promote competitive federalism among states
C. To make India a knowledge superpower by equipping its students with the necessary skills and quality knowledge
D. To shift the focus from inputs and programmes to outcomes from education

Q.17 What calls for further examination of rhetoric and reality?

A. The Draft National Education Policy, 2019 (DNEP)
B. No One Left Behind (NOLB)
C. New and reformistic approaches
D. Low learning attainment level in the country

Q.18 What does the author mean by "the weak linkages between education and employment"?

A. The potential risk of turning India's demographic dividend into a demographic disaster
B. The new age of the industrial revolution or the skilling age
C. Young people enter the workforce in India without professional technical knowledge or practical vocational skills
D. The gap between young people entering the workforce in India and people with suitable employment skills

Q.19 Our Indian education sector needs:

I. To resolve the elusive conundrum of the quantity-quality-equity triangle

II. To acknowledge the merit of education as an invaluable public good

III. More public investment

IV. Policy intervention in school education

A. Only I **B.** Both II and III
C. Both I and III **D.** I, III and IV

Q.20 According to the passage, which of the following statements is not true?

A. The accessibility of education is measured by the size and flow of students moving across the education system.
B. Equality can be gauged by the reduction or persistence of developmentally deprived population.
C. Quality of education can be understood from teaching-learning processes and developmental outcomes for children that are more conveniently implied by attainment scores.
D. Educational indicators are measurable by a battery of tests on students.

Q.21 A series is given with one term missing. Select the correct alternative from the given ones that will complete the series.

29, 35, 43, 53, ? , 79

A. 60 **B.** 55 **C.** 65 **D.** 57

Q.22 Ram started from point A and travelled forward 8 km to point B, then turned towards right and travelled 5 km to point C, and then turned right and travelled 7 km and then turned towards right and walked 5 km to point D. What is the total distance between A and D?

A. 1 km **B.** 7 km **C.** 15 km **D.** 8 km

Q.23 The price of motorcycle depreciates every year by 8%. If the value of the motorcycle after 2 years will be $Rs. 84640$, then what is the present value (in $Rs.$) of the motorcycle?

A. 90000 **B.** 102000 **C.** 110000 **D.** 100000

Q.24 If in some language TITLESHOOT is coded as "29235108662" and WARZONES is coded as "519865510", then what is the code for PLASTERISM?

A. 731102599190 **B.** 731102599104
C. 5258859096864 **D.** 2558859096864

Q.25 Two trains are moving in the same direction at speed of $54km/h$ and $92km/h$, their lengths are $400m$ and $360m$ respectively. What is the time taken (in seconds) by faster train to cross the slower train?

A. 60 **B.** 72 **C.** 81 **D.** 90

Q.26 If the proposition 'Allentrepreneurs are rich' is false, which of the following propositions can be claimed certainly to be true?

A. Some entrepreneurs are rich.
B. Some entrepreneurs are not rich.
C. No entrepreneur is rich.
D. All rich are entrepreneurs.

Q.27 Given below are some characteristics of reasoning. Select the code which expresses a characteristic which is not deductive in character-

A. The conclusion must be based on observation and experiment
B. The conclusion should be supported by the premise/premises
C. The conclusion must follow from the premise/premises necessarily
D. The argument may be valid or invalid

Q.28 Which one is most important for a teacher?

A. Expertise in subject content
B. Expertise in teaching skills
C. Rapport with students
D. Good health

Q.29 Given below are two statements (A and B), from those two statements two conclusions (i), (ii) are drawn. Select the code that states the conclusion/conclusions drawn validity (taking the premises singularly or jointly). **Statements:**
A) All greens are trees.B) No tree is a shrub.
Conclusions:I. No greens are shrubs.II. Some shrubs are greens.

Codes:

A. Both I and II **B.** Only I
C. Only II **D.** None of the above

Q.30 Which of the following statements is correct about ostensive definition?

A. A definition developed by showing someone an object and attaching a word to it.
B. A definition that specifies the purpose to a term by specifying a measurement procedure.
C. A definition that provides meaning to a term by specifying a measurement procedure.
D. A definition that attaches an emotive, positive or derogatory meaning to a term.

Ques (31-35):Direction: Following table shows the percentage distribution of votes amongst five candidates A, B, C, D and E and total votes cast (in hundred) during the year 2013 to 2018 of collage presidential election. Study the data carefully and answer the questions based on it.

Year	Percentage (%) of votes					Votes (in Hundred)
	A	B	C	D	E	
2013	36	12	18	24	10	420
2014	42	15	22	13	8	390
2015	24	21	28	11	16	378
2016	17	32	23	14	14	425
2017	16	18	20	24	22	478
2018	20	16	10	33	21	460

Q.31 What is the approximate average number of votes candidate A got per year from 2013 to 2015?

A. 120.00 **B.** 128.04 **C.** 135.24 **D.** 118.00

Q.32 What is the average number of votes a candidate gets in 2018?

A. 8.5 Thousand **B.** 8.4 Thousand
C. 7.6 Thousand **D.** 9.2 Thousand

Q.33 In the year 2015, 9000 voters wanted to cast their votes for candidate B, but some of them wrongly cast their votes. Find the percentage of wrongly casted votes which were supposed to be in favour of B.

A. 10.6% **B.** 11.8% **C.** 12% **D.** 8.8%

Q.34 If, out of the total number of voters in 2016 who fevered D, only 40% could successfully cast their votes and remaining was unsuccessful. Find the number of voters who appeared to cast their votes in favour of D:

A. 5950 **B.** 14750 **C.** 12875 **D.** 14875

Q.35 What is the percentage increase in the number of votes from 2013 to 2018?

A. $3\frac{1}{3}\%$ **B.** $9\frac{11}{21}\%$ **C.** $5\frac{4}{21}\%$ **D.** $1\frac{2}{21}\%$

Q.36 Assertion (A): Scientists warn that global warming may result in more extensive drought in the coming years.
Reason (R): Desalination has been proposed as one of the mitigation techniques for drought in India.

A. Both (A) and (R) are true and (R) is the correct explanation of (A)
B. Both (A) and (R) are true but (R) is not the correct explanation of (A)
C. (A) is correct and (R) is not correct
D. (A) is not correct and (R) is correct

Q.37 Match the following. List 1 deals with various conventions and summits. List 2 has the dates of ratifications.

List 1 (Conventions/Summit)	List 2 (Date of Ratification)
1. Intemational Treaty of Wetland	(i) 1971

Conservation Programme	
2. Montreal protocol	(ii) 1992
3. Earth summit	(iii) 1983
4. Kyoto Protocol	(iv) 1997

A. 1 – (i), 2 – (ii), 3 – (iii), 4 –(iv)
B. 1 – (i), 2 – (iv), 3 – (ii), 4 – (iii)
C. 1 – (i), 2 – (iii), 3 – (ii), 4 – (iv)
D. 1 – (iii), 2 – (ii), 3 – (iv), 4 – (i)

Q.38 If the polar ice starts melting, the length of day would:
A. Increases
B. Not be affected
C. Decreases
D. Increases first, then decreases

Q.39 In which year the world's population growth is expected to be zero, as per the report published by United Nations?
A. 2030 **B.** 2050 **C.** 2075 **D.** 2100

Q.40 Which of the following calamities cannot be caused by Earthquakes?
A. Floods **B.** Landslide
C. Cyclone **D.** Tsunami

Q.41 If you are in the CC field of an email, which of the other email address would you be able to see:
i. Sender's email address
ii. Other email addresses in CC
iii. Email addresses in BCC
A. Only i **B.** Only i and ii
C. Only i and iii **D.** All of them

Q.42 Which of the following best describes shareware?
A. Software available for free download
B. Software available for free download to copy users
C. Software available for free download, but needs to be paid later for continued use
D. Software available for free download for copy users but needs to be paid for continued use

Q.43 Which of the following is true about the National Mission in Education through ICT (NMEICT)?
A. It is a centrally sponsored scheme to enhance Gross Enrollment Ratio in higher education by making use of ICT.
B. The two major components are providing access and content generation.
C. Both A and B
D. None of them

Q.44 Arrange these in terms of access speed, from fastest to slowest memory.
i. Cache
ii. Hard Disk Drive
iii. USB
iv. RAM
A. i, ii, iii, iv **B.** i, iv, ii, iii
C. ii, iv, i, iii **D.** i, iv, iii, ii

Q.45 VRML stands for:
A. Visual Real Mark-up Language
B. Variety Register Machine Language
C. Virtual Reality Machine Language
D. Virtual Reality Modeling Language

Q.46 Assertion (A): Morality is caught, rather than taught.
Reason (R): Morality is not just a cognitive fact, but also effective and conative one.
A. Both A and R are true and R is the correct explanation of A
B. Both A and R are true and R is not the correct explanation of A
C. Only A is true
D. Both A and R are false

Q.47 Assertion (A): In urban areas, smog episodes occur frequently in winters.
Reason (R): In winters, a lot of biomass is burnt by people for heating purposes or to keep themselves warm.
Choose the correct answer from the code given below:
A. Both (A) and (R) are true and (R) is the correct explanation of (A)
B. Both (A) and (R) are true but (R) is not the correct explanation of (A)
C. (A) is true and (R) is false
D. Both (A) and (R) are false

Q.48 Match the List 1 with List 2. List 1 comprises the different learning programmes in India. List 2 lists down the various institutes related with the different learning programmes in India.

List 1	List 2
a) Oriental	(I) Tata Institute of Social Sciences
b) Non-Conventional	(ii) IIT Kanpur
C) Distance	(iii) Kuppuswami Sastri Institute
d) Conventional	(iv) IGNOU

A. a – (i), b – (ii), c – (iii), d – (iv)
B. a – (ii), b – (iii), c – (i), d – (iv)
C. a – (iii), b – (i), c – (iv), d – (ii)
D. a – (iii), b – (ii), c – (iv), d –(i)

Q.49 Consider the following statements about the National Assessment and Accreditation Council (NAAC).
1) NAAC is an autonomous body established in 1994 by the UGC with its headquarters in Delhi.
2) It was established as per recommendations of NPE (1986).
3) The prime function of NAAC is to assess and accredit institutions of higher learning, universities and colleges or their departments, schools, institutions, programmes etc.
Which of the following statements is/are correct?
A. Only 1 and 2 **B.** Only 2 and 3
C. Only 1 and 3 **D.** All of the above

Q.50 There is a lot of linguistic diversity in India. At the primary level, what should be done in multilingual classrooms to deal with problems related to this diversity?
A. Students must be fined when found speaking in their mother tongue or local language.
B. Admissions should not be given to those students who

speak other languages

C. The teacher must encourage children to communicate with each other through the means of language with expressions.

D. The teacher can ignore teaching in those schools.

// Smart Answer Sheet //

Correct Indicates percentage of students who answered questions correctly.

Skipped Indicates percentage of students who skipped questions.

Q.	Ans.	Correct	Skipped
1	C	49.44 %	4.67 %
2	D	26.54 %	14.02 %
3	C	30.37 %	13.74 %
4	B	31.96 %	16.08 %
5	C	23.83 %	15.89 %
6	A	56.82 %	15.98 %
7	C	48.04 %	16.54 %
8	B	41.03 %	16.82 %
9	C	34.77 %	19.62 %
10	D	59.63 %	17.1 %
11	B	28.22 %	20.94 %
12	C	18.04 %	21.21 %
13	C	48.6 %	18.97 %
14	B	31.59 %	18.6 %
15	C	35.7 %	18.97 %
16	C	29.25 %	24.86 %
17	A	39.63 %	25.7 %
18	D	11.4 %	26.54 %
19	C	16.54 %	27.67 %
20	B	16.36 %	28.59 %
21	C	66.82 %	22.25 %
22	A	42.9 %	24.11 %
23	D	21.03 %	28.04 %
24	B	44.95 %	27.76 %
25	B	32.43 %	31.78 %
26	B	28.69 %	22.71 %
27	A	23.08 %	27.67 %
28	B	30.65 %	24.49 %
29	B	36.73 %	24.02 %
30	A	13.74 %	27.94 %
31	C	26.64 %	32.89 %
32	D	24.02 %	34.11 %
33	B	24.86 %	36.26 %
34	D	9.35 %	37.38 %
35	B	25.51 %	35.99 %
36	B	33.36 %	26.55 %
37	C	30.47 %	28.88 %
38	A	20.84 %	25.23 %
39	D	19.72 %	26.26 %
40	C	35.23 %	24.68 %
41	B	36.26 %	26.26 %
42	D	25.79 %	27.2 %
43	C	49.72 %	27.1 %
44	D	20.09 %	25.98 %
45	D	25.42 %	25.7 %
46	A	38.41 %	26.82 %
47	B	20.84 %	27.38 %
48	C	35.14 %	28.5 %
49	B	18.6 %	28.6 %
50	C	32.43 %	26.54 %

Performance Analysis	
Avg. Score (%)	31.0%
Toppers Score (%)	100.0%
Your Score	

//Hints and Solutions//

1.

- A t-test is a type of inferential statistic which is used to determine if there is a significant difference between the means of two groups, which may be related in certain features.
- The t-test is one of the different tests that are used for the purpose of hypothesis testing. Z test determines the same but is used when the sample size is large.

Hence, the correct option is (C).

2.

- Research ethics is about the accuracy of results, use of scientific methods for objective results, also maintaining the confidentiality of the respondent's or participant's study or only revealing their study it if they have consented to do so.
- However, it should not be a quest for proving one's opinion right or political motives.

Hence, the correct option is (D).

3. John B. Watson (1878-1958) was the first to study how the process of learning affects our behaviour, and he formed the school of thought known as Behaviorism. Behavioural Psychology is basically interested in how our behaviour results from the stimuli both in the environment and within ourselves.

Options (A), (B) and (D) are a correct statement for the term learning except that study of behaviour is learning.

Hence, the correct option is (C).

4. Children in single-gender school would not find themselves comfortable while interacting with the opposite gender and it will result in restricted socialisation.

Socialization is very important for children, who begin the process at home with family and continue it at school. They are taught what will be expected of them as they mature and become full members of society. Socialization is also important for adults who join new social groups. Broadly defined, it is the process of transferring norms, values, beliefs, and behaviours to future group members.

Hence, the correct option is (B).

5.

- A normative study doesn't require hypothesis formulation as it studies a phenomenon about how it should be by suggesting improvements.
- For example, a normative study about a particular gadget would be about the review of its features and would recommend some improvements in future.

Hence, the correct option is (C).

6.

- A lecture method is a traditional method of teaching which involves the delivery of the content by the teacher.
- In order to make a lecture effective, receiving positive feedback from students is important.
- Without any feedback, a lecture is incompetent (lacked competence on part of the teacher), inconsequential (unrewarding), and futile.

Hence, the correct option is (A).

7.

- Confident stance of a teacher is enough to win the hearts of the students.
- A teacher becomes confident with good knowledge of his or her subject.
- Ensuring respect and obedience from the students doesn't require aggressive tone and exercise of authority.

Hence, the correct option is (C).

8.

- A teacher must appreciate and reinforce the attitude of enquiry, reflection, critical thinking, prior experience or knowledge, and motivation among students.
- This ensures a healthy learning environment in the classroom.
- Being submissive can hamper learning behaviour.

Hence, the correct option is (B).

9. Correct items have been matched against each other in the following table:

Choice Based Credit System	A student-centred approach to learning
Continuous and Comprehensive Evaluation	The developmental process of assessment
Teacher Support System	Learning guide and resources for teachers
Normative Assessment	Evaluation based on relative performance

Choice based credit system (CBCS), provides a learning platform wherein the student or knowledge seeker has the flexibility to choose their course from a list of elective, core and soft skill courses. This is a student-centric approach to learning or acquiring higher education.

Continuous and Comprehensive Evaluation (CCE) refers to a system of school-based evaluation of students that covers all aspects of students development. It is a developmental process of assessment which emphasizes on two fold objectives.

Support your teachers by following best practices for professional development focus on specific content, allow for active learning, and embed PD in the work itself (peer observation and feedback, co-teaching opportunities, teacher-based data teams, etc.)

Which is an assessment that is based on comparing the relative performances of students, either by comparing the performances of individual students within the group being tested or by comparing their performance with that of others of similar age, experience and background.

Hence, the correct option is (C).

10.

- Students learn when there is a positive environment for them to reform and improve.
- A progressive and liberal environment also helps students to express themselves.
- The learning environment in the classroom is vital to student success and influences the student in a number of ways. A negative learning environment or setting adversely affects student learning in many ways, such as low student achievement, poor behaviour, student anxiety, or depression.

Hence, the correct option is (D).

11.

- According to Little, 'Human communication is the process by which information is passed between people by means of previously agreed symbols, in order to produce the desired response'.
- Whereas Berlo tried to explain communication as S-M-C-R Model that stands for Sender-Message-Channel-Receiver. It is the basic communication process.

Hence, the correct option is (B).

12.

- Collective decision-making, self-expression, increasing one's effect, and elevating one's status is a part of group communication.
- Interpersonal Communication is also termed as dyadic communication.
- Interpersonal Communication is a universal form of face-to-face routine communication between two persons, both sending and receiving messages.
- It may be formal or informal, verbal or non-verbal. It takes place anywhere by means of words, sounds, facial expression, gestures, and postures. It is an effective communication situation because you can get immediate feedback.

Hence, the correct option is (C).

13.

- Effective communication within a classroom happens when the teacher is able to get his or her message across with the use of some effective medium.
- Effective communication in the classroom would help the teacher to be received and understood.
- It also helps to create a team spirit rather than creating disparity or polarisation.

Hence, the correct option is (C).

14. The communication process is the perfect guide toward achieving effective communication. When followed properly, the process can usually assure that the sender's message will be understood by the receiver. Although the communication process seems simple, it in essence is not. Certain barriers present themselves throughout the process. Those barriers are factors that have a negative impact on the communication process. Some common barriers include the use of an inappropriate medium (channel), incorrect grammar, inflammatory words, words that conflict with body language, and technical jargon. Noise is also another common barrier. Noise can occur during any stage of the process. Noise essentially is anything that distorts a message by interfering with the communication process. Noise can take many forms, including a radio playing in the background

Hence, the correct option is (B).

15.

- Certain disorders or diseases or other limitations could also prevent effective communication between the various channels of an organization.
- The shrillness of voice, dyslexia, etc. are examples of physiological barriers to effective communication.

Hence, the correct option is (C).

16. It can be deciphered from the following lines, "The Draft National Education Policy, 2019 (DNEP) envisions an India-centered education system that contributes directly to transforming our nation sustainably into an equitable and vibrant knowledge society, by providing high-quality education to all. The NITI Aayog particularly has shifted the policy focus from inputs and programmed to outcomes from education. It has promoted competitive federalism among states to improve their educational indicators that are measurable by a battery of tests on students."

Hence, the correct option is (C).

17. The passage states, "But any serious work on 'No One Left Behind' (NOLB) may ask for new and reformistic approaches. The DNEP has provided some hope, but it calls for further examination of rhetoric and reality. The DNEP must be read in the context of the current economic and educational climate in order to be able to gauge the essential path and pace needed to make its vision a reality."

Hence, the correct option is (A).

18. It can be deciphered from the following lines, "On the one hand, we are in another new age of industrial revolution or the skilling age. On the other, at present, roughly one million young people enter the workforce in India each month, but a majority of them are just raw hands without professional technical knowledge or practical vocational skills. The weak linkages between education and employment carry the potential risk of turning India's demographic dividend into a demographic disaster."

Hence, the correct option is (D).

19. It can be deciphered from the following lines, "In the education sector, the elusive conundrum of the quantity-quality-equity triangle has remained unresolved. Although the merit of education as an invaluable public good is well recognised, the public investment for it has remained low. It is relevant to explore how the DNEP has addressed some of the major areas for policy intervention in school education."

Hence, the correct option is (C).

20. The passage states, "It has promoted competitive federalism among states to improve their educational indicators that are measurable by a battery of tests on the student. It is relevant to explore how the DNEP has addressed some of the major areas for policy intervention in school education, namely Access, which can be measured by the size and flow of students moving across the education system, Equity, which can be gauged by the reduction or persistence of developmentally deprived population, and Quality, which can be understood from teaching-learning processes and developmental outcomes for children that are more conveniently implied by attainment scores."

Hence, the correct option is (B).

21. In this question, we show that first number is subtracted from second number and second number subtracted from third number and so on. Now we get:

35 - 29 = 6

43 – 35 = 8

53 – 43 = 10

? – 53 = 12

? = 12 + 53

? = 65

79 – 65 = 14

Hence, the correct option is (C).

22. This is the figure for the given problem.

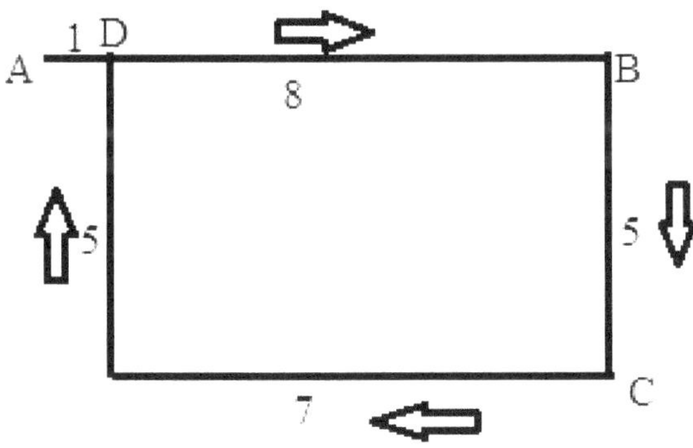

AD= AB - DB= 8-7 = 1km
Hence, the correct option is (A).

23. Rate of depreciation $= 8\%$
Value of motorcycle after two-year $= 84640$
Let the present value of motorcycle be x.
Then $x \times \frac{92}{100} \times \frac{92}{100} = 84640$
$x = \frac{846400000}{92\times92} = 100000$

Hence, the correct option is (D).

24. In code language, each number show the unit digit of each letter of word.

For TITLESHOOT:

T(20), I(9), T(20), L(12), E(5), S(19), H(8), O(15), O(15), T(20)

⇒ T(2+0), I(9),T(2+0), L(1+2), E(5), S(1+9), H(8), O(1+5), O(1+5), T(2+0)

⇒29235108662

For WARZONES
W(23), A(1), R(18), Z(26), O(15), N(14), E(5), S(19)

⇒ W(2+3), A(1), R(1+8), Z(2+6), O(1+5), N(1+4), E(5), S(1+9)

⇒519865510

Similarly,
PLASTERISM is coded as
P(16), L(12), A(1), S(19), T(20), E(5), R(18), I(9), S(19), M(13)

⇒ P(1+6), L(1+2), A(1), S(1+9), T(2+0), E(5), R(1+8), I(9), S(1+9), M(1+3)

⇒731102599104

Hence, the correct option is (B).

25. Given: Speed of trains $= 54km/h$ and $92km/h$
Their relative speed $= 92-54$
$= 38km/h$
$\because 1m/s = (5/18)km/h$
∴Their relative speed $= 38 \times 5/18$
Total distance to travel by the faster train to cross the other train
$= 400 + 360$
$= 760m$
∴Total time needed to travel this distance by the faster train = $\frac{760\times18}{5\times38}$
$- 72s$
Hence, the correct option is (B).

26. All entrepreneurs are rich ıs a Universal positive (A-type) proposition.

In the event that all-inclusive positive proclamation is false than certainly specific negative (O type) suggestion will be valid. Because there is a contradictory relationship between A and O. Contradictory opposition is the relation between two propositions having the same subject but differing in both quality and quantity.

Hence, the correct option is (B).

27. Deductive reasoning, also deductive logic, is the process of reasoning from one or more statements to reach a logical conclusion. Deductive reasoning goes in the same direction as that of the conditionals, and links premises with conclusions.

For reasoning to be deductive, the conclusion must be based on observation and experiment, the conclusion should not be supported by the premise/premises, it is not necessary for the conclusion to follow the premise/premises, it has got nothing to do with validity of an argument.

Hence, the correct option is (A).

28. Teachers are referred to as the transmitters, inspirers, and promoters of man's eternal quest for knowledge. The status of the teacher reflects the socio-cultural ethos of the society as it is said that no people can rise above the level of their teachers.

- The teacher to play multiple roles in a teaching-learning process i.e., manager, facilitator, counselor, producer, and leader, etc.
- He has to manage all the activities in a classroom that are designed around a learner as the learner is the center of the teaching-learning process.
- The most important for a teacher is to use his teaching skills effectively as his content knowledge will be of no use if he is not able to present it in a systematic and interesting manner.
- A good teacher is one who can make the maximum use of the minimal resources available to teach the students to provide a joyful learning experience.
- So, a teacher has to be most importantly an expert in teaching skills which will help them to present the content knowledge they had of their concerned subject.
- Also, the teacher has to be on a good rapport with the students so that the students can share their problems with their teachers and can ask their doubts without being hesitant.
- The other qualities of a teacher like his good health, his clothes, his voice modulation, etc. are the secondary qualities of being a good teacher.

So, it is concluded that expertise in teaching skills is most important for a teacher.

Hence, the correct option is (B).

29.

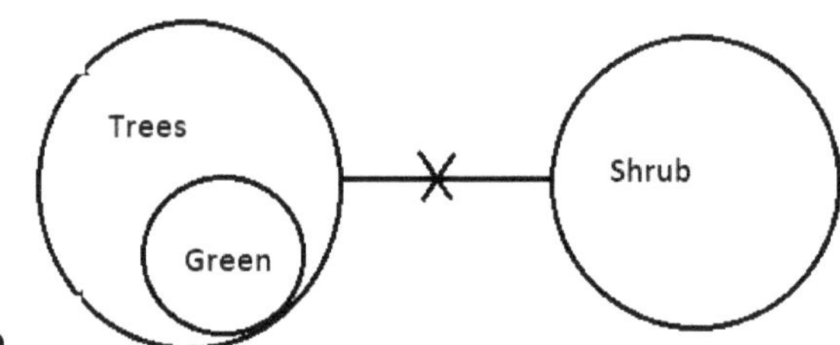

(i) No green is a shrub follows as all green are tree and no tree is shrub, so no green is a shrub is true.

(ii) Some shrubs are green does not follow, as no tree is shrub and all green are trees, so some shrubs are green does not follow.

Hence, the correct option is (B).

30.

- Ostensive definition: A definition developed by showing someone an object and attaching a word to it.
- This sort of definition is frequently utilized where the term is hard to characterize verbally, either in light of the fact that the words won't be comprehended or in light of the idea of the term.
- For example, defining red by pointing out red objects- apples, roses, etc.

Hence, the correct option is (A).

31. Average vote received by A from 2013 to 2015.

$= \frac{1}{3}\left(420 \times \frac{36}{100} + 390 \times \frac{42}{100} + 378 \times \frac{24}{100}\right)$

$= \frac{1}{30}(42 \times 36 + 39 \times 42 + 37.8 \times 24)$

$= \frac{1}{30}(1512 + 1638 + 907.2)$

$= \frac{1}{30} \times 4057.2 = 135.24$

Hence, the correct option is (C).

32. The average number of votes a candidate received in 2018.

$= \frac{\text{Total Votes}}{\text{No. of candidates}} = \frac{460}{5}$

$= 92$ Hundred

$= 9.2$ Thousand

Hence, the correct option is (D).

33. A number of votes received by \(B\) in 2015.

$= 378 \times \frac{21}{100} = 7938$

Wrongly casted votes against $B = 9000 - 7938 = 1062$

Percentage of wrongly casted votes against $B =$ $\frac{1062}{9000} \times 100 = 11.8\%$

Hence, the correct option is (B).

34. Votes received by D in 2016

$= 425 \times \frac{14}{100} = 59.5 = 5950$

40% of total votes $= 5950$

total votes $= 5950 \times \frac{100}{40} = 14875$

Hence, the correct option is (D).

35. Percentage increase $= \frac{460-420}{420} \times 100$

$= \frac{200}{21}$

$= 9\frac{11}{21}\%$

Hence, the correct option is (B).

36.

- Desalination has been proposed as one of the techniques to mitigate drought conditions in some areas.
- NITI Aayog has proposed that in order to address the country's water woes, desalination plants should be set up along India's vast coastline.
- So, Both A and R are true.
- But Reason is not the correct explanation of Assertion, as both the statements are talking about drought but with different causes.

Hence, the correct option is (B).

37.

- International treaty of wetland conservation programme also known as Ramsar Convention on Wetlands was signed in the year 1971 to save the wetlands.
- Montreal Protocol was signed in the year 1983 to protect the ozone layer by phasing out the substances that are harmful to ozone depletion.
- Earth summit was first signed in 1992
- Kyoto Protocol was signed in 1997 to reduce greenhouse gases emission.

Hence, the correct option is (C).

38. If polar ice starts melting, water would start accumulating in the oceans near the equator, thus decreasing the speed of the earth rotation. Hence, the length of the day will increase.

Hence, the correct option is (A).

39. By 2100, the world's population growth is expected to be zero.

As per the World's Population Prospect 2019 by United Nations population growth continues at the global level, but the rate of increase is slowing, and the world's population could cease to grow around the end of the century.

Hence, the correct option is (D).

40.

- Cyclones cannot be caused by an Earthquake.
- Earthquakes can cause Tsunami, landslides and flood.
- Tsunami is the waves caused by the sudden movement of the ocean due to earthquakes.
- Cyclone Fani caused damage in India.

Hence, the correct option is (C).

41.

- Recipients market in CC field can see email addresses of the sender and other recipients in CC, but not bcc.
- CC stands for Carbon copy and BCC stands for Blind Carbon Copy.

Hence, the correct option is (B).

42. Shareware refers to commercial software that is copyrighted, but which may be copied for others for the purpose of their trying it out with the understanding that they will pay for it if they continue to use it.

Hence, the correct option is (D).

43.

- NMEICT is a centrally sponsored scheme to enhance Gross Enrolment Ratio in higher education by making use of ICT.
- The two major components are providing access and content generation.

Hence, the correct option is (C).

44. In terms of memory speed hierarchy, the path would be as follows:

- Processor Registers > Processor Cache > RAM > USB/Flash > Hard Drive > tape backup.

Hence, the correct option is (D).

45. VRML (Virtual Reality Modeling Language, pronounced vermal or by its initials, originally before 1995 known as the Virtual Reality Markup Language) is a standard file format for representing 3-dimensional (3D) interactive vector graphics, designed particularly with the World Wide Web in mind.

Hence, the correct option is (D).

46.

- It is true that morality is caught rather than taught because morality is not just a cognitive ability (mental) but also affective (emotional) and conative behaviour (based on personal motivation).
- Both statements are right and rightly correlated with each other.

Hence, the correct option is (A).

47. In urban areas, smog episodes occur very frequently in winters is true. As this smog occurs due to many reasons like pollution, burning of biomass/plastic when sunlight and heat react with the different gases.

In winters, a lot of biomass is burnt by people for heating purposes or to keep themselves warm is also true. But it is not the only reason for the occurrence of smog in winters.

So, both the assertion and reason are true but the reason is not the correct explanation of the assertion.

Hence, the correct option is (B).

48.

- The oriental learning programme is instituted by Kuppuswami Sastri Institute.
- The non-conventional learning programme is instituted by the Tata Institute of Social Sciences.
- The conventional learning programme is instituted by IIT Kanpur.
- The distance learning programme is instituted by IGNOU.

Hence, the correct option is (C).

49.

- NAAC is an autonomous body established in 1994 by the UGC with its headquarters in Bangalore.
- It was established as per the recommendations of NPE (1986).
- The prime function of the NAAC is to assess and accredit institutions of higher learning, universities and colleges or their departments, schools, institutions, programs, etc.
- It regularly publishes manuals and promotion materials for assessment and accreditation.

50. Any teacher should enhance in his classroom the process of learning language through different means as well as should teach to respect each-others language.

Hence, the correct option is (C).

Mock Test 03

Q.1 For formulating the curriculum, which factor is most important?

A. Teachers ability
B. Children's capabilities and needs
C. National Ideology
D. Social and cultural Ideals

Q.2 If the majority of students in your class is weak you should:

A. Not care about intelligent students
B. Keep your speed of teaching fast so that students comprehension level may increase
C. Keep your teaching slow which can also be helpful to bright students
D. Keep your teaching slow along with some extra guidance to bright people

Q.3 A teacher can establish rapport with his pupil by:

A. Becoming a figure of authority
B. Impressing them with knowledge and skill
C. Playing the role of a guide with a desire to help them
D. Becoming a friend to the pupils

Q.4 A teacher can help the adolescent to overcome his special problems, and help him to adjust to the environment. Which of the following attitude, he should not make?

A. He should impart the right information about sex.
B. He should redirect the energies of the adolescent to fruitful channels through sports and other constructive activities.
C. He should have an unsympathetic attitude toward others.
D. He should have the right information about sex.

Q.5 All of the following are advantages of teaching machines except:

A. The control of cheating
B. Tracking of errors
C. The insurance of attention
D. Their universal use for different kinds of programmes

Q.6 The major objective of education is:

A. Reforming society
B. Making students disciplined
C. Developing inherent abilities/powers of students
D. Making students followers of teachers

Q.7 The teaching is not thought as a process of:

A. Directing the activities of people
B. Listening to the recitation of pupils
C. Indoctrinating adult ideas to young people
D. None of these

Q.8 According to Dewey, education is a:

A. Social need **B.** Personal need
C. Psychological need **D.** Theoretical need

Q.9 The term 'least restrictive environment' refers to the education of the:

A. Handicapped
B. Gifted
C. Early childhood youngsters
D. Retarded

Q.10 The Dalton Scheme of education is useful for which one of the following?

A. For infants **B.** For little children
C. For older children **D.** For all of these

Q.11 The most accurate statement about teaching machines is that:

A. B.F. Skinner began the movement for their use.
B. They were designed as an economy measure to replace teachers.
C. They are not as efficient as teachers in reinforcing responses.
D. They can be used for all learning programmes.

Q.12 The most important task is teaching is:

A. Making monthly reports and maintaining records
B. Making assignments and hearing recitations
C. Directing students in the development of experience
D. None of these

Q.13 Direction: Choose the correct answer from the following.

Assertion (A): To communicate well in the classroom is a natural ability.

Reason (R): Effective teaching in the classroom demands knowledge of the communication process.

A. Both (A) and (R) are true, and (R) is the correct explanation of (A)
B. Both (A) and (R) are true, but (R) is not the correct explanation of (A)
C. (A) is true, but (R) is false
D. (A) is false, but (R) is true

Q.14 When verbal and non-verbal messages are contradictory, it is said that most people believe in:

A. Indeterminate messages
B. Verbal messages
C. Non-verbal messages
D. Aggressive messages

Q.15 The reservation of seats for women in the Panchayat Raj Institutions is:

A. 30% of the total seats
B. 50% of the total seats
C. 33% of the total population
D. In proportion to their population

Q.16 Identify the main principle on which the Parliamentary System operates:

A. Responsibility of executive to the legislature
B. Supremacy of parliament
C. Supremacy of judiciary
D. The supremacy of constitution

Q.17 In the following questions, find the odd word/letters/number pair from the given alternatives.
A. SP **B.** NL **C.** ZW **D.** TQ

Q.18 Sunderban in Hooghly delta is known for:
A. Grasslands **B.** Conifers
C. Mangroves **D.** Arid forests

Q.19 In which parts of India groundwater is affected with arsenic contamination?
A. Haryana **B.** Andhra pradesh
C. Sikkim **D.** West Bengal

Q.20 It is believed that our globe is warming progressively. this global warming will eventually result in:
A. Increase in availability of usable land
B. Uniformity of climate at equator and poles
C. Fall in the sea level
D. Melting of polar ice

Q.21 Which one is like pole and pillar?
A. Beam **B.** Plank **C.** Shaft **D.** Timber

Q.22 The state - "Honesty is the best policy" is:
A. A fact **B.** A value
C. An opinion **D.** A value judgement

Q.23 The competency of an effective communicator can be judged on the basis of:
A. Personality of communicator
B. Experience in the field
C. Interactivity with the target audience
D. All of the above

Q.24 TV Channel launched for covering only Engineering and Technology subjects is known as:
A. Gyan Darshan **B.** Vyas
C. Eklavya **D.** Kisan

Q.25 The sentence "Men just don't want to vacate their seats of power" implies:
A. Lust for power
B. Desire to serve the nation
C. Conviction in one's own political abilities
D. Political corruption

Q.26 An investigator studied the census data for a given area and prepared a write-up based on them. Such a write-up is called:
A. Research paper **B.** Article
C. Thesis **D.** Research report

Q.27 The Government of India conducts Census after every 10 years. The method of research used in this process is:
A. Case study **B.** Developmental
C. Survey **D.** Experimental

Q.28 One of the essential characteristics of research is:
A. Replicability **B.** Generalizability
C. Usability **D.** Objectivity

Q.29 Effectiveness of teaching depends on:
A. Qualification of teacher
B. Personality of teacher
C. Handwriting of teacher
D. Subject understanding of teacher

Q.30 Which is an instant messenger that is used for chatting?
A. Altavista **B.** MAC
C. Microsoft Office **D.** Google Talk

Q.31 DVD technology uses optical media to store digital data. DVD is an acronym for:
A. Digital Vector Disc
B. Digital Volume Disc
C. Digital Versatile Disc
D. Digital Visualization Disc

Q.32 If DANCE is coded as GXQZH, then how will RIGHT be coded?
A. UFJEW **B.** SCKFX **C.** UEJWE **D.** UPWJE

Q.33 Which of the following Digital Initiatives has been launched under the National Mission on Education through ICT (NMEICT)?
i. SWAYAM Prabha
ii. National Digital Library
iii. National Academic Depository
iv. E-Yantra
A. (i) and (ii) only **B.** (iii) and (iv) only
C. (i), (ii), (iii) only **D.** (i), (ii), (iii) & (iv)

Q.34 The abbreviation DNS stands for:
A. Domain Name System
B. Dependent Name Server
C. Defense Nuclear System
D. Downloadable New Software

Q.35 The four major operations in scientific research are:
(a) Demonstration of co-variance
(b) Elimination of spurious relations
(c) Sequencing in terms of time-order
(d) Self-education
(e) Operationalization of personal choice
(f) Theorisation
A. (a), (b), (c) and (f) **B.** (b), (c), (d) and (e)
C. (a), (b), (c) and (d) **D.** (c), (d), (e) and (f)

Q.36 In the following question, find the odd word/letters/number from the given alternatives.
A. Softball **B.** Baseball
C. Cricket **D.** Basketball

Q.37 In a certain code, ROSE is written as @\%$# and PREACH is written as *@#18&, then how can SEARCH be written in that code?

A. $1235& **B.** $#2@3&
C. $#1@8& **D.** S#379@

Q.38 From among the given alternatives select the one in which the set of numbers is most like the set of numbers given in the question.

16,36,64

A. 4,9,144 **B.** 16,100,256
C. 25,49,121 **D.** 9,81,169

Q.39 The value of the research will be lost:

A. If a researcher feels agreement with an imaginary assumption
B. If a researcher becomes the prey to hallucination
C. If a researcher became prejudiced
D. All the above

Ques (40-42): Study the following table and answer the questions based on it.

Expenditures of a Company (in Lakh Rupees) per Annum Over the given Years.

Item of Expenditure

Year	Salary	Fuel and Transport	Bonus	Interest on Loans	Taxes
1998	288	98	3.00	23.4	83
1999	342	112	2.52	32.5	108
2000	324	101	3.84	41.6	74
2001	336	133	3.68	36.4	88
2002	420	142	3.96	49.4	98

Q.40 What is the average amount of interest per year which the company had to pay during this period?

A. $Rs. 36.66 lakhs$ **B.** $Rs. 33.72 lakhs$
C. $Rs. 34.18 lakhs$ **D.** $Rs. 32.43 lakhs$

Q.41 Identify the important element a teacher has to take cognizance of while addressing students in a classroom.

A. Avoidance of proximity
B. Voice modulation
C. Repetitive pause
D. Fixed posture

Q.42 The choice of communication partners is influenced by factors of:

A. Proximity, utility, loneliness
B. Utility, secrecy, dissonance
C. Secrecy, dissonance, deception
D. Dissimilarity, dissonance, deviance

Q.43 Choose the correct meaning of the sentence.

A person who renounces the world and practices self-discipline in order to attain salvation:

A. Sceptic **B.** Ascetic
C. Devotee **D.** Antiquarian

Q.44 If $4-2=8, 5-2=27$, and $6-2=64$ then $7-2$ equals to:

A. 25 **B.** 125 **C.** 55 **D.** 75

Q.45 Prema is Ajay's sister. Benita is Ajay's mother. Benjamin is Benita's father. Leela is Benjamin's mother. How is Prema related to Leela?

A. Daughter-in-law
B. Daughter
C. Grand Daughter
D. Great Grand Daughter

Q.46 The next term in the series:

2,7,28,63,126, _____ is

A. 215 **B.** 245 **C.** 276 **D.** 296

Q.47 The main objectives of student evaluation of teachers are:

1) To gather information about student weaknesses.
2) To make teachers take teaching seriously.
3) To help teachers adopt innovative methods of teaching.
4) To identify the areas of further improvement in teacher traits.

Identify the correct answer from the codes given below:

A. 1 and 2 only **B.** 2, 3 and 4 only
C. 1, 2 and 3 only **D.** 1 only

Q.48 Direction: Choose the correct answer from the following code.

Assertion (A): The purpose of higher education is to promote critical and creative thinking abilities among students.

Reason (R): These abilities ensure job placements.

A. Both (A) and (R) are true and (R) is the correct explanation of (A)
B. Both (A) and (R) are true but (R) is not the correct explanation of (A)
C. (A) is true but (R) is false
D. (A) is false but (R) is true

Q.49 Which of the following characteristics do not belong to an effective teacher/teaching. Identify the correct option.

A. A teacher is effective if he/she has the full confidence of the subject.
B. Teaching is always in a formal manner.
C. Teaching is a continuous process.
D. Teaching is an interaction between teacher and students.

Q.50 Learner centered approach to teaching and learning focuses on which of the following skills?

A. Learner needs
B. Subject matter
C. Development of skills
D. All of the above

// Smart Answer Sheet //

Correct Indicates percentage of students who answered questions correctly.

Skipped Indicates percentage of students who skipped questions.

Q.	Ans.	Correct	Skipped
1	B	42.24 %	7.4 %
2	D	57.4 %	26.72 %
3	C	52.53 %	29.42 %
4	C	43.14 %	27.98 %
5	D	32.13 %	31.77 %
6	C	48.01 %	32.5 %
7	C	42.96 %	29.78 %
8	A	42.78 %	33.03 %
9	A	25.27 %	30.87 %
10	C	22.74 %	32.68 %
11	A	25.45 %	30.33 %
12	C	45.49 %	30.14 %
13	D	29.42 %	35.38 %
14	C	43.14 %	34.12 %
15	B	31.59 %	35.74 %
16	D	25.09 %	35.2 %
17	B	44.4 %	34.84 %
18	C	30.69 %	36.1 %
19	D	18.23 %	29.06 %
20	D	35.2 %	31.95 %
21	A	43.5 %	31.23 %
22	D	40.61 %	30.51 %
23	D	45.31 %	33.57 %
24	C	39.89 %	29.97 %
25	A	45.31 %	25.81 %
26	B	47.83 %	30.69 %
27	C	57.22 %	29.78 %
28	D	44.04 %	32.13 %
29	D	41.16 %	35.92 %
30	D	36.28 %	36.46 %
31	C	36.28 %	33.4 %
32	A	34.12 %	32.49 %
33	D	38.99 %	28.52 %
34	A	32.67 %	33.76 %
35	A	41.7 %	28.88 %
36	D	22.38 %	31.23 %
37	C	25.63 %	39.35 %
38	B	19.86 %	40.07 %
39	D	37.73 %	37.18 %
40	A	31.77 %	38.27 %
41	B	35.02 %	37.72 %
42	A	29.42 %	37.01 %
43	B	50.9 %	27.8 %
44	B	47.47 %	32.49 %
45	D	33.94 %	30.32 %
46	A	24.37 %	30.86 %
47	B	42.06 %	36.28 %
48	B	44.4 %	31.05 %
49	B	27.26 %	33.39 %
50	D	40.79 %	32.5 %

Performance Analysis	
Avg. Score (%)	43.0%
Toppers Score (%)	100.0%
Your Score	

//Hints and Solutions//

1.

- For formulating the curriculum, children's capabilities and needs are most important.
- In curriculum development, we think about the type of learning experiences to be given to a child at various ages and grade levels.
- It needs systematic and sequential planning to widen the sphere of the learning experience at each level by keeping in view the principles of integration and correlation.
- The curriculum is usually concerned with two questions.

Hence, the correct option is (B).

2. If the majority of students in your class are weak you should keep your teaching slow along with some extra guidance to bright pupils. Every individual is unique with different IQ levels. Some students have the capability of grabbing fast and memorizing for a long. Others have less picking capacity. In an organization, school or college, both the active and weak students study. Teachers and professors are supposed to take care of each and everybody as per their specific needs. Weak students or slow learners require extra attention. Punishing a weak student won't provide the necessary solution.

Hence, the correct option is (D).

3. A teacher can establish rapport with his pupil by playing the role of a guide with a desire to help them. Learn something about your students' interests, hobbies, and aspirations. Create and use personally relevant class examples. Arrive to class early and stay late and chat with your students. Explain your course policies and why they are what they are.

Hence, the correct option is (C).

4. He should have an unsympathetic attitude toward others.

The teacher must perform any task correctly. In the case of teenagers, they are new to work and have a lot of problems. The teacher gave him many answers to his questions and in adult age, he was more successful because of knowledge.

Hence, the correct option is (C).

5. All of the following are advantages of teaching machines except their universal use for different kinds of programmes.

There are many advantages to the use of teaching machines. They are particularly useful in subjects that require drill, such as arithmetic or a foreign language. Users can proceed at their own pace and also have an opportunity to review their work.

Hence, the correct option is (D).

6. The major objective of education is developing inherent abilities/powers of students.

The main objective of teacher education is to develop a skill to stimulate experience in the thinking, under an artificially created environment, less with material resources and more by the creation of an emotional atmosphere.

Hence, the correct option is (C).

7. The teaching is not thought of as a process of indoctrinating adult ideas to young people. Indoctrination is the process of inculcating a person with ideas, attitudes, cognitive strategies, or professional methodologies (see doctrine). Humans are a social animal species inescapably shaped by cultural context, and thus some degree of indoctrination is implicit in the parent-child relationship and has an essential function in forming stable communities of shared values.

Hence, the correct option is (C).

8. Simply put, Dewey stated that human experiences- past, present, and future- influence the capacity to learn. He once said: 'Education is a social process. Education is, not a preparation for life; education is life itself. Dewey formulated "social efficiency" as the aim of education in view of the changing tenor of society. This change has been brought by the application of science to the means of production and distribution, by the rise of great manufacturing centres and by the rapid growth of means of communication. The school must take cognizance of these changes to fit the child in this changed situation in an effective manner.

Hence, the correct option is (A).

9. The term "least restrictive environment" refers to the education of the handicapped. Least Restrictive Environment (LRE) is the requirement in federal law that students with disabilities receive their education, to the maximum extent appropriate, with nondisabled peers and that special education student is not removed from regular classes unless, even with supplemental aids and services, education in regular classes cannot be achieved satisfactorily.

Hence, the correct option is (A).

10. The Dalton scheme of education is useful for older children. The Dalton scheme is a method of education by which pupils work at their own pace, and receive individual help from the teacher when necessary. There is no formal class instruction. Students draw up time-tables and are responsible for finishing the work on their syllabuses or assignments.

Hence, the correct option is (C).

11. The most accurate statement about teaching machines is that B.F. Skinner began the movement for their use. Developed by behavioural scientist B.F. Skinner, the machine and its many iterations made it possible for students to move through lessons at their own pace. The machine would pose a question, then offer a reward, usually in the form of encouragement, for answering correctly.

Hence, the correct option is (A).

12. The most important task in teaching is directing students in the development of experience. For students to be successful in self-directed learning, they must be able to engage in self-reflection and self-evaluation of their learning goals and progress in a unit of study.

Hence, the correct option is (C).

13.

- Effective teaching demands knowledge of communication in the following ways:
- Effective communication can be maintained using different audio-video techniques in the classroom.
- Effective communication demands careful use of nonverbal cues in the classroom.
- Using an honest and tactful tone will also add to effective communication in the classroom.

Hence, the correct option is (D).

14. When verbal and non-verbal messages are contradictory, it is said that most people believe in the non-verbal messages. The non-verbal messages include actions, gestures and movement of hands, facial expression etc.

Hence, the correct option is (C).

15. The 50% reservation for women in Panchayati Raj institutions is an important part of this empowerment of women. As per provisions contained in article 243 D of the Constitution, 1/3rd of the seats of Panchayati Raj Institutions and 1/3rd offices of the Chairperson at all levels of Panchayati Raj Institutions covered by Part IX of the Constitution are reserved for women. The following states have made legal provision for 50% reservation for women among members and Sarpanches: Andhra Pradesh, Bihar, Chhattisgarh, Jharkhand, Kerala, Maharashtra, Orissa, Rajasthan, Tripura and Uttarakhand. A statement giving the position about the Elected Women Representatives in all States and UTs as per the state of Panchayat report 2007-08 commissioned by the Ministry of Panchayati Raj is given in Annexure.

Hence, the correct option is (B).

16. The first and foremost feature of Indian Sovereignty is that the Constitution is the supreme law of the land; and all state organs including parliament, judiciary, states, etc. are bound by it. They must act within the limits laid down by the Constitution. This is called the Doctrine of Constitutional Supremacy. Parliamentary sovereignty (also called parliamentary supremacy or legislative supremacy) is a concept in the constitutional law of some parliamentary democracies. It holds that the legislative body has absolute sovereignty and is supreme over all other government institutions, including executive or judicial bodies.

Hence, the correct option is (D).

17. check every option respectively

$$S \overset{-3}{\rightarrow} P$$

$$Z \overset{-3}{\rightarrow} W$$

$$T \overset{-3}{\rightarrow} Q$$

But,

$$N \overset{-2}{\rightarrow} L$$

Hence, the correct option is (B).

18. The Sundarbans is a cluster of low-lying islands in the Bay of Bengal, spread across India and Bangladesh, famous for its unique mangrove forests. This active delta region is among the largest in the world, measuring about 40,000 sq km.

Hence, the correct option is (C).

19. In India, the states of West Bengal, Jharkhand, Bihar, Uttar Pradesh, Assam, Manipur and Chhattisgarh are reported to be most affected by arsenic contamination of groundwater above the permissible level.

Hence, the correct option is (D).

20. The Arctic's melting land ice and glaciers contribute to the sea-level rise happening. It results from the collision of colder air masses from the Arctic with warmer air.

Hence, the correct option is (D).

21. A beam is a structural member that carries a bending load that carries a vertical load on its longitudinal axis. Beam, in engineering, is basically a concrete piece of wood, a beam of a house, a plow, loom, or a balance in building construction, a beam is a horizontal member that carries a load that can be a brick Which is a stone wall above the base, in this case the beam is often called a lintel.

Hence, the correct option is (A).

22. A value judgment is the part of reasoning and it means a judgment of correctness or falseness. When a person thinks and provides his judgment on a certain type of concept, which is related to its rightness, then this judgment becomes value judgment.

Hence, the correct option is (D).

23. The competency of an effective communicator can be judged on the basis of the:

-Personality of the communicator

-Experience in the field

-Interactivity with the target audience

Being able to communicate effectively is perhaps the most important of all life skills. It is what enables us to pass information to other people, and to understand what is said to us. You only have to watch a baby listening intently to its mother and trying to repeat the sounds that she makes to understand how fundamental is the urge to communicate.

Hence, the correct option is (D).

24. Single technology is joint teaching between IIT and IGNOU. It was inaugurated on 26 January 2003 by Professor Murali Manohar Joshi, Honorable Minister, Human Resource Development, Science and Technology and Ocean Development.

Hence, the correct option is (C).

25. The sentence "Men just don't want to vacate their seats of power" implies "Lust for power". The lust for power has been an important and recurring theme in western historiography.

Hence, the correct option is (A).

26. An investigator studied the census data for a given area and prepared a write-up based on them. Such a write-up is called an article. A research paper is a piece of academic writing that provides analysis, interpretation, and argument based on in-depth independent research. Writing a research paper requires you to demonstrate a strong knowledge of your topic, engage with a variety of sources, and make an original contribution to the debate.

Hence, the correct option is (B).

27. The Census method is the method of statistical enumeration where all members of the population are studied. It can collect this information by surveying all households in the country using the census method. In our country, the Government conducts the Census of India every ten years.

Hence, the correct option is (C).

28. Scientific knowledge is objective. Simple objectivity means the ability to see and accept facts as they are, not as one might wish they were. To be objective, one has to protect oneself against one's own prejudices, beliefs, desires, values ,and preferences.

Hence, the correct option is (D).

29. Subjectivity is not characteristic of a good question paper. Subject knowledge has a very important role to play because high-quality teaching rests on teachers understanding the subjects they are teaching, knowing the structure and sequencing of concepts, developing factual knowledge essential to each subject, and guiding their pupils into the different ways of knowing that subjects provide: subjects create disciplined ways of knowing.

Hence, the correct option is (D).

30. Google Talk provides an instant messaging service that includes both text and voice communication. The instant messaging service is popularly known as "gtalk", "gchat", or "gmessage" to its users.

Hence, the correct option is (D).

31. DVD (abbreviation for Digital Versatile Disc or Digital Video Disc) is a digital optical disc data storage format invented and developed in 1995 and released in late 1996. Rewritable DVDs (DVD-RW, DVD+RW, and DVD-RAM) can be recorded and erased many times.

Hence, the correct option is (C).

32.

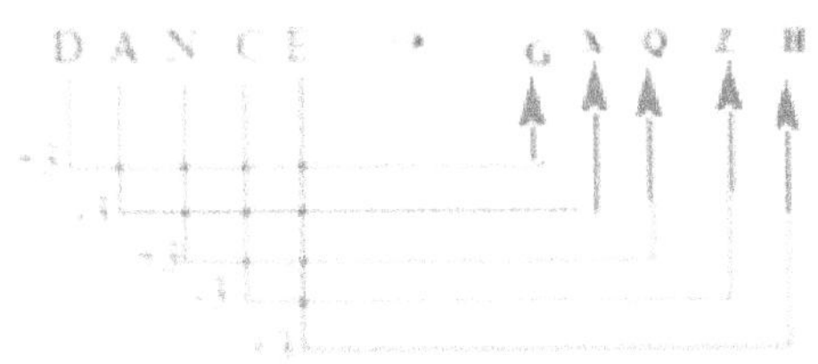

Similarly,

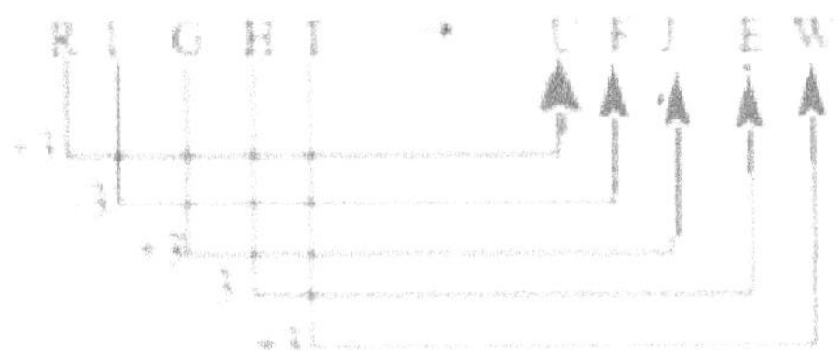

Hence, the correct option is (A).

33. SWAYAM Prabha: A project for operationalizing 32 Direct to Home (DTH) Television Channels for providing high-quality educational content to all teachers, students, and citizens across the country interested in lifelong learning.

National Digital Library: The objective is to integrate several national and international digital libraries in one single web-portal.

National Academic Depository: To provide all the details of academic awards online.

E-Yantra: An annual competition for students.

All the above-mentioned initiatives have been taken under the NMEICT. The other top initiatives are Swayam, E-Kalpa, Campus Connectivity, Virtual Labs, etc.

Hence, the correct option is (D).

34. Domain Name System (DNS) is a hierarchical and decentralized naming system for computers or any other services connected through the internet.

Hence, the correct option is (A).

35. The four major operations in scientific research are:

(a) Demonstration of co-variance: Covariance is the measure of the change of one variable with the change in the second variable. Scientific research demonstrates the effect of co-variance.

(b) Elimination of spurious relations: It is a really important operation in scientific research. The relation between the variables should be valid and logically, nothing suspicious should be there.

(c) Sequencing in terms of time-order: Every research should be in time order.

(f) Theorisation: To provide relevant theory is the other operation of scientific research.

Hence, the correct option is (A).

36. Basketball is different from others. In softball, baseball and cricket, bat and ball are used. While only ball is used in basketball.

Hence, the correct option is (D).

37. As
ROSE
@%$#

PREACH
*@#18&

Therefore,
SEARCH
$#1@8&

Hence, the correct option is (C).

38. $(16,36,64) = [4^2, (4+2)^2, (4+2+2)^2]$
The set of numbers which is most similar to the above case is:
$(16,100,256) = [4^2, (4+6)^2, (4+6+6)^2]$
Hence, the correct option is (B).

39. Value neutrality should be maintained by every researcher in conducting research. They should be impartial and devoid of imaginary assumptions and prejudices. So, it can be lost if all of the given situations happened.

Hence, the correct option is (D).

40. Average amount of interest paid by the Company during the given period

= Rs. $\left[\frac{23.4+32.5+41.6+36.4+49.4}{5}\right]$ lakhs

= $Rs.\left[\frac{183.3}{5}\right]$ lakhs

= $Rs. 36.66\ lakhs$.

Hence, the correct option is (A).

41. Out of the given options, voice modulation plays an important while delivering the lectures. The voice modulation helps the students to understand the seriousness of that particular question or topic. So, voice modulation is an essential element a teacher has to take cognizance of while addressing students in a classroom.

Hence, the correct option is (B).

42. The choice of communication partners is influenced by various factors - Proximity, utility, loneliness. Proximity means a sense of closeness/connection to the partner. Utility means seeking benefit out of communication and loneliness means the person is alone and he needs to talk to some other person. Therefore, these factors play important role in influencing the choice of the communication partner.

Hence, the correct option is (A).

43. One word substitution is Ascetic.
Sceptic: a person inclined to question or doubt accepted opinions.Ascetic: characterized by severe self-discipline and abstention from all forms of indulgence, typically for religious reasons.Devotee: a person who is very interested in and enthusiastic about someone or something.Antiquarian: relating to or dealing in antiques or rare books.

Hence, the correct option is (B).

44. In the given question, all follows a same pattern

$4 - 2 = 2^3 = 8$

$5 - 2 = 3^3 = 27$

$6 - 2 = 4^3 = 64$

$7 - 2 = 5^3 = 125$

Hence, the correct option is (B).

45.

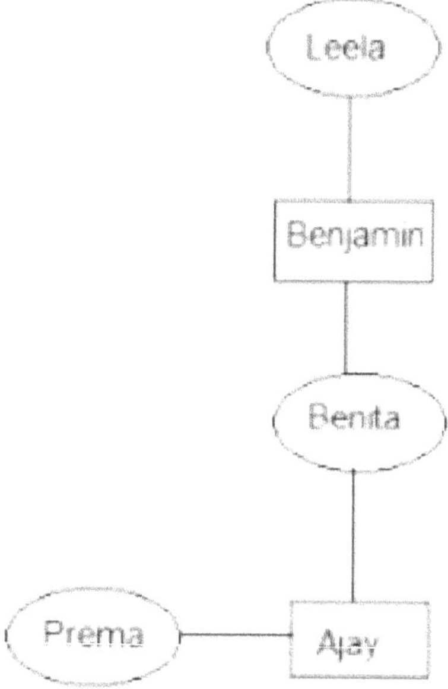

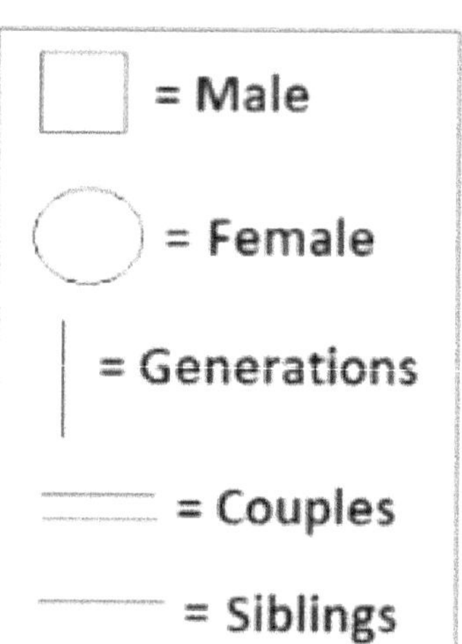

Prema is Great Grand Daughter of Leela.

Hence, the correct option is (D).

46. $(2^3-1) = 7$

$(3^3+1) = 28$

$(4^3-1) = 63$

$(5^3+1) = 126$

$(6^3-1) = 215$

So, the next term of series will be 215.

Hence, the correct option is (A).

47. The main objective of evaluation of teachers by student includes helping the teachers to adopt the innovative method of teaching, also assist the teacher in identifying their area of improvement. The student can evaluate the teacher on their teaching skills. But to gather information about student weaknesses cannot be the objective. So, option (1) is not at all. Other 3 options can be there.

Hence, the correct option is (B).

48. The purpose of higher education is to promote critical and creative thinking abilities among students so that they can become self-dependent. These abilities will help them to think independently, develops creativity, and also ensure job placements. Therefore, both the statements are correct, but the only reason is not the correct explanation of the assertion.

Hence, the correct option is (B).

49. Teaching can be done in a formal as well as in an informal manner. Therefore, option (B) is incorrect. Other options are correct.

The distinction made is largely administrative. Formal education is linked with schools and training institutions; non-formal with community groups and other organizations; and informal covers what is left, e.g. interactions with friends, family and work colleagues.

Hence, the correct option is (B).

50. A learner-centered approach to teaching and learning focuses on:

(i) Learner needs

(ii) Subject matter determining by both teachers and students

(iii) Employment of indirect ways of teaching

(iv) Focus is on the development of skills.

Hence, the correct option is (D).

Mock Test 04

Q.1 The term 'Yellow journalism' refers to:

A. Sensational news about terrorism and violence

B. Sensational news and exaggeration to attract readers/viewers

C. Sensational news about arts and culture

D. Sensational newsprints in yellow paper

Q.2 Informal fallacies deal with the logic of

A. Technical Structure

B. Meaning of Language

C. Invalid form

D. Form of argument

Q.3 The next term of the series $\sqrt{3}$, $\sqrt{12}$, $\sqrt{27}$ is

A. $\sqrt{39}$ **B.** $\sqrt{32}$ **C.** $\sqrt{54}$ **D.** $\sqrt{48}$

Q.4 Which of the following certain qualities and traits of learners can impact the way of learning?

1) Intelligence

2) Attitude

3) Motivation

4) Attraction

Select the correct answer using the code given below-

A. 1 and 2 only **B.** 1 and 3 only

C. 1, 2 and 3 only **D.** All of the above

Q.5 From the following list of statements identify the set which has negative implications for 'research ethics'-

1) A researcher critically looks at the findings of another research.

2) Related studies are cited without proper references.

3) Research findings are made the basis for policymaking.

4) Conduct of practitioner is screened in terms of reported research evidence.

5) A research study is replicated with a view to verify the evidence from other researches.

6) Both policy making and policy implementing processes are regulated in terms of preliminary studies.

A. 1, 2 and 3 **B.** 2, 3 and 4

C. 2, 4 and 6 **D.** 1, 3 and 5

Q.6 Direction: In the question below is given a three statement followed by two conclusions numbered I and II. You have to assume everything in the statement to be true, then consider the two conclusions together and decide which of them logically follows beyond a reasonable doubt from the information given in the statement.

Give answer:

Statements:

a. Some Jackets are Shirts.

b. Some Shirts are Sarees.

c. All Socks are Sarees.

Conclusions:

I. Some Shirts are Socks.

II. All Socks being Shirt is a possibility.

Code:

A. Neither Conclusions I nor II follows

B. Conclusions I and II follow

C. Either Conclusion I or II follows

D. Only Conclusion II follows

Q.7 The internal perception is done by which of the following factors?

A. Sense organs **B.** Mind

C. Assumption **D.** None of the above

Q.8 In a certain code language "CONSTRUCTION" is written as "EMPQVPWAVGQL". What will be the code for "DESTRUCTION" in the same language?

A. FCURTSERKMP **B.** EFTVSVDVJPO

C. FCURTSFSLOQ **D.** None of the above

Q.9 Truth and falsity are attributes of

A. Propositions **B.** Arguments

C. Opinions **D.** Debates

Q.10 Direction: In the question below are given two or three statements followed by two conclusions numbered I and II. You have to take the given statements to be true even if they seem to be at variance with commonly known facts and then decide which of the given conclusions logically follows from the given statements, disregarding commonly known facts.

Give answer:

Statements:

Some flowers are red.

Some roses are flowers.

Conclusions:

I. All roses being red is a possibility.

II. Some flowers can never be roses.

A. If only conclusion I follows

B. If only conclusion II follows

C. If either conclusion I or II follows

D. If neither conclusion I or II follows

Q.11 Which of the following is not a principle of effective communication?

A. Persuasive and convincing dialogue

B. Participation of the audience

C. One way transfer of information

D. Strategic use of grapevine

Q.12 In a joint family, there is a father, a mother, 3 married sons and one unmarried daughter. Of the sons, two have 2 daughters each, and one has a son. How many female members are there in the family?

A. 2 **B.** 3 **C.** 6 **D.** 9

Q.13 In a classroom, a communicator's trust level is determined by

A. The use of hyperbole
B. The change of voice level
C. The use of abstract concepts
D. The eye contact

Q.14 Direction: In the question below, consist of six sentences. The first and sixth sentence are given in the beginning. The middle four sentences in each have been removed and jumbled up. These are labelled as P, Q, R and S. Find out the proper order for the four sentences.

S_1: A force exists between everybody in the universe.

P: Normally it is very small but when one of the bodies is a planet, like earth, the force is considerable.

Q: It has been investigated by many scientists including Galileo and Newton.

R: Everything on or near the surface of the earth is attracted by the mass of earth.

S: This gravitational force depends on the mass of the bodies involved.

S_6: The greater the mass, the greater is the earth's force of attraction on it. We can call this force of attraction gravity.

The Proper sequence should be-

A. PRQS **B.** PRSQ **C.** QSRP **D.** QSPR

Q.15 Which type of communication involves "Open door policy"?

A. Formal communication
B. Informal communication
C. Visual communication
D. Non-verbal communication

Q.16 Which of the following is not a water- borne disease?

A. Typhoid **B.** Hepatitis **C.** Cholera **D.** Dengue

Q.17 Which of the following programmes of the Ministry of Human Resource and Development promotes life skill training among young people?

A. Samgra Shiksha
B. Adolescent Education Programme
C. Operation Blackboard
D. Swayam Prabha

Q.18 Direction: In the following question, the Assertions (A) and Reason(R) have been put forward. Read both the statements carefully and choose the correct alternative from the following-

Assertion(A): Bangladesh imports jute from India.

Reason(R): Bangladesh has most of the jute mills.

A. Both A and R are true and R is the correct explanation of A.
B. Both A and R are true but R is NOT the correct explanation of A.
C. Both A and R are false.
D. A is false but R is true.

Q.19 "Male and female students perform equally well in a numerical aptitude test." This statement indicates-

A. Research hypothesis
B. Null hypothesis
C. Directional hypothesis
D. Statistical hypothesis

Q.20 Jean Piaget gave a theory of cognitive development of humans on the basis of his

A. Fundamental Research
B. Applied Research
C. Action Research
D. Evaluation Research

Q.21 Direction: In the series, look for the degree and direction of change between the numbers. In other words, do the numbers increase or decrease, and by how much?

Look at this series- $2,1,(1/2),(1/4)$, ... What number should come next?

A. (1/3) **B.** (1/8) **C.** (2/8) **D.** (1/16)

Q.22 The mean of the ages of the father and his son is 27 years. After 18 years, the father will be twice as old as his son. Their present ages are

A. 42, 12 **B.** 40, 14 **C.** 30, 24 **D.** 36, 18

Q.23 Which sequence of research steps is logical in the list given below?

A. Problem formulation, Analysis, Development of Research design, Hypothesis making, Collection of data, Arriving at generalizations and conclusions
B. Development of Research design, Hypothesis making, Problem formulation, Data analysis, Arriving at conclusions and data collection
C. Problem formulation, Hypothesis making, Development of a Research design, Collection of data, Data analysis and formulation of generalizations and conclusions
D. Problem formulation, Deciding about the sample and data collection tools, Formulation of hypothesis, Collection and interpretation of research evidence

Q.24 Which one of the following is not a search engine?
[Haryana Constable, 2018]

A. Google **B.** Chrome **C.** Yahoo **D.** Bing

Q.25 Which is the type of measurement scale that is used to measure the non-numeric concepts?

A. Ratio Scale **B.** Interval Scale
C. Nominal Scale **D.** Ordinal Scale

Q.26 Two numbers are in the ratio $3:5$. If 9 is subtracted from the numbers, the ratio becomes $12:23$. The numbers are

A. 30,50 **B.** 36,60 **C.** 33,55 **D.** 42,70

Q.27 When media companies are owned by non-media business houses, it is called

A. Chain ownership

B. Joint Stock ownership
C. Conglomerate media ownership
D. Business ownership

Q.28 Which one of the following is not a scheme or program to strengthen higher education in India?

A. IGNOU
B. National Council of Teachers 1995
C. Operation Blackboard
D. National Literacy Mission

Q.29 What was the main agenda of the Incheon Declaration held by UNESCO in 2015?

A. Life Long Learning
B. Inclusive Education
C. Equitable Quality Education
D. All of the above

Q.30 JPEG stands for

A. Joint Photo Electronic Group
B. Joint Picture Electronic Group
C. Joint Photographic Experts Group
D. Joint Picture Expert Group

Ques (31-34):Direction: Read the following passage carefully and answer questions:

The literary distaste for politics, however, seems to be focused not so much on the largely murky practice of politics in itself as a subject of literary representation but rather more on how it is often depicted in Literature, i.e., On the very politics of representation. A political novel often turns out be not merely a novel about politics but a novel with a politics of its own, for it seeks not merely to show us how things are but has fairly definite ideas about how things should be, and precisely what one should think and do in order to make things move in that desired direction. In short, it seeks to convert and enlist the reader to a particular cause or ideology; it often is (in an only too familiar phrase) not literature but propaganda. This is said to violate the very spirit of literature which is to broaden our understanding of the world and the range of our sympathies rather than to narrow them down through partisan commitment. As John Keats said, 'We hate poetry that has a palpable design upon us'. Another reason why politics does not seem amenable to the highest kind of literary representation seems to arise from the fact that politics by its very nature is constituted of ideas and ideologies. If political situations do not lend themselves to happy literary treatment, political ideas present perhaps an even greater problem in this regard. Literature, it is argued, is about human experiences rather than about intellectual abstractions; it deals in what is called the 'felt reality' of human flesh and blood, and in sap and savours (rasa) rather than in arid and lifeless ideas. In an extensive discussion of the matter in her book Ideas and the Novel, the American novelist Mary McCarthy observed that 'ideas are still today felt to be unsightly in the novel' though that was not so in 'former days', i.e., in the 18th and 19th centuries. Her formulation of the precise nature of the incompatibility between ideas on the one hand and the novel on the other betrays perhaps a divided conscience in the matter and a sense of dilemma shared by many writers and readers: 'An idea cannot have loose ends, but a novel, I almost think, needs them. Nevertheless, there is enough in common for the novelists to feel ... the attraction of ideas while taking up arms against them – most often with weapons of mockery.'

Q.31 When confronted with signing a big card, the author felt like "a rabbit in the headlight". What does this phrase mean?

A. A state of confusion | **B.** A state of pleasure
C. A state of anxiety | **D.** A state of pain

Q.32 A political novel reveals

A. The Reality of the things
B. Writer's perception
C. The Particular ideology of the readers
D. The spirit of literature

Q.33 The constructs of politics by its nature is

A. Prevalent political situation
B. Ideas and Ideologies
C. Political propaganda
D. Understanding of human nature

Q.34 Literature deals with

A. Human-experiences in politics
B. Intellectual abstractions
C. Dry and empty ideas
D. Felt the reality of human life

Q.35 Communication is considered as meaningful only if some elements are present in the procedure. Which of the following elements will be appropriate in communication?

A. Process | **B.** Interaction
C. Social context | **D.** All of the above

Q.36 Direction: In the following question, two statements are given each followed by two conclusions I and II. You have to consider the statements to be true even if they seem to be at variance from commonly known facts. You have to decide which of the given conclusions, if any, follows from the given statements.

Statement:

1. All young scientists are open-minded.
2. No open-minded men are superstitious.

Conclusions:

I. Some young scientist are superstitious.
II. No young scientist are superstitious.

A. Conclusion I follows
B. Conclusion II follows
C. Neither I nor II follows
D. Both I and II follows

Q.37 Which of the following are the tools of good governance?

1. Social Audit
2. Separation of Powers
3. Citizen's Charter
4. Right to Information

Select the correct answer from the codes given below:

A. 1 and 2 | **B.** 1, 2 and 3

C. 1, 3 and 4 **D.** 1,2,3 and 4

Q.38 The maximum number of fake institutions/ universities as identified by the UGC in the year 2014 are in the State/ Union territory of

A. Bihar **B.** Uttar Pradesh
C. Tamil Nadu **D.** Delhi

Q.39 Warrior is related to sword, a carpenter is related to saw, the farmer is related to plough. In the same way, the author is related to

A. Book **B.** Fame **C.** Reader **D.** Pen

Q.40 Which of the following could be considered to be an advantage of using e-learning?

A. Web-based learning promotes active and independent learning
B. Web-based learning promotes dependent learning
C. E-learning doesn't appeal to all learning styles
D. Learning through the Internet on individual computers allows for wider access, but it can also easily lead to isolation

Q.41 Imagine you are working in an educational institution where people are of equal status. Which method of communication is best suited and normally employed in such a context?

A. Horizontal Communication
B. Vertical communication
C. Corporate communication
D. Cross communication

Q.42 Which of the following emphasized that education needs to be managed in an atmosphere of utmost intellectual rigor, seriousness of purpose and of freedom essential for innovation and creativity?

A. National Policy on Education – 1968
B. National Policy on Education – 1986
C. NITI Aayog – Three Year Action Agenda (2017-18 to 2019-20)
D. Draft National Education Policy – 2019

Q.43 The purpose of Gurukul system of education is to

A. Promote equality and excellence
B. Minimise stress in learning
C. Empowering for future learning
D. Encourage self-help

Q.44 Direction: Answer the questions based on the data given:

For a country, CO_2 emission (million metric tons) from various sectors are given in the following table.

Sector	Population	Electrical Power Production (GW)*
1951	20	10
1961	21	20
1971	24	25
1981	27	40
1991	30	50
2001	32	80
2011	35	100
		1 GW = 1000 million watt

By what percentage the power production increased 1951 from 2011 to?

A. 100 **B.** 300 **C.** 600 **D.** 900

Ques (45-46):Direction: Answer the questions based on the data given:

For a country, CO_2 emission (million metric tons) from various sectors are given in the following table.

Sector	Power	Industry	Commercial	Agriculture	Domestic
2005	500	200	150	80	100
2006	600	300	200	90	110
2007	650	320	250	100	120
2008	700	400	300	150	150
2009	800	450	320	200	180

Q.45 What is the percentage growth of CO_2 emissions from power sector from 2005 to 2009?

A. 60 **B.** 50 **C.** 40 **D.** 80

Q.46 Which sector has recorded maximum growth in CO_2 emissions from 2005 to 2009?

A. Power **B.** Industry
C. Commercial **D.** Agriculture

Q.47 Which of the following indoor plant helps to improve indoor air quality?

A. Areca Palm **B.** Lady Palm
C. Dragon Tree **D.** All of the above

Q.48 The primary source of organic pollution in fresh water bodies is

A. Run-off urban areas
B. Run-off agricultural forms
C. Sewage effluents
D. Industrial effluents

Q.49 Which uses only two symbols 0 and 1?

A. Binary number system
B. Decimal number system
C. Hexadecimal number system
D. Octal number system

Q.50 Which of the following is not the salient feature of the industrial policy developments since 1991?

A. The scope of the private sector has been enormously expanded
B. Public sector has been withdrawing partially or fully from several of the enterprises by divestment
C. The Indian industry is increasingly exposed to foreign competition
D. Monopoly or dominant position for the public sector in most of the industries and control of the commanding heights of the economy by the public sector

// Smart Answer Sheet //

Correct Indicates percentage of students who answered questions correctly.

Skipped Indicates percentage of students who skipped questions.

Q.	Ans.	Correct	Skipped
1	B	46.55 %	8.02 %
2	B	35.86 %	23.83 %
3	D	44.1 %	24.5 %
4	C	48.33 %	24.28 %
5	C	27.17 %	28.73 %
6	D	28.95 %	27.84 %
7	B	43.43 %	25.39 %
8	A	48.11 %	25.61 %
9	A	36.75 %	25.17 %
10	A	50.56 %	27.17 %
11	C	53.45 %	24.5 %
12	D	36.08 %	24.05 %
13	D	47.44 %	24.94 %
14	D	24.05 %	23.61 %
15	B	59.24 %	25.84 %
16	C	31.18 %	23.83 %
17	B	35.19 %	27.84 %
18	C	30.96 %	28.28 %
19	B	39.87 %	22.94 %
20	A	49.22 %	20.27 %
21	B	57.24 %	25.17 %
22	A	50.11 %	24.95 %
23	C	56.79 %	24.28 %
24	B	54.57 %	23.83 %
25	D	24.28 %	26.28 %
26	C	33.85 %	27.84 %
27	C	38.31 %	24.72 %
28	C	33.18 %	24.06 %
29	D	52.34 %	26.5 %
30	C	38.75 %	24.28 %
31	A	36.97 %	29.4 %
32	B	33.85 %	29.85 %
33	B	46.55 %	28.95 %
34	D	50.11 %	23.61 %
35	D	60.13 %	26.28 %
36	B	42.76 %	25.17 %
37	C	49.44 %	25.17 %
38	B	47.44 %	27.17 %
39	D	35.86 %	30.96 %
40	A	26.95 %	33.85 %
41	A	34.74 %	32.74 %
42	B	28.95 %	30.74 %
43	A	31.63 %	33.4 %
44	D	46.33 %	24.49 %
45	A	36.08 %	28.95 %
46	D	35.41 %	25.84 %
47	D	49.44 %	26.28 %
48	C	34.52 %	26.5 %
49	A	42.76 %	30.07 %
50	D	36.97 %	27.4 %

Performance Analysis	
Avg. Score (%)	43.0%
Toppers Score (%)	100.0%
Your Score	

//Hints and Solutions//

1. 'Yellow journalism' refers to sensational news and exaggeration to attract readers/viewers. It is the type of journalism that does not report complete real news, instead of that, it exaggerates the real issue.

Hence, the correct option is (B).

2. Informal fallacies dealt with the logic of the meaning of language. It means that our focus is not on the form of the argument, but on the meaning of the language.

Hence, the correct option is (B).

3. Given, $\sqrt{3},\ \sqrt{12},\ \sqrt{27}$

$\Rightarrow\ \sqrt{3},\ \sqrt{4\times 3},\ \sqrt{9\times 3}$

$\Rightarrow\ \sqrt{3},\ 2\sqrt{3},\ 3\sqrt{3},\ are\ in\ A.P.$

where $a = \sqrt{3}\ \ and\ d = 2\sqrt{3} - \sqrt{3} = \sqrt{3}$

$\therefore$ The Fourth term is $T_4 = a + 3d = \sqrt{3} + 3\times\sqrt{3} = 4\sqrt{3} = \sqrt{16\times 3} = \sqrt{48}$

Hence the correct option is (D).

4. Certain traits and personal qualities of learner can bring about differences in his/her learning. Certain qualities and traits of learners such as their level of intelligence, their attitudes, their motivation, their learning styles, aptitudes, their readiness to take risks, etc. can impact the way they learn.

Hence the correct option is (C).

5. Research Ethics is the analysis of the ethical issues which are reported by the people or researchers involved in that research of the particular topic. These ethics are influenced by negative implications that include the studies are cited without proper references, the conduct of practitioner that is screened in terms of reported research evidence, both policy making and policy implementing processes are regulated in terms of preliminary studies.
Hence, the correct option is (C).

6. As per the Venn diagram, Conclusions II are true.

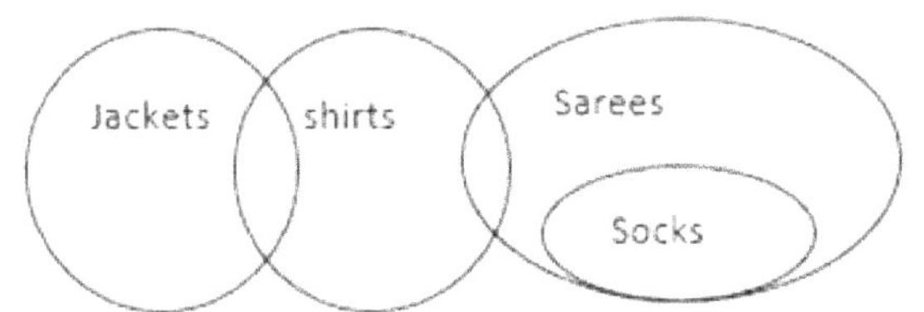

(i) Some Shirts are Socks does not follow as there is not a direct relation between shirts and socks.

(ii) All Socks being Shirt is a possibility follows.

Hence the correct option is (D).

7. According to Charvaka, perception is held to be two kinds internal and external. External perception is done by external sense organs and internal perception is done by internal sense organs i.e. mind.
Hence, the correct option is (B).

8.

C(+2)	O(−2)	N(+2)	S(−2)	T(+2)	R(−2)	U(+2)	C(−2)	T(+2)	I(−2)	O(+2)	N(−2)
E	M	P	Q	V	P	W	A	V	G	Q	L

D(+2)	E(−2)	S(+2)	T(−2)	R(+2)	U(−2)	C(+2)	T(−2)	I(+2)	O(−2)	N(+2)
F	C	U	R	T	S	E	R	K	M	P

Hence, the correct option is (A).

9. Truth and falsity are the attributes of propositions. A proposition is a sentence that is either true or false. If a proposition is true, then we can assume that its truth value is true, and if a proposition is false, we can assume its truth value is false. So, the statement can either be true or false.
Hence, the correct option is (A).

10.

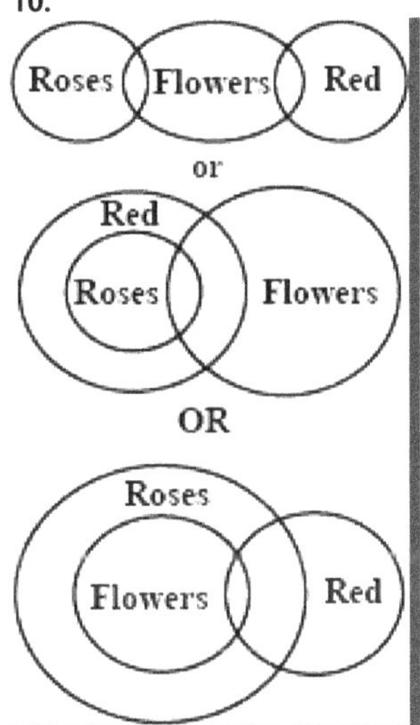

The above figure shows different possibilities of representation of given statements.

From the second figure, we can see that, all roses can be red. Thus conclusion I is correct.

From the third figures, we can see that, all flowers can be roses. Thus conclusion II is wrong.

Hence the correct option is (A).

11. Effective communication is a way of transferring information, thoughts and ideas to create understanding between sender and receiver. Communication is a persuasive and convincing dialogue which involves the participation of the audience through the strategic use of informal communication, also known as grapevine communication. Communication cannot be possible in one-way because it includes dispensing of information to another

person.
Hence, the correct option is (C).

12. The female members in the family are mothers, wives of 3 married sons unmarried daughters and 2 daughters of each of the two sons.

Number of female members $= (1 + 3 + 1 + 2 \times 2) = 9$

Hence, the correct option is (D).

13. In a classroom, a communicator's trust level is determined by the eye contact. It brings out the confidence in the person to ask or present his/her opinions in a much better way.
Hence, the correct option is (D).

14. The first statement in the sequence should be the one that best connects with S1. It should be a continuation or extension of S1.

Q is first in the sequence: S1 starts telling us that a young man was trapped on the Himalayas overnight. Q continues S1's story. It says that when the man arrived at the hospital his body temperature was 22 degrees and he showed no signs of life.

Q is followed by S: S tells us what happened after Q. It says that after he was brought to the hospital, he was immediately connected to a heart-lung machine.

S is followed by R: R continues the story told by S. It says that two hours after being connected to the machine, his body temperature had risen to normal.

R is followed by P: P continues R's point. It says that once his body temperature became normal, the patient came back to life and needed some days in ICU. S6 provides a conclusion to the story by saying that he suffered no after-effects and the resuscitation was a success.

Thus, the correct sequence is Q S P R.

Hence, the correct option is (D).

15. Open door policy is a part of informal communication, and it makes a person more confident and forthcoming with their creativity and ideas. Informal communication is based on social relationships, which is generally formed in any workplace.

Hence, the correct option is (B).

16. Cholera is the infection of the small intestine by some strains of the bacteria Vibrio cholera. The bacteria are transmitted between humans through the fecal-oral route, a bite of contaminated food or a sip of contaminated water. Amoebiasis is an infection caused by the amoebas of the Entamoeba group. Amoebiasis can be transmitted by ingestion of water contaminated with faeces containing amoebic cysts. Asthma, however, cannot be transmitted from person to person.

Hence, the correct option is (C).

17. The Adolescence Education Programme (AEP) is an important initiative that aims to empower young people with accurate, age-appropriate and culturally relevant information, promote healthy attitudes and develop skills to enable them to respond to real-life situations in positive and responsible ways.

Hence, the correct option is (B).

18. When Bangladesh was created after the partitioning of India, the areas of jute production went to Bangladesh while the jute mills were left in India. So, India imports raw jute from Bangladesh.

Hence the correct option is (C).

19. A null hypothesis is a hypothesis used in statistics which refers that no statistical significance difference exists in a set of given observation or populations. So, 'Male and female students perform equally well in a numerical aptitude test' is a case of null hypothesis.
Hence, the correct option is (B).

20. Piaget's theory of cognitive development is a comprehensive theory about the nature and development of human intelligence. Piaget's theory is based on four stages i.e. sensorimotor stage, preoperational stage, concrete operational stage, formal operational stage.

Fundamental Research aims to improve scientific theories for an improved understanding of natural phenomena. Piaget's idea is based on his fundamental research.

Hence, the correct option is (A).

21. This is a simple division series each number is one-half of the previous number.

In other terms to say, the number is divided by 2 successively to get the next result.

$4/2 = 2$

$2/2 = 1$
$1/2 = 1/2$
$(1/2)/2 = 1/4$
$(1/4)/2 = 1/8$ and so on.

Hence, the correct option is (B).

22. Let present age of father $= x$ years

Let present age of son $= y$ years $\frac{x+y}{2} = 27$

$\Rightarrow x + y = 54 \ldots\ldots(1)$
After 18 years, Father's age $= (x + 18)$ years

Son's age $= (y + 18)$ years So, $x + 18 = 2(y + 18)$
$\Rightarrow x + 18 = 2y + 36$
$\Rightarrow x - 2y = 18 \ldots\ldots(2)$
Putting value of 1 in (2), $\Rightarrow 54 - y - 2y = 18$

$\Rightarrow 3y = 36$
$y = 12, x = 42$
Present age of father $= 42$ years

Present age of son $= 12$ years

Hence, the correct option is (A).

23. The correct sequence of research steps is as follows:

a) Formulation of Problem

b) Making of Hypothesis

c) Development of a research design,

d) Collection of data,

e) Data analysis

f) Formulation of generalizations and conclusions.
Hence, the correct option is (C).

24. Chrome is a web browser. Google, Yahoo and Bing are the search engines.

Hence, the correct option is (B).

25. The measurement of a non-numeric concept is through an ordinal scale. It measures the items in an ordered range of ranking from highest to the lowest.

Ratio Scale has an absolute or true zero of measurement. It represents the actual number of variables.

Interval Scale is established as making units equal. Example: Fahrenheit scale

A nominal Scale is assigning numbers or symbols to events to label them.

Hence, the correct option is (D).

26. Given,

Two numbers are in the ratio is $3:5$

$$\frac{3x-9}{5x-9} = \frac{12}{23}$$

$$69x - 207 = 60x - 108$$

$$69x - 60x = 207 - 108$$

$$9x = 99$$

$$x = 11$$

So, the numbers are $33,55$.
Hence, the correct option is (C).

27. A media conglomerate describes companies that own large numbers of companies in various mass media such as television, radio, publishing, movies, and the Internet. As of 2008, The Walt Disney Company is the world's largest media conglomerate, with News Corporation, Viacom and Time.

Hence, the correct option is (C).

28. All the listed programmes and schemes were established to strengthen higher education in India except operation blackboard whose aim was to fulfil and provide basic infrastructure for primary schools.
Hence, the correct option is (C).

29. The agenda of the Incheon Declaration held by UNESCO in 2015 is to set out a new vision for education for the next 15 years. This new vision is fully captured by the proposed SDG 4 "Ensure inclusive and equitable quality education and promote lifelong learning opportunities for all".
Hence, the correct option is (D).

30. JPEG (often seen with its file extension . jpg or . jpeg) stands for "Joint Photographic Experts Group", which is the name of the group who created the JPEG standard.

Hence, the correct option is (C).

31. When confronted with signing a big card, the author felt like "a rabbit in the headlight". It was a state of confusion and we can clearly get that after reading the second sentence of the paragraph.

Hence, the correct option is (A).

32. A political novel only talks about the writer's perception.

Hence, the correct option is (B).

33. The constructs of politics by its nature is all about ideas and ideologies. Another reason why politics does not seem amenable to the highest kind of literary representation seems to arise from the fact that politics by its very nature is constituted of ideas and ideologies.

Hence, the correct option is (B).

34. Literature deals with the felt reality of human life.

Literature, it is argued, is about human experiences rather than about intellectual abstractions; it deals in what is called the 'felt reality' of human flesh and blood, and in sap and savours (rasa) rather than in arid and lifeless ideas.

Hence, the correct option is (D).

35. Process is used to exchange information properly between the sender and a receiver to achieve the desired result.

Interaction is a process of linking senders and receiver. The concept of interaction is central for understanding the concept of process in the communication.

Social context consists of a set of rules which govern the origin, flow and effect of messages.
Hence, the correct option is (D).

36.

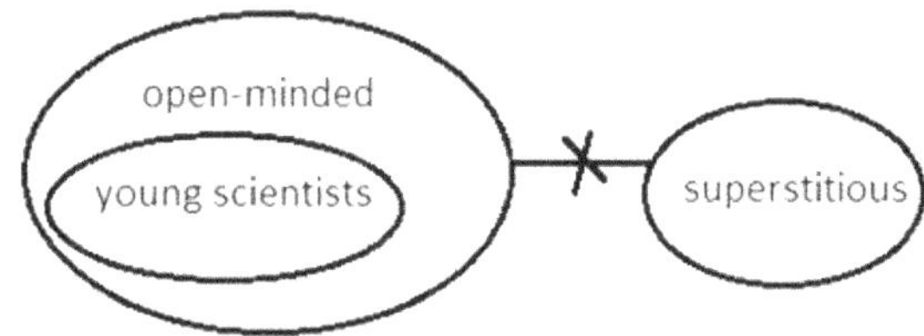

As per the above Venn-diagram, only conclusion II follows.

Hence the correct option is (B).

37. Good governance includes:

1. Social Audit

2. Citizen's Charter

3. Right to Information

Hence, the correct option is (C).

38. Presently, there are 23 fake universities on the records of the commission which are functioning in contravention of the provisions of the UGC Act, 1956. The act, under section 22(1) states that a degree can be awarded only by a university established under a central, State/Provincial Act or an institution deemed to be a university under section 3 of the UGC act or an institution empowered by an act of parliament to confer the degree. Among the fake universities, most are located in Delhi (7) and Uttar Pradesh (8).

Hence, the correct option is (B).

39. A warrior cannot war without the help of a sword, a carpenter cannot work without a saw, and farmer cannot do farming without a plough. The same way the author cannot do anything without a pen.

Hence, the correct option is (D).

40. Advantages of E-Learning

- You are able to link the various resources in several varying formats.
- It is a very efficient way of delivering courses online.
- Due to its convenience and flexibility, the resources are available from anywhere and at any time.
- Everyone, who is a part-time student or are working full time, can take advantage of web-based learning.
- Web-based learning promotes active and independent learning.
- As you have access to the net 24x7, you can train yourself anytime and from anywhere also.
- It is a very convenient and flexible option; above all, you don't have to depend on anyone for anything.
- Not only can you train yourself on a day to day basis, but also on weekends or whenever you have the free time to. There is no hard and fast rule.
- Through discussion boards and chats, you are able to interact with everyone online and also clear your doubts if any.
- The video instructions that are provided for audio and video learning can be rewound and seen and heard again and again if you do not happen to understand the topic the first time around.

Hence, the correct option is (A).

41. Horizontal communication is the transmission of information between people, divisions, departments or units within the same level of the organizational hierarchy. You can distinguish it from vertical communication, which is the transmission of information between different levels of the organizational hierarchy.

Hence, the correct option is (A).

42. In relation to Elementary Education, the followings are the major objectives of the National Policy of Education 1986 are mainly-

The National Policy on Education – 1986 emphasized that education needs to be managed in an atmosphere of utmost intellectual rigour, the seriousness of purpose and of freedom essential for innovation and creativity.

Universal retention of children up to 14 years of age and a sustainable improvement in the quality education to enable all children to achieve essential levels of learning.

Hence the correct option is (B).

43. The main purpose of the Gurukul system is to promote equality and excellence in the education system. The Gurukuls were the system of education in which the student was admitted during the initial of his/her education and they stayed at the teacher's place till their education is complete.

Hence, the correct option is (A).

44. Percentage (%) increase in power production from 1951 to 2011

$=\frac{(\text{Power Production in 2011}) - (\text{Power Production in 1951})}{(\text{Power Production in 1951})} \times 100\%$

$=\frac{(100-10)}{10} \times 100\%$

$= 900\%$

Hence, the correct option is (D).

45. Growth of CO_2 from power sector during 2005 to $2009 = 800 - 500 = 300$ (Just take values of 2009 and 2005 and subtract them)

Percentage growth $= \frac{(\text{Value in 2009})-(\text{Value in 2005})}{(\text{Value in 2005})} \times 100\%$

Percentage growth $= \frac{800-500}{500} \times 100$

$= \frac{300}{500} \times 100 = 60\%$

Hence, the correct option is (A).

46. According to the given formula:

Percentage growth $= \frac{(\text{Value in 2009})-(\text{Value in 2005})}{(\text{Value in 2005})} \times 100\%$

Power $\% = \frac{800-500}{500} \times 100 = 60\%$

Industry $\% = \frac{450-200}{200} \times 100 = 125\%$

Commercial $\% = \frac{320-150}{150} \times 100 = 113\%$

Agriculture $\% = \frac{200-80}{80} \times 100 = 150\%$

Domestic $\% = \frac{180-100}{100} \times 100 = 80\%$

So, the agriculture sector has recorded maximum growth in CO_2 emission from 2005 to 2009

Hence, the correct option is (D).

47. A study by NASA confirms that common houseplants are the natural air purifiers. These include aloe vera, areca palm, lady palm, dragon tree, bamboo among others.

Hence, the correct option is (D).

48. Organic pollutants originate from domestic sewage (raw or treated), urban run-off, industrial (trade) effluents and farm wastes. Sewage effluents is the greatest source of organic materials discharged to freshwaters.

Hence, the correct option is (C).

49. A binary number is a number expressed in the base - 2 numeral system or binary numeral system, which uses only two symbols typically " 0" (zero) and " 1" (one). The base - 2 numeral system is a positional notation with a radix of 2. Each digit is referred to as a bit.

Hence, the correct option is (A).

50. In India, the major LPG (Liberalisation, Privatisation, Globalisation) Reforms, 1991 were:

The industrial reforms of 1991 do not give a monopoly or dominant position to public sector rather it encouraged private entities to grow and contribute to the national economy.

Liberalisation- To allow private entities to deal in sectors previously owned solely by public entities by waving off-license requirements and easing laws.

Privatisation- Encouraging private investment in government entities by devesting and withdrawing capital from public companies.

Globalisation- Opening national doors to the world so that Indian companies can participate in international markets and exposed to foreign competition.

Hence the correct option is (D).

Mock Test 05

Q.1 Which of the following is not a type of Research?

A. Exploratory **B.** Explanatory
C. Applied **D.** Variable

Q.2 Kindergarten (kg) system of education is indebted to:

A. Dewey **B.** Froebel **C.** Plato **D.** Spencer

Q.3 The first important step in teaching is

A. Planning of representation of topic or subject
B. Organizing the background of students for the subject
C. Organizing the material to be taught
D. Knowing the background of students

Q.4 Classroom discipline can be maintained effectively by

A. Knowing the cause of indiscipline and handling it with stern hand
B. Providing a program which is according to the need and interest of pupils
C. By giving punishment for even smallest sins
D. None of these

Q.5 Which of the following statements defines the main objectives of Research?

A. Research should be highly focused and feasible
B. Research makes accurate use of concepts
C. Research is done to find out the hidden truth
D. All of the above

Q.6 The function of a teacher is in the order of

A. Guiding the child, helping him towards progress and evaluation
B. Checking homework, guiding him and assigning further task
C. Mentor, helping hand, learner
D. None of these

Q.7 Which of the following is responsible for uniformity in the curriculum at a higher level in India?

A. University Grants Commission (UGC)
B. National Council for Educational Research and Training (NCERT)
C. Ministry of Education
D. All India Council for Technical Education (AICTE)

Q.8 Which of the following statements, regarding the term ICT is/are TRUE?

P: ICT is an acronym that stands for Indian Classical Technology.

Q: Converging technologies that exemplify ICT include the merging of audio-visual, telephone and computer networks through a common cabling system.

[UGC NET Sociology, 2018]

A. P only **B.** Q only
C. P and Q **D.** Neither P nor Q

Q.9 Which of the following institutions is responsible for the implementation of reforms in teaching profession?

A. University Grants Commission (UGC)
B. National Council for Teacher Education (NCTE)
C. National Council for Educational Research and Training (NCERT)
D. National Institute of Educational Planning and Administration (NIEPA)

Q.10 Which of the following is a type of malware intentionally inserted into a software system that will set off a malicious function when specified conditions are met?

A. Worm **B.** Trojan
C. Spyware **D.** Logic bomb

Q.11 What is the name for a webpage address?

[UGC NET Sociology, 2017]

A. Domain **B.** Directory
C. Protocol **D.** URL

Q.12 A cluster of propositions with a structure that exhibits, some inference is called?

A. An inference **B.** An argument
C. An explanation **D.** A valid argument

Q.13 In a row of forty children, R is eleventh from the right end and there are fifteen children between R and M. What is $M's$ position from the left end of the row?

A. 14th **B.** 15th
C. 13th **D.** None of these

Q.14 A group of 210 students appeared in some test. The mean of students is found to be 60. The mean of the remaining students is found to be 78. The mean of the whole group will be

A. 80 **B.** 76 **C.** 74 **D.** 72

Q.15 From the list of learning outcomes indicated below, identify those which are said to be high-level outcomes:

(a) Learning facts and rules
(b) Showing the ability to analyze and synthesize
(c) Awareness, responding and valuing
(d) Imitation, manipulation and precision
(e) Articulation and naturalization
(f) Organization and characterization

Select the correct answer from the options given below:

A. (b), (e) and (f) **B.** (a), (b) and (c)
C. (b), (c) and (d) **D.** (a), (c) and (f)

Q.16 Assertion (A): Indoor air pollution is a serious health hazard

Reason (R): The dispersal of air pollutants is rather limited in an indoor environment

Choose the correct answer from the code given below-

A. Both (A) and (R) are true and (R) is the correct explanation of (A)

B. Both (A) and (R) are true but (R) is the not correct explanation of (A)

C. (A) is true and (R) is false

D. Both (A) and (R) are false

Q.17 Direction: This question has an assertion (A) and a reason (R). Find out how (A) and (R) are related.

Assertion (A): People population control measures do not necessarily help in checking environmental degradation.

Reason (R): The relationship between population growth and environmental degradation is rather complex.

Choose the correct answer from the following:

A. Both (A) and (R) are true and (R) is the correct explanation of (A)

B. Both (A) and (R) are true but (R) is not the correct explanation of (A)

C. (A) is true but (R) is false

D. A) is false but (R) is true

Q.18 A is the brother of B. B is the brother of C. C is the husband of D. E is the father of A. D is related to E as:

A. Daughter **B.** Daughter-in-law

C. Sister-in-law **D.** Sister

Q.19 Which of the following are Central Universities?

1. Pondicherry University
2. Vishwa Bharati
3. H.N.B. Garhwal University
4. Kurukshetra University

Select the correct answer from the code given below-

A. 1, 2 and 3 **B.** 1, 3 and 4

C. 2, 3 and 4 **D.** 1, 2and 4

Q.20 The University Grants Commission was established with which of the following aims?

1) Promotion of research and development in higher education

2) Identifying and sustaining institutions of potential learning

3) Capacity building of teachers

4) Providing autonomy to each and every higher educational institution in India

Select the correct answer from the codes given below

A. 1, 2, 3 and 4 **B.** 1, 2 and 3

C. 2, 3 and 4 **D.** 1, 2 and 4

Q.21 Which term will replace the question mark in the series :

$ABD,\ DGK,\ HMS,\ MTB,\ SBL,?$

A. ZKU **B.** ZCA **C.** ZKW **D.** KZU

Q.22 A deductive argument is invalid if

A. Its premises and conclusions are all false

B. Its premises are true its conclusion is false

C. Its premises are false but its conclusion is true

D. Its premises and conclusions are all true

Q.23 "Education is the manifestation of perfection already in man" was stated by which personality?

A. M.K. Gandhi **B.** R.N. Tagore

C. Swami Vivekanand **D.** Sri Aurobindo

Q.24 Rahul said, "The boy in that picture is the brother of the daughter of my paternal grandfather's only son". How is the boy in the picture related to Rahul?

A. Cousin **B.** Father **C.** Nephew **D.** Brother

Q.25 Ram travels 14 km South, turns right and travels 8 km and then again turns left and covers another 9 km. He then turns to the left and travels another 8 km. He then turns to the left and travels another 9 km. How far and in which direction is he from the starting point to endpoint of his journey?

A. 14 km, East **B.** 23 km, North

C. 14 km, South **D.** 23 km, West

Q.26 The next term in the series -1, 5, 15, 29, ? is:

A. 36 **B.** 47 **C.** 59 **D.** 63

Q.27 The South Asia University is situated in the city of

A. Colombo **B.** Dhaka

C. New Delhi **D.** Kathmandu

Q.28 What is Sri Prakasa Committee (1959) most commonly known for?

A. Promoting Formal Education

B. Promoting Adult Education

C. Promoting Value Education

D. Promoting Distance Education

Ques (29-33):Direction: Read the following passage carefully and answer the question.

If India has to develop her internal strengths, the nation has to focus on the technological imperatives, keeping in mind three dynamic dimensions: the people, the overall economy and the strategic interests. These technological imperatives also take into account a 'fourth' dimension, time, an offshoot of modern-day dynamism in business, trade, and technology that leads to continually shifting targets. We believe that technological strengths are especially crucial in dealing with this fourth dimension underlying continuous change in the aspirations of the people, the economy in the global context, and the strategic interests. The progress of technology lies at the heart of human history. Technological strengths are the key to creating more productive employment in an increasingly competitive market place and to continually upgrade human skills. Without a pervasive use of technologies, we cannot achieve the overall development of our people in the years to come. The direct linkages of technology to the nation's strategic strengths are becoming more and more clear, especially since the 1990s. India's own strength in a number of core areas still puts it in a position of reasonable strength in the geopolitical context. Any nation aspiring to become a developed one needs to have strengths in various strategic technologies and also the ability to continually upgrade them through its own creative strengths. For people-oriented actions as well, whether for the creation of large scale productive employment or for ensuring nutritional and health security for people or for better living conditions, technology is the only vital input. The absence of greater technological impetus could lead to lower productivity and wastage of precious natural resources. Activities with low productivity or low-value addition, in the final analysis, hurt the poorest most. The technological imperatives to lift our people to a new life, and to life, they are entitled to be important. India, aspiring to become a major economic power in terms of trade and increase in GDP, cannot succeed on the strength of turnkey projects designed and built abroad or only through large-scale imports of plant machinery, equipment and know-how. Even while being alive to the short-term realities, medium and long-term strategies to develop core technological strengths within our industry are vital for envisioning a developed India.

Q.29 According to the above passage, which of the following are indicative of the fourth dimension?

1) Aspirations of people
2) Modern day dynamism
3) Economy in the global context
4) Strategic interests

Code:

A. 1, 2 and 3 only **B.** 2, 3 and 4 only
C. 1, 3 and 4 only **D.** 1, 2 and 4 only

Q.30 Differentiation between acceptance and non-acceptance of certain stimuli in classroom communication is the basis of ***[UGC NET Home Science, 2018], [UGC NET Sociology, 2018]***

A. Selective expectation of performance
B. Selective affiliation to peer groups
C. Selective attention
D. Selective morality

Q.31 The introduction of career courses in schools and colleges aims at

A. Developing the ability to make the intelligent choice of jobs
B. Providing professional knowledge to students
C. Increasing general knowledge
D. All of the above

Q.32 While delivering a lecture if there is some disturbance in the class, then a teacher should

A. Keep quiet for a while and then go on
B. Not bother about what is happening in the class
C. Punish those causing disturbance
D. All of these

Q.33 You are a teacher of literature. A chapter of a book deals with a biography of a scientist and his works. In this situation, what would you do with the chapter?

A. You would ask the students to read themselves
B. You would request the science teacher, to teach this chapter to the students
C. You would consult other books concerning the scientist and then teach the lesson to the student
D. All of the above

Q.34 Which of the following is the cause of semantic barrier in communication?

A. Body language **B.** Homophones
C. Gestures **D.** All of the above

Q.35 Which of the following is not a renewable natural resource?

A. Clean air **B.** Freshwater
C. Fertile soil **D.** Salt

Q.36 Assertion (A): Sustainable development is critical to well being of human society.

Reason (R): Environmentally sound policies do not harm the environment or deplete natural resources.

Choose the correct code:

A. Both (A) and (R) are correct and (R) is the correct explanation of (A)
B. Both (A) and (R) are correct, but (R) is not the correct explanation of (A)
C. (A) is true and (R) is false
D. (A) is false and (R) is true

Q.37 A person walks $10\ m$ in front and $10\ m$ to the right. Then every time turning to his left, he walks $5,\ 15$ and $15\ m$ respectively. How far is he now from his starting point?

A. $16\ m$ **B.** $15\ m$ **C.** $10\ m$ **D.** $5\ m$

Q.38 Which of the following features is included in nonverbal communication?

Select from the code to indicate your answer

a) Appearance
b) Body language
c) Sound
d) Report
e) Job description

A. (b), (c) and (d)
B. (a), (b) and (c)
C. (a), (c) and (d)
D. (a), (b), (c), (d) and (e)

Ques (39-43):Direction: The table below embodies data on the production, exports and per capita consumption of rice in country P for the five years from 2012 to 2016.

Year-wise Production, Exports and Per Capita Consumption of Rice			
Year	**Production (in million kg)**	**Exports (in million kg)**	**Per Capita Consumption (in kg)**
2012	186.5	114	36.25
2013	202	114	35.2
2014	238	130	38.7
2015	221	116	40.7
2016	215	88	42

The percentage increase in the consumption of rice over the previous year was the highest in which year?

Where, Per Capita Consumption = (Consumption in million kg) ÷ (Population in million) and consumption (in million kg) = Production – Exports

Q.39 The percentage increase in the consumption of rice over the previous year was the highest in which year?

[UGC NET Sociology, 2018]

A. 2013 **B.** 2014 **C.** 2015 **D.** 2016

Q.40 What is the population of the country in the year 2014 (in million)?

[UGC NET Home Science, 2018], [UGC NET Sociology, 2018]

A. 2.64 **B.** 2.72 **C.** 2.79 **D.** 2.85

Q.41 The ratio of exports to consumption in the given period was the highest in the year:

[UGC NET Home Science, 2018], [UGC NET Sociology, 2018]

A. 2012 **B.** 2013 **C.** 2014 **D.** 2015

Q.42 In which year, the population of the country was the highest?

[UGC NET Sociology, 2018]

A. 2013 **B.** 2014 **C.** 2015 **D.** 2016

Q.43 What is the average consumption of rice (in million kg) over the years $2012-2016$?

[UGC NET Home Science, 2018], [UGC NET Sociology, 2018]

A. 104 **B.** 102.1 **C.** 108 **D.** 100.1

Q.44 Which feature in Microsoft Word is used for adding 'Table of Contents'?

A. Insert **B.** Review
C. View **D.** References

Q.45 Printers can be broadly classified into two major categories. Which of the following are the two major categories?

A. Impact and Non-Impact Printer
B. Primary and Secondary Printer
C. Dynamic and Static Printer
D. Digital and Analog Printer

Q.46 In a certain code language, "BORROW" is written as "769965" and "BOMB" is written as "7647". How is "WOMB" written in that code language?

A. 5647 **B.** 5467 **C.** 5677 **D.** 5776

Q.47 The research method that relies on the experience of human beings is known as

A. Narrative method
B. Ethnographic method
C. Phenomenological method
D. Historical method

Q.48 'Greed Game Political Populism' is popularly known as which of the following movements?

A. Chipko Movement
B. Apikko Movement
C. Jungle Bachao Andolan
D. Tehri Dam Conflict

Q.49 TEQIP (Technical Education Quality Improvement Programme) was launched by MHRD in which of the following years?

A. 2002 **B.** 2006 **C.** 2012 **D.** 2018

Q.50 A is sister of B. F is daughter of G. C is mother of B. D is father of C. E is mother of D. A is related to D as

A. Daughter **B.** Daughter-in-law
C. Sister **D.** Granddaughter

// Smart Answer Sheet //

Correct Indicates percentage of students who answered questions correctly.

Skipped Indicates percentage of students who skipped questions.

Q.	Ans.	Correct	Skipped
1	D	62.36 %	4.4 %
2	B	39.84 %	18.68 %
3	D	47.8 %	20.88 %
4	B	48.9 %	20.06 %
5	D	67.86 %	22.52 %
6	A	47.8 %	23.35 %
7	A	36.26 %	23.63 %
8	B	39.56 %	23.9 %
9	D	43.68 %	21.43 %
10	D	32.14 %	24.73 %
11	D	59.34 %	21.15 %
12	B	44.78 %	19.78 %
13	A	42.03 %	22.26 %
14	D	34.07 %	20.33 %
15	A	21.7 %	21.71 %
16	A	33.52 %	20.33 %
17	A	37.64 %	24.17 %
18	B	62.36 %	24.73 %
19	A	41.76 %	21.98 %
20	B	54.95 %	16.75 %
21	C	56.04 %	20.61 %
22	B	46.43 %	20.05 %
23	C	52.2 %	20.6 %
24	D	44.51 %	20.05 %
25	C	45.6 %	25.55 %
26	B	34.07 %	24.17 %
27	C	57.97 %	21.98 %
28	C	29.95 %	18.95 %
29	C	32.69 %	28.57 %
30	C	50.0 %	23.63 %
31	B	34.89 %	26.1 %
32	A	48.08 %	25.0 %
33	C	50.0 %	25.55 %
34	B	30.49 %	18.69 %
35	D	31.04 %	23.36 %
36	A	31.59 %	20.33 %
37	D	49.45 %	20.06 %
38	B	41.48 %	24.18 %
39	B	32.42 %	30.49 %
40	C	29.67 %	33.24 %
41	A	19.78 %	32.97 %
42	D	26.65 %	29.67 %
43	D	28.02 %	33.24 %
44	D	15.11 %	20.88 %
45	A	37.09 %	23.07 %
46	A	47.8 %	21.71 %
47	C	25.82 %	24.18 %
48	C	28.57 %	22.53 %
49	A	30.22 %	25.82 %
50	D	39.01 %	25.83 %

Performance Analysis	
Avg. Score (%)	42.0%
Toppers Score (%)	100.0%
Your Score	

//Hints and Solutions//

1. Variable research simply refers to a person, place, thing, or phenomenon that you are trying to measure in some way.

Exploratory research is to gain familiarity with a phenomenon or achieve new insights into it.

Explanatory research is the research whose primary purpose is to explain or elaborate on how the events occur to build, elaborate, or extend.

Applied research is a research phenomenon that tries to add the basics of a discipline by eliminating the theory.

Hence, the correct option is (D).

2. The Kindergarten (kg) system of education is indebted to Froebel. Friedrich Froebel, the German educationalist, is best known as the originator of the 'Kindergarten system'.

The purpose of education is to encourage and guide man as a conscious, thinking and perceiving.

Hence, the correct option is (B).

3. The first important step in teaching is knowing the background of students. Background knowledge is an essential component in learning because it helps us make sense of new ideas and experiences.
Hence, the correct option is (D).

4. Providing a program which is according to the need and interest of pupils. Interest is a powerful motivational process that energizes learning, guides academic and career trajectories, and is essential to academic success.

Hence, the correct option is (B).

5. The objective of Research is to make accurate use of concepts. Research can also be done to find out the hidden truth. Research's objective should be highly focused and feasible.
Hence, the correct option is (D).

6. The function of a teacher is in the order of guiding the child, helping him towards progress and evaluation. It is to help students learn by imparting knowledge to them and by setting up a situation in which students can and will learn effectively.
Hence, the correct option is (A).

7. The University Grants Commission is responsible for uniformity in the curriculum at a higher level in India. The University Grants Commission (UGC) came into existence on 28th December 1953 and became a statutory Organization of the Government of India by an Act of Parliament in 1956, for the coordination, determination and maintenance of standards of teaching, examination and research in university education.
Hence, the correct option is (A).

8. ICT stands for Information and Communications Technology.

The converging technologies that exemplify Information and Communications Technology include the merging of audio-visual, telephone and computer networks through a common cabling system.

Hence, the correct option is (B).

9. The National Institute of Educational Planning and Administration (NIEPA) is responsible for the implementation of reforms in the teaching profession. National Institute of Educational Planning and Administration was established in the year 1962 as UNESCO Asian Centre for Educational Planners, Administrators and Supervisors which later became the Asian Institute of Educational Planning and Administration in 1965, which was later converted into the National Staff College for Educational Planners and Administrators in 1973, which was again rechristened as National Institute of Educational Planning and Administration (NIEPA) in the year 1979.

Hence, the correct option is (D).

10. A logic bomb is a piece of code intentionally inserted into a software system that will set off a malicious function when specified conditions are met. For example, a programmer may hide a piece of code that starts deleting files (such as a salary database trigger), should he or she ever be terminated from the company.

Hence, the correct option is (D).

11. URL is the name for a webpage address. URL stands for Uniform Resource Locater.
Hence, the correct option is (D).

12. A cluster of propositions with a structure that exhibits, some inference is called as an argument. An argument is any group of assumptions which is claimed to follow from the others work, that are regarded as providing some common ground for the truth of that research.
Hence, the correct option is (B).

13. Given,

$R's$ position $= 11$th from right

$= M's$ position

$= (11 + 15 + 1)$

$= 27$th from right

$= (40 - 27 + 1)$

$= 14$th from left

Hence, the correct option is (A).

14. Given,

$1/3$ of 210 students $= 70$

Mean of 70 students $= 60$

So, total of 70 student $= 70 \times 60 = 4200$

Mean of 140 students $= 78$

So, total of 140 students $= 140 \times 78 = 10920$

Total of 210 student $= 4200 + 10920 = 15120$

So, mean of whole group $= 15120/210 = 72$

Hence, the correct option is (D).

15. Learning outcomes which are said to be high-level outcomes are:

- Showing the ability to analyze and synthesize.
- Articulation and naturalization.
- Organization and characterization.

Learning outcomes are statements that describe significant and essential learning that learners have achieved, and can reliably demonstrate at the end of a course or program. In other words, learning outcomes identify what the learner will know and be able to do by the end of a course or program.

Hence, the correct option is (A).

16. Indoor Air pollution causes serious health problems such as respiratory problems and even cancer. There, it is a serious hazard. The dispersal of air pollutants is limited because it does not get space in the indoor environment.
Hence, the correct option is (A).

17. People population control measures do not necessarily help in checking environmental degradation as many environmental degradation problems are natural like floods, landslides, erosion etc. So, the relationship between population growth and environmental degradation is rather complex.
Hence, the correct option is (A).

18. A, B, C are brothers and their father is E. C is married to D. So, D is daughter-in-law of E.

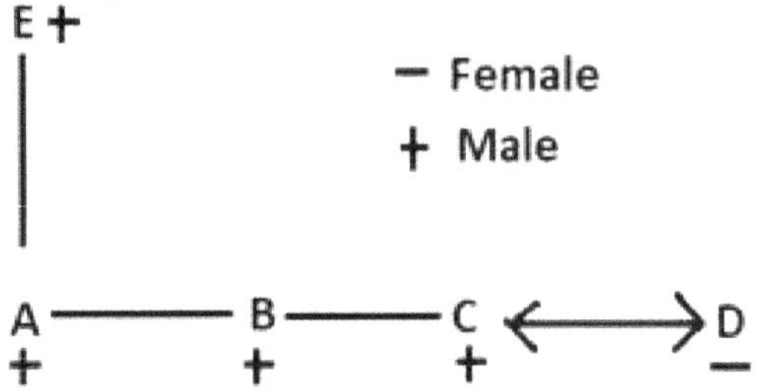

Hence, the correct option is (B).

19. Pondicherry University, Viswa Bharati and HNB Garhwal university all come under central universities. A Central University in India is established by Act of Parliament and are under the purview of the Department of Higher Education in the Union Human Resource Development Ministry. Universities in India are recognized by the University Grants Commission (UGC). The number of central universities published by the UGC includes 43 central universities as on April 2015.
Hence, the correct option is (A).

20. The University Grants Commission was established in the year 1956. UGC is the statutory organization which was established with the aim for the determination and maintenance of standards of teaching, different examination and research in Universities/Colleges. It is formed to regulates and transform higher education in India.
Hence, the correct option is (B).

21. The pattern followed here is

$\Rightarrow A + 1 = B, B + 2 = D$

$\Rightarrow D + 3 = G, G + 4 = K$

$\Rightarrow H + 5 = M, M + 6 = S$

$\Rightarrow M + 7 = T, T + 8 = B$

$\Rightarrow S + 9 = B, B + 10 = L$

Similarly,

$\Rightarrow Z + 11 = K, K + 12 = W$

Hence, the next term in the series is " ZKW".
Hence, the correct option is (C).

22. A deductive argument is invalid if its premises are true and its conclusion is false. A deductive argument is an argument that is given by the arguer to be deductively valid, i.e., to provide a surety of the truth of the conclusion provided that the argument's premises are also true. Premises should provide strong support for the conclusion.
Hence, the correct option is (B).

23. "Education is the manifestation of perfection already in man" this is the very famous quotation by Swami Vivekanand. This quotation was originally part of a letter written to Singaravelu Mudaliyar (Kidi) from Chicago, United States, dated 3 March 1894.
Hence, the correct option is (C).

24. From the given information in the question,

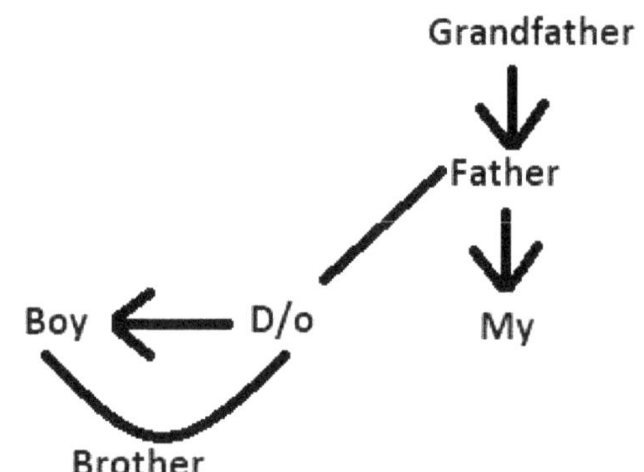

Hence, the correct option is (D).

25. From the information given in the question,

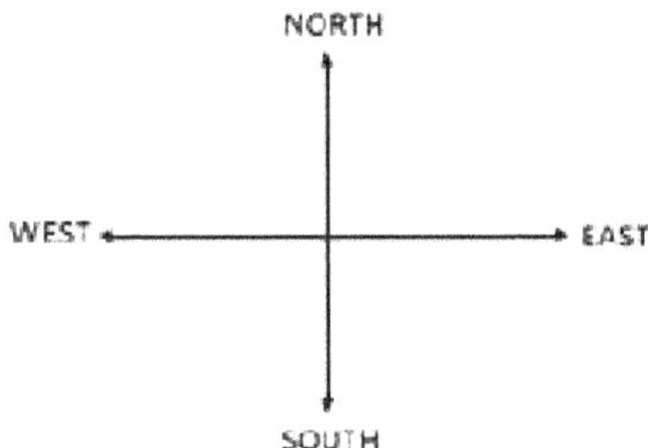

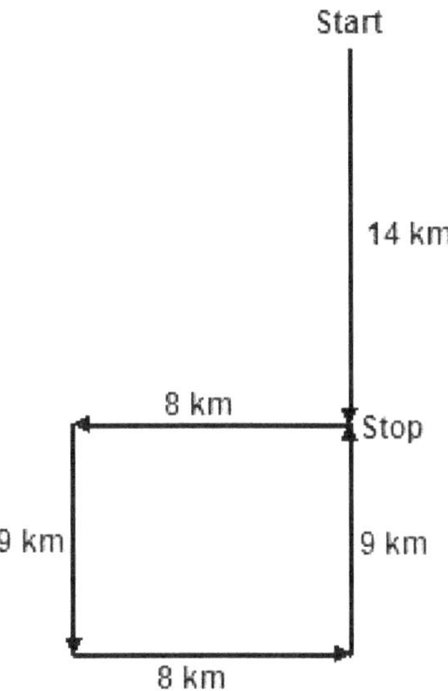

We find the distance between the starting and endpoint is 14 km and the direction is south.

Hence the correct option is (C).

26. The pattern followed here is:

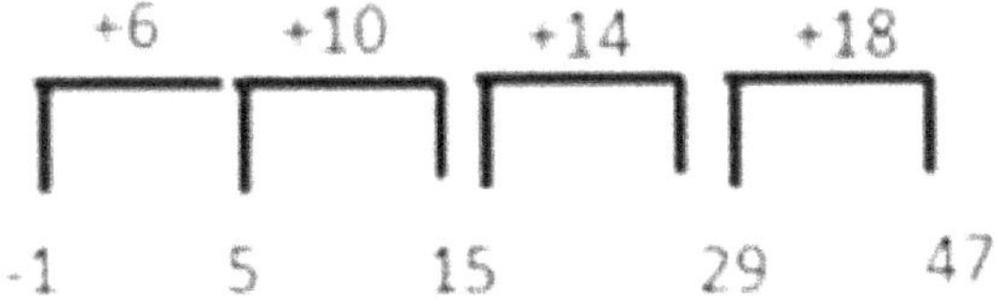

→ -1 + 6 = 5 (We have to add 6 to get 5 from -1)
→ 5 + 10 = 15 (6 + 4 = 10) (We have to add 10 to get 15 from 5)
→ 15 + 14 = 29 (10 + 4 = 14) (We have to add 14 to get 29 from 15)
→ 29 + 18 = 47 (14 + 4 = 18)
So, next term in the series is 47.
Hence, the correct option is (B).

27. The South Asia University current campus is Akbar Bhawan Campus in Chanakyapuri, New Delhi.
South Asian University (SAU) is an International University established by the eight Member States of the South Asian Association for Regional Cooperation (SAARC) in 2010. The eight countries are Afghanistan, Bangladesh, Bhutan, India, Maldives, Nepal, Pakistan and Sri Lanka.
Hence, the correct option is (C).

28. The Committee on Religious and Moral Instructions (1959) known as Sri Prakasa Committee recommended the teaching of moral and spiritual values in educational Institutes, thereby promoting value education. The recommendations were not paid much attention.
Hence, the correct option is (C).

29. As mentioned in the passage, "We believe that technological strengths are especially crucial in dealing with this fourth dimension underlying continuous change in the aspirations of the people, the economy in the global context, and the strategic interests." Thus, the highlighted elements are indicative of the fourth dimension, the fourth dimension is an offshoot or an extension of "modern-day dynamism" and not one of its indicators.

Hence the correct option is (C).

30. Acceptance and non-acceptance of certain stimuli in classroom communication is the basis of selective attention. It is the process of focusing on a particular object in the environment for a certain period of time.

Hence the correct option is (C).

31. The introduction of career courses in schools and colleges aims at providing professional knowledge to students. Professional knowledge requires one to combine subject matter expertise, pedagogical knowledge, and an understanding of students and their learning processes, all for the purposes of increasing student achievement.
Hence, the correct option is (B).

32. While delivering a lecture if there is some disturbance in the class, then a teacher should keep quiet for a while and then go on.
Hence, the correct option is (A).

33. You would consult other books concerning the scientist and then teach the lesson to the student. The purpose of a literature review is to demonstrate that your research question is meaningful.
Hence, the correct option is (C).

34. Homophones are words with the same pronunciation but different meanings which might have different spelling too.

For example- Words buy, by and bye. They have the same pronunciation, but different meanings and spellings.
Hence, the correct option is (B).

35. Salt is non-renewable natural resources. Any resources can be said as renewable only if it is self-replenishing. Salt is being formed by a natural process in the earth.
Hence, the correct option is (D).

36. Sustainable development is critical to the well-being of human society is definitely true, as any development brings some change to the well-being of humans.

Environmentally sound policies do not harm the environment or deplete the natural resources is also true, as these policies will save the environment which will help in sustainable development.

Both (A) and (R) are correct, and R is the correct explanation.

Hence, the correct option is (A).

37.

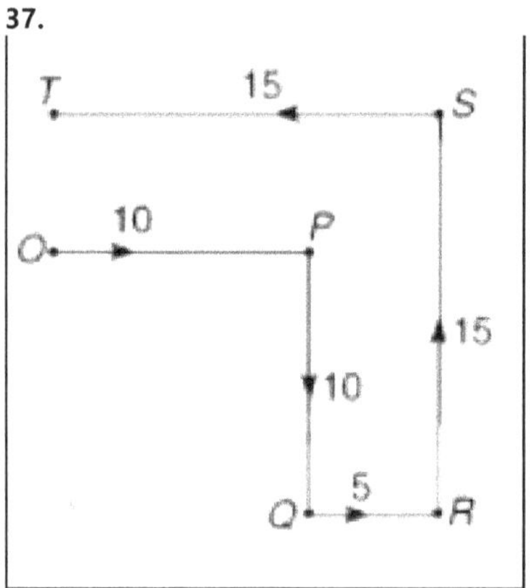

The starting point is O and endpoint is T

$\therefore$ $T's$ distance from the starting point O is OT which is $5m$.

Hence, the correct option is (D).

38. Non-verbal communication is all about the body language of the speaker. In appearance, it includes clothing, hairstyle, neatness of the speaker. In body language, it consists of facial expressions, gestures and postures. In sound, it includes voice tone, volume and speech rate. Report and job description are part of written communication.
Hence, the correct option is (B).

39. Thus, percentage increase was highest in $2014.$
Consumption = Production $-$ Export

$2012,$ consumption $= 186.5 - 114$ million $kg = 72.5$ million kg

$2013,$ consumption $= 202 - 114$ million kg $= 88$ million kg

$2014,$ consumption $= 238 - 130$ million kg $= 108$ million kg

$2015,$ consumption $= 221 - 116$ million kg $= 105$ million kg

$2016,$ consumption $= 215 - 88$ million kg $= 127$ million kg

Now, find out the percentage increase,

$\%$ increase in $2013 =$ (previous year value-recent year value)
$= \frac{88-72.5}{72.5} \times 100\% = 21.38\%$
$\%$ increase in $2014 =$ (previous year value-recent year value)
$= \frac{108-88}{88} \times 100\% = 22.72\%$
$\%$ increase in $2015 =$ (previous year value-recent year value)
$= \frac{105-108}{105} \times 100\% = -2.8\% \Rightarrow$ Decrease (So, discard)
$\%$ increase in $2016 =$ (previous year value-recent year value)
$= \frac{127-105}{105} \cdot 100\% = 20.95\%$
Hence, the correct option is (B).

40. Per capita consumption $= \frac{\text{Consumption}}{\text{Population}}$

Population $= \frac{\text{Consumption}}{\text{Per capita consumption}}$

Population $= \frac{108}{38.7} = 2.79$ million
Hence, the correct option is (C).

41. Consumption = Production $-$Export

$2012,$ consumption $= 186.5 - 114$ million $kg = 72.5$ million kg

$2013,$ consumption $= 202 - 114$ million $kg = 88$ million kg

$2014,$ consumption $= 238 \cdot 130$ million $kg = 108$ million kg

$2015,$ consumption $= 221 - 116$ million kg $= 105$ million kg

$2012, \frac{\text{Exports}}{\text{Consumption}} = \frac{114}{72.5} = 1.57$

$2013, \frac{\text{Exports}}{\text{Consumption}} = \frac{114}{88} = 1.3$

$2014, \frac{\text{Exports}}{\text{Consumption}} = \frac{130}{108} = 1.2$

$2015, \frac{\text{Exports}}{\text{Consumption}} = \frac{116}{105} = 1.1$

Thus for 2012 ratio is maximum.
Hence, the correct option is (A).

42. Consumption = Production $-$ Export

$2013,$ consumption $= 202 - 114$ million $kg = 88$ million kg

$2014,$ consumption $= 238 - 130$ million $kg = 108$ million kg

$2015,$ consumption $= 221 - 116$ million $kg = 105$ million kg

$2016,$ consumption $= 215 - 88$ million $kg = 127$ million kg

Population $= \frac{\text{Consumption}}{\text{Per Capita consumption}}$

$2013,$ Population $= \frac{88}{35.2} = 2.5$ million

2014, Population $= \frac{108}{38.7} = 2.79$ million

2015, Population $= \frac{105}{40.5} = 2.59 million$

2016, Population $= \frac{127}{42} = 3 million$

Thus, Population in 2016 is max.
Hence, the correct option is (D).

43. Consumption = Production $-$ Export

Consumption in the following years are as following:

$2012: 72.5$ million Kg

$2013: 88$ million kg

$2014: 108$ million Kg

$2015: 105$ million Kg

$2016: 127$ million Kg

Average $= (72.5 + 88 + 108 + 105 + 127) 500.5/5 = 100.1$ million kg
Hence, the correct option is (D).

44. For adding table of contents, click on the tab 'References' to add the 'table of contents. The references tab also helps to add footnotes, citations, and bibliography.
Hence, the correct option is (D).

45. Printers can be broadly classified into two categories - Impact and Non-Impact Printers.

Impact Printers- It is a printer that strikes a print head against an ink ribbon to mark the paper. Common examples -dot-matrix and daisy-wheel printers.

Non-Impact Printers- These printers print the characters without using ribbon. Common examples- Laser and Inkjet Printers.
Hence, the correct option is (A).

46. Here each letter is coded with a specific number as:

'B' is 7

'O' is 6

'R' is 9

'R' is 9

'O' is 6

'W' is 5

and,

'B' is 7

'O' is 6

'M' is 4

'B' is 7

Each letter is represented by a number.

Using code for BORROW and BOMB, we have

W = 5

OMB = 647

Hence,

WOMB's code is 5647

Hence, the correct option is (A).

47. The phenomenological method aims to describe, understand and interpret the meanings of experiences of human life. It focuses on research questions such as what it is like to experience a particular situation.
Hence, the correct option is (C).

48. The tribals of Singhbhum district of Bihar started the protest when the government decided to replace the natural sal forests with the highly-priced teak. This movement was called Jungle Bachao Andolan or "Greed Game Political Populism".
Hence, the correct option is (C).

49. It was launched by MHRD in 2002 to upscale and support the ongoing efforts in improving the quality of technical education. TEQIP Phase I (2003-09) and TEQUIP Phase II were implemented with the assistance of the World Bank.
Hence, the correct option is (A).

50. From the information given,

it can be concluded,

A is the sister of B and their mother is C.

D is their grandfather and E is their great-grandmother.

So, A is the grand-daughter of D.

Hence, the correct option is (D).

Mock Test 06

Q.1 Functional Leadership Theory is associated with-

A. Hackman, Walton, and McGrath
B. Bernard and Ordway Tead
C. Koontz and O'Donnell
D. Alford and Beatty

Q.2 When planning to do as social research, it is better to:

A. Approach the topic with an open mind
B. Do a pilot study before getting stuck into it
C. Be familiar with the literature on the topic
D. Forget about theory because this is a very practical

Q.3 The aim of vocationalization of education is:

A. Making liberal education job-oriented
B. Converting liberal education into vocational education
C. Preparing students for a vocation along with knowledge
D. Giving more importance to vocational than general education

Q.4 A researcher divides the populations into PG, graduates and 10 + 2 students and using the random digit table he selects some of them from each. This is technically called

A. Stratified sampling
B. Stratified random sampling
C. Representative sampling
D. None of these

Q.5 NAAC is an autonomous institution under the aegis of:

A. UGC **B.** CSIR **C.** AICTE **D.** ICSSR

Q.6 Under the Air Quality Index in India, which of the following pollutants is not included?

A. Carbon monoxide
B. Fine particulate matter
C. Ozone
D. Chlorofluorocarbons

Q.7 Which of the following is considered a major source of pollution in the rivers of India?

A. Unregulated small-scale industry
B. Untreated sewage
C. Agricultural run-off
D. Thermal power plants

Q.8 The attitude of the teacher that affects teaching pertains to

A. Affective domain
B. Cognitive domain
C. Conative domain
D. Psychomotor domain

Q.9 Maximum participation of students during teaching is possible through

A. Lecture method
B. Demonstration method
C. Inductive method
D. Textbook method

Q.10 Direction: Choose the correct answer from the following code:

Assertion (A): All teaching should aim at ensuring learning.

Reason (R): All learning results from teaching.

A. Both (A) and (R) are true, and (R) is the correct explanation of (A)
B. Both (A) and (R) are true, but (R) is not the correct explanation of (A)
C. (A) is true, but (R) is false
D. (A) is false, but (R) is true

Q.11 Effective teaching means:

A. Love, cooperation, sympathy, affection and encouragement were given to students
B. Corporal punishment was given to students at the time of moral offences
C. Individualized instruction and open classroom discussion
D. Both (A) and (C)

Q.12 A good teacher is one who ________.

A. Gives useful information
B. Explains concepts and principles
C. Gives printed notes to students
D. Inspires students to learn

Q.13 Which of the following statements about teaching aids are correct?

1) They help in retaining concepts for a longer duration.
2) They help students learn better.
3) They make the teaching-learning process interesting.
4) They enhance rote learning.

Select the correct answer from the codes given below:

A. 1, 2, 3 and 4 **B.** 1, 2 and 3
C. 2, 3 and 4 **D.** 1, 2 and 4

Q.14 Greater the handicap of the students coming to the educational institutions, the greater the demand on the

A. Family **B.** Society **C.** Teacher **D.** State

Q.15 Which one of the following pedagogy approach refers to an approach in which students explores topics in greater depth during class time, and ICT education tools technologies like online videos are used to 'deliver the content' outside of the classroom to students.

A. Flipped Classroom Approach
B. Brainstorming Approach
C. ICT based approach
D. Two-way approach

Q.16 In a particular code, HOSPITALS is coded as HSOLSAPTI. The code of BIOLOGICALS will be:

[UGC NET Sociology, 2016]

A. BLICOALIOSG **B.** BOLGICAILOS
C. SBLAOILOBCG **D.** BSILOALCOIG

Q.17 In the series $1,5,13,25,41,$....... the next term is

A. 59 **B.** 63 **C.** 61 **D.** 68

Q.18 At present, a mother is 3 times older than her son. After 5 years, the sum of their ages will be 70 years. The age of the mother after 10 years will be:

[UGC NET Sociology, 2016]

A. 40 **B.** 55 **C.** 45 **D.** 60

Q.19 AYD, BVF, DRH, GMJ, ? the next term is:

A. GLK **B.** HLM **C.** LHM **D.** KGL

Q.20 C and D are sisters. A and B are brothers. E is son of A and brother of D. B is related to C as:

A. Brother **B.** Son
C. Uncle **D.** Father-in-law

Q.21 The best way of providing value education is through:

A. Discussions on scriptural texts
B. Lectures/discourses on values
C. Seminars/symposia on values
D. Mentoring/reflective sessions on values

Q.22 Direction: Match List-I and List-II and select the correct answer from the codes given below:

List-I	List - II
(a) Flood	1. Lack of rainfall for sufficient duration
(b)Drought	2. Tremors produced by the passage of vibratory waves through the rocks of the earth
(c) Earthquake	3. A vent through which moulted substances come out
(d)Volcano	4. Excess rain and uneven distribution of water

A. (a) - 4, (b) - 1, (c) - 2, (d) - 3
B. (a) -2, (b) - 3 (c)-4, (d) - 1
C. (a) - 3, (b) - 4, (c) - 2, (d) - 1
D. (a) - 4, (b) - 3, (c) - 1, (d) - 2

Q.23 Given below are some characteristics of reasoning. Select the code that states a characteristic that is not of deductive reasoning.

A. The conclusion must be based on observation and experiment.
B. The conclusion should be supported by the premise/premises.
C. The conclusion must follow from the premise/premises necessarily.
D. The conclusion must follow from the premise/premises necessarily.

Q.24 Among the following propositions two are related in such a way that they cannot both be true but can both be false. Select the code that states those two propositions.

Propositions:

A) Every student is attentive.

B) Some students are attentive.

C) Students are never attentive.

D) Some students are not attentive.

A. (A) and (B) **B.** (A) and (C)
C. (B) and (C) **D.** (C) and (D)

Q.25 If the statement 'None but the brave wins the race' is false which of the following statements can be claimed to be true?

A. All brave persons win the race.
B. Some persons who win the race are not brave.
C. Some persons who win the race are brave.
D. No person who wins the race is brave.

Q.26 Directions: Read the passage and answer the question that follows:

Development is about expanding the capabilities of the disadvantaged, thereby improving their overall quality of life. Based on this understanding, Maharashtra, one of India's richest States, is a classic case of a lack of development which is seen in its unacceptably high level of malnutrition among children in the tribal belts. While the State's per capita income has doubled since 2004, its nutritional status has not made commensurate progress.

Poor nutrition security disproportionately affects the poorest segment of the population. According to NFHS 2015-16, every second tribal child suffers from growth restricting malnutrition due to chronic hunger. In 2005, child malnutrition claimed as many as 718 lives in Maharashtra's Palghar district alone. Even after a decade of double-digit economic growth (2004-05 to 2014-15), Palghar's malnutrition status has barely improved.

In September 2016, the National Human Rights Commission issued notice to the Maharashtra government over reports of 600 children dying due to malnutrition in Palghar. The government responded, promising to properly implement schemes such as Jascha Baccha and Integrated Child Development Services to check malnutrition. Our independent survey conducted in the Vikramgad block of the district last year found that 57%, 21%, and 53% of children in this block were stunted, wasted, and underweight, respectively; 27% were severely stunted. Our data challenges what Maharashtra's Women and Child Development Minister said in the Legislative Council in March — that "malnutrition in Palghar had come down in the past few months, owing to various interventions made by the government."

Stunting is caused by an insufficient intake of macro-and micro-nutrients. It is generally accepted that recovery from growth retardation after two years is only possible if the affected child is put on a diet that is adequate in nutrient requirements. A critical aspect of nutrient adequacy is diet diversity, calculated by different groupings of foods consumed with the reference period ranging from one to 15 days. We calculated a 24-hour dietary diversity score by counting the number of food groups the child received in the last 24 hours. The eight food groups include cereals, roots, and tubers; legumes and nuts; dairy products; flesh foods; eggs; fish; dark green leafy vegetables; and other fruits and vegetables.

In most households, it was rice and dal which was cooked most often and eaten thrice a day. These were even served at teatime to the children if they felt hungry. There was no milk, milk product, or fruit in their daily diets. Even the adults drank black tea as milk was unaffordable. Only 17% of the children achieved a minimum level of diet diversity — they received four or more of the eight food groups. This low dietary diversity is a proxy indicator for the household's food security too as the children ate the same food cooked for adult members.

Which of the following is/are true as per the passage?

I. India's situation is worse than in some of the world's poorest countries — Bangladesh, Afghanistan, or Mozambique.

II. Development is more than just economic growth.

III. On average, the nutrition expenditure as a percentage of the Budget has drastically declined from 1.68% in 2012-13 to 0.94% in 2018-19.

A. Only II
B. Only I and II
C. Only II and III
D. Only I and III

Ques (27-30):Directions: Read the passage and answer the question that follows:

Development is about expanding the capabilities of the disadvantaged, thereby improving their overall quality of life. Based on this understanding, Maharashtra, one of India's richest States, is a classic case of a lack of development which is seen in its unacceptably high level of malnutrition among children in the tribal belts. While the State's per capita income has doubled since 2004, its nutritional status has not made commensurate progress.

Poor nutrition security disproportionately affects the poorest segment of the population. According to NFHS 2015-16, every second tribal child suffers from growth restricting malnutrition due to chronic hunger. In 2005, child malnutrition claimed as many as 718 lives in Maharashtra's Palghar district alone. Even after a decade of double-digit economic growth (2004-05 to 2014-15), Palghar's malnutrition status has barely improved.

In September 2016, the National Human Rights Commission issued notice to the Maharashtra government over reports of 600 children dying due to malnutrition in Palghar. The government responded, promising to properly implement schemes such as Jascha Baccha and Integrated Child Development Services to check malnutrition. Our independent survey conducted in the Vikramgad block of the district last year found that 57%, 21%, and 53% of children in this block were stunted, wasted, and underweight, respectively; 27% were severely stunted. Our data challenges what Maharashtra's Women and Child Development Minister said in the Legislative Council in March — that "malnutrition in Palghar had come down in the past few months, owing to various interventions made by the government."

Stunting is caused by an insufficient intake of macro-and micro-nutrients. It is generally accepted that recovery from growth retardation after two years is only possible if the affected child is put on a diet that is adequate in nutrient requirements. A critical aspect of nutrient adequacy is diet diversity, calculated by different groupings of foods consumed with the reference period ranging from one to 15 days. We calculated a 24-hour dietary diversity score by counting the number of food groups the child received in the last 24 hours. The eight food groups include cereals, roots, and tubers; legumes and nuts; dairy products; flesh foods; eggs; fish; dark green leafy vegetables; and other fruits and vegetables.

In most households, it was rice and dal which was cooked most often and eaten thrice a day. These were even served at teatime to the children if they felt hungry. There was no milk, milk product, or fruit in their daily diets. Even the adults drank black tea as milk was unaffordable. Only 17% of the children achieved a minimum level of diet diversity — they received four or more of the eight food groups. This low dietary diversity is a proxy indicator for the household's food security too as the children ate the same food cooked for adult members.

Q.27 What could possibly be a/some possible reason/s for such extreme food insecurity among tribal households as has been shown in the passage?

I. Loss of their traditional dependence on forest livelihood.

II. Weak implementation of public nutrition schemes.

III. A worsening agriculture situation.

A. Only II
B. Only I and II
C. Only II and III
D. All of the above

Q.28 Which of the following strengthens the claim that the nutrition indicators fare poorly in India?

I. Stunting declined from 46.3% in 2005 to 34.4% in 2016.

II. As per an NHFS survey, wasting rates have increased from 16.5% to 25.6% over a period of 10 years.

III. The underweight rate (36%) has remained static in the last 10 years.

A. Only I
B. Only III
C. Only I and II
D. Only II and III

Q.29 What is ironic about the situation mentioned in paragraph 1?

A. States do not have adequate resources to feed the poor even when there are enough resources with the Centre.
B. Even though states may be classified as rich with a high per capita income, they may not really be developed.
C. Development of states depends on sustained economic growth which in turn leads to high per capita income.
D. The level of malnutrition is abnormally high in states which have a high growth level and better than average per capita income.

Q.30 As per the passage, which of the following is/are needed for an adequate meal?

I. Macro and micronutrients

II. Multiple food groups

III. High level of Intermittent fasting

A. Only II
B. Only I and III
C. Only I and II
D. Only II and III

Q.31 The e-content generation for undergraduate courses has been assigned by the Ministry of Human Resource Development to-

A. INFLIBNET
B. Consortium for Educational Communication
C. National Knowledge Commission
D. Indira Gandhi National Open University

Q.32 National Educational Alliance for Technology (NEAT) implementing agency is which among the following organisations?

A. UGC **B.** AICTE
C. ISRO **D.** Niti Aayog

Q.33 Education as a subject of legislation figures in which of the following lists?

A. Union List **B.** State List
C. Concurrent List **D.** Residuary Powers

Q.34 CSS stands for

A. Cascading Style Sheets
B. Collecting Style Sheets
C. Comparative Style Sheets
D. Comprehensive Style Sheets

Q.35 Symbols A-F are used in which one of the following?

A. Binary number system
B. Decimal number system
C. Hexadecimal number system
D. Octal number system

Q.36 A new Laptop has been produced that weightless, is smaller and uses less power than previous Laptop models. Which of the following technologies has been used to accomplish this?

[UGC NET Sociology, 2018]

A. Universal Serial Bus Mouse
B. Faster Random-Access Memory
C. Blu Ray Drive
D. Solid State Hard Drive

Q.37 Indian government's target of producing power from bio-power by the year 2022 is

A. 15 GW **B.** 10 GW **C.** 50 GW **D.** 25 GW

Q.38 Which of the following is the largest source of water pollution in major rivers of India?

A. Untreated sewage
B. Agriculture run-off
C. Unregulated small scale industries
D. Religious practices

Q.39 Who among the following is the ultimate authority to interpret the Indian Constitution?

A. Parliament
B. Supreme Court of India
C. President
D. Chief Justice of India

Q.40 Autonomy in higher education implies freedom in:

A. Finance
B. Administration
C. Policy-making
D. Curriculum development

Q.41 National Council for Women's Education was established in:

A. 1951 **B.** 1958 **C.** 1964 **D.** 1970

Q.42 Which one of the following is not situated in New Delhi?

A. Indian Institute of Advanced Studies
B. Indian Council of Cultural Relations
C. Indian Council of Scientific Research
D. National Council of Educational Research and Training

Q.43 Which of the following can the problems and techniques be classified into?

A. Game theory **B.** Network analysis
C. Inventory control **D.** All of these

Ques (44-45):Direction: For a country CO_2 emission (million metric tons) from various sectors are given in the following table. Answer the questions based on the data given:

CO_2 emissions (million metric tons)					
Sector	**Power**	**Industry**	**Commercial**	**Agriculture**	**Domestic**
2005	500	200	150	80	100
2006	600	300	200	90	110
2007	650	320	250	100	120
2008	700	400	300	150	150
2009	800	500	320	200	180

Q.44 What is the average annual growth rate of power generation in the power sector?

A. 12.57% **B.** 16.87% **C.** 30.81% **D.** 50.25%

Q.45 What is the percentage contribution of the power sector to the total CO_2 emissions in the year 2008?

A. 30.82% **B.** 41.18% **C.** 51.38% **D.** 60.25%

Q.46 Which of the following is true about the Tippit table?

A. It is a table of random digits
B. It is used for sampling methods
C. Both (A) and (B)
D. None of the above

Q.47 Every communicator has to experience-

A. Manipulated emotions
B. Anticipatory excitement
C. The issue of homophiles
D. Status dislocation

Q.48 Attitudes, actions and appearances in the context of classroom communication are considered as:

A. Verbal **B.** Non-verbal
C. Impersonal **D.** Irrational

Q.49 In the classroom, the teacher sends the message either as words or images. The students are really-

A. Encoders **B.** Decoders
C. Agitators **D.** Propagators

Q.50 Positive classroom communication leads to-

A. Coercion **B.** Submission
C. Confrontation **D.** Persuasion

// Smart Answer Sheet //

Correct Indicates percentage of students who answered questions correctly.

Skipped Indicates percentage of students who skipped questions.

Q.	Ans.	Correct	Skipped
1	A	54.93 %	6.26 %
2	C	28.36 %	21.79 %
3	A	29.25 %	22.39 %
4	B	45.37 %	22.99 %
5	A	32.84 %	26.26 %
6	D	31.34 %	26.27 %
7	B	49.85 %	24.48 %
8	A	31.34 %	26.27 %
9	B	33.73 %	25.08 %
10	C	35.52 %	26.57 %
11	D	58.21 %	23.58 %
12	D	59.4 %	23.59 %
13	B	55.52 %	23.88 %
14	C	57.31 %	22.99 %
15	A	18.21 %	25.07 %
16	D	28.96 %	25.97 %
17	C	55.82 %	25.97 %
18	B	37.91 %	27.76 %
19	D	62.69 %	22.98 %
20	C	53.43 %	20.9 %
21	D	37.91 %	20.6 %
22	A	45.67 %	22.39 %
23	A	32.24 %	23.58 %
24	B	40.6 %	22.68 %
25	B	23.88 %	26.57 %
26	A	25.37 %	32.24 %
27	D	19.7 %	31.05 %
28	D	37.01 %	28.36 %
29	B	30.15 %	30.45 %
30	C	40.0 %	28.96 %
31	B	22.09 %	22.69 %
32	B	34.93 %	23.28 %
33	C	49.25 %	21.79 %
34	A	48.66 %	22.09 %
35	C	54.63 %	26.27 %
36	D	35.52 %	23.58 %
37	B	35.52 %	23.88 %
38	A	54.93 %	26.26 %
39	B	15.22 %	25.08 %
40	D	22.99 %	33.43 %
41	B	39.4 %	31.94 %
42	A	24.18 %	27.46 %
43	D	32.24 %	32.54 %
44	A	26.27 %	29.85 %
45	B	34.33 %	31.94 %
46	C	43.58 %	28.96 %
47	B	35.82 %	25.37 %
48	B	49.25 %	24.48 %
49	B	45.67 %	26.57 %
50	D	39.1 %	25.08 %

Performance Analysis	
Avg. Score (%)	42.0%
Toppers Score (%)	98.0%
Your Score	

//Hints and Solutions//

1. Functional Leadership Theory is associated with Hackman, Walton, and McGrath. It is a particularly useful theory for addressing specific leader behaviours expected to contribute to organizational or unit effectiveness. This theory argues that the leader's main job is to see that whatever is necessary to group needs is taken care of.
Hence, the correct option is (A).

2. When planning to do social research, it is better to be familiar with the literature on the topic. Social Research is a method used by social scientists and researchers to learn about people and societies so that they can design products/services that cater to various needs of the people.

Hence, the correct option is (C).

3. Vocational education prepares individuals for jobs. It has adequate employment potentialities. It helps in broadening of horizon. According to the recommendation of the Secondary Education Commission (1952-53), the aim of the vocationalisation of education is to improve the vocational efficiency of the students.
Hence, the correct option is (A).

4. Division of population on the basis of class, income, education level etc is called stratification and every member of each stratum has an equal chance of being selected by the researcher. In this way characteristics of various strata are identified and studied.

Hence, the correct option is (B).

5. The National Assessment and Accreditation Council (NAAC) was established in 1994 as an autonomous institution of the University Grants Commission (UGC) with its Head Quarter in Bengaluru.

Hence, the correct option is (A).

6. Air Quality Index (AQI) is categorized into six categories, namely: Good, Satisfactory, Moderately polluted, Poor, Very poor, and Severe.

The AQI is proposed for eight pollutants like (Particulate Matter) PM_{10}, (Particulate Matter) $PM_{2.5}$, (Nitrogen dioxide) NO_2, (Sulphur dioxide) SO_2, (Carbon monoxide) CO, (Ozone) O_3, (Ammonia) NH_3, and (Lead) Pb. So, Chlorofluorocarbons (CFC) is not included.
Hence, the correct option is (D).

7. The main source of freshwater pollution can be attributed to the discharge of untreated waste mainly sewage effluents and run-off from agricultural fields. Industrial growth, urbanization, and the increasing use of synthetic organic substances have serious and adverse impacts on freshwater bodies.
Hence, the correct option is (B).

8. The affective domain includes how we deal with things emotionally, such as feelings, values, appreciation, enthusiasms, motivations, and attitudes. It is the part of the system for addressing, identifying, and understanding how people learn. So, the attitude of teachers affects teaching pertains to the affective domain.
Hence, the correct option is (A).

9. Maximum participation of students during teaching is possible through the demonstration method. A demonstration is a process of teaching someone how to make or do something in a step-by-step process. Demonstration often occurs when students have a hard time connecting theories to actual practice or when students are unable to understand applications of theories.
Hence, the correct option is (B).

10. All teaching should aim at ensuring learning. It is a correct statement. Teaching is an activity aimed at bringing about meaningful learning through a method that is morally and pedagogically (educationally) acceptable.

All learning results from teaching it is not a correct statement. Learning in a particular way using distinctive modes for thinking, relating, and creating. The concept of students having particular learning styles has implications for teaching strategies. All learning outcomes from Personal characteristics, Academic characteristics, Social/emotional characteristics, and Cognitive characteristics. Therefore Assertion (A) is correct and Reason (R) is not a correct statement.
Hence, the correct option is (C).

11. Effective teaching means:

Love, cooperation, sympathy, affection, and encouragement are given to students. Individualized instruction and open classroom discussion.

Hence, the correct option is (D).

12. A good teacher is one who inspires students to learn new things. Students who are not motivated will not learn effectively and in turn, they won't retain information or participate and may even become disruptive.
Hence, the correct option is (D).

13. Teaching aids like charts, boards, projectors, etc make the teaching-learning process interesting, which will further help the student to learn better and retain concepts for a longer duration. The student's retention power is increased through these different audio and video teaching aids.
Hence, the correct option is (B).

14. Greater the handicap of the students coming to the educational institutions, the greater the demand on the teacher. A teacher is the one who will understand the problems of the students and as the number of students increases in the educational institution, the demand for teachers also increases.
Hence, the correct option is (C).

15. Flipped classroom approach is a modern approach that deals with students are asked to do some homework before the class and then they learn that topic in-depth with live examples with the help of the instructor.
Hence, the correct option is (A).

16. In this logic, the order is like the first alphabet comes first, then the last alphabet, then the second alphabet from the front and second last alphabet and so on.

Like: H comes first, then S (last alphabet), then O (second alphabet), then L (second last alphabet) and so on.

In the required pattern, B comes first, then S (last alphabet), then I (second alphabet), then L (second last alphabet) and so on.

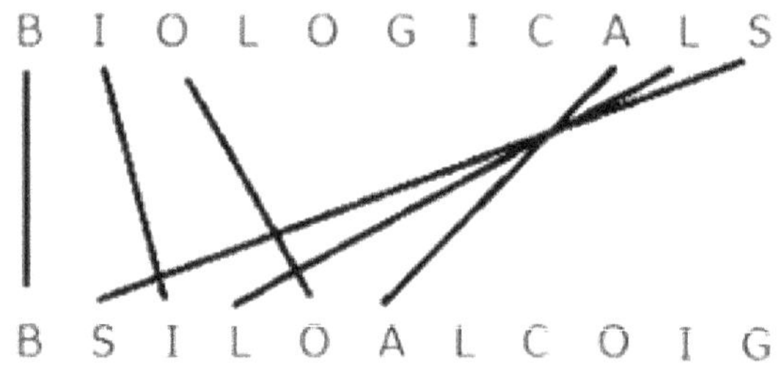

Hence, the correct option is (D).

17. The pattern is $+4, +8, +12, +16 \ldots \ldots$

So, missing term = $41 + 20 = 61$

Hence, the correct option is (C).

18. Let the age of mother be $'m'$ and that of son be $'s'$.

$m = 3s$

After 5 years, mother's age $= m + 5$ and son's age $= s + 5$.

Sum after 5 years,

$(m + 5) + (s + 5) = 70$ and $m = 3s$

$m + s = 70 - 10 = 60$

and $4s = 60 \Rightarrow s = 15$ and $m = 45$

Mother's age after 10 years $= 45 + 10 = 55$.
Hence, the correct option is (B).

19. Taking the first alphabet of every word,

A +1 = B + 2 = D + 3 = G + 4 = K

Taking the second alphabet of every word,

Y – 3 = V – 4 = R – 5 = M – 6 = G

Taking the third alphabet of every word,

D + 2 = F + 2 = H + 2 = J + 2 = L

So, AYD, BVF, DRH, GMJ, KGL

Hence, the correct option is (D).

20.

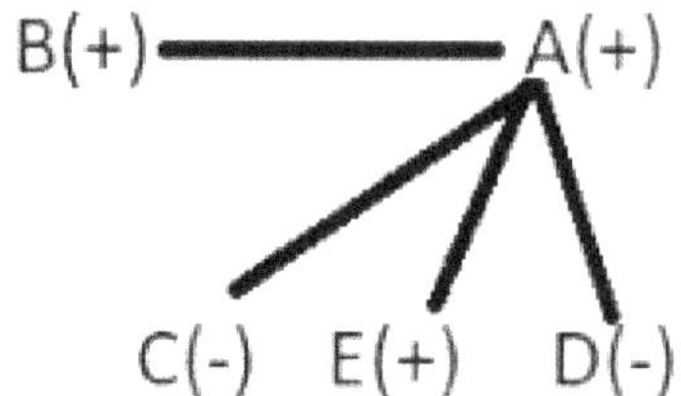

So, B is the uncle of C.
Hence, the correct option is (C).

21. Value Education is the process by which people (in higher institutes, the teacher) gives values to the students/others. Mentoring or reflective session on values is the best way for providing value education.

Hence, the correct option is (D).

22.

- **Flood**: It occurs an overflow of water on land which is usually a dry and uneven distribution of water.
- **Drought**: It is a period of abnormally low rainfall for a long duration, Lack of rainfall for sufficient duration.
- **Earthquake**: Its produced by the passage of vibratory waves through the rocks of the earth.
- **Volcano**: A vent through which moulted substances come out.

Hence, the correct option is (A).

23. In deductive reasoning, the conclusion is supported by the premises and must follow the premises is true. It is not based on observations and experiments. The argument may be valid or invalid is also true.

Hence, the correct option is (A).

24. An (All) and E (No) propositions are contrary. They both cannot be true, but both can be false. Therefore, A proposition- Every student is attentive and E proposition- Students are never attentive are correct options.

Hence, the correct option is (B).

25. If None but the brave wins the race' is false, it means brave does not win the race. According to the AIEO rule, the true statement must be a statement of Some-not (O statement).

Hence, the correct option is (B).

26. Statements I and III have not been mentioned in the passage and are incorrect.

Statement II is correct as can be concluded from the first paragraph of the passage.

Hence, the correct option is (A).

27. All the statements are valid as all give probable reasons for the prevailing condition of food insecurity.

Hence, the correct option is (D).

28. Statement I is positive and weakens the claim.

Statements II and III are negative and show the poor state of nutrition in India.

Hence, the correct option is (D).

29. An urban heat island (UHI) is an urban area or metropolitan area that is significantly warmer than its surrounding rural areas due to human activities.

The temperature difference is usually larger at night than during the day and is most apparent when winds are weak.

The UHI decreases air quality by increasing the production of pollutants such as ozone and decreases water quality as warmer waters flow into area streams and put stress on their ecosystems. Hence, the correct option is (B).

30. 'Stunting is caused by an insufficient intake of macro-and micro-nutrients. It is generally accepted that recovery from growth retardation after two years is only possible if the affected child is put on a diet that is adequate in nutrient requirements. A critical aspect of nutrient adequacy is diet diversity, calculated by different groupings of foods consumed with the reference period ranging from one to 15 days.'

As per the highlighted points, I and II are correct while III has not been mentioned in the passage.

Hence, the correct option is (C).

31. The e-content generation for undergraduate courses has been assigned by the Ministry of Human Resource Development to Consortium for Educational Communication. E-content is launched on seven subjects Anthropology, English, Hindi, Mathematics, Photography, Environmental Studies, and History.

Hence, the correct option is (B).

32. NEAT objective is to use Artificial Intelligence to make learning more personalised and customised as per the requirements of the learner for better learning outcomes in higher education.

All India Council for Technical Education (AICTE) under MHRD, the national level regulator for technical education in the country, would be the implementing agency for NEAT programme.

Hence, the correct option is (B).

33. Education as a subject of legislation figures in the Concurrent List. The Concurrent List is a list of 52 items given in the Seventh Schedule of the Constitution of India. It includes the power to be considered by both the central and state government.

Hence, the correct option is (C).

34. CSS stands for Cascading Style Sheet. It is a mechanism of adding style to a web document. CSS is used to define the font, font size, font weight, its position, and other visual settings.

Hence, the correct option is (A).

35. Symbols A-F are used in hexadecimal number system. It has 16 digits. 0 to 9 and A=10, B=11, C=12, D= 13, E= 14, F=15.

Hence, the correct option is (C).

36. A new Laptop has been produced that weightless, is smaller and uses less power than previous Laptop models that might be using solid-state hard drive. This device store data on flash memory.

Hence, the correct option is (D).

37. The Government of India has set a target of installing 175 GW of renewable energy capacity by the year 2022, which includes 100 GW from solar, 60 GW from wind, 10 GW from bio-power and 5 GW from small hydro-power.

Hence, the correct option is (B).

38. Untreated sewage is the largest source of water pollution in major rivers of India. Untreated sewage also poses a lot of diseases. It poses a major risk to human health since it contains waterborne pathogens that can cause serious human illness.

Hence, the correct option is (A).

39. As per Article 141, the law declared by the Supreme Court of India is to be binding on each court within the Indian territory as it's the apex court of the nation. The final judicial authority of interpreting the constitution as well as for deciding questions on national law and local bylaws. The implementation of rule of law is vested on the SC.

Hence, the correct option is (B).

40. Curriculum development can be defined as the step-by-step process used to create positive improvements in the courses offered by a school, college, or university. The world changes every day and new discoveries have to be roped into the education curricula.

Hence, the correct option is (D).

41. National Council on Women's Education, established by the Government of India in 1958. The committee presented its recommendations, The Centre and State Governments should give priority to the education of girls.

Hence, the correct option is (B).

42. The Indian Institute of Advanced Study (IIAS) is a research institute based in Shimla, India. It was set up by the Ministry of Education, Government of India in 1964 and it started functioning on 20 October 1965.

Hence, the correct option is (A).

43. Game theory, Network analysis, Inventory control are the following theories in which problems and techniques can be classified.

Hence, the correct option is (D).

44. In 2005 to $2006: \frac{100}{500} \times 100 = 20\%$

In 2006 to $2007: \frac{50}{600} \times 100 = 8.33\%$

In 2007 to $2008: \frac{50}{650} \times 100 = 7.69\%$

In 2008 to $2009: \frac{100}{700} \times 100 = 14.28\%$

Average Annual growth rate $= \frac{50.30}{4} = 12.57\%$

Hence, the correct option is (A)

45. % contribution of power sector to total CO_2 emissions in the year 2008 $= \frac{700}{1700} \times 100 = 41.18\%$

Hence, the correct option is (B).

46. Tippit table was published by L.H.C. Tippett in 1927. It is a table of random digits and uses for the sampling method.

Hence, the correct option is (C).

47. Every communicator has to experience anticipatory excitement. Anticipatory excitement describes the feeling when something is coming what one feels can happen. In anticipatory communication, the procedure is set to identify some areas of interest an individual/group will be interested in discussing based upon the common expected interests.

Therefore, every communicator has to experience anticipatory excitement.

Hence, the correct option is (B).

48. Attitudes, actions and appearances in the context of classroom communication are considered as Non-verbal communication. Non-verbal communication denotes our facial expressions, gestures, eye contact, posture, and tone of voice that we speak. It is the procedure in which the messages are sent and received without using words, either spoken or written.

Hence, the correct option is (B).

49. In the classroom, the teacher sends the messages either as words or images. The students are decoders who, try to understand what is told by the teacher. They decode the words of the teacher and then understand them according to their convenience.

Hence, the correct option is (B).

50. In case of final decision making regarding Anti Defection of an MP, Speaker and Chairman in Lok Sabha and Rajya Sabha acts as the final authority.

Coercion refers to the action or practice of persuading someone to do something by using force or threats.

Submission is a state of mind in which people cannot any longer do what they want to do because they have been influenced by someone else.

Confrontation is a situation in which people or groups with opposing ideas or opinions disagree angrily:

Persuasion is the act to influence someone to do something or to change their mind. Therefore, positive classroom communication leads to persuasion.

Hence, the correct option is (D).

Mock Test 07

Q.1 Which among the following is used for making Gunny bags, Hessians, Cordage, and Carpets?

A. Cotton
B. Jute
C. Wool
D. Polyester

Q.2 Where does a computer add and compare data?

A. Hard disk
B. Floppy disk
C. Memory chip
D. CPU

Q.3 The process of cultivating silkworm is called

A. Sericulture
B. Carding
C. Drawing
D. Spinning

Q.4 Which of the following grows best in a black soil and warm climate?

A. Cotton
B. Flax
C. Jute
D. Coconut

Q.5 Direction: Choose the correct option with the help of Assertion (A) and Reason (R).

Assertion (A): The initial messages to students in the classroom by a teacher need not be critical to establishing interactions later.

Reason (R): More control over the communication process means more control over what the students are learning.

A. Both (A) and (R) are true, and (R) is the correct explanation of (A)
B. Both (A) and (R) are true, but (R) is not the correct explanation of (A)
C. (A) is true, but (R) is false
D. (A) is false, but (R) is true

Q.6 Which of these should be avoided during the delivery of a speech?

A. Confidence
B. Clarity
C. Pauses
D. Rudeness

Q.7 Which of these should be avoided for an effective speech?

A. Determination of the purpose
B. Selection of message
C. Lack of interest
D. Selection of theme

Q.8 Which of these factors is not required to determine the purpose of speech?

A. Providing information
B. Discouragement
C. Accepting ideas
D. Entertainment

Q.9 Which of these ingredients is not required for selection of theme?

A. Planning
B. Disorganisation
C. Preparation
D. Organisation

Q.10 Which of these should be avoided for an effective speech?

A. Planning of speech
B. Preparation of speech
C. Long sentences
D. Organisation

Q.11 Which of the following set of statements reflects the basic characteristics of teaching?

(i) Teaching is the same as training.

(ii) There is no difference between instruction and conditioning when we teach.

(iii) Teaching is related to learning.

(iv) Teaching is a 'task' word while learning is an 'achievement' word.

(v) Teaching means giving information.

(vi) One may teach without learning taking place.

A. (i), (ii) and (iii)
B. (iii), (iv) and (vi)
C. (ii), (iii) and (v)
D. (i), (iv) and (vi)

Q.12 Which combination of methods of teaching is likely to optimize learning?

A. Lecturing, discussions and seminar method
B. Interactive discussions, planned lectures and PowerPoint based presentations
C. Interactive lecture sessions followed by buzz sessions, brainstorming and projects
D. Lecturing, demonstrations and PowerPoint based presentations

Q.13 Direction: Choose the correct option with the help of Assertion (A) and Reason (R).

Assertion (A): Teaching aids have to be considered as effective supplements to instruction.

Reason (R): They keep the students in good humor.

Choose the correct answer from the codes given below:

A. Both (A) and (R) are true and (R) is the correct explanation of (A)
B. Both (A) and (R) are true, but (R) is not the correct explanation of (A)
C. (A) is true, but (R) is false
D. (A) is false, but (R) is true

Q.14 Which of the following learner characteristics are likely to influence the effectiveness of teaching aids and evaluation systems to ensure positive results?

[UGC NET Sociology, 2016]

A. Learner's family background, age and habitation
B. Learner's parentage, socio-economic background and performance in learning of the concerned subject
C. Learner's stage of development, social background and personal interests
D. Learner's maturity level, academic performance level and

motivational dispositions

Q.15 From the following list of statements, select those which indicate the characteristics and basic requirements of teaching.

i. Teaching implies communication.

ii. Teaching is like selling goods.

iii. Teaching means managing and monitoring.

iv. Teaching implies influencing others.

v. Teaching requires convincing others.

vi. There can be no teaching without infrastructural support.

Choose the correct answer from the code given below:

A. i, iii and iv **B.** i, ii and iii

C. iv, v and vi **D.** ii, v and vi

Q.16 Which of the following teaching methods involves a group of experts coming together for the discussion and learning of specific techniques and topics?

A. Demonstration Method

B. Lecture Method

C. Discussion Method

D. Seminar Method

Q.17 As per the HDR 2015, in HDI India ranked:

A. 137th **B.** 134th **C.** 130th **D.** 127th

Q.18 Consider the following reasons which are responsible to keep India at the bottom of the Human Development:

I. rapid increase in population

II. large number of adult illiterates and low gross enrolment ratio

III. inadequate government expenditure on education and health

Which of the following statement(s) is/are correct?

A. Only I **B.** Only II

C. Both I and II **D.** Neither I nor II

Q.19 Full form of LCD?

A. Light Crystal Display

B. Liquid Compact Display

C. Light Compact Display

D. Liquid Crystal Display

Q.20 The educational institutions, libraries, hospitals, and industries store the concerned

A. Operating system **B.** Word processing

C. Data management **D.** Informing system

Q.21 Which of the following is not an output device?

A. Printer **B.** Speaker

C. Monitor **D.** Keyboard

Q.22 Which of the following institutions are empowered to confer or grant degrees under the UGC Act, 1956?

1) A university established by an Act of Parliament

2) A university established by an Act of Legislature

3) A university/institution established by a linguistic minority

4) An institution which is a deemed to be university

Select the correct answer from the codes given below:

A. 1 and 2 **B.** 1, 2 and 3

C. 1, 2 and 4 **D.** 1,2,3 and 4

Q.23 Correlation Analysis aims to present the:

A. Variation among the variables

B. Association among the variables

C. Differentiation among variable

D. Significance of the variables

Q.24 Vitamin which is not found in Fruits and Vegetables is:

A. Vitamin A **B.** Vitamin B1

C. Vitamin B6 **D.** Vitamin B12

Q.25 There are four kinds of factors that influence the environment – topographic, climatic, edaphic, and biotic. Out of these, which is also known as physiographic factors?

A. Topographic **B.** Climatic

C. Edaphic **D.** Biotic

Q.26 In a row of 74 girls, Shweta is 27th from left end. Palak is 7th to the right of Shweta. What is Palak's position from the right end of the row?

A. 40 **B.** 41 **C.** 42 **D.** 44

Q.27 Which number should come next in the series, 48, 24, 12, ...?

A. 8 **B.** 6 **C.** 4 **D.** 2

Q.28 Nisin is used as:

A. Antimicrobial agent **B.** Emulsifier

C. Stabilizer **D.** Sweetner

Q.29 In a company, all Mondays and Sundays are off. If a month starts with a Monday and has 31 days then how many off will be there in that month?

A. 7 **B.** 8 **C.** 9 **D.** 5

Q.30 Numbering the citations linked to footnotes or endnotes is done in which of the following formats?

A. APA style format

B. Chicago style format

C. MLA style format

D. Harvard style format

Q.31 Find the number of triangles in the given figure?

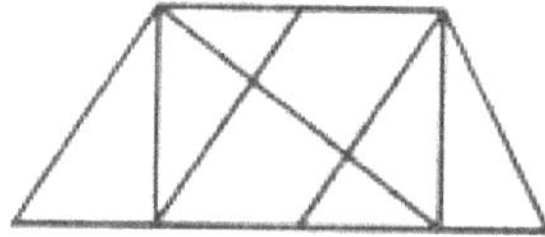

A. 8 **B.** 12 **C.** 12 **D.** 14

Q.32 dB (decibel) is the measurement of___________.

A. Building materials **B.** Sound

C. Water weight **D.** Natural Light

Q.33 A party consists of a grandmother, father, mother, four sons, and their wives and one son and two daughters to each of the sons.

How many females are there is all?

A. 14 **B.** 16 **C.** 18 **D.** 24

Q.34 The statements below are followed by two conclusions labeled I and II, Assuming that the information in the statements is true, even if it appears at variance with generally established tacts, decide which conclusion(s) logically and definitely follow(s) from the information given in the statements.

Statements:

1) Some owls are horses.

2) Some horses are hares.

Conclusions:

I. Some owls are hares.

II. Some hares are owls.

A. Only conclusion II follows

B. Only conclusion I follows

C. Both conclusions follow

D. Neither conclusion I nor conclusion II follows

Q.35 Introducing Rakesh to her husband a woman said, "His brother's father is the only son of my grandfather". The woman is related to Rakesh as:

[UGC NET Sociology, 2018]

A. Aunt **B.** Mother

C. Sister **D.** Daughter

Ques (36-40):Direction: Study the following table chart carefully and answer the question given beside.

The following table represents the Maximum marks of five subjects and marks obtained by five students in five subjects.

Students	Physics (Out of 75)	Mathematics (Out of 100)	Chemistry (Out of 75)	Biology (Out of 75)	English (Out of 120)
Ragini	56	65	45	38	95
Rohan	60	52	62	55	88
Sohan	50	78	70	58	88
Mohini	55	82	65	66	110
Mohan	42	96	64	72	104

Q.36 Marks obtained by Ragini in Chemistry and Biology together is what percent of the marks obtained by Mohini in Physics and Mathematics together?

A. 66.23% **B.** 60.58% **C.** 58.34% **D.** 54.32%

Q.37 Find the respective ratio of the marks obtained by all the students in Mathematics and marks obtained by all the students in Chemistry.

A. 293 : 351 **B.** 373 : 306

C. 351 : 293 **D.** 306 : 373

Q.38 Find the difference between the percentage of marks obtained by Mohan in English and that of Rohan in Physics.

A. 6.67% **B.** 4.59% **C.** 5.53% **D.** 3.12%

Q.39 Find the sum of marks obtained by Rohan in all the subjects.

A. 515 **B.** 427 **C.** 611 **D.** 317

Q.40 Find the overall percentage of Sohan in all the subjects.

A. 62.7% **B.** 58.4% **C.** 77.3% **D.** 79.1%

Q.41 P and Q are brothers. R and S are sisters. P's son is S's brother. How is Q related to R?

A. Uncle **B.** Brother

C. Father **D.** Grandfather

Q.42 The total number of central universities in India in April 2015 was:

A. 14 **B.** 27 **C.** 43 **D.** 8

Ques (43-46):Direction: Carefully read and answer the following quotation:

In terms of labour, for decades the relatively low cost and high quality of Japanese workers conferred considerable competitive advantage across numerous durable goods and consumer electronics industries (eg. Machinery, automobiles, televisions, radios). Then labour-based advantages shifted to South Korea, then to Malaysia, Mexico and other nations. Today, China appears to be capitalizing best on the basis of labour. Japanese firms still remain competitive in markets for such durable goods, electronics and other products, but the labour force is no longer sufficient for competitive advantage over manufacturers in other industrializing nations. Such shifting of labour-based advantage is clearly not limited to manufacturing industries. Today, a huge number of IT and service jobs are moving from Europe and North America to India, Singapore, and like countries with relatively well- educated, low - cost workforces possessing technical skills. However, as educational levels and technical skills continue to rise in other countries, India, Singapore, and like nations enjoying labour-based competitive advantage today are likely to find such advantage cannot be sustained through emergence of new competitors.

In terms of capital, for centuries the days of gold coins and later even paper money restricted financial flows. Subsequently regional concentrations were formed where large banks, industries and markets coalesced. But today capital flows internationally at rapid speed. Global commerce no longer requires regional interactions among business players. Regional capital concentrations in places such as New York, London and Tokyo still persist, of course, but the capital concentrated there is no longer sufficient for competitive advantage over other capitalists distributed worldwide. Only if an organization is able to combine, integrate and apply its resources (eg. Land, labour, capital, IT) in an effective manner that is not readily imitable by competitors can such an organization enjoy competitive advantage sustainable overtime. In a knowledge-based theory of the firm, this idea is extended to view organizational knowledge as a resource with atleast the same level of power and importance as the traditional economic inputs. An organization with superior knowledge can achieve competitive advantage in markets that appreciate the application of such knowledge. Semiconductors, genetic engineering,

Pharmaceuticals, software, military warfare, and like knowledge-intensive competitive arenas provide both time-proven and current examples. Consider semiconductors (e.g. computer chips), which are made principally of sand and common metals. These ubiquitous and powerful electronic devices are designed within common office buildings, using commercially available tools, and fabricated within factories in many industrialized nations. Hence, land is not the key competitive resource in the semiconductor industry.

Q.43 Which country enjoyed competitive advantages in automobile industry for decades?

A. South Korea
B. Japan
C. Mexico
D. Malaysia

Q.44 Why labour-based competitive advantages of India and Singapore cannot be sustained in IT and service sectors?

A. Due to diminishing levels of skill
B. Due to capital-intensive technology making inroads
C. Because of new competitors
D. Because of shifting of labour- based advantage in manufacturing industries

Q.45 How can an organization enjoy competitive advantage sustainable overtime?

A. Through regional capital flows
B. Through regional interactions among business players
C. By making large banks, industries and markets coalesced
D. By effective use of various instrumentalities

Q.46 What is required to ensure competitive advantages in specific markets?

A. Access to capital
B. Common office buildings
C. Superior knowledge
D. Common metals

Q.47 Session of the parliament is summoned by:

A. The speaker of the Lok sabha and the chairman of the Rajya sabha
B. The president
C. The prime minister
D. The speaker of the Lok sabha

Q.48 What is a Research Design?

A. A way of conducting research that is not grounded in theory
B. The choice between using qualitative or quantitative methods
C. The style in which you present your research findings e.g. a graph
D. A framework for every stage of the collection and analysis of data

Q.49 Which one of the following is a non-probability sampling?

A. Simple random
B. Purposive
C. Systematic
D. Stratified

Q.50 UNESCO published some professional requirements of a teacher, which of these are:

A. Mastery over the subject and competency for teaching
B. Innovativeness in approach and teaching strategies
C. Justice to the profession of teaching
D. All of the Above

// Smart Answer Sheet //

Correct Indicates percentage of students who answered questions correctly.

Skipped Indicates percentage of students who skipped questions.

Q.	Ans.	Correct / Skipped	Q.	Ans.	Correct / Skipped	Q.	Ans.	Correct / Skipped	Q.	Ans.	Correct / Skipped	Q.	Ans.	Correct / Skipped
1	B	38.64 % / 0.0 %	11	B	22.73 % / 48.86 %	21	D	40.91 % / 48.86 %	31	D	15.91 % / 48.86 %	41	A	40.91 % / 48.86 %
2	D	34.09 % / 48.86 %	12	C	32.95 % / 48.87 %	22	C	27.27 % / 48.87 %	32	B	48.86 % / 48.87 %	42	C	23.86 % / 48.87 %
3	A	48.86 % / 48.87 %	13	B	15.91 % / 48.86 %	23	B	29.55 % / 48.86 %	33	A	43.18 % / 48.87 %	43	B	43.18 % / 48.87 %
4	A	37.5 % / 48.86 %	14	D	35.23 % / 48.86 %	24	D	28.41 % / 48.86 %	34	D	26.14 % / 48.86 %	44	C	21.59 % / 48.86 %
5	D	15.91 % / 48.86 %	15	A	43.18 % / 48.87 %	25	A	25.0 % / 48.86 %	35	C	38.64 % / 48.86 %	45	D	19.32 % / 48.86 %
6	D	45.45 % / 48.87 %	16	D	30.68 % / 48.87 %	26	B	18.18 % / 48.87 %	36	B	23.86 % / 48.87 %	46	C	25.0 % / 48.86 %
7	C	46.59 % / 48.86 %	17	C	15.91 % / 48.86 %	27	B	50.0 % / 48.86 %	37	B	38.64 % / 48.86 %	47	B	14.77 % / 48.87 %
8	B	44.32 % / 48.86 %	18	C	42.05 % / 48.86 %	28	A	22.73 % / 48.86 %	38	A	28.41 % / 48.86 %	48	D	42.05 % / 48.86 %
9	B	46.59 % / 48.86 %	19	D	30.68 % / 48.87 %	29	C	36.36 % / 48.87 %	39	D	34.09 % / 48.86 %	49	B	29.55 % / 48.86 %
10	C	47.73 % / 48.86 %	20	C	30.68 % / 48.87 %	30	B	13.64 % / 48.86 %	40	C	22.73 % / 48.86 %	50	D	30.68 % / 67.05 %

Performance Analysis	
Avg. Score (%)	50.0%
Toppers Score (%)	96.0%
Your Score	

//Hints and Solutions//

1. Jute fiber is one of the cheapest and coarsest, and its main use is as a packaging material for agricultural and industrial products. Important products of jute are Gunny bags, Hessians, Cordage and Carpets. As a packing material, jute is very cheap, strong and durable.

Hence, the correct option is (B).

2. A central processing unit (CPU) is the electronic circuitry within a computer that carries out the instructions of a computer program by performing the basic arithmetic, logical, control, and input/output (I/O) operations specified by the instructions.

Hence, the correct option is (D).

3. Sericulture, or silk farming, is the cultivation of silkworms to produce silk. Although there are several commercial species of silkworms likely Bombyx mori (the caterpillar of the domestic silkmoth) is the most widely used and intensively studied silkworm.

Hence, the correct option is (A).

4. Cotton grows best in black soil and a warm climate. Cotton fiber comes from cotton plants and cotton crops are usually grown at places having black soil and a warm climate.

Hence, the correct option is (A).

5. The fundamental aspect to teacher and student success is the teacher's ability to communicate with students, parents and colleagues. Teachers must have quality communication skills to assist their students to achieve success in their academic studies. More control over the communication process means more control over what the students are learning.

Hence, the correct option is (D).

6. Presentation or speech should be delivered with confidence. Delivery must be with clarity and precision. A good speaker always pauses on punctuation marks.

Hence, the correct option is (D).

7. Four principles must be followed for an effective speech. They are: analysis of audience and occasion, determine the purpose, selection of message or theme and speech delivery.

Hence, the correct option is (C).

8. Three main factors are required to determine the purpose of the speech. They are: providing information, to make acceptance of ideas and entertainment.

The general purpose of any speech will be either to Inform, Motivate/Persuade, or Entertain your audience. As soon as you know the general purpose of your speech you can develop your Specific Purpose Statement (What the speaker will accomplish). Your Specific Purpose Statement is used to develop your speech.

Hence, the correct option is (B).

9. Three main ingredients are required for the selection of message or theme. They are planning, preparation and organisation.

Hence, the correct option is (B).

10. It is worthwhile to prepare the matter carefully. Use short sentences. Information should be conveyed in least possible words without leaving out anything important.

Hence, the correct option is (C).

11. As we all know that teaching is a process where a teacher imparts hi/her knowledge to the students in order to make students learn.

Teaching is related to learning here is the correct alternative because all the teaching is related with learning. Teaching can be acquired only by learning and teaching can be done to make the students learn.

Teaching is a 'task' word while learning is an 'achievement' word – this statement is also correct because teaching is a task and it can be performed in order to make the student learn and improve their behavior while learning is an achievement because an individual or students acquire a number of behavior and knowledge in order to modify their behavior so it is an achievement for the student.

One may teach without learning taking place- This statement also corrects because teaching may occur without the learning takes place. It is the work of a teacher to teach but learning depends upon the students if they are not ready to acquire knowledge then learning cannot be happen.

Hence, the correct option is (B).

12. Interactive lectures are the lecture where a teacher can at least break the lecture once in order to engage the student in teaching learning process. To make the interactive lectures interesting a teacher should employ the buzz session in between the lecture in order to discuss or give the feedback to the students.

If brainstorming and projects employed with the interactive lecture then it can be an icing on the cake. Brain storming is a method of teaching where efforts are made for finding conclusion by gathering lots of ideas by the students and then the project is given to the students so that student will learn by doing under the guidance of the teacher.

Hence, the correct option is (C).

13. Option (B) is absolutely correct because according to (A) assertion teaching aids have to be considered as effective supplements to instruction because with the help of teaching aids teaching can be imparted in the best possible manner without making much effort with teaching skills of a teacher.

Reason(R): yes, it is right that teaching keeps the students in good humor the mind of the student diverted in observing the various teaching aids like projector, slides, tapes, etc. and their irrelevant activities controlled up to an extent. But Reason (R) is not the correct explanation of Assertion (A) as both the sentences are different but the topics are the same.

Hence, the correct option is (B).

14. Yes, it is rightly said that the leaners maturity level, academic performance and motivational disposition all have a big influence in the effectiveness of teaching aids and evaluation system in the following ways:

i) If the maturity level of the learner is low to the extent of teacher employs teaching aid during his/her then it will hinder the effectiveness of teaching and learning and vice-versa.

ii) If the learner is low or weak in his/her academic learning then it also hinders the effectiveness of teaching because a weak learner find himself/herself difficult to understand the teaching aid which influences the effectiveness of teaching.

iii) Motivational nature or behavior of students also influences the effectiveness of teaching aid because if the learner is low motivated then he feels difficult to understand the teaching which is delivered with the helps of teaching aid and if a learner is highly motivated then he accepts the teaching through teaching aids easily.

Hence, the correct option is (D).

15. i. According to the first statement teaching is that activity where the teacher imparts his/her knowledge to the pupils in order to make the learners learn and it is only possible when proper communication between teacher and student takes place.

ii. The third statement is related to managing and monitoring students because teaching is the activity where the teacher teaches and manages his/her pupils and also monitors their activities through the whole teaching-learning process.

iii. Now according to the fourth statement teaching implies influencing others means in the teaching process it is very important for a teacher that he/she can influence others (students and management) through their teaching strategies in order to make the teaching-learning process effective.

Hence, the correct option is (A).

16. Seminar Method involves the exchange of information by the experts on specific techniques and concepts. It also provides guidance to a group working on a research project.

Demonstration Method is where the instructor actually performs an operation /task and shows the students what to do, how to do it.

The Lecture Method is a formal or a semi-formal method in which the instructor gives overview about the topic just by dictating.

Discussion Method is a method in which solutions are developed by discussing within a group.

Hence, the correct option is (D).

17. India ranked 130th among 188 countries in Human Development Report 2015 released by the United Nations Development Programme (UNDP). India's HDI rank between 2009 and 2014 has risen six positions.

Hence, the correct option is (C).

18. The following are the reasons to keep India at the bottom of human development:

(a) rapid increase in population.

(b) large number of adult illiterates and low gross enrolment ratio.

(c) high drop-out rates.

(d) inadequate government expenditure on education and health.

(e) large proportion of underweight children as well as under nourished people.

(f) very poor sanitation facilities and low access to essential life saving medicines.

Hence, the correct option is (C).

19. The Full form of LCD is Liquid Crystal Display. A liquid-crystal display (LCD) is a flat-panel display or other electronically modulated optical devices that uses the light-modulating properties of liquid crystals. Liquid crystals do not emit light directly, instead of using a backlight or reflector to produce images in color or monochrome.

Hence, the correct option is (D).

20. The educational institutions, libraries, hospitals, and industries store concerned with Data management.

Data management is the process of ingesting, storing, organizing and maintaining the data created and collected by an organization. Effective data management is a crucial piece of deploying the IT systems that run business applications and provide analytical information to help drive operational decision-making and strategic planning by corporate executives, business managers and other end users.

Hence, the correct option is (C).

21. The keyboard is not an output device of a computer.

The computer is a very versatile machine. It can easily process different types of data. To work with these data, we require different types of devices. These devices can help us enter data into the computer. These devices are called input and output devices. They mainly cover devices like mouse, keyboard, printer, speaker, joystick, etc which can be used with a computer.

The devices that are used to display the information of the results are known as output devices. While the devices whose main function is to give instructions and data to the computer are called input devices. Today we are going to discuss these devices in detail. This is to help you have a basic idea about input and output devices. This will also help you with the questions on computer aptitude in banking exams. We will start with the output devices. Input and Output (I/O) Devices. The computer is a very versatile machine. ... These devices are called input and output devices. They mainly cover devices like mouse, keyboard, printer, speaker, joystick, etc which can be used with a computer.

Hence, the correct option is (D).

22. Institutions that are empowered to confer or grant degrees under the UGC Act, 1956 are university established by an Act of Parliament, established by an Act of Legislature, institution which is a deemed to be a university.

Hence, the correct option is (C).

23. Correlation Analysis:

- Correlation analysis is a statistical method used to evaluate the strength of the relationship between two variables.
- Correlation explores the type (positive, negative, or none) and degree of association (magnitude of closeness) between two quantitative variables with available statistical data.
- This analysis is fundamentally based on the assumption of a linear relationship between the quantitative variables.
- Correlational studies are carried out either to help explain important human behaviors or to predict likely outcomes.

Therefore, correlation analysis aims to present the association among the variables.

Hence, the correct option is (B).

24. Vitamin B12 is not found in fruits. Vitamin B12 is a nutrient that helps keep the body's nerve and blood cells healthy and helps make DNA, the genetic material in all cells. Fish, meat, poultry, eggs, milk, and other dairy products are the best sources of vitamin B12.

Hence, the correct option is (D).

25. Topographic factors can also be known as physiographic factors which include altitude, direction of mountain chains, plateaus, plains, lakes, rivers, sea level, and valleys etc.

Hence, the correct option is (A).

26. Total number of girls = 74

Shweta's position from left end = 27th

Palak's position from left end = 27 + 7 = 34th

Thus, Palak's position from right end = (74+1) - 34 = 41

Hence, the correct option is (B).

27. It is a simple division series in which each number is one-half of the previous number. We can also say that each number is divided by 2 to arrive at the next number;

On dividing 48 by 2, we get 24.

On dividing 24 by 2, we get 12.

So, on dividing 12 by 2, we will get 6.

Hence, the correct option is (B).

28. Nisin is a polycyclic antibacterial peptide produced by the bacterium Lactococcus lactis that is used as a food preservative.

It has 34 amino acid residues, including the uncommon amino acids lanthionine (Lan), methyllanthionine (MeLan), di-dehydroalanine (Dha), and di-dehydroamino butyric acid (Dhb).

These unusual amino acids are introduced by posttranslational modification of the precursor peptide. In these reactions, a ribosomally synthesized 57-mer is converted to the final peptide.

Hence, the correct option is (A).

29. It is given that all Mondays and Sundays are off.

If a month starts with a Monday and has 31 days, then the number of Mondays = 5

But the number of Sundays = 4

Thus, total off days = 4+5 = 9

Hence, the correct option is (C).

30. Chicago format almost always has footnotes or endnotes. Both footnotes and endnotes are common writing tool features implemented when using various citation styles. They provide writers with a clear method in directing the reader to further information on the research topic and additional citations. Though the terms are sometimes used interchangeably, footnotes and endnotes have a few key differences. Footnotes are found at the bottom of a page and endnotes are located at the end of a complete document, or sometimes at the end of a chapter or section.

Hence, the correct option is (B).

31. The figure may be labeled as shown:

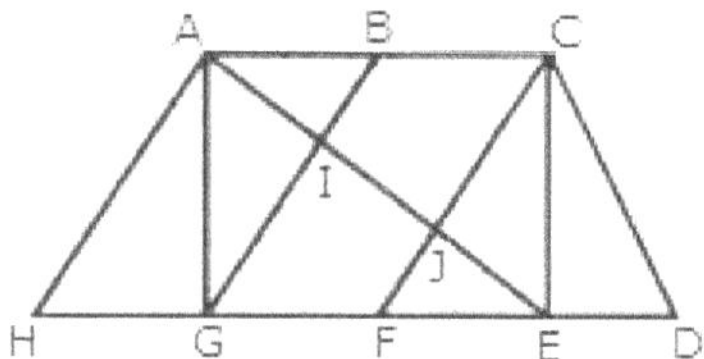

The simplest triangles are AHG, AIG, AIB, JFE, CJE and CED i.e., 6 in number

The triangles composed of two components each are ABG, CFE, ACJ, and EGI i.e., 4 in number.

The triangles composed of three components each are ACE, AGE, and CFD i.e., 3 in number.

There is only one triangle i.e., AHE composed of four components.

Therefore, There are 6 + 4 + 3 + 1 = 14 triangles in the given figure.

Hence, the correct option is (D).

32. The scale of measurement of sound is Decibel or dB. Levels of 30 dB are considered quiet and levels 85 dB are considered noisy.

Hence, the correct option is (B).

33. A grandmother is one female, the mother is another, the wives of four sons are the four females and two daughters of all four sons are eight females.

So, in all, there are 1+1+4+8 = 14 females.

Hence, the correct option is (A).

34. The least possible Venn diagram is:

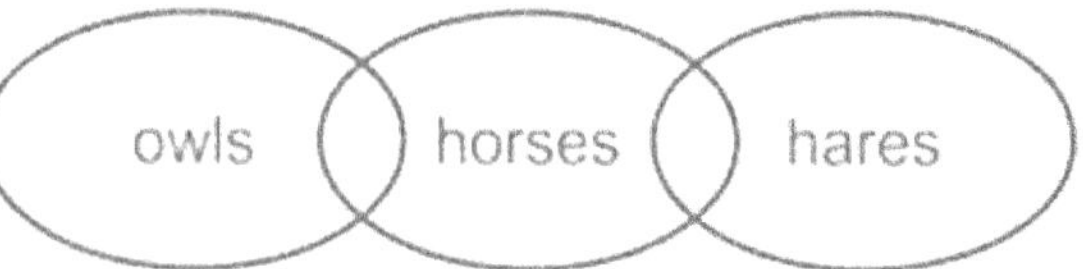

I. Some owls are hares → False (It can be possible, but it is not definite)

II. Some hares are owls → False (It can be possible, but it is not definite)

Hence, neither conclusion I nor conclusion II follows.

Hence, the correct option is (D).

35. Only son of woman's grandfather----Woman's father,

Man's brother's sister----Man's father.

So, a man's father is a woman's father i.e. woman is the man's sister.

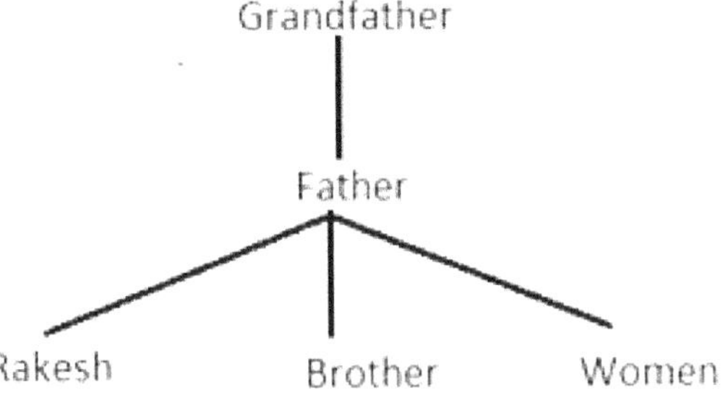

Hence, the correct option is (C).

36. Marks obtained by Ragini in Chemistry and Biology together $= 45 + 38 = 83$

Marks obtained by Mohini in Physics and Mathematics together $= 55 + 82 = 137$

Required $\% = \frac{83}{137} = 60.58\%$

Hence, the correct option is (B).

37. Marks obtained by all the students in Mathematics = 65 + 52 + 78 + 82 + 96 = 373

Marks obtained by all the students in Chemistry = 45 + 62 + 70 + 65 + 64 = 306

Required ratio = 373 : 306

Hence, the correct option is (B).

38. Percentage of marks obtained by Mohan in English

$= \frac{104}{120} \times 100 = 86.67\%$

Percentage of marks obtained by Rohan in Physics

$= \frac{60}{75} \times 100 = 80\%$

Required difference $= 86.67 - 80 = 6.67\%$

Hence, the correct option is (A).

39. Sum of marks obtained by Rohan in all the subjects = 60 + 52 + 62 + 55 + 88 = 317

Hence, the correct option is (D).

40. Total marks in all the subjects $= 75 + 100 + 75 + 75 + 120 = 445$

Marks obtained by Sohan in all the subjects $= 50 + 78 + 70 + 58 + 88 = 344$

Required $\% = \frac{344}{445} \times 100 = 77.3\%$

Hence, the correct option is (C).

41. P and Q are brothers. R and S are sisters. P's son is S's brother. We will draw the flow chart of given information as follows, a circle around the alphabet indicates that that person is a lady.

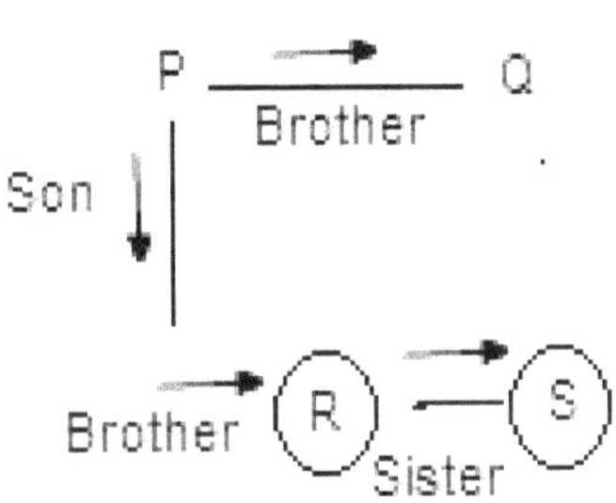

Q uncle of R.

Hence, the correct option is (A).

42. There are 43 central universities in India out of these 40 central universities fall under the ministry of Human Resource Development and one central university each under the Ministry of Agriculture, Ministry of shipping, Ministry of External Affairs.

Hence, the correct option is (C).

43. According to the first sentence of the passage, "In terms of labour, tor decades the relatively low cost and high quality of Japanese workers conferred considerable competitive advantage across numerous durable goods and consumer electronics industries (e.g. Machinery, automobiles, televisions, radios)." This clearly states that the automobile industry was one of those countries which enjoyed competitive advantages in automobile industry for decades.

Hence, the correct option is (B).

44. According to the second paragraph of the passage, "However, as educational levels and technical skills continue to rise in other countries, India, Singapore, and like nations enjoying labour-based competitive advantage today are likely to find such advantage cannot be sustained through emergence of new competitors." This segment states that since the competitors in the technical field are growing, the labour-based competitive advantages of India and Singapore cannot be sustained in IT and service sectors.

Hence, the correct option is (C).

45. According to the second last paragraph of the passage, "Only if an organization is able to combine, integrate and apply its resources (e.g. Land, labour, capital, IT) in an effective manner that is not readily imitable by competitors can such an organization enjoy competitive advantage sustainable overtime." This sentence means that if the resources are efficiently used by organizations, in a way which is not harnessed by the competitors, they can enjoy competitive advantage overtime.

Hence, the correct option is (D).

46. According to the second last paragraph of the passage, "An organization with superior knowledge can achieve competitive advantage in markets that appreciate the application of such knowledge." Hence, to ensure competitive advantages in specific markets, superior knowledge is required.

Hence, the correct option is (C).

47. The President is an Integral Part of the Parliament. The Parliament consists of the Lok Sabha, Rajya Sabha and the President. He is the head of the executive and enjoys certain powers.

He can address the Parliament at the beginning of the first session after each general year and the first session of each year. He can summon or prorogue the Parliament or dissolve the Lok Sabha. He is empowered to call for a Joint meeting of both the Houses of the Parliament to resolve a deadlock regarding the bill or any other question.

Hence, the correct option is (B).

48. Research design is a framework for every stage of collection and analysis of data. It is overall strategy to integrate various components and constitute the analysis of data. It Research design is the "blue print" of the study. It defines the type and subtype of the study. Research design is designed to seek answers to research questions.

Hence, the correct option is (D).

49. Non-probability sampling is also known as random sampling and is divided into two main types viz., accidental and purposive sampling. Non-probability sampling represents a group of sampling techniques that help researchers to select units from a population that they are interested in studying.

Hence, the correct option is (B).

50. Teachers are one of the most influential and powerful forces for equity, access and quality in education and key to sustainable global development. However, their training, recruitment, retention, status and working conditions remain preoccupying. Moreover, there is a worldwide shortage of well-trained teachers.

UNESCO has made the supply of well-trained, supported and qualified teachers one of its top priorities. This focus has been reinforced by Sustainable Development Goal 4: Quality Education through the Education 2030 Framework for Action, which has a target calling for a substantial increase in qualified teachers through the betterment of their training, recruitment, retention, status, working conditions and motivation.

The professional requirement of a teacher as explained in the UNESCO publication are mastery over the subject and competency for teaching, innovativeness in approach and teaching strategies and justice to the profession.

Hence, the correct option is (D).

Mock Test 08

Q.1 Which model of communication is a one-way process where the sender is the one who sends the message but the receiver does not give feedback or response?

A. Horizontal model　　**B.** Transactional model
C. Linear model　　**D.** Interactional model

Q.2 To communicate effectively with students, teachers should not use which of the following methods?

(a) Affinity-seeking strategies
(b) Immediacy behaviors
(c) Humor
(d) Collaborative filters
(e) Technical words
(f) Ambiguous statement

A. (a) and (f) only　　**B.** (a), (b) and (c)
C. (a), (c) and (d)　　**D.** (d), (e) and (f)

Q.3 Assertion (A): Synchronous media requires the audience to be present when the media is being broadcasted or performed.

Reasoning (R): Media that takes place in real-time such as live television or radio is known as synchronous media.

A. Assertion is true and reasoning is false
B. Assetion is False and reasoning is true
C. Assertion is true and reasoning is the correct explanation of (A)
D. Assertion is true and reasoning is not the correct explanation of (A)

Q.4 Match the following List 1 with List 2 with correct responses.

List 1	List 2
a. Intrapersonal communication	(i) It is the communication where more than two individuals are involved in exchange of ideas, skills and interests.
b. Mass communication	(ii) It is a face to face communication between two persons.
c. Interpersonal communication	(iii) It uses mechanical devices that multiply messages and take it to a large number of people simultaneously.
d. Group communication	(iv) It is the communication within an individual, including talking to oneself.

A. a-iv, b-iii, c-ii, d- i　　**B.** a-iii, b-ii, c-i, d-iv
C. a-iv, b-iii, c-i, d-ii　　**D.** a-iv, b-i, c-ii, d-iii

Q.5 'Information overload' can be categorized as a _____ barrier to communication.

A. Psychological　　**B.** Physiological
C. Social　　**D.** Cultural

Q.6 Direction: Select the odd word from the given alternatives.

A. Stream　**B.** Rivulet　**C.** River　**D.** Valley

Q.7 Direction: A series is given with one missing term. Select the correct alternative from the given ones that will complete the series.

NOM, QRP, TUS, ?

A. WAX　**B.** HUT　**C.** WXV　**D.** WTU

Q.8 Ram and Sam start walking towards North from the same point and cover 20 metres. After that, Ram turns to his left and Sam to his right. After sometime. Ram walks 10 metres, in the same direction in which he turned. On the other hand, Sam walks only 7 metres. Later. Ram turns towards his left and Sam to his right. Both walk 25 metres forward. How far is Ram from Sam now?

A. 17 metres　　**B.** 5 metres
C. 10 metres　　**D.** 20 metres

Q.9 Direction: A series is given with one missing term. Select the correct alternative from the given ones that will complete the series.

5, 11, 24, 51, 106, ?

A. 122　**B.** 217　**C.** 221　**D.** 115

Q.10 If ' $BUDDHISM$ ' is coded as ' $DWFFJKUO$ ', then ' $CHRISTIAN$ ' will be coded as which of the following codes?

A. $EITJUVKBP$　　**B.** $EJTKUVJCO$
C. $EJTKVUJCP$　　**D.** $EJTKUVKCP$

Ques (11-15):Direction: Read the passage carefully and choose the best answer to each question out of the four alternatives.

It is not good manners to stop a person on the street or in a shop, or in the performance of any duty and to talk to him for ten, fifteen, or twenty minutes just to pass the time of day. We can tell that a person is in a hurry to get somewhere, or he is doing something, and we know enough not to interrupt him for any length of time. Yet some of us think nothing of calling someone on the telephone, interrupting him without a thought about what he may be doing, and chattering away, forgetting about time or anything else. Perhaps we don't consider our telephone conversation an interruption because we don't see what we have interrupted. Naturally, we must observe the common courtesies over the telephone. But we must remember that one of the courtesies of telephoning is to be brief.

Never ask anybody to guess who you are? The person you are telephoning may not be in a guessing mood. If you know him, you may want to ask after the state of his health and that of his family, but as soon as you possibly can, go get on with your business. He certainly wants to know why you are telephoning him. When you are finished with your business, you might take moment to observe the natural courtesies of conversation, expressing your thanks before ending your call.

From the way the telephone is used in your home, you would hardly suspect that this is an instrument on which very important business transactions are conducted. There are times when even you are called upon to be business-like, brief, and effective on the telephone.

Q.11 How can we make the best use of a telephone?

A. By being elaborate
B. By being brief, effective and business-like
C. By observing the courtesies
D. By not being business-like

Q.12 We interrupt people on the telephone because:

A. We are thoughtless
B. We enjoy doing it
C. We forget about the time
D. We don't consider our telephone call an interruption

Q.13 When we telephone, we must:

A. Be business-like
B. Ask people to guess who you are
C. Chatter away
D. Not bother about the time we spend

Q.14 Which of the following statement/s is true?

(i) We know enough to interrupt someone.
(ii) We don't know enough to interrupt someone.
(iii) We can interrupt anyone on the telephone.
(iv) We can interrupt anyone anytime we want.

A. Only (i) **B.** Only (ii)
C. (iii) & (iv) **D.** Only (iv)

Q.15 It is not good manners to:

A. Stop a person on the street to pass time
B. Stop a person in the shop to pass time
C. Stop a person during duty to pass time
D. All of the above options

Q.16 Which of the following statements is/are correct with respect to Internet and Intranet?

i. The number of users in the Intranet is limited.
ii. Internet is a wide network of computers & open to all.
iii. Intranet uses internet protocols such as TCP/IP and FTP.
iv. Internet is safer than Intranet.

A. (i), (ii) and (iii) only
B. (ii), (iii) and (iv) only
C. (i) and (iv) only
D. All of the above

Q.17 Which of the following is an example of proprietary system software?

A. Linux
B. Microsoft Internet explorer
C. Microsoft windows
D. Microsoft office

Q.18 Which of the following initiatives has been implemented by MHRD under NMEICT Programme to incorporate Robotics into engineering education with the main objective of providing hands on application of Computer science, mathematics and engineering principles?

A. E-Kalpa **B.** E-Yantra
C. E-Shodh Sindhu **D.** E-Acharya

Q.19 Which of the following file extensions is used for the Bitmap Image File?

A. .btp **B.** .bit **C.** .bmp **D.** .btm

Q.20 What is the full form of HTTP?

A. Hyper Text Transfer Protocol
B. Hyper Text Transition Protocol
C. Hyper Text Transfer Program
D. Hyper Text Transition Program

Q.21 Direction: Study the following statements carefully.

Statement I: Smog comprises of smoke & fog and soot comprises of soil, dust and smoke.

Statement II: Smog is the particulate matter whereas soot is the ground-level ozone.

A. Both Statements I and II are true
B. Only Statement I is true
C. Only Statement II is true
D. Both Statements I and II are false

Q.22 As a part of the 'Go Green Initiative', Indian Railways has planned to set up a solar power plant of _____ by 2020-21.

A. 100 Mega Watt **B.** 1000 Mega Watt
C. 150 Mega Watt **D.** 1500 Mega Watt

Q.23 The Deccan Thorn Forest covers which of the following states in India?

A. Maharashtra **B.** Andhra Pradesh
C. Karnataka **D.** All of them

Q.24 Which of the following goals fall in the list of United Nations Sustainable Development Goals?

i. Good Health and Well Being
ii. Peace and Justice Strong Institutions
iii. Clean Water and Sanitation
iv. Partnerships to achieve the Goal

A. (i), (ii) and (iii) only
B. (ii), (iii) and (iv) only
C. (i), (iii) and (iv) only
D. All of the above

Q.25 Who secured the top rank in The Human Development Report 2020?

A. Sweden **B.** Norway
C. Switzerland **D.** Austria

Q.26 The Vice–President is the ex-officio Chairman of the_____.

A. Rajya Sabha
B. Lok Sabha
C. Planning Commission

D. National Development Council

Q.27 The three-tier Panchayat Raj system in India was proposed by the:

A. Balwant Rai Mehta Committee
B. Ashok Mehta Committee
C. Royal Commission
D. None of the above

Q.28 Is it permissible to conduct the election for the post of President of India when one or more State Assemblies are dissolved?

A. Yes, can be conducted
B. Not possible to conduct
C. Parliament permission is needed
D. With the permission of the Election Commission of India

Q.29 Statements:

a) Some chairs are tables.

b) Some tables are sofas.

c) All sofa is a bed.

Conclusions:

(i) Some beds are chairs.

(ii) Some tables are beds.

(iii) Some sofas are chairs.

(iv) All beds are sofas.

A. Only (iv) follows
B. Only (ii) follows
C. Only (i) and (ii) follows
D. Only (i) and (iv) follows

Q.30 The term "closure" in Parliamentary terminology implies:

A. The end of a session of Parliament
B. Stoppage of debate on a motion
C. End of a day's proceedings
D. None of the above

Ques (31-35):Direction: Study the following table carefully and answer the questions based on it:

Years	Percentage of students qualified(%)					Total no. of candidate qualified
	Science (%)	Arts (%)	Commerce (%)	Engineering (%)	Management (%)	
2013	40	24	19	8	9	780
2014	42	15	18	12	13	650
2015	45	20	20	7	8	500
2016	45	15	16	10	14	620
2017	35	19	15	12	19	900
2018	42	18	14	14	12	850

Q.31 What is the average number of students qualified in Science per year from 2013 to 2015?

A. 260 **B.** 270 **C.** 280 **D.** 275

Q.32 If in the year 2015,160 Arts student participated in the exam, then the percentage of disqualified students from Arts in the year 2015 is:

A. 36.5% **B.** 38.5% **C.** 37.5% **D.** 35%

Q.33 What is the average number of students qualified in 2018 per subject?

A. 170 **B.** 200 **C.** 180 **D.** 195

Q.34 If out of the total number of students who appeared in the engineering exam 2016, only 40% qualified. Find the number of engineering student appeared in the exam that year:

A. 133 **B.** 144 **C.** 155 **D.** 167

Q.35 What is the percentage increase in the number of qualified students from 2013 to 2018?

A. $9\frac{37}{39}\%$ **B.** $8\frac{38}{39}\%$ **C.** $8\frac{1}{37}\%$ **D.** $9\frac{1}{9}\%$

Q.36 If the Governor of a state wants to resign before his or her term expiration, whom shall he/she writes to?

A. Prime Minister **B.** President
C. Vice President **D.** Chief Minister

Q.37 Which of the following was launched in 2013 with the purpose to provide strategic funding to eligible state higher educational institutions?

A. Rashtriya Madhyamik Shiksha Abhiyan
B. All India Council for Technical Education
C. Sarva Shiksha Abhiyan
D. Rashtriya Uchchatar Shiksha Abhiyan

Q.38 Which of the following is not the main functions of the National Testing Agency?

A. To identify experts and institutions in setting examination questions
B. To produce and disseminate information and research on education and professional development standards
C. To research on the finance and marketing related topics
D. To lead proficient, straightforward, and universal benchmarks tests to survey the competency of possibility for affirmation and enlistment purposes

Q.39 Experimental research is often used for which of the following statements?

(a) Where there is an involvement of two or more variables.

(b) Where manipulation of one variable causes change in results.

(c) Where the magnitude of correlation yields good results.

(d) Where the prediction of results is somewhat known.

A. (a), (b), (c), (d) **B.** (a), (b), (c)
C. (a), (b), (d) **D.** (b), (c), (d)

Q.40 Which of these is true about ethnography?

(a) Ethnography studies a group or culture of a group.

(b) Participant observation can be included while doing ethnography.

(c) Ethnography as a method is appropriate for qualitative research as well as quantitative research.

(d) It is not a holistic study.

(e) It emerged as an important method in anthropology for studying the culture of 'other' subjects.

A. (a), (b), (c) and (e) **B.** (b), (c), (d) and (e)
C. (a), (b), (d) **D.** (a), (b), (e)

Q.41 MHRD works through which of the following departments?

(a) Department of School Education & Literacy.

(b) Department of Physical and Mental Health.

(c) Department of Higher Education.

A. (a) and (b) **B.** (a) and (c)
C. (a), (b), (c) **D.** (b) and (c)

Q.42 In the following table, Set-I mentions an apex level institution in India while Set-II indicates their establishment date. Match the two sets and give your answer.

Set-I	**Set-II**
(a) University Grant Commission (UGC)	1995
(b) All India Council of Technical Education (AICTE)	1955
(c) National Council of Teacher Education (NCTE)	1994
(d) National Assessment and Accreditation Council (NAAC)	1945

A. a-i, b-iv, c-iii, d-ii **B.** a-ii, b-iv, c-i, d-iii
C. a-ii, b-i, c-iii, d-iv **D.** a-i, b-iv, c-ii, d-iii

Q.43 International Literacy Day is celebrated every year on which of the following dates?

A. 8th September **B.** 8th August
C. 10th July **D.** 12th December.

Q.44 The President can be removed from office by a process of impeachment for 'violation of the Constitution'. Consider the following statements in this regard:

1. Constitution does not define the meaning of the phrase 'violation of the Constitution'.
2. The impeachment charges to be initiated should be signed by 100 MPs in the case of Lok sabha and 50 MPs in the case of Rajya Sabha.
3. The impeachment is a quasi-judicial procedure in Parliament.

Select the correct answer from given below:

A. 1 and 2 only **B.** 1 and 3 only
C. 2 and 3 only **D.** 1, 2 and 3

Q.45 Higher Education is the responsibility of which of the following governments?

A. Only State
B. Only Centre
C. Both Centre and States
D. None of the above

Q.46 Match the following combination of evaluation approaches with their correct meaning correctly.

List-I	**List-II**
Formative Evaluation	Evaluation carried at the end of the course
Criteria-Referenced Evaluation	Evaluation of individual performance in comparison to others
Summative Evaluation	Evaluation against specific standards
Norm-Referenced Evaluation Course	Evaluation carried throughout the

A. (i)-a, (ii)-c, (iii)-d, (iv)-b
B. (i)-d, (ii)-c, (iii)-a, (iv)-b
C. (i)-a, (ii)-b, (iii)-d, (iv)-c
D. (i)-d, (ii)-b, (iii)-a, (iv)-c

Q.47 Which of the following factor(s) affect the process of teaching?

(i) Experience of a teacher

(ii) Subject matter of teaching

(iii) Classroom environment

(iv) Human relation skill

A. (i), (ii) and (iii) only
B. (ii) and (iv) only
C. (i), (iii) and (iv) only
D. All of the above

Q.48 Which of the following statements is not true about teaching?

A. Classroom teaching is the most effective method of teaching
B. Teaching is a comprehensive process
C. Teaching can be made effective by making use of teaching aids
D. Teaching requires expertise and experience

Q.49 Bhandarkar Oriental Research Institute, one of the institutes that provide oriental learning programs in India is located in which of the following cities?

A. Pune **B.** Mumbai
C. Bengaluru **D.** Hyderabad

Q.50 What is the full form of NIEPA?

A. National Institute of Educational Planning and Administration
B. National Institute of Educational Program and Assessment
C. National Institute of Educational Planning and Assessment
D. None of the above

// Smart Answer Sheet //

Correct Indicates percentage of students who answered questions correctly.

Skipped Indicates percentage of students who skipped questions.

Q.	Ans.	Correct	Skipped
1	C	53.97 %	1.59 %
2	D	34.92 %	30.16 %
3	C	57.14 %	30.16 %
4	A	55.56 %	31.74 %
5	B	19.05 %	31.74 %
6	D	49.21 %	30.16 %
7	C	61.9 %	31.75 %
8	A	47.62 %	30.16 %
9	B	47.62 %	31.75 %
10	D	42.86 %	30.16 %
11	B	47.62 %	30.16 %
12	D	42.86 %	30.16 %
13	A	52.38 %	30.16 %
14	B	34.92 %	30.16 %
15	D	63.49 %	30.16 %
16	A	36.51 %	30.16 %
17	C	22.22 %	30.16 %
18	B	49.21 %	30.16 %
19	C	38.1 %	30.15 %
20	A	60.32 %	31.74 %
21	B	22.22 %	30.16 %
22	B	36.51 %	30.16 %
23	D	42.86 %	30.16 %
24	D	55.56 %	28.57 %
25	B	36.51 %	30.16 %
26	A	41.27 %	30.16 %
27	A	44.44 %	31.75 %
28	A	22.22 %	31.75 %
29	B	44.44 %	30.16 %
30	B	14.29 %	30.15 %
31	B	25.4 %	31.74 %
32	C	25.4 %	31.74 %
33	A	36.51 %	31.74 %
34	C	28.57 %	31.75 %
35	B	33.33 %	31.75 %
36	B	50.79 %	30.16 %
37	D	49.21 %	30.16 %
38	C	33.33 %	30.16 %
39	B	31.75 %	30.15 %
40	D	19.05 %	30.16 %
41	B	39.68 %	31.75 %
42	B	49.21 %	30.16 %
43	A	44.44 %	30.16 %
44	B	22.22 %	31.75 %
45	C	63.49 %	30.16 %
46	B	33.33 %	31.75 %
47	D	38.1 %	31.74 %
48	A	39.68 %	28.57 %
49	A	44.44 %	31.75 %
50	A	42.86 %	30.16 %

Performance Analysis	
Avg. Score (%)	50.0%
Toppers Score (%)	100.0%
Your Score	

//Hints and Solutions//

1. The linear model of communication is considered as a one-way process in which the sender sends a message to the receiver but at that time receiver is not present to give feedback or any type of response.

The Horizontal model of communication is the communication in which information is delivered to the people working at the same level of an organizational hierarchy.

A transactional model of communication is the communication in which the information is exchanged between the sender and receiver where each sender/receiver takes turns to send/receive the message.

The Interactional model of communication is the communication where information has exchanged both ways between sender and receiver.

Hence, the correct option is (C).

2. Collaborative filters, Technical words, and Ambiguous statements must not be a part of effective communication because they affect the quality of communication.

Technical words are considered as jargons in business communication and ambiguous statement are those statements whose meaning is not clear.

Collaborative filters are the predictive process behind the recommendation engine.

Hence, the correct option is (D).

3. Synchronous media takes place in real-time and the audience is present when media is broadcasted or performed. This media helps to share the information at the same time i.e. information broadcasting and the audience is present at the same time to receive the information.

Example: Video conferencing.

Hence, the correct option is (C).

4. Intrapersonal communication is a communication that takes place within an individual, including talking to oneself.

Mass communication is a communication that uses mechanical devices that multiply messages and take them to a large number of people simultaneously.

Interpersonal communication is a face to face communication between two persons.

Group communication is communication where more than two individuals are involved in the exchange of ideas, skills, and interests.

Hence, the correct option is (A).

5. Physiological barriers to communication are related to the limitations of the human body and the human mind. These barriers include poor listening skills, information overload, inattention, emotions, poor retention, etc.

Hence, the correct option is (B).

6. Stream, Rivulet and River are all water bodies whereas Valley is a low area between hills or mountains. Thus, Valley is the odd word.

Hence, the correct option is (D).

7. N +3 = Q + 3 = T + 3 = W

O + 3 = R + 3 = U + 3 = X

M + 3 = P + 3 = S + 3 = V

Hence, the correct option is (C).

8. According to the question, Ram and Sam start walking towards the North from the same point and cover 20 metres. After that, Ram turns to his left and Sam to his right. After sometime. Ram walks 10 metres, in the same direction in which he turned. On the other hand, Sam walks only 7 metres. Later. Ram turns towards his left and Sam to his right. Both walk 25 metres forward.

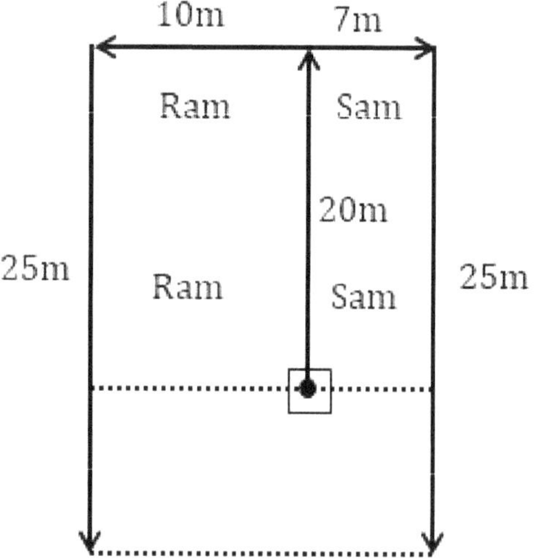

Required distance = (10 + 7 =) 17 metres.

Now, Ram is 17 metres far from Sam.

Hence, the correct option is (A).

9.

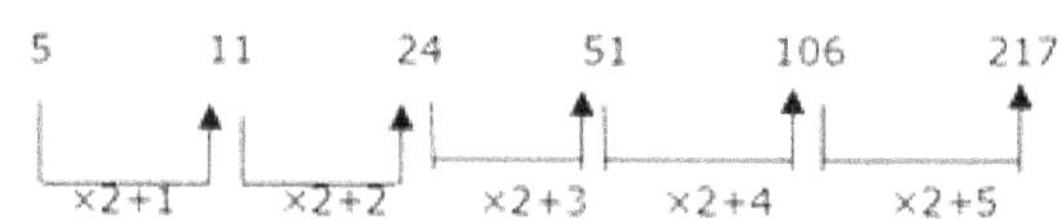

The next term is 217.

Hence, the correct option is (B).

10.

$$B \xrightarrow{+2} D$$
$$U \xrightarrow{+2} W$$
$$D \xrightarrow{+2} F$$
$$D \xrightarrow{+2} F$$
$$H \xrightarrow{+2} J$$
$$I \xrightarrow{+2} K$$
$$S \xrightarrow{+2} U$$
$$M \xrightarrow{+2} O$$

Similarly,

$$C \xrightarrow{+2} E$$
$$H \xrightarrow{+2} J$$
$$R \xrightarrow{+2} T$$
$$I \xrightarrow{+2} K$$
$$S \xrightarrow{+2} U$$
$$T \xrightarrow{+2} V$$
$$I \xrightarrow{+2} K$$
$$A \xrightarrow{+2} C$$
$$N \xrightarrow{+2} P$$

So, $CHRISTIAN$ will be coded as $EJTKUVKCP$.

Hence, the correct option is (D).

11. As per the last line of the passage, "There are times when even you are called upon to be business-like, brief, and effective on the telephone".

Hence, the correct option is (B).

12. The answer lies in the following lines of the passage, "Perhaps we don't consider our telephone conversation an interruption because we don't see what we have interrupted".

Hence, the correct option is (D).

13. As given in the last line of the passage, "There are times when even you are called upon to be business-like, brief, and effective on the telephone".

Hence, the correct option is (A).

14. Option B is correct as given in the above-mentioned lines.

Option A is incorrect as given in the following line of the passage, "We can tell that a person is in a hurry to get somewhere, or he is doing something, and we know enough not to interrupt him for any length of time".

Option C is incorrect as given in the following lines, "Yet some of us think nothing of calling someone on the telephone, interrupting him without a thought about what he may be doing, and chattering away, forgetting about time or anything else".

Option D is incorrect as it is suggested in the passage that we should not interrupt anyone just like that.

Hence, the correct option is (B).

15. The answer lies in the following line of the passage, "It is not good manners to stop a person on the street or in a shop, or in the performance of any duty and to talk to him for ten, fifteen or twenty minutes just to pass the time of day".

Hence the correct option is (D).

16. Intranet:

The number of users in the Intranet is limited.

The Intranet is safer than the Internet.

Intranet uses internet protocols such as TCP/IP and FTP.

Internet:

Internet is a wide network of computers & open to all.

Hence, the correct option is (A).

17. Proprietary software is any software that is copyrighted and bears limits against use, distribution and modification that are imposed by its publisher, vendor or developer. Proprietary software remains the property of its owner/creator and is used by end-users/organizations under predefined conditions.

Examples of proprietary software include Microsoft Windows, Adobe Flash Player, PS3 OS, iTunes, Adobe Photoshop, Google Earth, macOS (formerly Mac OS X and OS X), Skype, WinRAR, Oracle's version of Java and some versions of Unix.

Hence, the correct option is (C).

18. E-Yantra: Initiative has been implemented by MHRD under NMEICT Programme to incorporate Robotics into engineering education.

E-Kalpa: It includes courses based on Design.

E-Shodh Sindhu: International e-journal and e-books are made available to all the higher educational institutions through this program.

E-Archaya: It is the official repository of NMEICT e-content and all content produced under NMEICT.

Hence, the correct option is (B).

19. A Bitmap image is stored as a series of tiny dots which are known as pixels. Each pixel is a very small square that is assigned a specific color, and then these are arranged in a pattern to form the image. The file extension is ".bmp".

Hence, the correct option is (C).

20. The Hyper Text Transfer Protocol (HTTP) is an application protocol for distributed, collaborative, hypermedia information systems.

Note:- HTTP is the foundation of data communication for the World Wide Web. Hyper Text is a structured text that uses logical links (hyperlinks) between nodes containing text.

Hence, the correct option is (A).

21. Smog and soot are the two kinds of air pollution.

Smog or ground-level ozone occurs when fossil fuels react with sunlight.

Soot or particulate matter is made up of tiny particles of chemicals, soil, dust, or allergens, in the form of gas or solids.

Hence, the correct option is (B).

22. As a part of the 'Go Green Initiative', Indian Railways has planned to set up a solar power plant of 1000 MW by 2020-21. The initiative will help Indian Railways to generate about 10 percent of its electrical energy from renewable sources. As of now, 71.19 MW of solar plants have already been installed over rooftops at service buildings and railway stations.

Hence, the correct option is (B).

23. Deccan thorn forests (thorn forests) are found in South India and northern Sri Lanka. Historically, this area was previously covered with tropical dry deciduous forest, but now it is left in small pieces. The vegetation here has a forest-like southern tropical thorn bush. It is spread in the Indian states of Tamil Nadu, Andhra Pradesh, Karnataka and Maharashtra and is also found in northern Sri Lanka.

Hence, the correct option is (D).

24. There are 17 Sustainable Development Goals listed by the United Nations. Here is the list:

No Poverty, Zero Hunger, Good Health and Well-being, Quality Education, Responsible Consumption and Production Industry, Innovation and Infrastructure, Reduced Inequality, Sustainable Cities and Communities, Climate Action, Life Below Water, Life on Land, Peace and Justice Strong Institutions, Partnerships to achieve the Goal, Gender Equality, Clean Water and Sanitation, Affordable and Clean Energy, Decent Work and Economic Growth.

Hence, the correct option is (D).

25. According to the report, Norway topped the Human Development Index, followed by Ireland, Switzerland, Hong Kong, and Iceland in 2020.

Hence, the correct option is (B).

26. Articles 64 and 89 (1) provide that the Vice-President of India shall be ex-officio Chairman of the Council of States i.e., Rajya Sabha, and shall not hold any other office of profit.

Hence, the correct option is (A).

27. It was based on the recommendation of the Balwant Rai Mehta committee. It came into force with effect from April 24, 1993. It has a 3-tier system of Panchayati Raj for all States having a population of over 20 lakh.

Hence, the correct option is (A).

28. Article 55 is conspicuously silent on whether there will be a representation of all or each State in the Presidential election, although there is a vacancy in the Electoral College. It only provides for "the different States." Since there is no guarantee to ensure non-vacancy in the Presidential Electoral College, the phrase, "the elected members of Legislative Assemblies of States" means only those who are actually in office at the time of the Presidential Election.

so, the 11th AMENDMENT was done in 1961 which Indemnify the President and Vice President Election procedure from a challenge on grounds of existence of any vacancies in the electoral college.

So, it can be said that YES, It is permissible to conduct the election for the post of President of India when one or more state Assemblies are dissolved.

Hence, the correct option is (A).

29.

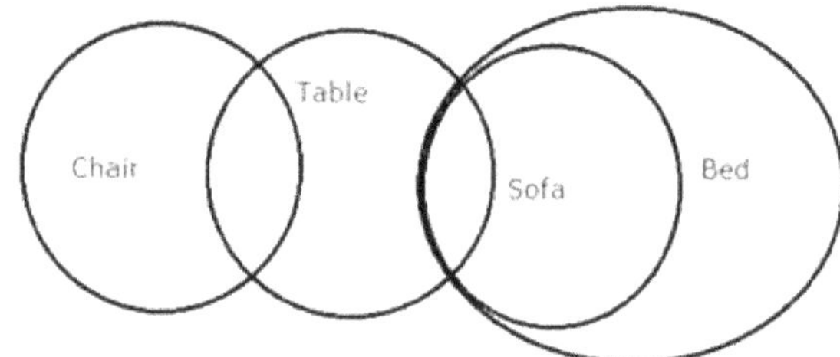

(i) Some beds are chairs do not follow as there is no direct relation between bed and chair.

(ii) Some tables are beds follows as from the diagram some part of the tables lies in bed.

(iii) Some sofas are chairs do not follow as there is no direct relation between sofa and chair.

(iv) All beds are sofas does not follow as some bed is sofa is true but not all.

Therefore, only conclusion 2 follows.

Hence, the correct option is (B).

30.

- The term "closure" in Parliamentary terminology implies the stoppage of debate on a motion.
- The closure is one of the means by which a debate may be brought to a close by a majority decision of the House, even though all Members wishing to speak have not done so.

Hence, the correct option is (B).

31. Required average

$$= \frac{1}{3}\left(780 \times \frac{40}{100} + 650 \times \frac{42}{100} + 500 \times \frac{45}{100}\right)$$
$$= \frac{1}{3}(312 + 273 + 225)$$
$$= \frac{810}{3} = 270$$

Hence, the correct option is (B).

32. Number of Arts students qualified in 2015

$$= 500 \times \frac{20}{100} = 100$$

Percentage of disqualified students $= \frac{160-100}{160} \times 100$

$$= 37.5\%$$

Hence, the correct option is (C).

33. Average:
$= \frac{1}{5} \times \frac{850}{100}(42 + 18 + 14 + 14 + 12)$
$= \frac{17}{10} \times 100 = 170$
Hence, the correct option is (A).

34. Number of qualified students
$= 620 \times \frac{10}{100} = 62$
$40\% \equiv 62$
$100\% \equiv 62 \times \frac{100}{40} = 155$
Hence, the correct option is (C).

35. Percentage increase:
$= \frac{850-780}{780} \times 100$
$= \frac{70}{780} \times 100$
$= \frac{700}{78} = \frac{350}{39}$
$= 8\frac{38}{39}\%$

Hence, the correct option is (B).

36. Article 156 in the Constitution relates to the term of office of Governor. As per this article, a Governor is elected by the President and should hold office for a term of 5 years. In case of early resignation, the Governor shall write to the President.

Hence, the correct option is (B).

37. Rashtriya Uchchatar Shiksha Abhiyan (RUSA) was launched in 2013 with the purpose to provide strategic funding to eligible state higher educational institutions.

The objectives of Rashtriya Uchchatar Shiksha Abhiyan (RUSA) are:

1) To improve the quality of state institutions by ensuring conformity to laid norms and standards.

2) It aims to provide equal development to all higher institutions and to rectify the weaknesses or loopholes in the higher education system.

3) To create new institutes by upgrading the existing autonomous colleges.

Hence, the correct option is (D).

38. NTA (National Testing Agency) has been built up as a chief, expert, self-ruling, and self-supported testing association to lead selection tests for affirmation/cooperation in higher instructive organizations. NTA is not related to research in the finance and marketing department. NTA research educational, professional, and testing systems to identify gaps in the knowledge systems and take steps for bridging them.

Hence, the correct option is (C).

39. Experimental research is conducted to study the cause and effect relationship of different phenomenon. This involves the manipulation of one or more variables to observe the change in effect. Correlation is the mutual relationship between the variables.

In experimental research, the magnitude of the correlation yields good results.

Hence, the correct option is (B).

40. Ethnography is a systematic study of people and culture. Ethnographic studies are extremely important for a qualitative researcher for a detailed study of the cultural phenomenon. The method was first introduced to the discipline of anthropology but later on, become popular in social sciences as well. Ethnography is a holistic study.

So, a, b and e are true about ethnography.

Hence, the correct option is (D).

41. MHRD works through two departments: The Department of school education & literacy and the Department of Higher Education. While the Department of School Education and Literacy is in charge of the improvement of school training and proficiency in the nation. Department of Higher Education deals with what is one of the biggest Higher Education frameworks of the world, soon after the United States and China.

Hence, the correct option is (B).

42. UGC (University Grants Commission) was established in the year 1956 as a statutory body through the Parliament Act for coordinating and maintaining the higher education standards in India.

AICTE (All India Council for Technical Education) was established in the year 1945 as an advisory body & as a statutory body through the Parliament Act for planning and development of technical education in India.

NCTE (National Council for Teacher Education) was established in the year 1995 to undertake and maintain the procedures and processes in the Indian Education System.

NAAC (National Assessment and Accreditation Council) was established in the year 1994 with the motive to evaluate the performances of universities and colleges in India.

Hence, the correct option is (B).

43. International Literacy Day is observed every year on 8 September. It aims to highlight the importance of literacy for the individual, community and society. There is a lack of literacy among the 77 million three million adults in the world even today.

Hence option (A) is correct.

44. Constitution does not define the meaning of the phrase 'violation of the Constitution'. The impeachment charges to be initiated should be signed by 25% of members of the house where the president gets the opportunity to represent his side.

No President has so far been impeached.

Hence, the correct option is (B).

45. Higher education is the responsibility of both the center and state governments. The Central Government is also responsible for considering an educational institution as "Deemed-to-be University" on the recommendations of the University Grants Commission.

Hence, the correct option is (C).

46. Formative Evaluation: Evaluation is carried throughout the course in the form of weekly assignments, discussion etc.

Summative Evaluation: Evaluation is carried at the end of the course in the form examinations.

Criteria-Referenced Evaluation: Evaluation is done against specific standards or criteria.

Norm-Referenced Evaluation: Evaluation of individual performance in comparison to others. It is to assess how a student performs in relation to other peers.

Hence, the correct option is (B).

47. There are various factors that affect teaching. These are the Experience of a teacher, educational qualification of a teacher, Subject matter of teaching, Classroom environment, Human relation skill, communication skill, method and technique of teaching, use of teaching aids.

Hence, the correct option is (D).

48. Effective teaching can take place outside the classroom also. It is not important that learning and teaching can take place in classrooms only.

So, Classroom teaching is the most effective method of teaching is not correct.

Correct statements:

1. Teaching is a comprehensive process.
2. Teaching can be made effective by making use of teaching aids.
3. Teaching requires expertise and experience.

Hence, the correct option is (A).

49.

- Bhandarkar Oriental Research Institute, one of the institutes that provide oriental learning programs in India is located in Pune, Maharashtra.
- Oriental Learning Programmes are related to and devoted to Indological Studies. This is concerning to the culture of Asia.

Hence, the correct option is (A).

50. NIEPA stands for National Institute of Educational Planning and Administration. It is a deemed university established by HRD Ministry to facilitate research in education in India and South Asia.

Hence, the correct option is (A).

Mock Test 09

Q.1 Artifacts that arise and affect the internal validity in research are:

(a) History

(b) Randomisation

(c) Maturity

(d) Instrumentation

(e) Experimental mortality

(f) Matching

A. (a), (b), (c) and (d) **B.** (a), (c), (d) and (e)

C. (b), (c), (d) and (f) **D.** (d), (e), (f) and (b)

Q.2 Environmental education should be taught in schools because

A. It will affect environmental pollution

B. It is an important part of life

C. It will provide job to teachers

D. We cannot escape from an environment

Q.3 There are two sets given below. Set –I specifies the types of research, while Set-II indicates their characteristics. Match the two and give your answer by selecting the appropriate code.

Set – I

(Research types)

1) Fundamental

2) research

3) Applied research

4) Action research

5) Evaluative research

Set – II

(Characteristics)

i. Find out the extent of perceived impact of an intervention

ii. Developing an effective explanation through theory building

iii. Improving an existing situation through use of interventions

iv. Exploring the possibility of a theory for use in various situations

v. Enriching technological resources

A. 1 - ii, 2 - iv, 3 - iii, 4 - i, 5-v

B. 1 - v, 2 - iv, 3-iii, 4 - ii, 5-i

C. 1 - i, 2 - ii, 3 - iii, 4 - iv, 5-v

D. 1 - ii, 2 - iii, 3 - iv, 4 - v, 5-i

Q.4 Which of the following is the correct definition of the 'Motif'?

A. It refers to creative activity, such as painting, music, literature, and dance

B. It refers to a design or figure that consists of recurring shapes or colours, as in architecture or decoration

C. It is visual art form such as painting or sculpture, producing works to be appreciated primarily for their beauty or emotional power

D. None of the above

Q.5 A researcher intends to explore the effect of possible factors for the organization of effective mid-day meal interventions. Which research method will be most appropriate for this study?

A. Historical method

B. Descriptive survey method

C. Experimental method

D. Ex-post-facto method

Q.6 In which language the newspapers have the highest circulation?

A. Gujarati **B.** Panjabi **C.** Hindi **D.** English

Q.7 'Sampling Cases' means

A. Sampling using a sampling frame

B. Identifying people who are suitable for research

C. Literally the researcher's brief case

D. Sampling of people, newspapers, television programmes etc.

Q.8 Which of the following organization looks after the quality of Technical and Management education in India?

A. NCTE **B.** MCI **C.** AICTE **D.** CSIR

Q.9 Match the items of the first set with that of the second set in respect of evaluation system.

Choose the correct code:

Set-I	Set-II
a. Formative evaluation	i. Evaluating cognitive and co-cognitive aspects with regularity
b. Summative evaluation	ii. Tests and their interpretations based on a group and certain yardsticks
c. Continuous and comprehensive evaluation	iii. Grading the final learning outcomes
d. Norm and criterion	iv. Quizzes and discussions

A. a-iv b-iii c-i d-ii **B.** a-i b-ii c-iii d-iv

C. a-iii b-iv c-ii d-i **D.** a-i b-iii c-iv d-ii

Q.10 Following are the main elements of the Choice Based Credit System. Identify the one which does not belong to the Choice Based Credit System (CBCs).

A. The assessment is done twice in a year

B. Students are given a choice to select from the available courses

C. Each course is assigned a specific credit

D. There are three main courses in CBCs-Main, Foundation and Elective

Q.11 Identify the category of evaluation that assesses the learning progress to provide continuous feedback to the students during instruction.

A. Placement **B.** Diagnostic

C. Formative **D.** Summative

Q.12 Normal BMI for adult Asians as suggested by WHO is

A. 18 – 23 kg/m² **B.** 18 – 28 kg/m²
C. 20 – 25 kg/m² **D.** 21 – 26 kg/m²

Q.13 Which of the following is not a hand printing technique?

A. Duplex **B.** Screen **C.** Block **D.** Stencil

Q.14 In the following two sets, teaching methods are indicated in set-I, while in set-II basic requirements for success / effectiveness are given. Match these two sets and select your answer from the codes given below:

Aggregates - I

(Teaching method)

1) Explain
2) Discussion in groups
3) thought process
4) customized instruction

Aggregate - II

(Basic Requirements of Success / Effectiveness))

i. Presentation in short terms with feedback
ii. Presenting a large number of ideas
iii. Communication of content in clear language
iv. Methodology of teaching-equipment
v. Case-based participation in participants

A. 1 - i 2 - ii 3 - iii 4 - iv
B. 1 - ii 2 - iii 3 - iv 4 - v
C. 1 - iii 2 - v 3 - ii 4 - i
D. 1 - iv 2 - ii 3 - I 4 - iii

Q.15 Which one of the following is considered a sign of motivated teaching?

A. Students asking questions
B. Maximum attendance of the students
C. Pin drop silence in the classroom
D. Students taking notes

Q.16 Anil played 8 cricket matches. The mean (average) of runs was found to be 80 runs. After playing four more matches, the mean of total runs was found to be 70 runs. Total runs scored in the last four matches:

A. 400 **B.** 300 **C.** 200 **D.** 100

Q.17 The next term in the series is:

5, 11, 21, 35, 53, ?, ...

A. 75 **B.** 90 **C.** 115 **D.** 125

Q.18 The area covered by forest in India is about:

A. 46% **B.** 33% **C.** 22% **D.** 19%

Q.19 If the code for ALLAHABAD is DPQGOIKKO, the code for BENGULURU will be:

A. ESBTBDIMF **B.** MBDBFEIST
C. EISMBTDBF **D.** ESBDFBTMI

Q.20 If $5\$125 = 25, 12\$48 = 4$ then what is the value of $4\$24 = ?$

A. 34 **B.** 35 **C.** 6 **D.** 5

Q.21 Gopal walks 20 m North. Then he turns right and walks 30 m. Then he turns right and walks 35 m. Again, he turns left and walks 15 m. Then he again turns left and walks 15 m. The shortest distance between his original position and final one is:

A. 65 m **B.** 55 m **C.** 40 m **D.** 45 m

Q.22 If two standard form categorical propositions with the same subject and predicate are related in such a manner that if one is undetermined the other must be undetermined, what is their relation?

A. Contrary **B.** Sub contrary
C. Contradictory **D.** Sub-altern

Q.23 Just as melting ice - cubes do not cause a glass of water to overflow, melting sea - ice does not increase oceanic volume.

What type of argument is it?

[UGC NET Sociology, 2017]

A. Analogical **B.** Hypothetical
C. Psychological **D.** Statistical

Q.24 Identify the type of reasoning shown in the following statements.

Statement 1: We see smoke coming out of the hills.

Statement 2: Wherever there is smoke, there is always a fire.

Conclusion: Therefore, hills have a fire.

A. Pratyaksha **B.** Upamana
C. Anumana **D.** Arthapatti

Q.25 Communication is a part of ______ skills.

A. Soft **B.** Hard **C.** Rough **D.** Short

Q.26 The technology used to provide the internet by transmitting data over wires of the telephone network is

A. Transmitter **B.** Diodes
C. HHL **D.** DSL

Q.27 Public Order as an item in the Constitution figures in

A. The Union List
B. The State List
C. The Concurrent List
D. The Residuary Powers

Q.28 Which of these should not be avoided for effective communication?

A. Noise **B.** Planning
C. Semantic problems **D.** Wrong assumptions

Q.29 Every type of communication is affected by its:

A. Reception **B.** Transmission
C. Non-regulation **D.** Context

Q.30 Ankit scored 32, 45 and 49 marks in Physics, English and Philosophy respectively. The maximum marks in each subject is 50. Determine his overall percentage for the three subjects.

A. 58 **B.** 50 **C.** 42 **D.** 84

Q.31 Who among the following is the chairman of Rajya Sabha?

A. President
B. Voice President
C. Prime Minister
D. Speaker of Lok Sabha

Q.32 A Lok Sabha speaker addresses his/ her resignation to whom among the following?

A. Deputy Speaker **B.** President
C. Prime Minister **D.** Law Ministry

Q.33 The University Grants Commission has a scheme for "Human Rights and values in Education". Under this scheme, which statement is incorrect among the following for 'Human Rights and Duties Education' component?

A. To establish value and wellness centers in schools
B. To encourage research activities
C. To develop interaction between society and educational institutions
D. To sensitize the citizens so that the norms and values of human rights are realized

Q.34 Where is Hemwati Nandan Bahuguna Garhwal University located?

A. Jammu and Kashmir
B. Himachal Pradesh
C. Uttarakhand
D. Bihar

Q.35 Which one of the following is not a natural fibre?

A. Cotton **B.** Nylon **C.** Flax **D.** Wool

Q.36 Which of the traditional textile motif is related to the French naut open work and Herringbone stitch techniques?

A. Chikankari of Lucknow
B. Kantha of West Bengalication
C. Pipli Applique Work
D. Rajasthani Embroidery

Q.37 Which of the following enables us to send the same letter to different person in MS Word?

A. Main join **B.** Mail copy
C. Mail insert **D.** Mail merge

Q.38 In a Computer a byte generally consists of:

A. 4 bits **B.** 8 bits **C.** 16 bits **D.** 10 bits

Q.39 One of the anthropogenic sources of gaseous pollutants chlorofluorocarbons (CFCs) in air is

A. Cement industry **B.** Fertiliser industry
C. Foam industry **D.** Pesticide industry

Q.40 Assertion (A): Indoor air pollution is a serious health hazard.

Reason (R): The dispersal of air pollutants is rather limited in indoor environment.

Choose the correct answer from the code given below:

A. Both (A) and (R) are true and (R) is the correct explanation of (A)
B. Both (A) and (R) are true but (R) is the correct explanation of (A)
C. (A) is true and (R) is false
D. Both (A) and (R) are false

Ques (41-45):Direction: Read the following passage carefully and give the suitable Answer.

The last great war, which nearly shook the foundations of the modern world, had little impact on Indian literature beyond aggravating the popular revulsion against violence and adding to the growing disillusionment with the 'humane pretensions' of the Western World. This was eloquently voiced in Tagore's later poems and his last testament, Crisis in Civilization. The Indian intelligentsia was in a state of moral dilemma. On the one hand, it could not help sympathizing with England's dogged courage in the hour of peril, with the Russians fighting with their backs to the wall against the ruthless Nazi hordes, and with China groaning under the heel of Japanese militarism; on the other hand, their own country was practically under military occupation of their own soil, and an Indian army under Subhas Bose was trying from the opposite camp to liberate their country. No creative impulse could issue from such confusion of loyalties. One would imagine that the achievement of Indian independence in 1947, which came in the wake of the Allies' victory and was followed by the collapse of colonialism in the neighboring countries of South-East Asia, would have released an upsurge of creative energy.

No doubt it did, but unfortunately it was soon submerged in the great agony of partition, with its inhuman slaughter of the innocents and the uprooting of millions of people from their homeland, followed by the martyrdom of Mahatma Gandhi. These tragedies, along with Pakistan's invasion of Kashmir and its later atrocities in Bangladesh, did indeed provoke a poignant writing, particularly in the languages of the regions most affected, Bengali, Hindi, Kashmiri, Punjabi, Sindhi and Urdu. But poignant or passionate writing does not by itself make great literature. What reserves of enthusiasm and confidence survived these disasters have been mainly absorbed in the task of national reconstruction and economic development. Great literature has always emerged out of chains of convulsions. Indian literature is richer today in volume, range and variety than it ever was in the past.

Q.41 What effect did the previous World War have on Indian literature?

A. It had no effect
B. This increased public anger against violence.
C. It rocked the foundation of literature
D. It gave strong support to the western world

Q.42 Whose expression did Tagore express in his last epic?

A. Supported Subhash Bose
B. Revealed the Polls of 'Human Releases' of Western World
C. Expressed his allegiance to England
D. Encouraged the emancipation of countries

Q.43 Vegetable which is not blanched before drying is:

A. Cauliflower **B.** Palak
C. Onion **D.** Tomato

Q.44 It is important to know some installation practices to know the problems on the job site. What is the fastening method for hanging cabinets in wood frame construction?

A. They were indifferent to the sufferings of the Russian people
B. They were in favor of Japanese military might
C. His indecisive sincerity encouraged creativity
D. He expressed sympathy for the courage of England

Q.45 What were the effects of the tragedy of Kashmir and Bangladesh?

A. Doubt of other countries
B. Continuity of rivalry
C. Battle cast
D. National reconstruction

Ques (46-50):Directions: Study the following table carefully to answer the questions.

Number of boys & girls enrolled in 5 different sports in academy during 6 different years (In thousand)

Course	Badminton		Wrestling		Tennis		Gymnastics		Archery	
Years	Boys	Girls	Boys	Girls	Boys	Girls	Boys	Girls	Boys	Girls
2011	7.2	6.3	13.3	3.2	15.5	6.1	12.6	4.1	2.7	1.1
2012	6.6	4.2	18.4	4.2	18.9	6.3	18.4	4.3	3.8	2.2
2013	10.6	5.8	27.4	12.8	23.2	8.8	19.3	10.3	5.7	3.5
2014	13.6	7.9	21.4	13.4	26.6	9.2	12.6	4.4	8.9	4.8
2015	16.8	6.4	12.6	5.2	27.9	12.4	24.4	6.2	14.8	3.2
2016	17.2	5.2	13.4	3.2	35.8	5.9	10.6	5.1	6.6	1.8

Q.46 What is the average number of boys enrolled in all the sports in the year 2011? (in thousands)

A. 10.26 **B.** 9.26 **C.** 10.62 **D.** 11.26

Q.47 What is the average number of girls enrolled in wrestling during all the years? (in thousands)

A. 6.5
B. 8
C. 7
D. None of these

Q.48 The difference between the number of boys and girls enrolled in Gymnastics during the year 2011, 2012 and 2013. (in thousands) is

A. 21.6 **B.** 316 **C.** 31.6 **D.** 216

Q.49 By what percent is the number of boys enrolled in Archery in 2015 is more than that of girls in the same course and in the same year?

A. 360.5 **B.** 260.5 **C.** 262.5 **D.** 362.5

Q.50 In the given years in which sport the number of boys enrolled showed a consistent increase?

A. Gymnastics
B. Tennis
C. Badminton
D. Archery

// Smart Answer Sheet //

Correct Indicates percentage of students who answered questions correctly.

Skipped Indicates percentage of students who skipped questions.

Q.	Ans.	Correct	Skipped
1	B	33.33 %	3.71 %
2	B	53.7 %	29.63 %
3	A	14.81 %	29.63 %
4	B	25.93 %	27.77 %
5	D	42.59 %	27.78 %
6	C	53.7 %	27.78 %
7	D	40.74 %	25.93 %
8	C	59.26 %	25.93 %
9	A	44.44 %	25.93 %
10	A	35.19 %	27.77 %
11	C	48.15 %	27.78 %
12	A	37.04 %	27.77 %
13	A	27.78 %	25.92 %
14	C	38.89 %	27.78 %
15	A	61.11 %	29.63 %
16	C	37.04 %	27.77 %
17	A	57.41 %	25.92 %
18	C	22.22 %	29.63 %
19	C	62.96 %	25.93 %
20	C	62.96 %	29.63 %
21	D	44.44 %	27.78 %
22	C	25.93 %	27.77 %
23	A	55.56 %	24.07 %
24	C	42.59 %	29.63 %
25	A	61.11 %	24.08 %
26	D	38.89 %	27.78 %
27	B	14.81 %	25.93 %
28	B	35.19 %	27.77 %
29	D	31.48 %	29.63 %
30	D	50.0 %	27.78 %
31	B	53.7 %	27.78 %
32	A	24.07 %	27.78 %
33	A	24.07 %	27.78 %
34	C	40.74 %	27.78 %
35	C	14.81 %	29.63 %
36	A	25.93 %	27.77 %
37	D	42.59 %	25.93 %
38	B	61.11 %	29.63 %
39	C	38.89 %	25.92 %
40	A	33.33 %	27.78 %
41	B	35.19 %	25.92 %
42	B	42.59 %	24.08 %
43	C	29.63 %	25.93 %
44	D	20.37 %	24.07 %
45	D	42.59 %	25.93 %
46	A	51.85 %	29.63 %
47	C	42.59 %	27.78 %
48	C	46.3 %	29.63 %
49	D	24.07 %	27.78 %
50	B	51.85 %	27.78 %

Performance Analysis	
Avg. Score (%)	45.0%
Toppers Score (%)	100.0%
Your Score	

//Hints and Solutions//

1. Confounds and artifacts are the two kinds of threats to the validity of socio-psychological research. The major threats to internal validity are history, maturation, testing, instrumentation, statistical regression, selection, experimental mortality, and selection-history interactions. Matching and randomization doesn't vary the treatment and outcome of the research.

Hence, the correct option is (B).

2. Environmental education should be taught in schools because it is an important part of life.

Environmental education helps students understand how their decisions and actions affect the environment, builds knowledge and skills necessary to address complex environmental issues, as well as ways we can take action to keep our environment healthy and sustainable for the future.

Hence, the correct option is (B).

3. Fundamental Research is concerned with the generalizations and with the formulation of theory building.

Applied Research is a socially useful application of knowledge generated to social concern. It is a form of systematic inquiry involving practical application.

Action Research is used by teachers, supervisors etc. to improve the quality of decision and actions. It lays stress on developing the present situations to make these better.

Evaluative Research determines the impact of social intervention. It analyses the effect of a particular program on a certain problem the program is trying to solve.
Hence, the correct option is (A).

4. The term 'Motif' refers to a design or figure that consists of recurring shapes or colors, as in architecture or decoration.

A motif is a recurring narrative element with symbolic significance. If you spot a symbol, concept, or plot structure that surfaces repeatedly in the text, you're probably dealing with a motif. They must be related to the central idea of the work, and they always end up reinforcing the author's overall message.

Hence, the correct option is (B).

5. To explore the effect of possible factors for the organization of effective mid-day meal interventions, ex-post-facto method is the most appropriate. This study allows the comparative study of mid-day meal. This research which is also known as after-the-fact research is an investigation that starts after the fact has occurred without interference from the researcher.

Hence, the correct option is (D).

6. The Hindi language newspapers have the highest circulation. The largest number of newspapers were published in Hindi (20,589), followed by English (7,596), Marathi (2,943), Urdu (2,906), Bengali (2,741), Gujarati (2,215), Tamil (2,119), Kannada (1,816), Malayalam(1,505) and Telugu (1,289).

Hence, the correct option is (C).

7. 'Sampling Cases' means sampling of people, newspapers, television programmes etc. A sampling case is a small group that is generalised for the whole population.

Hence, the correct option is (D).

8. AICTE organization looks after the quality of Technical and Management education in India. All India Council for Technical Education (AICTE) was set up in November 1945 as a national-level Apex Advisory Body to conduct a survey on the facilities available for technical education and to promote development in the country in a coordinated and integrated manner

Hence, the correct option is (C).

9. Formative assessment assists the students during the learning process. It includes quizzes, discussions, etc.

Summative assessment evaluates learning of the students at the end of an instructional unit. It is used to grade the final learning outcomes.

Continuous and comprehensive evaluation evaluates cognitive and co-cognitive aspects with regularity and also evaluates every aspect of the student during their presence at the college/school.

Norm and criterion-referenced tests evaluate interpretations based on a group and certain yardsticks.

Hence the correct option is (A).

10. The assessment under CBCs is done twice in a year i.e. Semester wise. Students are given a choice to select from the available courses, each course is assigned a specific credit and there are three main courses in CBCs-Main, Foundation and Elective are the main elements of the Choice Based Credit System (CBCs).

Hence, the correct option is (A).

11. The formative process determines learning progress to provide continuous feedback while instructing students. Formal education is best for reaching the formative process. Formative education is best to access the learning process.

Hence, the correct option is (C).

12. The normal BMI range for adult Asians suggested by the WHO is 18–23 kg / m^2. The body mass index (BMI) is a simple and the most commonly used index used to classify overweight and obesity. It is defined as a person's weight in kilograms divided by the square of his height in meters (kg/m^2).

Hence, the correct option is (A).

13. Duplex is not a hand printing technique. Duplex printing means that you can print on both sides of the paper with your printer either automatically or manually by turning the paper over after the first side has printed. To duplex print, your model will need to have the functionality built-in.

Hence, the correct option is (A).

14. Lecture - It is the process of lecturing in understandable languages.

Discussion in groups - It is the action or process of talking about a topic in groups to arrive at a conclusion or exchange ideas.

Brainstorming - Brainstorming is a group creativity technique through which attempts are made to formulate a conclusion for a particular problem by collating a list of relevant ideas contributed by its members.

Programmed Instruction - Programmed Instruction is a method of presenting new content to students in sorted order of controlled steps.

Hence, the correct option is (C).

15. (B), (C), (D) are not sign of motivated teaching as it doesn`t indicate the interest of students but students asking questions clearly indicate that students are getting what is being taught to them and thus ask questions.
Hence, the correct option is (A).

16. We know that, Average $= \frac{Sum\ of\ terms}{Number\ of\ terms}$

$\Rightarrow$Number of terms $= Average \times Sum\ of\ terms$

Runs after 8 matches $= 80 \times 8 = 640$ runs

After 12 matches $= 70 \times 12 = 840$ runs

Total runs scored in last four matches $= 840 - 640 = 200$

Hence, the correct option is (C).

17. This question follows the following pattern:

5 + 6 = 11

11+10 = 21

21+14 = 35

35+18 = 53

53+22= 75

Hence, the correct option is (A).

18. According to the 2019 report, the total forest cover of the country is 712,249 square kilometers (21.67 percent of India's total geographical area) from in 2017.

Hence, the correct option is (C).

19. This question follows the following pattern:

A + 3 = D

L + 4 = P

L + 5 = Q

A + 6 = G

H + 7 = O

A + 8 = I

B +9 = K

A + 10 = K

D + 11 = O

So, the code for BENGULURU will be:

B + 3 = E

E + 4 = I

N + 5 = S

G + 6 = M

U + 7 = B

L + 8 = T

U + 9 = D

R + 10 = B

U + 11 = F

Hence, the correct option is (C).

20. The pattern followed is that for $a\$b = \frac{b}{a}$ a

For example, $5\$125 = \frac{125}{5} = 25$

and $12\$48 = \frac{48}{12} = 4$

Similarly, $4\$24 = \frac{24}{4} = 6$

Hence, the correct option is (C).

21. According to the question, the total distance traveled by Gopal is shown in the following figure:

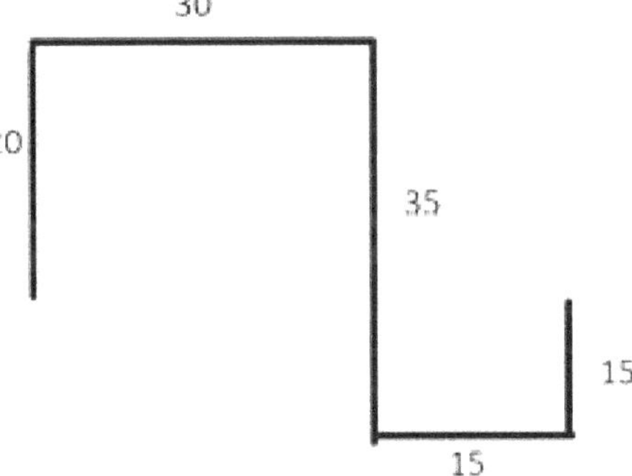

From the figure, the minimum distance between Gopal's initial position and the final position= 30m + 15m = 45m

Hence, the correct option is (D).

22. If two standard form categorical propositions with the same subject and predicate are related in such a manner that if one is undetermined the other must be undetermined, then this phenomenon is called as contradictory.

Hence, the correct option is (C).

23. This argument is analogical in nature. The analogy here is- Melting Ice cubes is compared with the melting sea – ice and glass of water is compared with the ocean. So, there is a similarity between the objects.

Hence, the correct option is (A).

24. Anumana is a method by which knowledge is derived from another knowledge. On the basis of our perceptual knowledge, we know that wherever there is smoke there is fire (the opposite might not be true). After knowing the invariable relation between the two we can logically deduce the presence of fire whenever we see smoke. This is anumana.
Hence, the correct option is (C).

25. Communication is a part of Soft skills. A list of soft skills includes more than communication, but good communication skills are typically connected to all areas of soft skills training, such as providing good customer service.

Hence, the correct option is (A).

26. The technology used to provide the internet by transmitting data over wires of the telephone network is Digital Subscriber Line (DSL).

Digital Subscriber Line (DSL) technology is a Copper Loop Transmission Technology. DSL (Digital Subscriber Line) is a technology for bringing high- bandwidth information to homes and small businesses over ordinary copper telephone lines. xDSL refers to different variations of DSL, such as ADSL, HDSL, and RADSL.

Hence, the correct option is (D).

27. The State List or List-II is a list of 59 items(after the 101st Constitutional amendment act, 2016, entry numbers 52 and 55 deleted). Initially, there were 66 items in the list in Schedule Seven to the Constitution of India. The legislative section is divided into three lists: Union List, State List and Concurrent List.

Hence, the correct option is (B).

28. Lack of planning must be avoided for effective communication. There are innumerable examples of people who would give an ill-planned, long winding lecture while a short presentation with tables or graphs would be sufficient.

Hence, the correct option is (B).

29. Every type of communication is affected by its context. Contexts can be similar, which sometimes might be confusing or overlapping. Communication will not be affected by reception or transmission.

Hence, the correct option is (D).

30. Total marks scored by Ankit in Physics, English and Philosophy respectively $= 32 + 45 + 49 = 126$

Total aggregate marks of the three subjects $= 3 \times 50 = 150$

$\therefore$ Required percentage $= \frac{126}{150} \times 100$

$= \frac{126}{3} \times 2 = 84\%$

Hence, the correct option is (D).

31. Voice President is the ex-officio chairman of Rajya Sabha; however, the deputy chairman is elected from amongst the Rajya Sabha's members.

Hence, the correct option is (B).

32. The Speaker of Lok Sabha has to address his letter of resignation to the Deputy Speaker.

The Deputy Speaker of the Lok Sabha is the second-highest legislative officer of the Lok Sabha, the lower house of the Parliament of India.

Hence, the correct option is (A).

33. The University Grants Commission has a scheme for "Human Rights and values in Education". Under this scheme, there is a provision to encourage the research activities in the higher institutes. The other guidelines listed are to develop interaction between society and educational institutions and to sensitize the citizens so that the norms and values of human rights are realized. To establish value and wellness centers in school is not a component listed in 'Human Rights & Duties Education' scheme.

Hence, the correct option is (A).

34. Hemwati Nandan Bahuguna Garhwal University is located in Garhwal (Uttarakhand). Earlier, it was a state university but has acquired a central university status with effect from 2009.

Hence, the correct option is (C).

35. A fiber is defined as a thin thread of a natural or artificial substance. Fiber is especially used to make cloth or rope.

Nylon is a man-made synthetic fiber prepared by the process of polymerization. The monomer used to prepare Nylon is E-caprolactam. Natural fibers like cotton, wool, flax, and silk are produced by plants and animals.

Hence, the correct option is (C).

36. Chikankari of Lucknow is a traditional embroidery style of Lucknow, Uttar Pradesh. In this art form, the French naut open work and Herringbone stitch techniques are used.

Hence, the correct option is (A).

37. Mail merge is used to send the same mail to different persons in MS Word. Mail merge is a way to create personalized letters and pre-addressed mailing labels. Microsoft Word can insert content from a database, spreadsheet into Word documents.

Hence, the correct option is (D).

38. A byte is a unit of digital information that most commonly consists of eight bits.

1 Byte = 8 bits

Hence, the correct option is (B).

39. Chlorofluorocarbons released into the atmosphere since the 1930s in various applications like in air-conditioning, refrigeration, blowing agents in foams, etc.One of the anthropogenic sources of gaseous pollutants chlorofluorocarbons (CFCs) in air is in Foam Industry.

Hence, the correct option is (C).

40. Indoor Air pollution causes serious health problems such as respiratory problems and even cancer. There, it is a serious hazard. The dispersal of air pollutants is limited because it does not get space in the indoor environment.

Hence, the correct option is (A).

41. According to the first few lines of the passage, "The Last World War, which almost shook the foundations of the modern world, had little impact on Indian literature beyond raising popular revolt against violence and linking the growing disenchantment with 'human pretense. Western' Of world "

This means that the last great war increased hatred against violence.

Hence, the correct option is (B).

42. The previous World War "associated growing disillusionment with the 'human pretense' of the Western world." And this was explicitly voiced in "Tagore's later poems and his last will, Crisis in Civilization".

Therefore, in his last testament, Tagore made it clear that the 'human pretense' of the Western world was exposed.

Hence, the correct option is (B).

43. Vegetables that do not require blanching before drying are onions, green peppers, and mushrooms. Water blanching: Bring a large pot of water (two-thirds full) to a rolling boil.

Hence, the correct option is (C).

44. The human intelligentsia, according to the passage during the period of the Great War, "could not help sympathizing with the dogged courage of England in times of crisis". This means that he expressed sympathy for England's courage during difficult times.

Hence, the correct option is (D).

45. According to the latter part of the passage, "The reserves of enthusiasm and confidence left in these disasters (divisions) have been largely absorbed in the task of national reconstruction and economic development.

Hence, the correct option is (D).

46. $\text{Required Avarage} = \frac{\text{Sum of boys enrolled in all the sports in the all year}}{\text{Number of Course}}$

$= \frac{7.2+13.3+15.5+12.6+2.7}{5}$

$= \frac{51.3}{5}$

$= 10.26$ (in thousand)

Hence, the correct option is (A).

47. Required Average $= \frac{\textit{Sum of girls enrolled in wrestling during all the years}}{\textit{Number of years}}$

$= \frac{3.2+4.2+12.8+13.4+5.2+3.2}{6}$

$= \frac{42}{6} = 7$ (in thousand)

Hence, the correct option is (C).

48. Year $2011,\ 2012$ and 2013 Gymnastics:

Boys $\Rightarrow\ 12.6 + 18.4 + 19.3 = 50.3$ thousand

Girls $\Rightarrow\ 4.1 + 4.3 + 10.3 = 18.7$ thousand

Difference $= 50.3 - 18.7 = 31.6$ thousand

Hence, the correct option is (C).

49. From the table,

$\text{Required percent (enrolled in Archery in 2015)} = \frac{\text{number of boys} - \text{number of girls}}{\text{number of girls}} \times 100$

$= \frac{14.8-3.2}{3.2} \times 100$

$= \frac{11.6}{3.2} \times 100 = 362.5$

Hence, the correct option is (D).

50. We can clearly observe from the table that the Tennis is the only sport in which enrollment of boys is increasing consistently.

Hence, the correct option is (B).

Mock Test 10

Q.1 A good communicator begins his/her presentation with a:
[UGC NET Sociology, 2017]

A. Complex question **B.** Non-sequitur
C. Repetitive phrase **D.** Ice-breaker

Q.2 The interaction between a teacher and students creates a zone of proximal:
[UGC NET Sociology, 2017]

A. Difference **B.** Confusion
C. Development **D.** Distortion

Q.3 A good question to know about your students' thinking could be:

A. Is your answer correct?
B. How did you get the answer?
C. Did you cross-check your answer with your partner?
D. Is your working same as given in the book?

Q.4 Communicative abilities embrace which of the following skills?

A. Linguistic skills **B.** Semantic skills
C. Cultural skills **D.** Both (A) and (B)

Q.5 _____ should be present sufficiently in a healthy house.

A. Clean and fresh air
B. Sunlight
C. Mosquitoes
D. Both (A) and (B)

Q.6 Which among the following is not a characteristic of newspapers?

A. The predominance of news-oriented content
B. Choice of the time of use
C. High cost
D. Textual medium

Q.7 In which of the following activities, potential for nurturing creative and critical thinking is relatively greater?
[UGC NET Sociology, 2018]

A. Preparing research summary
B. Presenting a seminar paper
C. Participation in research conference
D. Participation in a workshop

Q.8 From the list given below identify the learner characteristics which would facilitate teaching-learning system to become effective. Choose the correct code to indicate your answer.

1) Prior experience of learner
2) Learner's family lineage
3) Aptitude of the learner
4) Learner's stage of Development
5) Lerner's food habits and hobbies
6) Learner's religious affiliation

[UGC NET Sociology, 2017]

A. 1, 3 and 4 **B.** 4, 5 and 6
C. 1, 4 and 5 **D.** 2, 3 and 6

Q.9 Which of the following are the merits of radio as a means of communication?

I. Easy access
II. Portable
III. One-way communication

A. II only **B.** I and II
C. I only **D.** I, II, and III

Q.10 Assertion (A): Synchronous media requires the audience to be present when the media is being broadcasted or performed.

Reasoning (R): Media that takes place in real-time such as live television or radio is known as synchronous media.

A. The assertion is true and the reasoning is false.
B. The assertion is False and the reasoning is true.
C. The assertion is true and reasoning is the correct explanation of (A)
D. The assertion is true and the reasoning is not the correct explanation of (A).

Q.11 In which teaching method learner's participation is made optimal and proactive?

A. Discussion method
B. Buzz session method
C. Brainstorming session method
D. Project method

Q.12 A teacher who is not proficient in the local language or dialect will face _______ barrier in communication.

A. Psychological **B.** Physiological
C. Semantic **D.** Cultural

Q.13 Written communication is a part of which type of communication?

A. Verbal communication
B. Non-verbal communication
C. Both (A) and (B)
D. None of the above

Q.14 Which among the following reflects best the quality of teaching in a classroom?

A. Through the use of many teaching aids in the classroom
B. Through full attendance in the classroom
C. Through the quality of questions asked by students in classroom
D. Through observation of silence by the students in classroom

Q.15 One of the most powerful factors affecting teaching effectiveness is related to the:

A. Social system of the country

B. Economic status of the society
C. Prevailing political system
D. Educational system

Q.16 In series 1, 6, 15, 28, 45, ... the next term will be:

[UGC NET Sociology, 2017]

A. 66 B. 76 C. 56 D. 84

Q.17 The next term in the series ABD, DGK, HMS, MTB, ... is:

[UGC NET Sociology, 2017]

A. NSA B. SBL C. PSK D. RUH

Q.18 Assertion (A): Historical studies and the scriptures indicate that Indian woman enjoyed a comparatively high status during the early Vedic period and enjoyed equal rights to education.

Reason (R): References of learned ladies like Lopamudra, Apala, Urvasi, Ghosa, Sulabha, Lilabati, Maitreyi, Saswati, Kshana, Gargi and many others can be seen in the ancient scripts.

Choose the correct answer from the following:

A. Both, A and R are true and R is the correct explanation of A
B. Both, A and R are false
C. A is true but R is false
D. A is false but R is true

Q.19 A postman walked 20 m straight from his office, turned right, and walked 10 m. After turning left he walked 10 m and after turning right walked 20 m. He again turned right and walked 70 m. How far he is from his office?

[UGC NET Sociology, 2017]

A. 50 m. B. 40 m. C. 60 m. D. 20 m.

Q.20 Agricultural Produce (Grading and Marketing) Act (1937) is also:

A. PFA Act B. FPO Act
C. Agmark Act D. ISI Act

Q.21 The next term in the following series YEB, WFD, UHG, SKI, ? will be

A. TLO B. QOL C. QLO D. GQP

Q.22 The essence of effective communication is mentioned in which of the following statements?

A. The receiver gives feedback to the sender.
B. Sender and receiver both exchange information
C. Sender and receiver both attribute the same meaning to a message.
D. None of the above

Q.23 Consider the following statements regarding structure of NITI Aayog.

1) PM is its Chairman
2) Union Finance minister is its Vice-Chairperson
3) Chief Executive Officer, appointed by the PM
4) Ex-Officio Members: maximum of four members of the Union Council of Ministers to be nominated by the PM.

Which of the statements given above is/are correct?

A. 1, 2 and 3 only B. 2, 3 and 4 only
C. 1, 3 and 4 only D. 1, 2 and 4 only

Q.24 Direction: Each of the following questions has some conclusions. The conclusions are followed by some set of statements. Study the statements carefully and select the correct statement which follows the conclusion logically.

Conclusion:

Some machines are definitely not racks;

Some machines are wheels.

Statements:

I. No rack is pin; some pins are machines; all wheels are machines.

II. All racks are machines; No machine is a wheel; all wheels are pins.

III. All wheels are racks; No rack is a machine; all machines are pins.

IV. All machines are racks; all racks are wheels; all wheels are pins.

V. No rack is pin; all machines are racks; all wheels are pins.

A. Only statement V B. Only statement III
C. Only statement I D. Only statements II

Q.25 System software is the set of programs that enables the computer's hardware devices and _______ software to work together.

A. management B. processing
C. utility D. application

Ques (26-29):Directions: Study the graph and answer the questions:

Chart Title

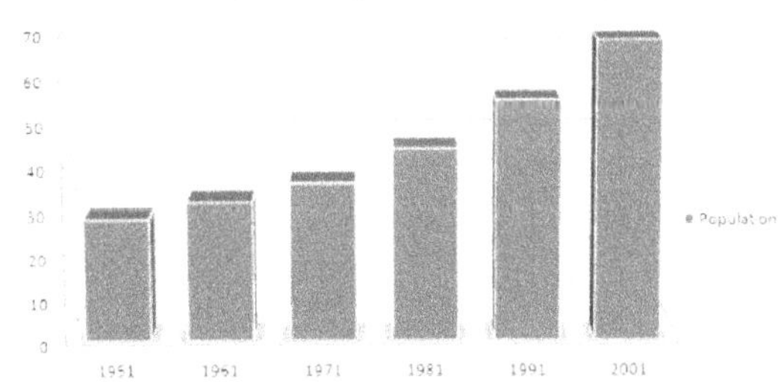

Q.26 The percent increase in population from 1991 to 2001 is:

A. 24.8 crores B. 20 crores
C. 13.6 crores D. 22.9 crores

Q.27 In which census year, the percent increase in population is highest as compared to that in the previous census year?

A. 1971 B. 1981 C. 1991 D. 2001

Q.28 In which census year, the percent increase in population is least as compared to that in the previous census year?

A. 1971 B. 1981 C. 1991 D. 1961

Q.29 Per year increase in population from the year 1951 to 2001 is:

A. 8100000 **B.** 7600000 **C.** 8900000 **D.** 6700000

Q.30 Esc key in a windows keyboard is not used to ________.

A. Close a dialog-box
B. Run a selected command
C. Cancel a command
D. Close a selected drop-down list

Q.31 Which of the following are the demerits of globalization of higher education?

1) Exposure to global curriculum
2) Promotion of elitism in education
3) Commodification of higher education
4) Increase in the cost of education

Select the correct answer from the codes given below:

A. 1 and 4 **B.** 1, 3 and 4
C. 2, 3 and 4 **D.** 1, 2, 3 and 4

Q.32 Which of the following statement/statements is/are true about Nalanda University?

a) Nalanda University is an international university.
b) It is located in Rajgir, Nalanda (Bihar).
c) It was established in November 2016.
d) It came into being by a special Act of the Indian Parliament – a testimony to the important status that Nalanda University occupies in the Indian intellectual landscape.
e) It offers graduate as well as post-graduate courses.

A. a, b, d **B.** a, b, e
C. b, c, d **D.** a, b, c, d, e

Q.33 Name the recent program launched as a part of the National Institute of Opening Schooling (NIOS) for untrained teachers.

A. Diploma in Elementary Education (D . El. Ed)
B. B . Ed.
C. NET
D. TET

Q.34 The Asian College of Journalism is located at ____.

A. Hyderabad **B.** Delhi
C. Chennai **D.** Mumbai

Q.35 Which of the following organizations deals with 'capacity building program' on Educational Planning?

A. NCERT **B.** UGC **C.** NAAC **D.** NUEPA

Q.36 Arrange the following in correct chronological order:

(a) Keshavananda Bharti Case
(b) Golaknath Case
(c) Minerva Mills Case
(d) Sajjan Singh Case

Select the correct answer using the codes given below:

A. (c), (b), (d), (a) **B.** (a), (d), (c), (b)
C. (d), (b), (a), (c) **D.** (b), (d), (c), (a)

Q.37 Which of the following is NOT correctly matched?

A. Public Health and Sanitation; State List
B. Census; Union List
C. Allocation of seats in the Council of States; Second Schedule
D. Anti-Defection; Tenth Schedule

Q.38 Human Rights Day is observed every year on

A. 20th January **B.** 30th December
C. 10th December **D.** 10th November

Q.39 Which of the following is correct about the Central Vigilance Commission?

A. It submits an annual report to the Union Government.
B. It does not have statutory status.
C. It was established in 1952
D. None of the above

Q.40 On the keyboard of the computer each character has an "ASCII" value which stands for:

A. Adaptable Standard Code for Information Change
B. American Stock Code for Information Interchange
C. African Standard Code for Information Interchange
D. American Standard Code for Information Interchange

Q.41 Which part of the Central Processing Unit (CPU) performs the calculation and makes decisions:

A. Alternate Local Unit
B. American Logic Unit
C. Alternating Logic Unit
D. Arithmetic Logic Unit

Q.42 "DPI" stands for:

A. Dots per inch **B.** Digits per unit
C. Dots pixel inch **D.** Diagrams per inch

Q.43 The process of laying out a document with text, graphics, headlines and photographs is involved in:

A. Deck Top Printing
B. Desk Top Printing
C. Deck Top Publishing
D. Desk Top Publishing

Q.44 Transfer of data from one application to another line is known as:

A. Dodgy Data Exchange
B. Dynamic Data Exchange
C. Dynamic Disk Exchange
D. Dogmatic Data Exchange

Q.45 The Chimmini Wildlife Sanctuary (CWS) is located in which state?

A. Uttrakhand **B.** Chhattisgarh
C. Himachal Pradesh **D.** Kerala

Q.46 The Grizzled Squirrel Wildlife Sanctuary (GSWS) is located in which state?

A. Uttrakhand **B.** Tamil Nadu
C. Gujarat **D.** Chhattisgarh

Q.47 The Orang National Park (ONP) is located in which state?

A. Manipur **B.** Mizoram **C.** Tripura **D.** Assam

Q.48 The Bori Wildlife Sanctuary (BWS) is located in which state?

A. Chhattisgarh **B.** Madhya Pradesh
C. Maharashtra **D.** Rajasthan

Q.49 Which of the following was India's First Biosphere Reserves?

A. Sunderbans **B.** Nanda Devi
C. Nilgiri **D.** Pachmarhi

Q.50 On 23 December 2005, the Government of India enacted the Disaster Management Act, which envisaged the creation of the National Disaster Management Authority. Who among the following heads this authority?

A. Home Minister of India
B. Prime Minister of India
C. Defence minister of india
D. President of India

// Smart Answer Sheet //

Correct Indicates percentage of students who answered questions correctly.

Skipped Indicates percentage of students who skipped questions.

Q.	Ans.	Correct	Skipped
1	D	60.98 %	7.31 %
2	C	68.29 %	17.08 %
3	B	58.54 %	17.07 %
4	A	12.2 %	17.07 %
5	D	75.61 %	14.63 %
6	C	60.98 %	17.07 %
7	C	36.59 %	17.07 %
8	A	75.61 %	17.07 %
9	B	39.02 %	17.08 %
10	C	60.98 %	17.07 %
11	D	26.83 %	17.07 %
12	C	60.98 %	17.07 %
13	A	48.78 %	17.07 %
14	C	68.29 %	14.64 %
15	D	60.98 %	17.07 %
16	A	65.85 %	17.08 %
17	B	56.1 %	17.07 %
18	A	68.29 %	14.64 %
19	A	43.9 %	14.64 %
20	C	56.1 %	17.07 %
21	B	70.73 %	17.07 %
22	C	43.9 %	14.64 %
23	C	41.46 %	14.64 %
24	C	46.34 %	17.07 %
25	D	46.34 %	17.07 %
26	C	29.27 %	17.07 %
27	D	63.41 %	14.64 %
28	A	29.27 %	14.63 %
29	A	34.15 %	17.07 %
30	B	58.54 %	17.07 %
31	C	56.1 %	14.63 %
32	A	41.46 %	17.08 %
33	A	65.85 %	17.08 %
34	C	31.71 %	17.07 %
35	D	39.02 %	17.08 %
36	C	41.46 %	17.08 %
37	C	31.71 %	17.07 %
38	C	58.54 %	17.07 %
39	A	58.54 %	17.07 %
40	D	68.29 %	17.08 %
41	D	78.05 %	17.07 %
42	A	56.1 %	17.07 %
43	D	36.59 %	17.07 %
44	B	58.54 %	17.07 %
45	D	46.34 %	17.07 %
46	B	29.27 %	17.07 %
47	D	41.46 %	17.08 %
48	B	46.34 %	17.07 %
49	C	36.59 %	17.07 %
50	B	41.46 %	17.08 %

Performance Analysis	
Avg. Score (%)	44.0%
Toppers Score (%)	94.0%
Your Score	

//Hints and Solutions//

1. A good communicator mostly begins his/her presentation with an ice breaker.

• Ice breaker can be any game or an activity which is used to introduce people to each other and to make them feel relaxed and comfortable.

• It is an effective way to begin a presentation or training session.

• Beginning with a complex question, repetitive phrase, or non-sequitur is not a good idea.

Hence, the correct option is (D).

2. • The interaction between teacher and students should create a sense of development between both the parties. Both of them should gain from the interaction.

• The interaction should neither create any difference between them nor any confusion.

• Even distortion of information should not take place between their interaction.

Hence, the correct option is (C).

3. Here the question mentioned in option (B) could be the best to know about the student's thinking as it is an open-ended question which:

- Discourages one-word answers.
- Provides detailed qualitative information.
- Requires an answer with proper explanation.
- Promotes divergent thinking, creativity and ingenuity.

Hence, the correct option is (B).

4. Communicative abilities include those skills which are defined with reference to the manner and mode in which the system is realized in use. Communicative abilities embrace linguistic skills but not the reverse. Essentially, they are ways of creating or recreating discourse in different modes.

Hence, the correct option is (A).

5. Sunlight and fresh air keep us healthy, thus a house should be made in such a way that it has an abundance of both.

Hence, the correct option is (D).

6. Characteristics of papers:

Power of news-situated substance: There are three kinds of content in papers: news, perspectives, and commercials. Of these news eclipses, the others since documents are principally implied for the dispersal of news.

Standard periodicity: Newspapers might be distributed day by day or week by week. Periodicity may shift, be that as it may, consistency ought to be kept. Each paper maintains a specific consistency in distribution.

The decision of the season of utilization: Unlike TV and radio, we can peruse papers whenever. Some read in the first part of the day while others at night after work. This office builds the fame of documents

Minimal effort: Compared to other media, the paper is a practical medium. Anyone can bear the cost of paper and use all over. Electronic media requires control supply and the new media need advanced innovation.

Literary medium: Text is the spirit of papers; however, they convey pictures and designs.

Hence, the high cost is not a characteristic of newspapers.

Hence, the correct option is (C).

7. The research conference is a meeting for researchers to present and discuss their creative ideas and work at a large level. The conference inculcates creativity and critical thinking among the participants more than the seminars, workshops, research summary.

Hence, the correct option is (C).

8. Following are the characteristics of the learner which facilitates the teaching-learning system to become effective are:

a) Prior or previous experience of the learner facilitates the teaching-learning process a lot because without students' good previous knowledge or learning a good teaching-learning process does not take place.

b) Aptitude of a learner: Student talent, behavior, or aptitude facilitates the teaching-learning process effectively.

c) Stage of development of a learner also affects the teaching-learning process if the learners are at the preschool level. His/her physical and intellectual development takes place very rapidly in comparison to another stage of development.

Hence, the correct option is (A).

9. There are several merits of radio as a source of communication as it is easily accessible, not much infrastructure or setup is needed for receivers.

It is very handy i.e. portable it can be carried anywhere i.e. it can be used on the way anywhere.

The only demerit mention in the option of the question is that it has a one-way communication system.

For example, if one is listening to the topic of any subject being taught on the radio then it is impossible for one to clear the doubts at the same time.

Hence, the correct option is (B).

10. Synchronous media takes place in real-time and the audience is present when media is broadcasted or performed. This media helps to share the information at the same time i.e. information broadcasting and the audience is present at the same time to receive the information.

Hence, the correct option is (C).

11. The project method is a learning method where the participation of the student is maximum in comparison to the teacher and the students here is an active learner. Students here find the solution by themselves to assigned projects. Students learn how to solve real-life problems with co-operation with each other.

Hence, the correct option is (D).

12.

- Semantic barriers to communication are often caused by the use of different languages.
- Low proficiency in the local language will cause semantic barriers to communication in the classroom.

Hence, the correct option is (C).

13. Verbal communication: verbal means the use of words in the communication process and in the design and formulation of messages. In verbal communication, the message is transmitted verbally, i.e, by making use of words, such as oral and written.

Hence, the correct option is (A).

14. The quality of teaching can be reflected in the best way through the quality of questions asked by the student. The quality of student's questions reflects the interest level and curiosity level of a student during the teaching-learning process.

The questions of the students give the teacher an idea about how much their student is grasping the content taught by the teacher which further allows the teacher to improve their teaching skills in order to make teaching more effective. Quality questions asked by the students ensures an effective teaching-learning process.

Hence, the correct option is (C).

15. Teaching effectiveness can be affected by the education system of the country. The education system of the country is divided into three main categories i.e. primary, secondary, and tertiary. Primary education covers the elementary prospects of the education system, secondary covers 10th, and 12th level while the tertiary level of the education covers graduate, postgraduate, and doctorate level courses. If all the three levels of education function well then only the education system should be improved in our country.

Hence, the correct option is (D).

16. This series follows the following sequence:

$$1 + 5 = 6$$

$$6 + 9 = 15$$

$$15 + 13 = 28$$

$$28 + 17 = 45$$

$$45 + 21 = 66$$

Therefore, 66 will be the next number.

Hence, the correct option is (A).

17. The pattern followed by first letter:

A + 3 = D,

D + 4 = H,

H+ 5 = M,

M + 6 = S,

The pattern followed by Second letter:

B + 5 = G,

G + 6 = M,

M + 7 = T,

T + 8 = B,

The pattern followed by Third letter:

D + 7 = K,

K+ 8 = S,

S + 9 = B,

B +10 = L,

Hence, the correct option is (B).

18. The Rig Veda provides ample evidence to prove the concept of equality of woman with men as regards access and capacity to acquire the highest knowledge. Both the assertion and reason are true and the reason given supports the assertion statement.

Hence, the correct option is (A).

19.

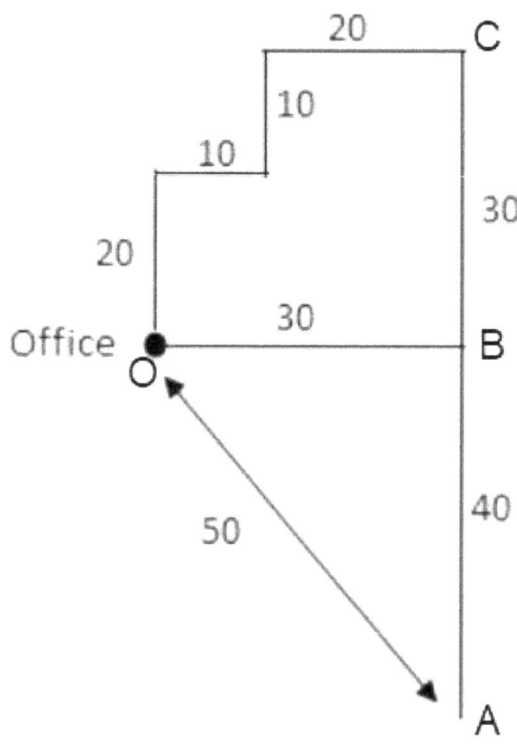

The distance between A and B is,

$$CB = CA - AB$$

$$AB = CA - CB$$

$$AB = 70 - 30 = 40 \text{ m}$$

On using Pythagoras theorem, we can find the distance between the office and the postman,

Let us take office as O.

$$OA = \sqrt{OB^2 + AB^2}$$

$$= \sqrt{30^2 + 40^2}$$

$$= \sqrt{900 + 1600}$$

$$= \sqrt{2500}$$

$$OA = 50 \text{ m}$$

Hence, the correct option is (A).

20. The AGMARK Head Office at Faridabad (Haryana) is legally enforced in India by the Agricultural Produce (Grading and Marking) Act of 1937 (and amended in 1986).

Hence, the correct option is (C).

21. According to qustion:

Y + 2 = W , E + 1 = F , B + 2 = D

W + 2 = U , F + 2 = H , D + 3 = G

U + 2 = S , H + 3 = K ,G + 2 = I

S + 2 = Q , K + 4 = O , I + 3 = L

So, QOL is the next term in the series.

Hence, the correct option is (B).

22. Communication is the act of conveying messages that contain certain meanings or actions and effective communication means that the sender and receiver both regard the same meaning to a particular message.

Hence, the correct option is (C).

23. Full-time Organisational Framework. In Addition to PM as its Chairman it will comprise:

A) Vice-Chairperson—to be appointed by the PM.

B) Members: all as full-time.

C) Part-time Members: maximum of 2, From leading universities, research Organizations and other relevant institutions in an ex-officio capacity. Part time members will be on a rotational basis.

D) Ex-Officio Members: maximum of 4 members of the Union Council Of Ministers to be nominated by the PM.

E) Chief Executive Officer: to be Appointed by the PM for a fixed Tenure, in the rank of Secretary to the Government of India.

F) Secretariat: as deemed necessary.

Hence, the correct option is (C).

24.

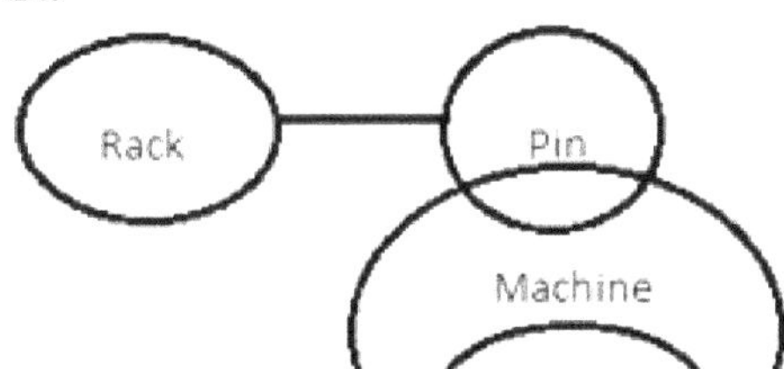

Hence, the correct option is (C).

25. System software is the set of programs that enables your computer's hardware devices and application software to work together.

Hence, the correct option is (D).

26. According to the given data,

The population in $1991 = 54.80$

The population in $2001 = 68.40$

So, the increase in Population

$= 68.40 - 54.80$

$= 13.6$ crores

Hence, the correct option is (C).

27. The percent increase in population is highest as compared to that in the previous census year is in $2001 = 24.8$

Hence, the correct option is (D).

28. The percent increase in population is least as compared to that in the previous census years is in 1971

$= [(36.14 \times 31.85) \times 100]$

$= 13.47\%$

Hence, the correct option is (A).

29. Per year increase in population from the year 1951 to 2001 is:

$= 68.40 - 27.90$

$= 40.5$ crores

So, the annual increase

$= \frac{40.5}{50}$ crores

$= \frac{40.5 \times 10000000}{50}$

$= 8100000$

Hence, the correct option is (A).

30. Esc key in a windows keyboard is not used to Run a selected command. The key (frequently labeled Esc) found on most computer keyboards and used for any of various functions, as to interrupt or cancel the current process or running program, or to close a pop-up window.

Hence, the correct option is (B).

31. Demerits of globalization of higher education are as follows:

- Promotion of elitism in higher education
- The commodification of higher education (It has become a saleable commodity)
- Increase in the cost of education (not affordable by everyone to study abroad)

Hence, the correct option is (C).

32.

- Nalanda University, an international university was established in November 2010.
- The University came into existence by a special Act of the Indian Parliament.
- It is located in Rajgir, Nalanda.
- Currently, it offers master's courses (postgraduate) only.

Hence, the correct option is (A).

33. It is a quality program of the National Institute of Open Schooling (NIOS) for in-service untrained teachers, which would provide a Diploma in Elementary Education (D. El. Ed). So far, 15 lakh teachers have enrolled. It is a Teacher Training Program designed for all untrained government, government-aided, and private unaided recognized in-service untrained teachers of elementary schools. With an aim to improve the education system, by training approximately 15 lakh untrained teachers by 31st March 2019.

Hence, the correct option is (A).

34. The Asian College of Journalism (ACJ) is a journalism school in Chennai, India, which offers postgraduate diploma courses in journalism.

Hence, the correct option is (C).

35. The National University of Educational Planning and Administration (NUEPA) is a premier organization dealing with capacity building and research in planning and management of education in India as well as in South Asia also.

Hence, the correct option is (D).

36. Sajjan Singh v. State of Rajasthan case 1965 conferred that parliament can amend any part of the Constitution. However, it was reversed in the 1967 Golaknath case that held that the Fundamental rights cannot be amended. In the 1973 case of Kesavananda Bharti, it held the basic structure doctrine. In the Minvera Mills v. Union of India case, the supreme court struck down the 39th amendment and deleted parts of the 42nd amendment.

Hence, the correct option is (C).

37. Correctly matched pairs in the given options are

A) Public Health and Sanitation State List

B) Census Union List

C) Anti-Defection Tenth Schedule

D) Allocation of seats in the Council of States is provided in the fourth schedule of the Indian constitution.

Hence, the correct option is (C).

38. On 10th December 1948, the Declaration of Human Rights was adopted by the General Assembly of the United Nations. Since then 10th December is observed as Human Rights Day.

Hence, the correct option is (C).

39. Central Vigilance Commission:-

1. It submits an annual report to the Union Government.

2. It is aimed at preventing corruption and was established by an executive resolution of Union Government in 1964.

3. Santhanam Committee on the Prevention of Corruption (1962-64) recommended its formation.

4. It was only recently in 2003 that a law was passed giving statutory status to CVC. This authorized the CVC as the 'Designated Agency' to receive written complaints about the disclosure on any allegation of corruption or misuse of office and recommend appropriate action.

Hence, the correct option is (A).

40. Stands for "American Standard Code for Information Interchange." ASCII is a character encoding that uses numeric codes to represent characters. These include upper and lowercase English letters, numbers, and punctuation symbols.

Hence, the correct option is (D).

41. An arithmetic-logic unit (ALU) is the part of a computer processor (CPU) that carries out arithmetic and logic operations on the operands in computer instruction words. In some processors, the ALU is divided into two units, an arithmetic unit (AU) and a logic unit (LU).

Hence, the correct option is (D).

42. DPI stands for 'dots per inch' – the number of little printed dots there is in an inch of your printed document. The larger the DPI, the larger the number of dots and therefore the clearer the print.

Hence, the correct option is (A).

43. Desk Top Publishing is the use of the computer and software to create visual displays of ideas and information. Desktop publishing documents may be for desktop or commercial printing or electronic distribution, including PDF, slideshows, email newsletters, electronic books, and the Web.

Hence, the correct option is (D).

44. Dynamic Data Exchange (DDE) is an interprocess communication system that allows data to be communicated or shared between the applications in operating systems such as

Windows. Dynamic Data Exchange makes use of shared memory and a set of commands, message formats, and protocols for communication and sharing.

Hence, the correct option is (B).

45. The Chimmini Wildlife Sanctuary (CWS) is located along the Western Ghats in Mukundapuram taluk of Thrissur District of Kerala. The sanctuary is an important bird area with 192 recorded avian species such as grey-headed bulbul, Indian rufous babbler, white-bellied blue-flycatcher, Ceylon frogmouth, Indian edible-nest swiftlet, Malabar trogon, and Loten's sunbird. The sanctuary also offers trekking paths for the adventure traveler.

Hence, the correct option is (D).

46. The Grizzled Squirrel Wildlife Sanctuary (GSWS) is located in the Virudhunagar and Madurai districts of Tamil Nadu and covers an area of 485.2 sq Kms. Over 240+ species of birds are seen in this sanctuary including 14 species of birds endemic to the Western Ghats, such as the critically endangered Oriental white-backed vulture and the long-billed vulture. In addition to grizzled giant squirrels, the sanctuary is home to numerous animals such as barking deer, bonnet macaque, common langur, elephants, flying squirrels, gaur, Indian giant squirrel, leopard, lion-tailed macaques, mouse deer, Nilgiri langur, and Nilgiri Tahrs. There are over 220 species of butterflies including many rare and endemic species. Some of the rare butterflies spotted here include Eversheds ace, Silver royal, Orange awlet, Hampsons hedge blue, etc.

Hence, the correct option is (B).

47. The Orang National Park (ONP) is located on the north bank of the Brahmaputra River in the Darrang and Sonitpur districts of Assam and covers an area of 78.81 square kilometers. The park has rich flora and fauna, including great Indian one-horned rhinoceros, pigmy hog, elephants, wild buffalo, and tigers. It is the only stronghold of rhinoceros on the north bank of the Brahmaputra river.

Hence, the correct option is (D).

48. The Bori Wildlife Sanctuary (BWS) is located in Hoshangabad District of Madhya Pradesh and covers an area of 518 square kilometers. It is an important transition zone between the forests of western and eastern India. The sanctuary is mostly covered in mixed deciduous and bamboo forests, part of the Eastern Highlands moist deciduous forests eco-region. It is home to tiger, leopard, wild boar, muntjac deer, gaur, chital deer, etc.

Hence, the correct option is (B).

49. Nilgiri Biosphere Reserve located in Tamil Nadu, Kerala, and Karnataka was the first biosphere reserve established in 1986.

Hence, the correct option is (C).

50. The Disaster Management Act, 2005 received the Presidential assent on 23 December 2005. It envisaged the creation of the National Disaster Management Authority with not more than nine members (including a Vice-Chairperson) and the Prime Minister of India as its chairperson.

Hence, the correct option is (B).

Mock Test 11

Q.1 As per Article 54, the President shall be elected by the members of an electoral college consisting of:

A. The elected members of Lok Sabha
B. The elected members of Rajya Sabha
C. The elected members of the Legislative Assembly
D. All of them

Q.2 Which of the following is not a private university?

A. Alliance University, Bangalore
B. Vinoba Bhave University, Bihar
C. Sri Sai University, Himachal Pradesh
D. Sharda University, Uttar Pradesh

Q.3 Who secured the lowest rank in The Human Development Report 2018?

A. Afghanistan **B.** Congo
C. Niger **D.** Kenya

Q.4 What was the rank of India in the Human Development Index 2018?

A. 142nd **B.** 136th **C.** 140th **D.** 130th

Q.5 Which of the following statements are correct in respect of NITI Aayog?

1) It is a constitutional body.
2) It is a statutory body.
3) It is neither a constitutional body nor a statutory body.
4) It is a think-tank.

Select the correct answer from the codes given below:

A. 1 and 4 **B.** 2 and 4
C. 3 and 4 **D.** 2, 3 and 4

Q.6 The components of a research design are:

(a) Comparison
(b) Control
(c) Reactivity
(d) Manipulation
(e) Non-representativeness
(f) Generalisation

A. (c), (d), (e) and (f) **B.** (b), (c), (d) and (e)
C. (a), (b), (d) and (f) **D.** (a), (c), (e) and (f)

Q.7 The table given below represents which type of the following frequencies?

Class (Marks)	Frequency
0-10	10
10-20	12
20-30	18

A. Grouped Frequency Distribution
B. Ungrouped Frequency Distribution
C. Cumulative Frequency Distribution
D. None of the above

Q.8 Which of the following is not true about the research problem?

I. A research problem is the research question which a researcher wants to solve.
II. A research problem should not be vague.
III. Research questions around social inequality should be avoided because they are sensitive.
IV. The researcher should have some knowledge about the topic one has chosen.

A. I, II, and III **B.** II, III, and IV
C. I, II, and IV **D.** All the above

Q.9 Which of the following research types focuses on ameliorating the prevailing situations?

[UGC NET Sociology, 2017]

A. Fundamental Research
B. Applied Research
C. Action Research
D. Experimental Research

Q.10 Which among the following is not the characteristic of research?

A. It is a scientific and systematic inquiry
B. It aims at finding new information
C. It helps to formulate new theories and concepts
D. It is limited to the academic domain

Q.11 Which of the following statement/s about the Applied research is/are correct?

I. Applied research is used to solve a practical problem.
II. It can be used to solve problems of the education system of developing countries.
III. Applied research is action-oriented.
IV. Applied research is also called fundamental research.

A. Only I **B.** I and II
C. I, II, and III **D.** None

Q.12 In finalizing a thesis writing format which of the following would form part of supplementary pages?

[UGC NET Sociology, 2017]

A. List of tables and figures
B. Table of contents
C. Conclusions of the study
D. Bibliography and Appendices

Q.13 Which of the following traditional textile motif is closely related to the embroidery art form of Gujarat and Sindh?

A. Chikankari of Lucknow
B. Kantha of West Bengal
C. Pipli Applique Work
D. Rajasthani Embroidery

Q.14 Which of the following factors are included in the theory Proposed by EL Thorndike?

A. Abstract intelligence
B. Concrete (technical) intelligence
C. Social intelligence
D. All of these

Q.15 A college-level assistant professor has planned his/her lectures with an intent to develop cognitive dimensions of students centered on skills of analysis and synthesis. Below, given are two sets of items Set – I consisting of levels of cognitive interchange and Set – II comprising basic requirements for promoting them. Match the two sets and indicate your answer by choosing the correct alternative from the code:

Set - I	Set - II
(Levels of Cognitive Interchange)	**(Basic requirements for promoting cognitive interchange)**
a. Memory level	i. Giving the opportunity for discriminating examples and non-examples of a point.
b. Understanding level	ii. Recording the important points made during the presentations.
c. Reflective level	iii. Asking the students to discuss various items of information.
	iv. Critically analyzing the points to be made and discussed.

A. a-ii b-iv c-i　　**B.** a-iii b-iv c-ii
C. a-ii b-i c-iv　　**D.** a-i b-ii c-iii

Q.16 Which of the following is a very popular art form is practiced by the Lohana Community?

A. Chamba Handkerchief
B. Banni and Heer Bharat
C. Kutch and Kathiawar Embroidery
D. Bagh Kashidakari

Q.17 Which one of the following statements is correct in the context of multiple–choice type questions?

A. They are more objective than true-false type questions.
B. They are less objective than essay type questions.
C. They are more subjective than short-answer type questions.
D. They are more subjective than true-false type questions.

Q.18 Which of the following is a signature art form of the tribal community of Gujarat?

A. Chamba Handkerchief
B. Banni and Heer Bharat
C. Kutch and Kathiawar Embroidery
D. Bagh Kashidakari

Q.19 Which of the following art form is believed to be auspicious, a symbol of happiness, prosperity, and Suhag of a married woman?

A. Phulkari of Punjab
B. Bagh Kashidakari
C. Kashida
D. Banni and Heer Bharat

Q.20 The missing term in series $1,4,27,16,?,36,343,$ is

A. 30　　**B.** 49　　**C.** 125　　**D.** 81

Q.21 Pointing to a photograph, a man said, "I have no brother, and that man's father is my father's son." Whose photograph was it?

A. His son　　**B.** His own
C. His father　　**D.** His nephew

Q.22 The STC rating is used to evaluate ________ of a space or material?

A. The flame resistance
B. The light refraction
C. The acoustical quality
D. The structural limit

Q.23 Which of the following is a non-Climacteric type of fruit?

A. Pineapple　　**B.** Litchi
C. Grape　　**D.** All of these

Q.24 Which is the staple vegetable in the Indian diet?

A. Tomato　　**B.** Cauliflower
C. Potato　　**D.** Chilli

Q.25 In pre-cooling, water is mostly removed by:

A. Convection　　**B.** Conduction
C. Radiation　　**D.** None of these

Q.26 At present, a person is 4 times older than his son and is 3 years older than his wife. After 3 years the age of the son will be 15 years. The age of the person's wife after 5 years will be:

A. 42　　**B.** 48　　**C.** 45　　**D.** 50

Q.27 Which of the following TCP/IP Internet protocol is diskless machine uses to obtain its IP address from a server?

A. RARP　　**B.** RIP　　**C.** ARP　　**D.** X.25

Q.28 A network that uses different technologies can be connected by using

A. Packets　　**B.** Switches　　**C.** Bridges　　**D.** Routers

Q.29 In the digital era, there is a fear that classroom communication may result in:

A. Stimulation　　**B.** passive adaptation
C. Quick adaptation　　**D.** Over-stimulation

Q.30 What of the following statements correctly defines the term gesticulation?

A. Use of gestures while speaking
B. Use of gestures while listening
C. Use of gestures while conversing
D. All of the above

Q.31 Which one of the following is the physical barrier to non-verbal communication?

A. Body language　　**B.** Stereotyping
C. Denotation　　**D.** Interpretation

Ques (32-35):Direction: Following data shows the percentage distribution of students in six different universities and the percentage distribution of boys and girls in each university. Study the data carefully and answer the question that follows.

Universities	% of students	% of boys	% of girls
A	12	55	45
B	15	60	40
C	8	40	70
D	28	75	25
E	17	20	80
F	20	64	36

Q.32 The ratio of the number of girls in university B to that of the number of boys in university D is:

A. $8:15$ **B.** $2:7$
C. $4:5$ **D.** Data inadequate

Q.33 The number of students in which university is the same as the total number of students in university A and university C together?

A. B **B.** F
C. C **D.** Data inadequate

Q.34 The number of students in university D is what percent more than that of university F?

A. 8% **B.** 22% **C.** 40% **D.** 55%

Q.35 The average number of students in a university is:

A. 750 **B.** 680
C. 435 **D.** Data inadequate

Q.36 Direction: Select the correct option according to the Assertion (A) and Reason (R).

Assertion (A): Teacher communication is central to classroom management.

Reason (R): Teacher communication behaviors should not be used to regulate the classroom behavior of students.

A. Both (A) and (R) are true
B. (A) is true, but (R) is false
C. Both (A) and (R) are true, but (R) is not the correct explanation of (A)
D. (A) is false, but (R) is true

Q.37 The term "Grapevine Communication" is related to

A. Formal Communication
B. Informal Communication
C. Written Communication
D. Vertical Communication

Q.38 In order to avoid catastrophic consequences of climate change, there is general agreement among the countries of the world to limit the rise in the average surface temperature of the earth compared to that of pre-industrial times by

A. 1.5°C to 2°C **B.** 2.0°C to 3.5°C
C. 0.5°C to 1.0°C **D.** 0.25°C to 0.5°C

Q.39 Match Set-1 and Set-2 and select the correct answer from the codes given below:

Set-1	Set-2
(a) Flood	1. Lack of rainfall of sufficient duration
(b) Drought	2. Tremors produced by the passage of vibratory waves through the rocks of the earth
(c) Earthquake	3. A vent through which molted substances come out
(d) Volcano	4. Excess rain and uneven distribution of water

A. (a)-4 (b)-1 (c)-2 (d)-3
B. (a)-2 (b)-3 (c)-4 (d)-1
C. (a)-3 (b)-4 (c)-2 (d)-1
D. (a)-4 (b)-3 (c)-1 (d)-2

Q.40 Which of the following statement is true with respect to the Phillips curve?

A. The Phillips curve shows the relationship between unemployment and inflation in an economy
B. The downward sloping curve of the Phillips curve is generally held to be valid only in the short run
C. Both (A) and (B)
D. None of the above

Q.41 Which of the following organizations brings out the publication known as 'World Economic Outlook'?

A. The International Monetary Fund
B. The United Nations Development Programme
C. The World Economic Forum
D. The World Bank

Q.42 Which of the following sequences of research steps is nearer to the scientific method?

A. Suggested solution of the problem, Deducing the consequences of the solution, Perceiving the problem situation, Location of the difficulty, and testing the solutions
B. Perceiving the problem situation, Locating the actual problem and its definition, Hypothesizing, Deducing the consequences of the suggested solution, and Testing the hypothesis in action
C. Defining a problem, Identifying the cause of the problem, defining a population, drawing a sample, collecting data, and Analysing results
D. Identifying the causal factors, Defining the problem, developing a hypothesis, selecting a sample, collecting data, and arriving at generalizations and Conclusions

Q.43 Which of the following set of statements best describes the nature and objectives of teaching?

Indicate your answer by selecting from the code.

1) Teaching and learning are integrally related.

2) There is no difference between teaching and training.

3) Concern of all teaching is to ensure some kind of transformation in students.

4) All good teaching is formal in nature.

5) A teacher is a senior person.

6) Teaching is a social act whereas learning is a personal act.

Code:

A. 1, 2 and 4 **B.** 2, 3 and 5
C. 1, 3 and 6 **D.** 4, 5 and 6

Q.44 Who developed the process of canning?

A. Nicolas Appert **B.** Louis Pasteur
C. Norman Borlaug **D.** Walter Hesse

Q.45 Find the average of the first 15 prime numbers?
A. 29.23 **B.** 18.77 **C.** 21.86 **D.** 19.5

Q.46 If cost price of 21 oranges is equal to the selling price of 18 oranges then profit percent is
A. $7\frac{1}{7}$ **B.** $5\frac{5}{9}$ **C.** $14\frac{2}{7}$ **D.** $7\frac{1}{3}$

Q.47 If A, B, and C can do a piece of work in 10 days. 5 days work of A is equal to 4 days work of B, C alone can do the same work in 20 days. In how many days A alone can do the same work.
A. 45 days **B.** 40 days **C.** 36 days **D.** 60 days

Q.48 A sum of money amounts to Rs. 4624 in 2 years and to Rs. 4913 in 3 years at compound interest. The sum is..
A. Rs. 4096 **B.** Rs. 4260 **C.** Rs. 4325 **D.** Rs. 4360

Q.49 The cost price of 20 articles is the same as the selling price of X articles. If the profit is 25%, then the value of X is :
A. 16 **B.** 18 **C.** 25 **D.** 15

Q.50 A person sells a table at 12.5% profit and a chair at a loss of 8.33% but on the whole, he has a profit of Rs. 25 on the other hand, if he sells the table at a loss of 8.33% and chair at a profit of 12.5, he neither gains nor loses. Find the cost price of the table?
A. 600 **B.** 500 **C.** 450 **D.** 360

// Smart Answer Sheet //

Correct Indicates percentage of students who answered questions correctly.

Skipped Indicates percentage of students who skipped questions.

Q.	Ans.	Correct	Skipped
1	D	41.67 %	2.08 %
2	B	35.42 %	47.91 %
3	C	12.5 %	47.92 %
4	D	20.83 %	50.0 %
5	C	22.92 %	47.91 %
6	C	37.5 %	47.92 %
7	A	27.08 %	50.0 %
8	C	8.33 %	47.92 %
9	C	25.0 %	50.0 %
10	D	47.92 %	47.91 %
11	C	35.42 %	45.83 %
12	D	31.25 %	47.92 %
13	D	18.75 %	47.92 %
14	D	27.08 %	47.92 %
15	C	27.08 %	47.92 %
16	B	18.75 %	47.92 %
17	A	29.17 %	50.0 %
18	C	39.58 %	47.92 %
19	A	29.17 %	47.91 %
20	C	39.58 %	47.92 %
21	A	20.83 %	47.92 %
22	C	22.92 %	50.0 %
23	C	12.5 %	47.92 %
24	C	31.25 %	50.0 %
25	B	18.75 %	50.0 %
26	D	29.17 %	50.0 %
27	A	22.92 %	47.91 %
28	D	29.17 %	50.0 %
29	D	22.92 %	47.91 %
30	A	6.25 %	47.92 %
31	A	29.17 %	47.91 %
32	B	12.5 %	47.92 %
33	B	33.33 %	45.84 %
34	C	22.92 %	47.91 %
35	D	31.25 %	47.92 %
36	B	20.83 %	47.92 %
37	B	41.67 %	47.91 %
38	A	22.92 %	50.0 %
39	A	43.75 %	50.0 %
40	C	39.58 %	50.0 %
41	A	20.83 %	50.0 %
42	B	14.58 %	50.0 %
43	C	39.58 %	50.0 %
44	A	20.83 %	47.92 %
45	C	25.0 %	50.0 %
46	C	29.17 %	47.91 %
47	A	14.58 %	50.0 %
48	A	20.83 %	47.92 %
49	A	16.67 %	47.91 %
50	D	6.25 %	50.0 %

Performance Analysis	
Avg. Score (%)	30.0%
Toppers Score (%)	100.0%
Your Score	

//Hints and Solutions//

1. The President of India is elected by the Members of an Electoral College consisting of:

(a) The elected members of both Houses of Parliament.

(b) The elected members ofthe Legislative Assemblies of the States [including National Capital Territory of Delhiand the Union Territory of Puducherry vide the Constitution (Seventieth Amendment)Act, 1992] (Article 54).

The members nominated to either House of Parliament orthe Legislative Assemblies of State including NCT of Delhi and Union Territory ofPuducherry is not eligible to be included in the Electoral College.

Hence, the correct option is (D).

2. All of the given options are private universities except Vinoba Bhave University. Vinoba Bhave University is a state public university. Vinoba Bhave University was established on 17 September 1992. It has the affiliation of approx 70 UG institutions and other professional and vocational institutions from the entire state.

In the Indian higher education sector, universities are classified into four types depending on the manner in which they were set up.

These are :

- Central Universities
- State Universities
- Deemed Universities
- Private Universities

Hence, the correct option is (B).

3. Looking at 2018 results, Norway, Switzerland, Australia, Ireland, and Germany lead the HDI ranking of 189 countries and territories, while Niger, the Central African Republic, South Sudan, Chad, and Burundi have the lowest scores in the HDI's measurement of national achievements in health, education, and income.

Hence, the correct option is (C).

4. India's HDI value for 2019 is 0.645 which puts it in the medium human development category. India has been positioned at 131 out of 189 countries and territories, according to the report. India had ranked 130 in 2018 in the index.
Hence, the correct option is (D).

5. NITI Aayog or the National Institutions for Transforming India is neither a constitutional body (deriving powers, functions from constitution) nor a statutory body passed through the act of parliament.

NITI Aayog has never been passed as an act of Parliament nor it has been mentioned anywhere in the Constitution thus it's definitely neither statutory nor a constitutional body. NITI Aayog is being seen as a think-tank that will foster cooperative federalism rather than take a top-down approach.

Hence, the correct option is (C).

6. Comparison, control, manipulation, and generalization are essential to research design. But reactivity in research is caused when the participant is aware of the research purpose. We seek representativeness in a good research design, not non-representativeness.
Hence, the correct option is (C).

7. A grouped frequency distribution is the organizing of raw data in table form, using classes (Class intervals) and frequencies. In an ungrouped frequency distribution, the data is given as individual data points. On the other hand, Cumulative frequency is the sum of the class and all classes below it in a frequency distribution. Thus, the above table represents the Grouped Frequency Distribution.

Hence, the correct option is (A).

8. All the statements are true except option C. Sensitive topics should also be explored because they might benefit society in some manner.

A research problem is a definite or clear expression [statement] about an area of concern, a condition to be improved upon, a difficulty to be eliminated, or a troubling question that exists in scholarly literature, in theory, or within existing practice that points to a need for meaningful understanding and deliberate investigation. A research problem does not state how to do something, offer a vague or broad proposition, or present a value question.

Hence, the correct option is (C).

9. Action research is a type of research that was started to solve an immediate problem or prevailing problems whereas the remaining types of research are for other purposes such as:

- Fundamental research aims to improve scientific theories for improved understanding.
- Experimental research is a study that strictly adheres to a scientific research design.
- Applied Research aims to apply the theories into practice.

Hence, the correct option is (C).

10. Research is a systematic and scientific inquiry to find new information. One reason for conducting research is to develop and evaluate concepts and theories. However, it is not just limited to the academic domain. It is quite a valuable activity for economic, social, political, and cultural domains as well.
Hence, the correct option is (D).

11. Applied research is used to solve a specific, practical problem of an individual or a group. This particular kind of research is used in business, medicine, and education in order to find solutions that may cure diseases, solve scientific problems, or develop technology.

Applied Research can be defined as research that encompasses the real-life application of natural science. It is directed towards providing a solution to specific practical problems and develop innovative technology.

In finer terms, it is the research that can be applied to real-life situations. It studies a particular set of circumstances, so as to relate the results to its corresponding circumstances.

Hence, the correct option is (C).

12. In finalizing a thesis writing format Bibliography and Appendices would form part of supplementary pages.

List of References/Bibliography: The list of references contains only the details of those works cited in the text. It includes sources not cited in the main text matter but is relevant to the subject of study, specifically in case of larger dissertations or thesis. Small research projects may need just a reference section to include all the literature that has been referred to in the report.

Appendices: The appendices help the author to authenticate the thesis and help the reader to check the data. The material that is usually put in the appendices is Original data, Long tables, Long quotations, Supportive legal decisions, laws, and documents, Illustrative material, Extensive computations, Questionnaires and letters, Schedules or forms used in collecting data, Case studies/histories, and Transcripts of interviews.

Hence, the correct option is (D).

13. Rajasthani Embroidery is closely related to the embroidery art form of Gujarat and Sindh. It is an ancient craft, which has transformed over time to reflect the prevailing social, material, and sometimes even the political mood of the times.

The term 'Motif' refers to a design or figure that consists of recurring shapes or colours, as in architecture or decoration. India is a land of diverse culture which also provided ample space for the evolution of diverse traditions of handicraft. They varied according to the place and geographical conditions.

Hence, the correct option is (D).

14. The multi-factor theory of intelligence was proposed by EL Thorndike. According to Thorndike, intelligence is not a single factor like general intelligence rather it is a combination of multiple factors. It includes abstract, concrete, and social intelligence.

Hence, the correct option is (D).

15. Memory level is a thoughtless and first level of teaching. It is concerned with mental ability or memory. It records the important points made during the presentations.

An understanding level helps to grasp the opinion, to perceives and comprehend the meaning. Also gives an opportunity for discriminating examples and non-examples of a point.

The reflective level includes deep thinking about something. It involves critically analyzing the points to be made and discussed.

Hence, the correct option is (C).

16. Banni and Heer Bharat are practiced by the Lohana community (Master of Swords' are an Indo-Aryan ethnic group). It is famous for its richness in color blending, color pallets, and design patterns.

Lohan as or 'Master of Swords' are an Indo-Aryan ethnic group and are a Suryavanshi Kshatriya community of India that originated in Iran and Afghanistan. In India, they mainly reside in Gujarat, Mumbai and other parts of the country. They have also spread to all parts of the world. It is a Pashtun sub-tribe of the Ghilzai tribe.

Hence, the correct option is (B).

17. Multiple-choice questions don't include subjective questions. So, option (C) and (D) doesn't follow. Also, the essay type questions are too lengthy to become multiple-choice questions. Therefore, option (B) is also eliminated. Now, it is clear that the multiple-choice type questions will have more objective than true-false type questions.

Hence, the correct option is (A).

18. Kutch and Kathiawar Embroidery is a signature art form of the tribal community of Kutch and Kathiawar (Gujarat). This art form is generally done in six styles: Suf, khaarek, paako, Rabari, Garasia Jat, and Mutava.

Hence, the correct option is (C).

19. Phulkari of Punjab is one of the famous embroidery traditions of Punjab. It is believed to be auspicious, a symbol of happiness, prosperity, and Suhag of a married woman. Phulkari has always played an important role in the lives of Punjabi girls. It was more like a precious personal gift meant for special family occasions, be it to welcome a newborn into the family or to gift the daughter during her nuptial ceremony. Traditional Phulkaris not only reflect the versatility, hard work, and creativity of the rural women but also represents the tradition and culture of Punjab.

Hence, the correct option is (A).

20. Pattern of the given series is:

$$1^3 = 1$$
$$2^2 = 4$$
$$3^3 = 27$$
$$4^2 = 16$$
$$5^3 = 125$$
$$6^2 = 36$$
$$7^3 = 343$$

So, the missing term is 125.

Hence, the correct option is (C).

21. The narrator has no brother, so he is the only son of his father, and his father's son is he himself. Hence, the narrator is the father of the man in the photograph, so the man in the photograph is his son.

Hence, the correct option is (A).

22. The Sound transmission class (STC) is used to evaluate the acoustical quality of a space or a material.

Acoustic quality is defined as the degree to which the totality of the individual requirements made on an auditory event are met.

Sound Transmission Class (STC) is an integer rating of how well a building partition attenuates airborne sound.STC gives a rough idea of how much sound a wall might stop. STC is the most common sound reduction measurement in use.

Hence, the correct option is (C).

23. Non-climacteric fruits are characterized by ripening transitions that do not strictly depend on a significant increase in ethylene production and an associated rise in respiration rate non-climacteric fruits include strawberry, grape, raspberry, cherry, citrus, strawberries, and cashews.

Hence, the correct option is (C).

24. Potato is the staple vegetable in the Indian diet. Potatoes are also a staple ingredient in Indian foods. They are a part of many dishes, such as samosas, pakoras, bhaji, aloo paneer, and stuffed paratha. One reason that they play such a large component in Indian cuisine is that potatoes are a vegetarian option and also a good filler starch. The staple foods of India are those that are fundamental to Indian cuisine. They are enhanced by the plethora of spices available.

Hence, the correct option is (C).

25. In pre-cooling, mostly water is removed by Conduction. With conduction, the heat is transferred within the product to its coldest surface. This is the direct movement of heat from one object to another by direct methods (from fresh produce to water or warmer to cooler).

Pre-cooling refers to the removal of field heat (quick cooling) after harvest. If not, harvest deterioration is faster at a higher temperature. Pre-cooling is done just above chilling and freezing temperature.

Hence, the correct option is (B).

26. Let at present a person's age be x.

According to the question,

Son's age $= \frac{x}{4}$

Wife's age $= x - 3$

After 3 years:

$\frac{x}{4} + 3 = 15$

$x + 12 = 15 \times 4$

$x + 12 = 60$

$x = 60 - 12$

$x = 48$ years

Son's present age $= \frac{x}{4} = \frac{48}{12} = 12$ years

Wife's present age $= x - 3 = 48 - 3 = 45$

After 5 years

Person's age $= 48 + 5 = 53$ years

Son's age $= 12 + 5 = 17$ years

Wife's age $= 45 + 5 = 50$ years

Hence, the correct option is (D).

27. RARP (Reverse Address Resolution Protocol) is a protocol by which a physical machine in a local area network can request to learn its IP address from a gateway server's Address Resolution Protocol (ARP) table or cache.

A network administrator creates a table in a local area network's gateway router that maps the physical machine (or Media Access Control - MAC address) addresses to corresponding Internet Protocol addresses.

When a new machine is set up, its RARP client program requests from the RARP server on the router to be sent its IP address. Assuming that an entry has been set up in the router table, the RARP server will return the IP address to the machine which can store it for future use.

Hence, the correct option is (A).

28. A network that uses different technologies can be connected by using Routers. A router is a networking device that forwards data packets between computer networks. Routers perform the traffic directing functions on the Internet. A data packet is typically forwarded from one router to another router through the networks that constitute an internetwork until it reaches its destination node.

Hence, the correct option is (D).

29. In the digital era, there is a fear that classroom communication may result in over-stimulation.

A stimulating classroom environment is one where students can learn through exploration and hands-on practice, be encouraged to think critically, and be provided with a variety of experiences.

Results suggest that though farmers are aware of long-term changes in climatic factors (temperature and rainfall, for example), they are unable to identify these changes as climate change. Note that these changes may be considered as passive response or adaptation strategies to climate change.

Over-stimulation happens when a child is swamped by more experiences, sensations, noise, and activity than she can cope with.

Hence, the correct option is (D).

30. Gesticulation is to make movements with your hands or arms, especially when you are expressing (with the help of gestures) something while speaking.

Hence, the correct option is (A).

31. The physical barrier to non-verbal communication is Body language. The factors that make communication less effective are non-verbal cues, gestures, posture, and general body language.

The physical barrier is the environmental and natural condition that acts as a barrier in communication in sending a message from sender to receiver. Organizational environment or interior workspace design problems, technological problems, and noise are the parts of physical barriers.
Hence, the correct option is (A).

32. Let, the total number of students in all universities together be x.

Required ratio $= \frac{\text{Number of girls in university B}}{\text{Number of boys in university D}}$

Number of girls in university B $= x \times \frac{15}{100} \times \frac{40}{100}$

Number of boys in university D $= x \times \frac{28}{100} \times \frac{75}{100}$

Required ratio $= \frac{x \times \frac{15}{100} \times \frac{40}{100}}{x \times \frac{28}{100} \times \frac{75}{100}} = \frac{15 \times 40}{28 \times 75} = \frac{2}{7}$

Hence, the correct option is (B).

33. From the table:

The total number of students in university A and university C together $= 12\% + 8\% = 20\%$

We conclude that the number of students in A and C together constitutes 20% of the total which is the same as in F.

Hence, the correct option is (B).

34. From the table:
Number of students in university $D = 28\%$
Number of students in university $F = 20\%$
According to the question,
Required percent

$= \frac{(\text{Number of students in university } D - \text{Number of students in university } F)}{\text{Number of students in university } F}$

Required percent $= \frac{28-20}{20} \times 100$

$= 8 \times 5 = 40\%$

Hence, the correct option is (C).

35. Average $= \frac{\text{Total no of students}}{6}$

As we have no information about the number of students, we cannot find the average number of students in a university.

Hence, the correct option is (D).

36. Teacher communication is central to classroom management. As a teacher, we already know that there are three components in the teaching-learning process i.e. teacher, student, and the communication between them. Communication is the process through which a teacher delivers his instructions whether orally, written, or in signs. It is the teacher who regulates his/her class upon the basis of his knowledge and that knowledge can only be delivered through the interaction between him and his students. So, Assertion is right.

Here given R (reason) is false because it is the behavior of the teacher which can be used for regulating the behavior of his/her student. It is the way of communication through which a teacher wants to deliver his ideas, knowledge, or command. It is the strategies of a teacher through which he/she delivers his ideas to student it is his body language and gestures which guides the behavior of students.
Hence, the correct option is (B).

37. Grapevine is a form of informal communication, operates both in internal and external informal channels which can contribute to and benefit the organization. It passes opinions, suspicions, and rumors that generally do not move through formal channels.

Hence, the correct option is (B).

38. Countries usually agree to limit the temperature rise to 1.5 to 2 degrees Celsius as compared to pre-industrial times recognizing that this would significantly reduce the risks and impacts of climate change.

Hence, the correct option is (A).

39.

Set-1	Set-2
(a) Flood	4. Excess rain and uneven distribution of water
(b) Drought	1. Lack of rainfall of sufficient duration
(c) Earthquake	2. Tremors produced by the passage of vibratory waves through the rocks of the earth
(d) Volcano	3. A vent through which molted substances come out

Hence, the correct option is (A).

40. Both (A) and (B) statement is true with respect to the Phillips curve.

The Phillips curve is an economic concept developed by A. W. Phillips stating that inflation and unemployment have a stable and inverse relationship. The theory claims that economic growth comes from inflation, which in turn should lead to more jobs and less unemployment.

It shows the trade-off between unemployment and inflation.

The downward sloping curve of the Phillips Curve is generally held to be valid only in the short run.

In the long run, the Phillips Curve is usually thought to be horizontal at the Non-Accelerating Inflation Rate of Unemployment (NAIRU).

Hence, the correct option is (C).

41. World Economic Outlook is a survey conducted and published by the International Monetary Fund. It is published twice and partly updated 3 times a year. It portrays the world economy in the near and medium context (4 years).

WEO (World Economic Outlook) forecasts include the macroeconomic indicators, such as GDP, inflation, current account, and fiscal balance of more than 180 countries around the globe. It also deals with major economic policy issues.

Hence, the correct option is (A).

42. The correct sequence of scientific research is as follows:

a) Perceiving the problem situation – First we represent, what is the problem or what problem we want to study.

b) Locating the actual problem and its definition – Define the problem by locating its causes.

c) Hypothesizing – Formulate the hypothesis. The hypothesis is a proposed explanation on the basis of some limited evidence.

d) Deducing the consequences of the suggested solution.

e) Testing the hypothesis in action.

Hence, the correct option is (B).

43. The nature and objectives of teaching are explained as under:

The two fundamental aspects of the education process are teaching and learning. Teaching helps the students to learn and acquire relevant skills. Learning involves the acquisition of habits, knowledge, and attitudes. Since teaching and learning are integrally related to each other, good teaching means maximum learning.

Teaching ensures some kind of transformation in students because, with the help of a good teacher, a student acquires good habits, knowledge, and attitudes.

Teaching is a social act because it can be done with a number of students or helps in the social development of students while learning is a personal act because it depends upon a student that how much he/she want to learn through the teaching process.

Hence, the correct option is (C).

44. Canning is a method of preserving food from spoilage by storing it in containers that are hermetically sealed and then sterilized by heat. The process was invented after prolonged research by Nicolas Appert of France in 1809, in response to a call by his government for a means of preserving food for the army and navy use.

Hence, the correct option is (A).

45. The first 15 prime numbers are: $2,3,5,7,11,13,17,19,23,29,31,37,41,43,47$

For average taking the sum of all numbers:

$$2+3+5+7+11+13+17+19+23+29+31+37+41+43+47=328$$

Average $=\frac{328}{15}=21.86$

Hence, the correct option is (C).

46. According to the question:

$$\frac{SP-CP}{CP}\times 100$$

$$=\frac{3}{21}\times 100$$

$$=14\frac{2}{7}$$

Hence, the correct option is (C).

47. The ratio of work efficiency of A and $B=4:5$

The ratio of days $A:B=5:4$

Let total work is 20 units.

1 day work of $C=1$ unit

10 days work of $C=10$ unit $\quad .....(i)$

Work done by A and B in 10 days $=20-10=10$ unit.

Let one day work of A is $4x$ unit and one day work of B is $5x$ unit.

One day work of A and B is $9x$ units

Therefore, 10 days work of A and $B=90x$

Putting in equation (i)

$$90x=10$$

$$x=\frac{1}{9}$$

One day work of $A=\frac{4}{9}$

A alone can do the 20 unit work in $=20\times\frac{9}{4}=45$ days.

Hence, the correct option is (A).

48. S.I. on Rs. 4624 for 1 year $=4913-4624=$ Rs. 289

Interest Rate $=\frac{100\times 289}{4624\times 1}=\frac{25}{4}$

Let the sum $=x$

$$\Rightarrow x\times\left(1+\frac{25}{4\times 100}\right)^2=4624$$

$$\Rightarrow x=\frac{4624\times 16\times 16}{17\times 17}$$

$\Rightarrow x=$ Rs. 4096

Hence, the correct option is (A).

49. Let CP of 1 article be Rs. 1

CP of 20 articles = 20

According to the question,

SP of X articles = CP of 20 articles = 20

Given,

Profit percent made on selling the articles = 25%

Therefore, SP of X articles = 125% of CP of X articles

20 = 125% of X

X = 16

Hence, the correct option is (A).

50. The purchase value of the table considered $=P$

The purchase price of the chair $=R$

$$12\frac{1}{2}\%\text{ of }P+\left(-8\frac{1}{3}\right)\text{ of }R=25$$

$$\left(-8\frac{1}{3}\%\right)\text{ of }P+12\frac{1}{2}\%\text{ of }R=0$$

or

$$\frac{25P}{2} - \frac{25R}{3} = 2500 \quad .....(i)$$

$$\frac{25P}{3} - \frac{25R}{2} = 0 \quad .....(ii)$$

$$\frac{25R}{2} = \frac{25P}{3} \Rightarrow R = \frac{2P}{3}$$

Putting the value of R in the equation (i)

$$P = 360$$

Hence, the correct option is (D).

Mock Test 12

Ques (1-5):Direction: Read the given passage carefully and answer the question that follows.

Much is still unknown about human behaviour. Unanswered questions remain and further research is necessary. Knowledge about motivation, leader behaviour, and change will continue to be of great concern to practitioners of management for several reasons: It can help improve the effective leadership of human resources; it can help in preventing resistance to change, restriction to output, and personnel disputes; and often it can lead to a more productive organization. Our intention has been to provide a conceptual framework that may be useful to you in applying the conclusions of the behavioural sciences. The value that a framework of this kind has is not in changing one's knowledge, but in changing one's behaviour in working with people.

We have discussed three basic competencies in influencing: diagnosing - being able to understand and interpret the situation you are attempting to influence; adapting - being able to adapt your behaviour and the resources you control to the contingencies of the situation; and communicating - being able to put the message in such a way that people can easily understand and accept it. Each of these competencies is different and requires a different developmental approach. For example, diagnosing is cognitive or of the mind in nature and requires thinking skills; adapting is behavioural in nature and requires behavioural practice; and communicating Is process-oriented and requires learning and interrelating the key steps in the process. Because these three competencies require different knowledge and skills, how do we continue the process that we started with?

The key to starting the process of changing behaviour is sharing what you have learned with other people in your own organization. Two things occur when people who work together all have a common language. First, they are able to give each other feedback and help in a very rational, unemotional way that affects behaviour. Second, when followers start to realize that if their manager is using situational leadership, it is not the manager, but their behaviour, that determines the leadership style to be used with them.

Q.1 Which of the following prohibits resistance to change?

A. Knowledge of leader behaviour
B. Removing the restriction on output
C. Personnel disputes
D. Non-productive organisation

Q.2 What is the value outcome of applying a theoretical framework of behavioural science?

A. Changes in one's own knowledge
B. Change in one's behaviour while working with others
C. Not understandable human behaviour
D. Emergence of a value-loaded framework

Q.3 Each of the basic competencies needs:

A. Exclusivity
B. Situational contingency
C. Inter-relation with other steps
D. A different approach in acquiring it

Q.4 What prompts changes in a person's behaviour?

A. Leadership style
B. Situational support to the managers
C. Sharing of learning outcomes with others in the organization
D. Segregation of competencies

Q.5 The inferences that can be drawn from the passage are:

a. Common language among people in an organization will ensure unbiased feedback

b. People are known for fluctuating behaviour

c. People's behaviour influences the leader

d. Emotions and human behaviour are separate and easily explicable

Choose the correct answer from the options given below:

A. a and b only　**B.** b and c only
C. c and d only　**D.** a and c only

Q.6 Who propounded the Socio-cultural theory of Human Development in 1978?

A. Lev Vygotsky　**B.** John B. Watson
C. B.F. Skinner　**D.** Auguste Comte

Q.7 UNDP (United nation development programme) annually releases HDR (Human development report) with how many composite indices?

A. 5　**B.** 6　**C.** 7　**D.** 9

Q.8 In most of the Indian big cities, the dominant source of air pollution is:

A. vehicular traffic　**B.** household smoke
C. thermal power plant　**D.** suburban trains

Q.9 Which of the following is not a biotic component of the ecosystem?

A. Air　**B.** Plants　**C.** Bacteria　**D.** Animals

Q.10 National Policy on Education, 1986 has introduced which reform in the education system?

A. Continuous and Comprehensive Evaluation
B. Scholastic Evaluation and Co-scholastic Evaluation
C. Formative and Summative
D. All of the above

Q.11 Highest academic decision making body of the University is:

A. Board of Studies　**B.** Faculty
C. Academic Council　**D.** BCUD

Q.12 The apex institution/institutions for engineering education and research in India is/are:

A. Indian Institutes of Technology
B. Indian Institutes of Information Technology
C. Indian Institute of Advanced Study
D. Association of Indian Universities

Q.13 Three kinds of universities in India are:

A. State Universities, Central Universities, Affiliating Universities
B. Unitary Universities, Technical Universities, General Education Universities
C. State Universities, Central Universities, Private Universities
D. Central Universities, State Universities, Deemed Universities

Q.14 Which one of the following statements is not correct about the University Grants Commission (UGC)?

A. It was established in 1956 by an Act of Parliament.
B. It is tasked with promoting and coordinating higher education.
C. It receives Plan and Non-Plan funds from the Central Government.
D. It receives funds from State Governments in respect of State Universities.

Q.15 Which factors influence the choice of communication partners?

A. Proximity, utility, loneliness
B. Utility, secrecy, dissonance
C. Secrecy, dissonance, deception
D. Dissimilarity, dissonance, deviance

Q.16 In the analog communication, content is considered to be:

A. Convergent **B.** Static
C. Physical **D.** Ethereal

Q.17 The types of organizational communication includes:

1. Internal communication
2. External communication
3. Interpersonal communication
4. Intra-personal communication

A. 1 and 2 **B.** 2, 3 and 4
C. 1, 2 and 3 **D.** All four

Q.18 Which of the following statements is true?

A. Motivated learners learn better than unmotivated
B. Girls learn better than boys
C. Children learn better than adults
D. Creative persons learn better than intelligent

Q.19 Marked price of an item is Rs. 800. On purchase of 1 item, discount is 15%, on purchase of 4 items, discount is 38%. Rajshri buys 5 items, what is the effective discount?

A. 33.4 percent **B.** 16 percent
C. 9 percent **D.** 17.5 percent

Q.20 The difference between simple and compound interests compounded annually on a certain sum of money for 2 years at 8% per annum is Rs. 40. What is the sum?

A. Rs. 12500 **B.** Rs. 6250
C. Rs. 25000 **D.** Rs. 18750

Q.21 Eleven friends spent Rs. 19 each on a tour and the twelfth friend spent Rs. 11 less than the average expenditure of all twelve of them. What is the total money (in Rs) spent by them?

A. 216 **B.** 227 **C.** 236 **D.** 247

Q.22 The missing term in the series $1,4,27,16,?,36,343$ is:

A. 30 **B.** 49 **C.** 125 **D.** 81

Q.23 One writes all numbers from 50 to 99 without the digits 2 and 7. How many numbers have been written?

A. 32 **B.** 36 **C.** 40 **D.** 38

Q.24 If STREAMERS is coded as UVTGALDQR, then KNOWLEDGE will be coded as:

A. MQPYLCDFD **B.** MPQYLDCFD
C. PMYQLDFCD **D.** YMQPLDDFC

Q.25 If we want to seek new knowledge of facts about the world, we must rely on the reason of the type:

A. Inductive **B.** Deductive
C. Demonstrative **D.** Physiological

Q.26 Direction: Consider the following statement and select the correct code stating the nature of the argument involved in it:

To suppose that the earth is the only populated world in the infinite space is as absurd as to assert that in an entire field of millet only one grain will grow.

A. Astronomical **B.** Anthropological
C. Deductive **D.** Analogical

Q.27 A is the father of B and C is the son of D. E is the brother of A. B is the sister of C. How is D related to E?

A. Daughter **B.** Brother
C. Brother-in-Law **D.** Sister-in-Law

Q.28 In a certain code language, 'GRABPONT' is written as 'NTIVVGLM'. What is the code for 'TMVLRBDE' in that code language?

A. VJVYFBGZ **B.** YJUXFBGZ
C. YJVXFBGZ **D.** YJVXFBHG

Q.29 "A man ought no more to value himself for being wiser than a woman if he owes his advantage to a better education than he ought to boast of his courage for beating a man when his hands were tied."

The above passage is an instance of-

A. Deductive Argument
B. Hypothetical Argument
C. Analogical Argument
D. Factual Argument

Q.30 Which of the following are the tools of good governance?

1. Social Audit
2. Separation of Powers
3. Citizen's Charter
4. Right to Information

Select the correct answer from the options given below:

A. 1 and 2 **B.** 1, 2 and 3
C. 1, 2 and 4 **D.** 1,2,3 and 4

Q.31 NMEICT stands for:

A. National Mission on Education through ICT
B. National Mission on E-governance through ICT
C. National Mission on E-commerce through ICT
D. National Mission on E-learning through ICT

Q.32 Learner-centred teaching means that:

A. learners are considered passive recipients and teacher has the 'right' knowledge
B. learners are slow in learning and teacher stresses completion of syllabus
C. learners are given an opportunity to construct knowledge and teacher is a guide in the learning process
D. learners know little and teaching involves transmission of facts to them

Ques (33-37):Direction: Read the table carefully and answer the following questions.

The following table gives information about the number of active pandemic cases and number of deaths due to pandemic in different cities.

CITY	TOTAL CASES	ACTIVE CASES	DEATHS
City 1	2332	1644	93
City 2	14630	3462	139
City 3	9888	3720	413
City 4	27900	17015	874
City 5	2800	1470	260

Q.33 What is the total percentage of active cases in city 2 and city 5?

A. 27.28% **B.** 28.29% **C.** 25.26% **D.** 26.25%

Q.34 Which of the following cities has encountered highest percentage of deaths?

A. City 1 **B.** City 3 **C.** City 4 **D.** City 5

Q.35 What the ratio between number of recovered cases in city 5 to number of recovered cases in city 1?

A. 119:214 **B.** 214:119
C. 89:137 **D.** 98:57

Q.36 Which of the following cities has encountered lowest percentage of deaths?

A. City 2 **B.** City 3 **C.** City 4 **D.** City 5

Q.37 Number of recovered cases in city 4 is what percentage of total number of cases in city 3?

A. 102.15% **B.** 101.5%
C. 101.24% **D.** 112.27%

Q.38 The type of research that involves looking at variables over an extended period of time is known as:

A. Cross-sectional area **B.** Time series
C. Longitudinal **D.** Latitudinal

Q.39 The aim of the research is/are:

I. Factual
II. Verifiable
III. Theoretical
IV. Ambiguous

Codes

A. I and II **B.** II and III
C. I, II, and III **D.** IV and I

Q.40 In the context of survey research, the following steps are taken in a certain order.

I. Sampling
II. Inference
III. Data analysis
IV. Data collection

Codes:

A. II, III, I, IV **B.** I, IV, III, II
C. III, II, IV, I **D.** IV, I, II, III

Q.41 Given below are two statements:

Statement I: Fundamental research is directed at exploring the applicability of truths and principles already established.

Statement II: Action research aims at ameliorating the ongoing conditions and practices.

In the light of the above statements, choose the most appropriate answer from the options given below:

A. Both Statement I and Statement II are correct
B. Both Statement I and Statement II are incorrect
C. Statement I is correct but Statement II is incorrect
D. Statement I is incorrect but Statement II is correct

Q.42 The characteristics of scientific method of research are:

a. Empiricism
b. Objectivity
c. Systematic
d. Secretive
e. Security related
f. Predictive

A. a, b, d and e **B.** c, d, e and f
C. d, e, f and a **D.** a, b, c and f

Q.43 Which one of the following cloud concepts is related to sharing and pooling the resources?

A. Polymorphism
B. Virtualization
C. Abstraction
D. None of the mentioned

Q.44 The objective of ICT is:

[Super TET Paper - I, 2019]

A. The establishment of smart schools

B. To increase the capacity of teachers
C. Both (A) and (B)
D. None of the above

Q.45 The expert person of Chemistry subject is included in making of computer assisted instruction in Chemistry, it means ________ technology of CAI used.

A. Hardware
B. Software
C. Courseware
D. Subject-ware

Q.46 Application of ICT in research is relevant in which of the following stages?

i) Survey of related studies

ii) Data collection in the field

iii) Data Analysis

iv) Writing the thesis

v) Indexing the references

Choose the most appropriate option from those given below:

A. (ii), (iv) and (v)
B. (i), (iii) and (v)
C. (i), (ii) and (iv)
D. (ii), (iii) and (iv)

Q.47 Which of the following statements is/are true?

A. Fibre optic cables are wooden fibres to provide high quality transmission.

B. Wireless communication provides anytime anywhere connection to both computers and telephones.

C. Mobile phones are capable of providing voice communication and also digital messaging service.

Choose the correct answer from the options given below:

A. A and C only
B. B and C only
C. A and B only
D. C only

Q.48 Synchronous communication takes place through which of the following technologies?

A. Video chat

B. Virtual classrooms

C. Audio conferencing

D. Wikis

E. Electronic mail

Choose the correct answer from the options given below:

A. A, B, and C only
B. B, C, and D only
C. C, D, and E only
D. A, D, and E only

Q.49 Which of the following disasters belong to the category of nuclear disasters?

a. Fukushima disaster

b. Chernobyl disaster

c. Three-mile Island incident

d. The love canal disaster

Choose the correct option:

A. (a), (b) and (c)
B. (a), (b) and (d)
C. (a), (c) and (d)
D. (b), (c) and (d)

Q.50 Teaching is defined as:

A. Facilitation of learning
B. Transmission of knowledge by teachers and its reception by the students
C. Reading the textbooks
D. Transmission of knowledge by teachers

// Smart Answer Sheet //

Correct Indicates percentage of students who answered questions correctly.

Skipped Indicates percentage of students who skipped questions.

Q.	Ans.	Correct	Skipped
1	A	43.27 %	1.67 %
2	B	53.54 %	1.9 %
3	D	52.25 %	1.53 %
4	C	61.24 %	1.2 %
5	D	54.25 %	1.28 %
6	A	53.36 %	1.59 %
7	A	60.12 %	1.72 %
8	A	81.48 %	0.0 %
9	A	85.05 %	0.0 %
10	A	67.25 %	1.7 %
11	C	44.63 %	1.22 %
12	A	62.73 %	1.57 %
13	C	50.51 %	1.95 %
14	D	69.41 %	1.21 %
15	A	67.73 %	1.65 %
16	B	48.0 %	1.15 %
17	C	46.67 %	1.25 %
18	A	53.23 %	1.51 %
19	A	28.41 %	4.42 %
20	B	50.0 %	1.91 %
21	A	50.71 %	1.96 %
22	C	77.09 %	0.0 %
23	A	68.92 %	1.68 %
24	B	76.82 %	0.0 %
25	A	87.97 %	0.0 %
26	D	64.16 %	1.33 %
27	D	50.11 %	1.94 %
28	C	31.9 %	3.01 %
29	C	76.3 %	0.0 %
30	C	18.25 %	4.19 %
31	A	60.04 %	1.78 %
32	C	66.22 %	1.6 %
33	B	85.28 %	0.0 %
34	D	17.49 %	3.92 %
35	B	45.67 %	1.6 %
36	A	54.58 %	1.02 %
37	C	89.7 %	0.0 %
38	C	76.38 %	0.0 %
39	C	56.58 %	1.43 %
40	B	41.94 %	1.81 %
41	D	61.54 %	1.55 %
42	D	26.81 %	4.63 %
43	B	47.8 %	1.52 %
44	C	63.55 %	1.72 %
45	B	11.29 %	3.25 %
46	B	17.67 %	4.48 %
47	B	64.78 %	1.79 %
48	A	41.18 %	1.66 %
49	A	44.86 %	1.82 %
50	A	55.8 %	1.86 %

Performance Analysis	
Avg. Score (%)	44.0%
Toppers Score (%)	69.0%
Your Score	

//Hints and Solutions//

1. The third and fourth sentences of the passage say - "Knowledge about motivation, leader behaviour, and change will continue to be of great concern to practitioners of management for several reasons: It can help improve the effective leadership of human resources; it can help in preventing resistance to change, restriction to output, and personnel disputes; and often it can lead to a more productive organization."

According to the above, we can clearly deduce that out of the given options, only knowledge of leader behaviour prohibits resistance to change (as asked in the question).

Hence, the correct option is (A).

2. The last two sentences of the first paragraph of the passage say - "Our intention has been to provide a conceptual framework that may be useful to you in applying the conclusions of the behavioural sciences. The value that a framework of this kind has is not in changing one's knowledge, but in changing one's behaviour in working with people."

Hence, the correct option is (B).

3. The second sentence of the second paragraph says - "Each of these competencies is different and requires a different developmental approach."

Let's look at the other options:

Exclusivity: Nowhere is exclusivity mentioned in the passage either directly or by way of inference

Situational contingency: The first sentence of the second paragraph contains the phrase - "adapting - being able to adapt your behaviour and the resources you control to the contingencies of the situation." Thus this is actually the defining feature of one of the three basic competencies in influencing, that is, defining but this is not a need of the three competencies

Inter-relation with other steps: The third sentence of the second paragraph contains the phrase - "...communicating Is process-oriented and requires learning and interrelating the key steps in the process". Thus this is actually a requirement of only one of the three basic competencies, called communicating but not a need for all three competencies.

Hence, the correct option is (D).

4. The first sentence of the third paragraph says - "The key to starting the process of changing behaviour is sharing what you have learned with other people in your own organization."

Let's look at the other options:

Leadership style: The concluding sentence of the passage says - "Second when followers start to realize that if their manager is using situational leadership, it is not the manager, but their behaviour, that determines the leadership style to be used with them." Thus leadership style is a change resulting from situation-based leadership and not something that prompts a change in behaviour

Situational support to the managers: Nowhere does the passage mention 'situational support'. The concluding sentence of the passage says - "Second when followers start to realize that if their manager is using situational leadership, it is not the manager, but their behaviour, that determines the leadership style to be used with them." Thus, situational leadership is a type of leadership and not something that prompts a change in behaviour

Segregation of competencies: Although according to the passage, each competency needs a different set of skills and knowledge, there is nothing mentioned about segregation of competencies in the passage either directly or by way of inference.

Hence, the correct option is (C).

5. The third paragraph of the passage says - "Two things occur when people who work together all have a common language. First, they are able to give each other feedback and help in a very rational, unemotional way that affects behaviour. Second, followers start to realize that if their manager is using situational leadership, it is not the manager, but their behaviour, that determines the leadership style to be used with them."

From the above, we can logically conclude that inferences a and c are valid.

Let's look at the other statements:

People are known for fluctuating behaviour: Nowhere is such a fact mentioned in the passage

Emotions and human behaviour are separate and easily explicable:

- The two opening sentences of the passage say - "Much is still unknown about human behaviour. Unanswered questions remain and further research is necessary."
- Also, the concluding paragraph states that a common language can help in giving unbiased and unemotional feedback.
- From the above, it is clear that this is not a valid inference.

Hence, the correct option is (D).

6. Lev Vygotsky propounded the Socio-cultural theory of Human Development in 1978.

Sociocultural theory of human development:

- The major theme of Vygotsky's theoretical framework is that social interaction plays a fundamental role in the development of cognition.
- Vygotsky (1978) states: "Every function in the child's cultural development appears twice: first, on the social level, and later, on the individual level; first, between people (interpsychological) and then inside the child (intrapsychological).
- Vygotsky's theory is comprised of concepts such as culture-specific tools, private speech, and the Zone of Proximal Development.

Hence, the correct option is (A).

7. UNDP (United nation development programme) annually releases HDR (Human development report) with 5 composite indices.

The report is based on 5 composite indices namely:

- Human development index
- Gender development index
- Multidimensional poverty index
- Gender inequality index
- Inequality-adjusted human development index

Hence, the correct option is (A).

8. In most of the Indian big cities, the dominant source of air pollution is vehicular traffic.

Air pollution:

- Air pollution is the modification of the air by mixing with some particles and gases that are injurious to health and wealth which is undesirable
- Air pollution is a common phenomenon nowadays with the advancement of technology
- It is dominated in urban areas more than rural areas.

Hence, the correct option is (A).

9. Air is not a biotic component of the ecosystem.

The ecosystem is defined as 'the sum total of living, non-living components; influences and events, surrounding an organism. The ecosystem comprises both living (biotic) and non-living (abiotic) components.

Hence, the correct option is (A).

10. Continuous and Comprehensive Evaluation (CCE) was introduced as a school-based evaluation system as per the Right of Children to Free and Compulsory Education Act, 2009 (RTE Act, 2009) which was implemented in April 2010. The national policy on education, 1986 has introduced continuous and comprehensive reform in the education system for the overall qualitative improvement.

The 'Continuous' aspect of CCE: It means continual and periodical assessment which will help in finding out the strengths and gaps in children's learning so that the teacher can plan on ways to enhance learning.

- A continual aspect includes the placement and formative evaluation, where placement evaluation means assessment of learners' progress on various aspects from the very beginning of instructions and formative evaluation means the evaluation of learners during the instructional process through various formal or informal methods of evaluation.
- The periodicity aspect includes the summative evaluation which is the evaluation of the performance of learners should be done frequently at the end of every unit or term

The 'Comprehensive' aspect of CCE: It implies that the evaluation of learners' performance is carried out in both scholastic and co-scholastic areas.

- Scholastic areas cover activities in curricular or subject-specific areas. The term 'Scholastic' refers to those activities, which are related to intellect or the brain. It is related to the assessment of learners in curricular subjects. It includes assignments, projects, practicals, etc.
- Co-scholastic areas include life skills, abilities in co-curricular areas, attitudes, and values. Various co-scholastic aspects are Life Skills, Attitudes, Human Values, Cocurricular activities, and Aesthetic, visual and performing arts.

Hence, the correct option is (A).

11. Highest academic decision making body of the University is academic Council.

The Academic Council shall be the principal academic body of the University and shall, subject to the provisions of the Act, Statutes, Ordinances, Regulations and Rules, co-ordinate and exercise general supervision over the academic policies of the University.

The Academic Council is the statutory bodies of the University. It shall consist of the following members:

- Vice-Chancellor as Chairperson
- All the Deans of Faculties and Heads of the Institutions
- Five Professors/Associate Professors of the University nominated by the Chancellor.
- Controller of Examinations
- Three educationists of repute from outside the University were nominated by the Chancellor.
- Three representatives of repute from amongst the Scientists / Educationists/ Technologists / Industrialists for their specialized knowledge co-opted by the Academic Council.
- The Registrar shall be the Member-Secretary.

Thus, the highest academic decision-making body of the University is Academic Council.

Hence, the correct option is (C).

12. The apex institution/institutions for engineering education and research in India is Indian Institutes of Technology.

Indian Institute of Technology:

- The Indian Institute of Technology, governed by the Institutes of technology act, 1961.
- The founder of IIT was Jawaharlal Nehru, founded in 1951 and is located in 23 cities in India.
- IITs are autonomous public technical and research universities located across India.
- The IITs are administered centrally by the IIT Council, an apex body established by the Government of India.
- IITs are coveted engineering institutions in India.

Hence, the correct option is (A).

13. Three kinds of universities in India are State Universities, Central Universities, Private Universities.

Central University: Central universities are set up by an act of Parliament. The President of India is a visitor to all central universities. The University Grants Commission (UGC) is the agency that provides funding for the maintenance and development of these universities. The University of Delhi, Allahabad University, Jawaharlal Nehru University (JNU), Aligarh Muslim University (AMU) are among the central universities.

State University: Universities set up or recognized by an act of the state legislature are known as state universities. State governments are responsible for the establishment of state universities and provide plan grants for their development and non-plan grants for their maintenance. Three of the country's oldest institutions of higher learning, the University of Calcutta, the University of Madras, and the University of Mumbai are state universities.

Private University: A private university is an institution of higher learning established through a state or central act by a sponsoring body, such as a society registered under the Societies Registration Act, 1860, or any other corresponding law for the time being in force in a state or a public trust or a company registered under Section 25 of the Companies Act, 1956. For an institution to be given the status of a private university, the state legislature conferring the status has to pass an act by which the institution will receive the status of a university. Private universities have to be recognized by the UGC so that the degrees awarded by them have to be of any value. Amity University, Lovely Professional University, Shoolini University, etc. are some examples of Private Universities.

Hence, the correct option is (C).

14. Statement 1: It was established in 1956 by an Act of Parliament.

- UGC was formally established only in November 1956 as a statutory body of the Government of India through an Act of Parliament for the coordination, determination, and maintenance of standards of university education in India.
- It provides recognition to universities in India and disburses funds to such recognized universities and college.

Statement 2: It is tasked with promoting and coordinating higher education.

- UGC is responsible for coordinating, determining, and maintaining standards of higher education.
- UGC has also constituted a Task Force to monitor concerns/grievances of students, teachers, and institutions and 'redress them accordingly'.

Statement 3: It receives Plan and Non-Plan funds from the Central Government.

- The University Grants Commission of India (UGC India) is a statutory body set up by the Government of India in accordance with the UGC Act 1956 under the Ministry of Education and is charged with coordination, determination, and maintenance of standards of higher education.

Statement 4: It receives funds from State Governments in respect of State Universities.

- Statement 4 is an incorrect statement as UGC doesn't receive any funds from State Governments in respect of State Universities.

Hence, the correct option is (D).

15. Proximity. utility, and loneliness influence the choice of communication partners.

Proximity:

- It deals with a person's positioning and physical closeness while communicating with others.
- One should move its proximity in response to the other person's body language.

Utility: It deals with how both the parties, who are engaged in communication, can satisfy each other.

Loneliness:

- While going through interaction, both parties (sender or receiver) must check whether the other person is feeling uncomfortable or some sort of loneliness.
- The speaker should try to communicate the information which is beneficial for both ends.
- So that the other person feels interested and not lonely.

Hence, the correct option is (A).

16. In the analog communication, content is considered to be static.

A communication system conveys information from its source to a destination and the concept of information is central to communication. There are many kinds of information sources, including machines as well as people and messages appear in various forms. There are two distinct message categories - analog and digital.

Analog Communication:

- An analog message is a physical quantity that varies with time, in a smooth and continuous fashion.
- Analog communication is the process of conveying (sending, receiving, and processing) of information including image, voice and video by using continuous signals or analog signals.
- Here the contents can be only linear and static not dynamic.
- For examples include, laser beams, microwave, etc.

Hence, the correct option is (B).

17. The communication which takes place at the organizational level, like in the corporates, non-profits, and government bodies is called organizational communication. There are three aspects of organization communication:

- Internal communication: Internal communication is upwards, downwards and cross ward in nature.

- External communication: External communication is related to the association between organization informality.
- Interpersonal communication: Interpersonal communication is concerned with relationships between employee

So, we conclude that all the above three are included in organizational communication.

Hence, the correct option is (C).

18. Motivated learners learn better than unmotivated learners.

Motivated learner: They are more excited to learn. Learning and participating in each learning activity is enjoyable for them.

Unmotivated learners: They do not find anything interesting in learning. They are usually indifferent about classes, marks, achievements, etc.

Hence, the correct option is (A).

19. Marked price of an item $=$ Rs. 800

Selling price of 4 items $= (1 - 0.38) \times 800 \times 4 =$ Rs. 1984

Selling price of 1 item $= (1 - 0.15) \times 800 =$ Rs. 680

Total Selling price of 5 items $= 1984 + 680 =$ Rs. 2664

Total Marked price $= 800 \times 5 =$ Rs. 4000

Discount $\% = \frac{discount}{Marked\ price} \times 100$

$= \frac{(4000-2664)}{4000} \times 100$

$= 33.4\%$

Hence, the correct option is (A).

20. We know that, for 2 years

$CI - SI = p\left(\frac{8}{100}\right)^2$

$\Rightarrow 40 = p\left(\frac{8}{100}\right)^2$

$\Rightarrow p = \frac{40\times10000}{64}$

$=$ Rs. 6250

Hence, the correct option is (B).

21. Given that,

Eleven friends spent Rs. 19 each.

Let, the average expenditure of all twelve of them is ' x'.

According to question,

$\frac{19\times11+(x-11)}{12} = x$

On solving we get,

$x = 18$

So, total money spent by them $= 18 \times 12 =$ Rs. 216

Hence, the correct option is (A).

22. Pattern of the given series is:

$1^3 = 1$

$2^2 = 4$

$3^3 = 27$

$4^2 = 16$

$5^3 = 125$

$6^2 = 36$

$7^3 = 343$

So, the missing term is 125.

Hence, the correct option is (C).

23. The number between 50 to 99= 50

The number between 50 to 99 having digits 2 and 7= 18

The number between 50 to 99 without the digits 2 and 7= 50-18= 32

Hence, the correct option is (A).

24. The first four-word is coded by adding 2 in the alphabetical series, the middle word is same, the last four words are coded by subtracting 1.

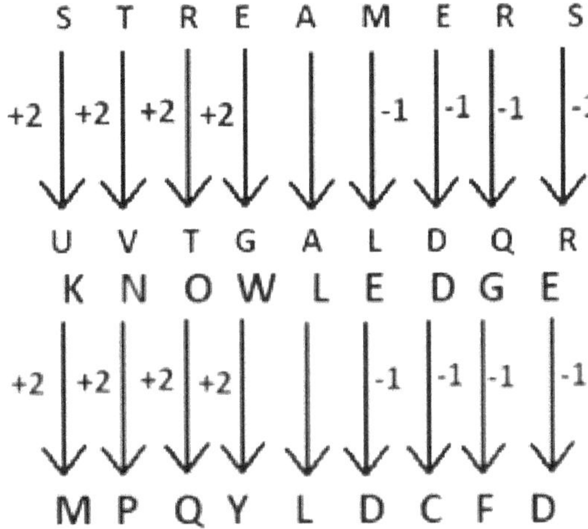

Hence, the correct option is (B).

25. Inductive reasoning is the one in which the premises seek to supply strong evidence for the truth of the conclusion. The truth of the conclusion of an inductive argument is probable, based upon the provided evidence. Inductive reasoning is known as hypothesis construction because the conclusions derived are based on current knowledge and predictions. So, if we want to seek new knowledge of facts about the world, we must rely on inductive reasoning.

Hence, the correct option is (A).

26. Here, we have given a comparison between one thing to another thing. Infinite space has been compared to the Millet field and Earth has been compared to a single grain.

So, the nature of the argument is Analogical.

Hence, the correct option is (D).

27. From the given information:

Symbol in Diagram	Meaning
○	Female
□	Male
═	Married Couple
—	Siblings
|	Difference of a generation

Based on the given data, we can draw a family tree:

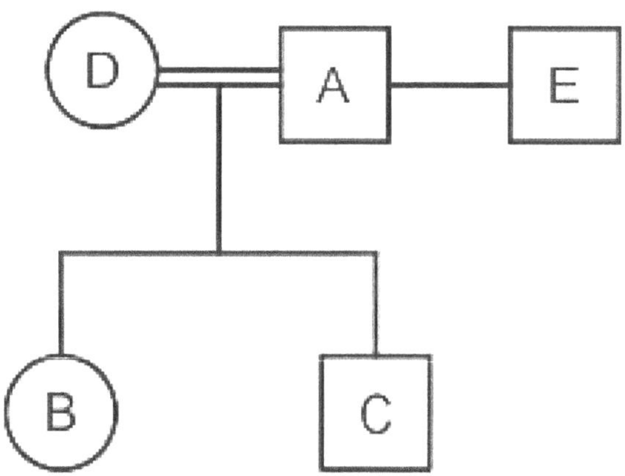

So, D is the sister in law of E.

Hence, the correct option is (D).

28. The positions of the letters according to the English alphabet series:

Alphabets	A	B	C	D	E	F	G	H	I	J	K	L	M
Positional value	1	2	3	4	5	6	7	8	9	10	11	12	13
Positional value	26	25	24	23	22	21	20	19	18	17	16	15	14
Alphabets	Z	Y	X	W	V	U	T	S	R	Q	P	O	N

The pattern for this code is as follows;

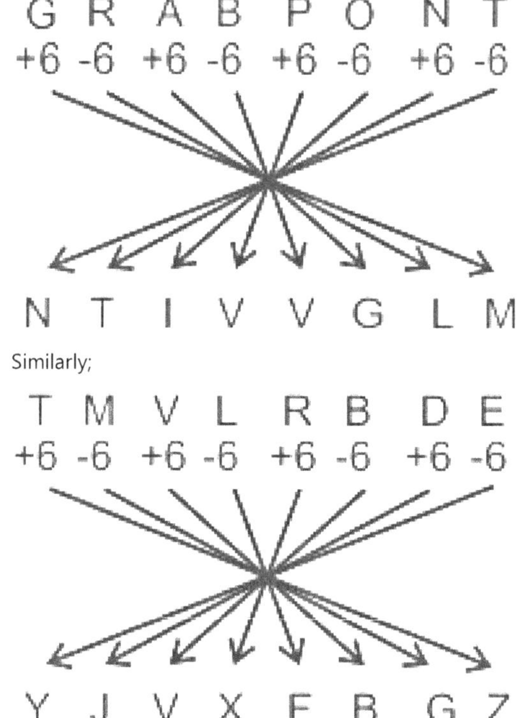

So, 'YJVXFBGZ' is the correct answer.

Hence, the correct option is (C).

29. The above passage is an Analogical argument because the man is comparing himself with the woman for the purpose of clarification.

Analogical Arguments (or Arguments by Analogy) are a from of Induction where a conclusion is derived from a comparison of similarities between two or more cases.

Hence, the correct option is (C).

30. Good governance includes:

1. Social Audit: A social audit is a formal review of a company's endeavors, procedures, and code of conduct regarding social responsibility and the company's impact on society. A social audit is an assessment of how well the company is achieving its goals or benchmarks for social responsibility.

2. Separation of Powers: Separation of powers is when the state is divided into three different governmental bodies (legislature, executive and judiciary); and all three bodies have separate and independent powers and areas of responsibility.

4. Right to Information: Right to Information empowers every citizen to seek any information from the Government, inspect any Government documents and seek certified photocopies thereof. Right to Information also empowers citizens to official inspect any Government work or to take the sample of material used in any work.

Hence, the correct option is (C).

31. NMEICT stands for National Mission on Education through Information and Communication Technology. It is an initiative taken by the Government of India to become a knowledge superpower by efficiently utilizing our human resource.

Hence, the correct option is (A).

32. Learner-centred teaching means that learners are given an opportunity to construct knowledge and teacher is a guide in the learning process.

It strongly believes that when children are given the freedom to work at their own pace, they develop the ability to assimilate the concepts efficiently.

Characteristics of the learner-centred approach of teaching:

- It stresses the importance of enquiry, observation and investigation.
- It takes into account learner's capabilities, capacities and learning styles.

Hence, the correct option is (D).

33. Given:

Number of total cases in city 2 and city 5 $= 14630 + 2800 = 17430$

Number of active cases in city 2 and city 5 $= 3462 + 1470 = 4932$

Formula used:

Percentage of active cases in a city $= \frac{\text{total number of active cases}}{\text{total cases}} \times 100$

Total percentage of active cases in city 2 and city 5 $= \frac{4932}{17430} \times 100 = 28.29\%$

Hence, the correct option is (B).

34. Given: Total number of cases and deaths in each city

Formula used:

Percentage of deaths in a city $= \frac{\text{total number of deaths}}{\text{total cases}} \times 100$

Percentage of deaths in a city 1 $= \frac{93}{2332} \times 100 = 3.98\%$

Percentage of deaths in a city 3 $= \frac{413}{9888} \times 100 = 4.17\%$

Percentage of deaths in a city 4 $= \frac{874}{27900} \times 100 = 3.13\%$

Percentage of deaths in a city 5 $= \frac{260}{2800} \times 100 = 9.28\%$

City with highest percentage of deaths is city 5.

Hence, the correct option is (D).

35. Formula used:

Number of recovered cases = Total cases - active cases - deaths

Number of recovered cases in city 1 $= 2332 - 1644 - 93 = 595$

Number of recovered cases in city 5 $= 2800 - 1470 - 260 = 1070$

Thus, ratio between number of recovered cases in city 5 to number of recovered cases in city 1 $= 1070 : 595 = 214 : 119$

Hence, the correct option is (B).

36. Given:

Total number of cases and deaths in each city

Formula used:

Percentage of deaths in a city $= \frac{= \text{total number of deaths}}{\text{total cases}} \times 100$

Percentage of deaths in a city 2 $= \frac{139}{14630} \times 100 = 0.95\%$

Percentage of deaths in a city 3 $= \frac{413}{9888} \times 100 = 4.17\%$

Percentage of deaths in a city 4 $= \frac{874}{27900} \times 100 = 3.13\%$

Percentage of deaths in a city 5 $= \frac{260}{2800} \times 100 = 9.28\%$

City with lowest percentage of deaths is city 2.

Hence, the correct option is (A).

37. Given:

Total number of cases in city 3 $= 9888$

Total number of cases in city 4 $= 27900$

Total number of active cases in city 4 $= 17015$

Total number of deaths in city 4 $= 874$

Formula used:

Number of recovered cases = Total cases - active cases - deaths

Number of recovered cases in city 4 $= 27900 - 17015 - 874 = 10011$

∴ Number of recovered cases in city 4 is what percentage of total number of cases in city 3 $= \frac{10011}{9888} \times 100 = 101.24$

Hence, the correct option is (C).

38. In the longitudinal study, data is collected over a period of time ranging from weeks, months, years, decades, etc. Firstly, the data is collected at the outset of the study and may repeat over an extended period of time. By allowing this, the researchers can experience how the variables change over time within the same strata.

Hence, the correct option is (C).

39. Research:

It is defined as the critical inquiry or investigation in seeking facts or principles. It is a systematic process that is used in developing more information on an already available topic or a completely new topic. It is considered as both an art or science.

Research is said to be inductive thinking that enhances the growth and development of ideas of thinking and inquiry.

Aims or objectives of the research:

1. Factual- Research includes the development of new ideas or redevelopment of existing ideas. Ideas generated are essentially factual and are based on principles. Research is descriptive in nature and is generally based on human values. Research is considered to be factual as it establishes a cause-and-effect relationship between the different variables in play.
2. Verifiable- Research is valid and verifiable. It implies that whatever research is conducted it can always be verified by other people. It is a very important aim as the research is always based on some data collection and analysis.
3. Theoretical- Research refers to the formulation of theories that are applicable universally, hence it is obviously theoretical. It includes an introduction or explanation of existing theories. This explains an important objective of research as theoretical.

From the above discussion, it can be observed that the correct answer is option (C).

Ambiguous- the term refers to something not having an obvious meaning. Research can not be ambiguous as it is the attainment of things with certainty.

Hence, the correct option is (C).

40. The correct order is: Sampling, Data collection, Data analysis, Sampling

Survey Research is defined as the process of conducting research using surveys that researchers send to survey respondents. The data collected from surveys is then statistically analyzed to draw meaningful research conclusions.

Hence, the correct option is (B).

41. Research is defined as careful consideration of a study regarding a particular concern or problem using scientific methods.

Statement I: Fundamental research is directed at exploring the applicability of truths and principles already established.

- Fundamental research is research for knowledge's sake; the aim is the generation of new knowledge irrespective of any use at the moment of discovery.
- Fundamental research is a type of research approach that is aimed at gaining a better understanding of a subject, phenomenon, or basic law of nature. This type of research is primarily focused on the advancement of knowledge rather than solving a specific problem.
- There may not be any immediate need or application of the new knowledge thus produced, nor it is conducted for an immediate gain or problem-solving.

Statement II: Action research aims at ameliorating the ongoing conditions and practices.

- There are two dimensions attached to this word Action Research. One is action, which is doing something, and Research, which is analyzing.
- When both the terms combine, it is of doing something to analyze or analyze to do something or doing something while analyzing.
- Action Research also means learning by doing.
- Action research is used in real-life situations, rather than any experimental studies,
- Its primary focus is to solve real-life problems through collective action.

So, Statement I is incorrect but Statement II is correct.

Hence, the correct option is (D).

42. The scientific method was first outlined by Sir Francis Bacon (1561-1626) to provide logical, rational problem solving across many scientific fields. The scientific method consists of systematic observation, classification, and interpretation of data.

Characteristics of the scientific method of research are:

Empiricism: It means knowledge comes only or primarily from sensory experience by doing in real-life settings.

Objectivity: It means that certain things, especially moral truths, exist independently of human knowledge or perception of them.

Systematic: Something people undertake in order to find out things in a systematic way, thereby increasing their knowledge. In addition to it 'Systematic Research,' it is based on logic and not relied on just beliefs.

Predictive: When something is predictable it means that it is likely to occur because it happened in the past.

Hence, the correct option is (D).

43. Virtualization is related to pooling and sharing in a cloud concept. Through this, the resources are shared. Through this type of computation, it is possible to run applications and services on a common distributed network. Abstraction is one of the critical concepts of cloud computing.

Hence, the correct option is (B).

44. Communicating information effectively by making use of appropriate technology is called Information and Communication Technology (ICT).

- It is an umbrella term that includes many communication devices such as radio, television, cellular phones, computers and network, satellite systems and so on.
- It is defined, as a "diverse set of technological tools and resources used to communicate, and to create, disseminate, store, and manage information."

Hence, the correct option is (C).

45. The expert person of Chemistry subject is included in making of computer assisted instruction in Chemistry, it means Software technology of CAI used.

Computer-Assisted Instruction: Some of the first computer-assisted instruction (CAI), developed by Patrick Suppes at Stanford University during the 1960s, set standards for subsequent instructional software.

Hence, the correct option is (B).

46. Information Technology (IT) and Information and Communication Technology (ICT) are very often interchangeably used in the context of modern technology infrastructure.

ICT is a broad and comprehensive term, which comprises information technology and communication technology. Information technology includes radio, television, computer and the Internet, teleconferencing, and mobile.

Hence, the correct option is (B).

47. Wireless communication provides anytime. anywhere connection to both computers and telephones is statement is true.

Optical fibers are used most often as a means to transmit light[a] between the two ends of the fiber and find wide usage in fiber-optic communications, where they permit transmission over longer distances and at higher bandwidths (data transfer rates) than electrical cables.

Hence, the correct option is (B).

48. Communication:

- Communication means passing information or sending massage to a target population.
- It contained five steps generally, Sender - Massage - Channel - Receiver - Feedback.
- Based on the time and place of communication it can be divided into Synchronous communication and Asynchronous communication.

Communication	Characteristics	Example
Synchronous communication	• Sender and receiver participating in the communication at the same time • No, start and stop bits • The place is not a factor, fast transmission	Video chat, Virtual classrooms, Audio conferencing, etc.
Asynchronous communication	• Sender and receive don't have to use the same clock system • Take more time for transmission • Send byte or character	Wikis, Electronic mail, virtual library, social networking, etc.

So, it is clear that A, B, and C only facilitate Synchronous communication.

Hence, the correct option is (A).

49. The Fukushima, the Chernobyl and the three-mile island incident belong to the category of nuclear disasters.

Natural and human-caused disasters affect thousands of people each year. Major adverse events such as these have the potential to cause catastrophic loss of life and physical destruction.

Nuclear Disasters: The main drawback of nuclear energy is the possibility of nuclear disasters. These occur in nuclear power plants. The consequences of such disasters can be extremely serious. A few of these nuclear disasters include:

The Fukushima Disaster: It took place in 2011 at the Fukushima Daiichi plant in northern Japan. It is the second-worst nuclear accident in the history of nuclear power generation. It is also known as the Fukushima nuclear accident or Fukushima Daiichi nuclear accident.

The Chernobyl Disaster: The 1986 accident at the Chernobyl nuclear power plant in Ukraine, then part of the former Soviet Union, is the only accident in the history of commercial nuclear power to cause fatalities from radiation. It was the result of a severely flawed reactor design, combined with human error.

Three-mile Island Incident: The Three Mile Island accident, that took place on March 28, 1979, was a meltdown at a nuclear power plant in Middletown, Pennsylvania. This was the most serious accident in U.S. commercial nuclear power plant operating history. It resulted from a combination of equipment malfunctions, design-related problems and human errors.

Hence, the correct option is (A).

50. Teaching is defined as 'facilitation of learning' or in other words, the main objective of teaching is to facilitate learning:

- Traditionally, teachers are the ones with knowledge and expertise in a particular field. They impart that knowledge through a variety of means to their students.
- Facilitators build on the knowledge base of the group of students to find the answers to questions.
- A facilitator is a person who assists a group of people in grasping at their common targets and in achieving them without any intervention on his/her behalf.
- Therefore, when we say the teacher has to play the role of a facilitator in the classroom, this means that the teacher should not be the king who controls the activities of the learners.
- He /she should grant the learners some space to let the spirits of creativity and innovation.

- In other words, the learners must get involved in active participation that would be represented in argumentative discussions and teamwork activities, so that the process of learning becomes comprehensive.

Hence, the correct option is (A).

Mock Test 13

Ques (1-5):Direction: Read the given passage carefully and answer the following question.

At the turn of the century, a dominant conception of the child as learner was that he was cognitively an "empty organism" responding more or less randomly to stimulation, and characteristically learning when specific responses were connected with specific stimuli through the meditation of pleasure or pain. The organism itself, it was believed, would do nothing to learn or think if it were not impelled to such activity by primary drives like hunger or thirst or by externally applied motives like reward and punishment. Experimenters in the laboratory were connecting correct responses of animals to puzzle boxes by giving or withholding food and teachers in the classroom were connecting correct responses of children to problem cards by giving or withholding approval.

In pointing to this aspect of the turn - of - the - century view of the learner, I do not mean to derogate the historic achievement of the connectionist formulation of learning. But the essential point is a conception of the learner as an ideationally empty organism associating discrete stimuli and responses through the operation of rewards and punishments under the control of the teacher. Both the stimulus - what was supposed to be learned - an the response - what was actually learned - were believed to be determined by the teacher.

It was no accident that the materials and methods of instruction and the form of the classroom were teacher - centred. The teacher was necessarily placed in front of the classroom - sometime on a dais or platform - and the pupils in chairs rigidly fastened to the floor in straight rows facing forward so they would not turn away from the only source of the learning experience: the teacher. Given this contemporary vision of the learner, what could be a more eminently practical and sensible image of the ideal learning environment? Indeed, there is a letter by John Dewey dating from this period in which he complains that when he was trying to equip his new school according to his different conception of child as learner, he was unable to find any other kind of classroom furniture.

Q.1 What did John Dewey say of child learning?

A. Teacher as the only source of knowledge
B. The learner should be given incentives for learning
C. The existing educational environment was ideal
D. The focus should be on child as a learner

Q.2 What was expected of pupils during those early days?

A. To create an ideal learning environment
B. To be in the forefront of the classroom
C. Be attentive towards classroom teaching
D. To place the teacher on the higher pedestal

Q.3 The connectionist formula placed importance on:

A. Withholding negative stimuli
B. Teacher-centric motivation
C. Search for specific responses
D. Doing experiments in laboratories

Q.4 The basic idea behind laboratory experiments was related to:

A. Motivating the child with reward and punishment
B. Considering hunger and thirst as negligible in impact
C. Animals and children having the same drive
D. Teachers controlling children

Q.5 The early child was thought of as:

A. Intelligent enough to know both pain and pleasure
B. Having no power of cognition
C. Not amenable to specific stimuli
D. Having motivational effect in a random way

Q.6 In which type of education system, students with special educational needs have to be adjusted with the existing school environment?

A. Integrated
B. Inclusive
C. Special and Inclusive
D. Integrated and Inclusive

Q.7 The ultimate goal of education is to:

A. develop problem-solving skills among students
B. make students economically productive
C. cultivate the habit of maintaining good relationships
D. prepare knowledgeable individuals

Q.8 Main feature of distance education is:

A. Face to face learning
B. Counseling sessions and study centers
C. Compulsory attendance
D. Easy to get the degree

Q.9 Which one of the following institutions were established as a consequence to the closure of inter-University Board brought in for cooperation among the university in the field of education and allied areas?

A. Association of Central Universities
B. University Grants Commission
C. IIAS, Shimla
D. Association of Indian Universities

Q.10 Select the period in which India became a centre of higher learning.

A. Gupta Period **B.** Buddha Period
C. Mughal Period **D.** British Period

Q.11 Which model of communication is a one way process where sender is the one who sends the message but receiver does not give feedback or response?

A. Horizontal model **B.** Transactional model
C. Linear model **D.** Interactional model

Q.12 All are the components of listening except:

A. Hearing

B. Attending-being attentive

C. Answering

D. Understanding and remembering

Q.13 Educational TV was first introduced in India in the year

A. 1961 **B.** 1959 **C.** 1968 **D.** 1969

Q.14 Match the following List 1 with List 2 with correct responses.

List 1	**List 2**
a. Intrapersonal communication	(i) It is the communication where more than two individuals are involved in exchange of ideas, skills and interests.
b. Mass communication	(ii) It is a face to face communication between two persons.
c. Interpersonal communication	(iii) It uses mechanical devices that multiply messages and take it to a large number of people simultaneously.
d. Group communication	(iv) It is the communication within an individual, including talking to oneself.

A. a-iv, b-iii, c-ii, d- i **B.** a-iii, b-ii, c-i, d-iv

C. a-iv, b-iii, c-i, d-ii **D.** a-iv, b-i, c-ii, d-iii

Q.15 'Information overload' can be categorized as _____ barrier to communication.

A. Psychological **B.** Physiological

C. Social **D.** Cultural

Q.16 What will come in place of question mark (?) in the following number series?

8, 27, 125, ?, 1331, 2197

A. 49 **B.** 343 **C.** 64 **D.** 512

Q.17 Which two signs should be interchanged to make the given equation correct?

12 ÷ 4 + 148 × 4 - 18 = 67

A. + and – **B.** - and ÷ **C.** × and ÷ **D.** × and +

Q.18 Sum of the square of two numbers is 625. While the difference between these two numbers is 17. Find the sum of two numbers .

A. 31 **B.** 17.5 **C.** 16.25 **D.** 24.25

Q.19 Select the odd word from the given alternatives.

A. Stream **B.** Canal **C.** River **D.** Valley

Q.20 A series is given with one missing term. Select the correct alternative from the given ones that will complete the series.

$NOM, QRP, TUS, ?$

A. WAX **B.** HUT **C.** WXV **D.** WTU

Q.21 A series is given with one missing term. Select the correct alternative from the given ones that will complete the series.

5, 11, 24, 51, 106,?

A. 122 **B.** 217 **C.** 221 **D.** 115

Q.22 Direction: Given below are three statements (a), (b) and (c). From the given statements, four conclusions, (i), (ii), (iii) and (iv) are drawn. Select the correct option which states that conclusions logically follow from the given statements.

Statements:

(a) Some chairs are tables.

(b) Some tables are sofas.

(c) All sofa is a bed.

Conclusions:

(i) Some beds are chairs.

(ii) Some tables are beds.

(iii) Some sofas are chairs.

(iv) All beds are sofas.

Code:

A. Only (iv) follows

B. Only (ii) follows

C. Only (i) and (ii) follows

D. Only (i) and (iv) follows

Q.23 Match the following methods of teaching with its effective use:

List A	**List B**
a. Inspire, ignites, stimulates, thinking Reasoning in students	1. Discussion
b. Sharing ideas, stimulates thinking together	2. Lecture help
c. Understands others points of view, clarification, Comprehension, new ideas are generated.	3. Collaboration
d. Self-learning confidence building, active Participation in discussion.	4. Seminar

A. a - 1, b - 2, c - 3, d - 4

B. a - 2, b - 3, c - 4, d - 1

C. a - 1, b - 4, c - 2, d - 3

D. a - 2, b - 3, c - 1, d - 4

Q.24 Direction: Given below are two statements:

Statement I: Use of support materials during teaching can replace teaching act if used carefully.

Statement II: Online methods are effective supplements for improving quality of teaching and learning.

In the light of the above statements, choose the correct answer from the options given below:

A. Both Statement I and Statement II are true

B. Both Statement I and Statement II are false

C. Statement I is correct but Statement II is false

D. Statement I is incorrect but Statement II is true

Q.25 A college level assistant professor has planned his/her lectures with an intent to develop cognitive dimensions of students centered on skills of analysis and synthesis. Below, given are two sets of items Set – I consisting of levels of cognitive interchange and Set – II comprising basic requirements for promoting them. Match the two sets and indicate your answer by choosing the correct alternative from the code:

Set – I (Levels of Cognitive	**Set – II (Basic requirements for promoting cognitive interchange)**

Interchange)	
a. Memory level	i. Giving the opportunity for discriminating examples and non-examples of a point.
b. Understanding level	ii. Recording the important points made during the presentations
c. Reflective level	iii. Asking the students to discuss various items of information
	iv. Critically analyzing the points to be made and discussed

A. a - ii, b - iv, c - i **B.** a - iii, b - iv, c - ii
C. a - ii, b - i, c - iv **D.** a - i, b - ii, c - iii

Q.26 Massive Open Online Courses (MOOCs) are:

A. flexible and open form of self-directed, online learning designed for mass participation
B. flexible and open form of teacher-directed, online learning designed for mass participation
C. flexible and open form of self-directed, off-line learning designed for mass participation
D. flexible and open form of teacher-directed, off-line learning designed for mass participation

Q.27 Educationist and their special educational contribution — choose correct:

A. Louis Braille	(1) Handicapped learners
B. Helen Kellar	(2) Deaf learners
C. Thomas Edison	(3) Dumb and Deaf learners
D. Lal Adwani	(4) Blind learners

A. A - (2), B - (4), C - (1), D - (3)
B. A - (3), B - (2), C - (4), D - (1)
C. A - (4), B - (3), C - (2), D - (1)
D. A - (2), B - (1), C - (3), D - (4)

Q.28 The study of living organisms with the environment is known as __________.

A. Ecosystem **B.** Environment
C. Community **D.** Ecology

Q.29 What is the climate pattern in areas of limited size or immediate surroundings of plant and animal?

A. Mixed climate **B.** Macroclimate
C. Microclimate **D.** Segmented climate

Q.30 What is untreated sewage?

A. Raw sewage **B.** Treated Sewage
C. Pollutants **D.** Wastewater

Q.31 In which of the countries per capita use of water is maximum?

A. USA **B.** European Union
C. China **D.** India

Q.32 Who among the following, propounded the concept of paradigm?

A. Peter Haggett **B.** Von Thunen
C. Thomas Kuhn **D.** John K. Wright

Q.33 A variable that is manipulated is known as:

A. Confounding variable
B. Control variable
C. Dependent variable
D. Independent variable

Q.34 Which of the following is susceptible to the issue of research ethics?

[UGC NET Sociology, 2017]

A. Inaccurate application of statistical techniques
B. Inaccurate application of statistical techniques
C. Choice of sampling techniques
D. Reporting of research findings

Q.35 The _______ of a research article is placed near its beginning.

A. summary **B.** abstract
C. synopsis **D.** preface

Q.36 Among the following which one is not instructional material?

A. printed study guide **B.** Overhead projector
C. Audio podcast **D.** Youtube video

Q.37 Which of the following terms is related to the digital learning environment for design?

A. e-Vidwan **B.** e-Acharya
C. e-Kalpa **D.** e-Yantra

Q.38 The binary equivalent of $(-23)_{10}$ is ?

A. 111010010 **B.** 111010001
C. 111010111 **D.** 111110001

Q.39 e-Shodh Sindhu provides access to scholarly articles, e-journals and e-books at:

A. Primary education level
B. Secondary education level
C. Higher education level
D. Research level only

Q.40 An Integrated text-to-speech and text-to-braille system for the visually impaired provided by C-DAC is:

A. Sakshat **B.** e-Drishti
C. Shruti Drishti **D.** Gyan Darshan

Q.41 The ratio of two numbers a and b is 3 : 7. After adding 9 to each number, the ratio becomes 9:17. The numbers a and b are:

A. (8, 42) **B.** (9, 21) **C.** (15, 35) **D.** (18, 42)

Ques (42-46):Direction: In the following table, the number of employees working in five companies and their corresponding ratio of male and female employees have been given. Study the table carefully and answer the questions that follow.

Company	Number of employees	Male : Female
L	500	12 : 8
M	700	15 : 5
N	900	4 : 1
O	1200	13 : 12
P	1400	9 : 5

Q.42 The total number of male employees working in companies N and P together is:

A. 1620 **B.** 1820 **C.** 1700 **D.** 1600

Q.43 The number of female employees in company M is:

A. 175 **B.** 275 **C.** 325 **D.** 525

Q.44 What is the average number of employees in all companies together?

A. 930 **B.** 940 **C.** 650 **D.** 850

Q.45 The number of female employees working in company O is what percent of total employees working in that company?

A. 24% **B.** 12% **C.** 48% **D.** 15%

Q.46 What is the ratio between the number of females in company P and number of females in company L?

A. 5:2 **B.** 2:7 **C.** 4:9 **D.** 3:7

Q.47 What should come in the place of question mark '?' in the following number series?

100, ?, 28, 16, 10, 7

A. 52 **B.** 34 **C.** 62 **D.** 93

Q.48 Direction: In the question below, there are two statements followed by two conclusions numbered I and II. You have to take the given statements to be true even if they seem to be at variance with commonly known facts. Read all the conclusions and then decide which of the given conclusions logically follows from the given statements disregarding the commonly known facts.

Statements:

Some spades are diamond.

Only few diamond are club.

Conclusions:

I. All diamond are club.

II. Some spades are club.

A. Only conclusion I follows

B. Only conclusion II follows

C. Both I and II follow

D. Neither I nor II follows

Q.49 Which of the following is NOT a "greenhouse gas" (GHG)?

A. Oxygen **B.** Carbon dioxide

C. Water vapour **D.** Methane

Q.50 A teacher proposes to find out the effect of praise and encouragement during a teaching learning session based on Skinner's theory of reinforcement. What type of research will it belong to?

A. Fundamental research

B. Evaluative research

C. Action research

D. Applied research

// Smart Answer Sheet //

Correct Indicates percentage of students who answered questions correctly.

Skipped Indicates percentage of students who skipped questions.

Q.	Ans.	Correct	Skipped
1	D	89.9 %	0.0 %
2	D	58.32 %	1.63 %
3	B	29.23 %	3.26 %
4	C	18.01 %	3.36 %
5	B	53.96 %	1.89 %
6	A	76.92 %	0.0 %
7	A	59.61 %	1.02 %
8	B	60.32 %	1.63 %
9	D	49.05 %	1.55 %
10	A	44.37 %	1.12 %
11	C	61.31 %	1.9 %
12	C	85.2 %	0.0 %
13	B	30.02 %	3.79 %
14	A	66.07 %	1.92 %
15	B	54.4 %	1.57 %
16	B	81.26 %	0.0 %
17	D	40.35 %	1.47 %
18	A	58.19 %	1.49 %
19	D	53.66 %	1.53 %
20	C	60.87 %	1.6 %
21	B	56.89 %	1.89 %
22	B	69.66 %	1.0 %
23	D	18.38 %	4.05 %
24	D	43.68 %	1.24 %
25	C	46.1 %	1.46 %
26	A	48.12 %	1.89 %
27	C	63.59 %	1.78 %
28	D	86.28 %	0.0 %
29	C	59.65 %	1.31 %
30	D	59.99 %	1.64 %
31	B	65.16 %	1.44 %
32	C	87.53 %	0.0 %
33	D	78.19 %	0.0 %
34	D	44.19 %	1.28 %
35	B	52.15 %	1.98 %
36	B	87.11 %	0.0 %
37	C	80.3 %	0.0 %
38	B	46.49 %	1.32 %
39	C	65.57 %	1.81 %
40	C	30.43 %	4.07 %
41	D	55.05 %	1.03 %
42	A	20.81 %	3.79 %
43	A	49.2 %	1.59 %
44	B	42.48 %	1.92 %
45	C	66.03 %	1.14 %
46	A	55.39 %	1.63 %
47	A	51.36 %	1.12 %
48	D	43.7 %	1.83 %
49	A	41.88 %	1.05 %
50	D	45.4 %	1.53 %

Performance Analysis	
Avg. Score (%)	36.0%
Toppers Score (%)	61.0%
Your Score	

//Hints and Solutions//

1. According to the passage "Given this contemporary vision of the learner, what could be a more eminently practical and sensible image of the ideal learning environment? Indeed, there is a letter by John Dewey dating from this period in which he complains that when he was trying to equip his new school according to his different conception of the child as a learner, he was unable to find any other kind of classroom furniture."

It can be concluded that John Dewey wanted to equip the school by keeping in mind the conception of child as a learner.

Hence, the correct option is (D).

2. The correct answer is to place the teacher on the higher pedestal.

The second sentence of the concluding paragraph says "The teacher was necessarily placed in front of the classroom sometimes on a dais or platform - and the pupils in chairs rigidly fastened to the floor in straight rows facing forward so they would not turn away from the only source of the learning experience: the teacher"

From the above, we can logically conclude that the main idea behind learning in the early days was that the pupils should place the teacher on a high platform or pedestal.

All other characteristics of learning in those days, like the students fastened to the floor and facing forward so that they were attentive, were means to fulfil the above.

Hence, the correct option is (D).

3. The connectionist formula placed importance on teacher-centric motivation.

The second paragraph of the passage mentions "the connectionist formulation of learning. But the essential point is a conception of the learner as an ideationally empty organism associating discrete stimuli and responses through the operation of rewards and punishments under the control of the teacher. Both the stimulus what was supposed to be learned and the response what was actually learned - were believed to be determined by the teacher."

Hence, the correct option is (B).

4. The opening paragraph of the passage says the following about the historic conception of the child:

cognitively an "empty organism" responding more or less randomly to stimulation.

characteristically learning when specific responses were connected with specific stimuli through the meditation of pleasure or pain

would do nothing to learn or think if it were not impelled to such activity by primary drives like hunger or thirst or by externally applied motives like reward and punishment.

Experimenters in the laboratory were connecting correct responses of animals to puzzle boxes by giving or withholding food and teachers in the classroom were connecting correct responses of children to problem cards by giving or withholding approval.

Teachers controlling children: This was the main idea behind the learning process in historical times but not behind the laboratory experiments.

Hence, the correct option is (C).

5. The opening paragraph of the passage says the following about the historic conception of the child:

Cognitively an "empty organism" responding more or less randomly to stimulation.

Characteristically learning when specific responses were connected with specific stimuli through the meditation of pleasure or pain.

Would do nothing to learn or think if it were not impelled to such activity by primary drives like hunger or thirst or by externally applied motives like reward and punishment.

Thus we can logically conclude that the early child was thought of as having no power of cognition.

Hence, the correct option is (B).

6. "In integrated education system" students with special educational needs have to be adjusted to the existing school environment.

- In India, "integrated education" has been provided mainly to students with mild disabilities who are considered "easy" to include in regular school programs.
- In the "integrated education" model "whenever possible, students with disabilities attend a regular school".
- Integration signifies the process of interaction of disabled children with normal children in the same educational settings.
- The emphasis, however, is upon the student to fit the system rather than the system to adapt to meet the educational needs of a student.
- Students with severe disabilities, in a majority of cases, do not attend a school, or in rare cases, attend a special school.
- In integrated schools, children of all backgrounds learn side by side in the same classrooms every day.

Hence, the correct option is (A).

7. The ultimate goal of education is to develop problem-solving skills among students.

Problem-solving is a process of overcoming difficulties that appear to interfere with the attainment of a goal.

- It is a mental process and is part of the larger problem process that includes problem finding and problem shaping.

- Problem-solving is a higher-order cognitive process that requires the modulation and control of more routine or fundamental skills.
- Problem Solving is the framework or pattern within which creative thinking and reasoning take place. It is a basic skill needed by today's learners.

Hence, the correct option is (A).

8. Main feature of distance education is counseling sessions and study centers.

Distance Education, or distance learning, is a field of education that focuses on the pedagogy and andragogy, technology, and instructional systems design that aims to deliver education to students who are not physically "on-site".

Distance Education "is a process to create and provide access to learning when the source of information and the learners are separated by time and distance, or both." In other words, distance learning is the process of creating an educational experience of equal qualitative value for the learner to best suit their needs outside the classroom.

Hence, the correct option is (B).

9. the Association of Indian Universities were established as a consequence to the closure of IUB brought in for cooperation among the university in the field of education and allied areas.

Association of Indian Universities (AIU):

- The Inter-University Board (later known as the Association of Indian Universities) was established in 1925 to promote university activities, by sharing information and cooperation in the field of education, culture, sports and allied areas.
- The AIU has been acting as a representative body of universities of India to liaise with the universities and the government (central as well as state) and to coordinate among the universities and the other apex higher education organizations of the world.
- It works for the cause of higher education. It assesses the courses, syllabi, standards and credits of foreign universities pursued abroad and equates them in relation to various courses offered by Indian universities.
- It is mainly concerned with the recognition of Degrees/Diplomas awarded by the Universities in India, which are recognized by the UGC, New Delhi, and abroad for the purpose of admission to higher degree courses in Indian Universities.

Hence, the correct option is (D).

10. India became a center of higher learning in the Gupta Period.

- The Gupta period was a gradual evolution. Education as a system of knowledge was confined to the Brahmanic class in the Gupta age.
- Formal education was available in Brahmin asramas, hermitages, and in some extends to Buddhist and Jaina monasteries. In the former, it would have been restricted to the upper castes.
- Theoretically, the period of studentship at the former lasted over many years, but it is unlikely that most would spend long periods as students. Learning was a personalized experience involving teachers and pupils.
- The emphasis was on memorizing texts such as parts of the Vedas and gaining familiarity with the contents of the Dharmasastras and subjects such as grammar, rhetoric, prose and verse composition, logic, and metaphysics. But much else was included in Sanskrit learning, such as astronomy, mathematics, medicine, and astrology.

Hence, the correct option is (A).

11. The linear model of communication is considered as a one-way process in which sender sends a message to the receiver but at that time receiver is not present to give feedback or any type of response.

Horizontal model of communication is the communication in which information is delivered to the people working at the same level of an organisational hierarchy.

Transactional model of communication is the communication in which the information is exchanged between the sender and receiver where each sender/receiver takes turn to send/receive the message.

Interactional model of communication is the communication where information is exchanged both ways between sender and receiver.

Hence, the correct option is (C).

12. All are the components of listening except answering.

The listening process involves four stages: Hearing, Attending-being attentive, Understanding and remembering, and responding.

Hence, the correct option is (C).

13. Educational TV was first introduced in India in the year 1959.

Educational television or learning television is the use of television programs in the field of distance education. Many children's television series are educational, ranging from dedicated learning programs to those that indirectly teach the viewers. Some series are written to have a specific moral behind every episode, often explained at the end by the character that learned the lesson.

Hence, the correct option is (B).

14. The correct combination is - a-iv, b-iii, c-ii, d- i

Intrapersonal communication is a communication that takes place within an individual, including talking to oneself.

Mass communication is a communication that uses mechanical devices that multiply messages and take them to a large number of people simultaneously.

Interpersonal communication is a face to face communication between two persons.

Group communication is the communication where more than two individuals are involved in the exchange of ideas, skills and interests.

Hence, the correct option is (A).

15. 'Information overload' can be categorized as Physiological barrier to communication.

Physiological barriers to communication are related to the limitations of the human body and the human mind. These barriers include poor listening skills, information overload, inattention, emotions, poor retention etc.

Hence, the correct option is (B).

16. The given series is the cube of prime numbers:

$2^3 = 8$

$3^3 = 27$

$5^3 = 125$

$7^3 = 343$

$11^3 = 1331$

$13^3 = 2197$

∴ The value of ? is 343.

Hence, the correct option is (B).

17. (A) + and –

Given expression: 12 ÷ 4 + 148 × 4 - 18 = 67

After interchanging the symbols, we get:

L.H.S = 12 ÷ 4 - 148 × 4 + 18

= 3 - 37 + 18

= 21 - 37

= -16 ≠ R.H.S

(B) - and ÷

Given expression: 12 ÷ 4 + 148 × 4 - 18 = 67

After interchanging the symbols, we get:

L.H.S = 12 - 4 + 148 × 4 ÷ 18

= 12 - 4 + 148 × 0.22

= 12 - 4 + 32.89

= 44.89 - 4

= 40.89 ≠ R.H.S

(C) × and ÷

Given expression: 12 ÷ 4 + 148 × 4 - 18 = 67

After interchanging the symbols, we get:

L.H.S = 12 × 4 + 148 ÷ 4 - 18

= 12 × 4 + 37 - 18

= 48 + 37 - 18

= 85 - 18

= 67 = R.H.S

(D) × and +

Given expression: 12 ÷ 4 + 148 × 4 - 18 = 67

After interchanging the symbols, we get:

L.H.S = 12 ÷ 4 × 148 + 4 - 18

= 3 × 148 + 4 - 18

= 444 + 4 - 18

= 448 - 18

= 430 ≠ R.H.S

So, '× and ÷' is the correct answer.

Hence, the correct option is (D).

18. Given

sum of the square of numbers $= 625$

difference between two number $= 17$

Formulal:

$$(a+b)^2 = a^2 + b^2 + 2ab$$

A.M of two numbers $= \frac{(a+b)}{2}$

Calculation:

Let two numbers be x and y respectively.

So, $x^2 + y^2 = 625$ ... (1)

and $x - y = 17$

$\Rightarrow (x-y)^2 = 17^2$

$\Rightarrow x^2 + y^2 - 2xy = 289$

From equation (1)

$\Rightarrow 625 - 2xy = 289$

$\Rightarrow xy = 168$ ... (2)

As we know,

$$(x+y)^2 = x^2 + y^2 + 2xy$$

From equation (1) and (2)

$$(x+y)^2 = 625 + 336 = 961$$

$\Rightarrow x + y = 31$

Hence, the correct option is (A).

19. Valley is the odd one out because all others are fluid flowing bodies and valley is a typical landform.

Hence, the correct option is (D).

20. $N \overset{+3}{\rightarrow} Q \overset{+3}{\rightarrow} T \overset{+3}{\rightarrow} W$

$O \overset{+3}{\rightarrow} R \overset{+3}{\rightarrow} U \overset{+3}{\rightarrow} X$

$M \overset{+3}{\rightarrow} P \overset{+3}{\rightarrow} S \overset{+3}{\rightarrow} V$

Hence, the correct option is (C).

21.

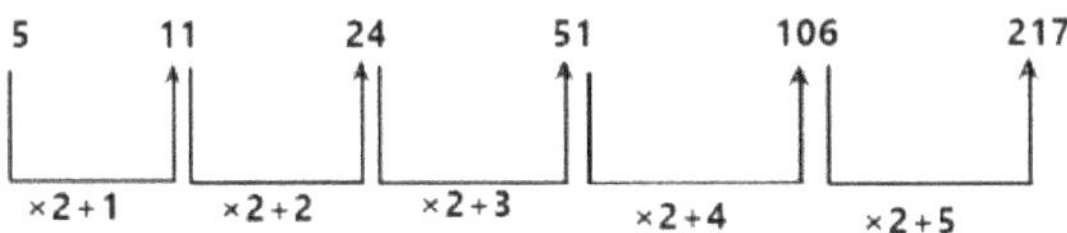

The next term is 217.

Hence, the correct option is (B).

22.

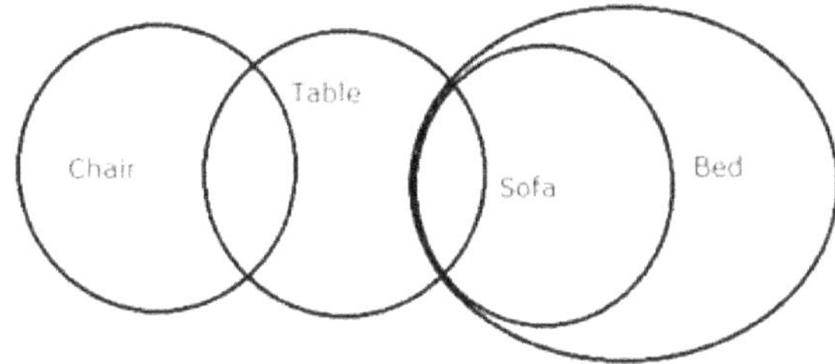

(i) Some beds are chairs does not follow as there is no direct relation between bed and chair.

(ii) Some tables are beds follows as from the diagram some part of the tables lies in bed.

(iii) Some sofas are chairs does not follow as there is no direct relation between sofa and chair.

(iv) All beds are sofas does not follow as some bed are sofa is true but not all.

Therefore, only conclusion (ii) follows.

Hence, the correct option is (B).

23.

List A	**List B**
a. Inspire, ignites, stimulates, thinking Reasoning in students	Lecture help
b. Sharing ideas, stimulates thinking together	Collaboration
c. Understands other's points of view, clarification, Comprehension, new ideas are generated.	Discussion
d. Self-learning confidence building, active participation in the discussion.	Seminar

A lecture is an educational instruction delivered by faculty to students in a typical classroom setting. The instructions are long speeches on the subject matter/topic within the curriculum selected by the Instructor.

Collaboration is a practice whereby individuals engage cooperatively to serve common purposes. It includes knowledge and workspace sharing with mutual efforts.

Discussion is a conversation on a topic among a group where the topic is analyzed critically between the members through a series of purposeful talk/debate and information sharing in order to solve a problem or get into a consensus after arriving at a definite conclusion at the end of discussion.

A seminar is a formal academic meeting of a group under a distinguished expert or panel where discourse is made on the stated topic or the theme of the seminar. It is an interactive session where the participants actively engage in the topic of the seminar.

Hence, the correct option is (D).

24. Teaching is a process in which one individual teaches or instructs another individual. Teaching is considered as the act of imparting instructions to the learners in the classroom situation. It is watching systematically. Dewey:- considers it as a manipulation of the situation, where the learner will acquire skills and insight with his own initiation.

Statement I: Use of support materials during teaching can replace teaching act if used carefully.

- Support materials cannot replace teaching.
- Support materials are merely an augmentation to teaching.
- They can help in the process of learning, but they certainly cannot replace the power of teaching.
- It is significant that we remember, teaching is more than just facilitating knowledge. Teaching also guides, mentors, and inspires students. Teaching itself is a power that cannot be replaced by support materials of any kind.

Thus, the statement I is incorrect.

Statement II: Online methods are effective supplements for improving the quality of teaching and learning.

- Online learning may take several forms in delivering and supporting curricula.
- At the most basic level, online learning resources may simply provide a mechanism for learners to engage asynchronously with content delivered in a lecture in either video or audio form. This form of content delivery often referred to as a podcast, can be used to reexamine areas of a lecture that may have seemed unclear or to deliver content in lieu of a classroom presentation.
- Alternatively, online resources may be explicitly integrated or blended with in-class activities, as in the flipped curriculum approach where students interact with videos, audio clips, or readings prior to a classroom session to provide core knowledge and content that informs applications during the in-class session.
- Finally, online learning may provide the full mechanism for delivering and assessing knowledge and skills as occurs with massive open online courses (MOOCs).

Thus, the statement II is incorrect.

Hence, the correct option is (D).

25. The activities of teaching and learning may be organized at various levels of abstraction; ranging from the use and application of simple mental powers to the most complex ones. Such organizations are distinguished and labeled as 'forms and levels' of teaching. There are three identifiable levels of teaching and learning activities: Memory level, understanding level, and Reflective level. Morris L. Biggie (1976) has added one more level under the rubric 'autonomous development'.

Set – I (Levels of Cognitive Interchange)	**Set – II (Basic requirements for promoting cognitive interchange)**
a. Memory level	ii. Recording the important points made during the presentations
b. Understanding level	i. Giving the opportunity for discriminating examples and non-examples of a point.
c. Reflective level	iv. Critically analyzing the points to be made and discussed

Hence, the correct option is (C).

26. MOOCs are a flexible and open form of self-directed, online learning designed for mass participation.

MOOC (Massive Open Online Courses):

- Massive open online courses (MOOCs) are one of the most prominent trends in higher education in recent years. The term 'MOOCs' represents open access, global, self-directed, free, video-based instructional content, videos, problem sets, and forums released through an online platform to high volume participants.
- MOOCs (Massive Open Online Courses) provides a new way of learning, which is open, participatory, distributed, and lifelong.
- The MHRD, Government of India has also started a MOOCs platform called SWAYAM (Study Webs of Active-Learning for Young Aspiring Minds).

Hence, the correct option is (A).

27. An educationist is someone who works within an educational system in various roles and responsibilities that facilitate teaching, learning, assessment, research, curriculum development, and policy among others.

A. Louis Braille	(4) Blind learners
B. Helen Kellar	(3) Dumb and Deaf learners
C. Thomas Edison	(2) Deaf learners
D. Lal Adwani	(1) Handicapped learners

Hence, the correct option is (C).

28. The study of living organisms with the environment is known as Ecology. Ecology is the study of the relationship between living organisms and the environment. It also deals with the interaction of living organisms with each other.

Hence, the correct option is (D).

29. Microclimate refers to the climatic condition of the immediate surroundings of plants and animals while Macroclimate is the climatic pattern over a large area or on local, global, and regional levels.

Hence, the correct option is (C).

30. Untreated sewage refers to wastewater that contains harmful waterborne pathogens and bacteria and which has not yet gone through a sewage treatment plant. Raw sewage originates from broken toilet pipes, overspills, industry leakages and heavy storms.

Hence, the correct option is (C).

31. The European Union (EU) is a political and economic union of 28-member states that are located primarily in Europe. So, per capita use of water is highest in European Union.

Hence, the correct option is (B).

32. A paradigm is a standard, perspective, or set of ideas. A paradigm is a way of looking at something.

Concept of Paradigm:

- The historian of science Thomas Kuhn gave it its contemporary meaning.
- Kuhn fathered, defined and popularized the concept of "paradigm shift".
- In his book, The Structure of Scientific Revolutions (first published in 1962), Kuhn defines a scientific paradigm as: "universally recognized scientific achievements that, for a time, provide model problems and solutions for a community of practitioners".
- He adopted the word to refer to the set of concepts and practices that define a scientific discipline at any particular period of time.
- According to him scientific advancement is a series of peaceful interludes punctuated by intellectually violent revolutions.
- Therefore, it is a change in the way of thinking from one form to another.

Hence, the correct option is (C).

33. The variable that is changed in an experiment is called the manipulated variable. Sometimes, it is also called an independent variable.

Hence, the correct option is (D).

34. Research ethics is specifically related to the analysis of ethical issues that are raised when people are involved as participants in research.

The reporting of research findings is susceptible to the issue of research ethics, as there cannot be any distortion with the findings.

Whereas the other three options are not susceptible to the issue of research ethics because these are not influenced by research ethics.

Hence, the correct option is (D).

35. The abstract of a research article is placed near its beginning.

An abstract is a brief summary of a research article, thesis, review, conference proceeding, or any in-depth analysis of a particular subject and is often used to help the reader quickly ascertain the paper's purpose.

When used, an abstract always appears at the beginning of a manuscript or typescript, acting as the point of entry for any given academic paper or patent application. Abstracting and indexing services for various academic disciplines are aimed at compiling a body of literature for that particular subject.

Hence, the correct option is (B).

36. Overhead projector is not an instructional material. The printed study guide has instructional material in the form of notes from a particular topic. The audio podcast is the material which contains useful information in audio form. YouTube video is the medium through which the instructional material is provided in the form of audio as well as video.

Hence, the correct option is (B).

37. e-KALPA: Creating Digital-learning Environment for Design also called e-Kalpa is an initiative of the Ministry of Human Resources, Government of India as part of the National Mission in Education through Information and Communication Technology (NMEICT).

This project presents three initiatives –

- providing digital online content for design,
- a social networking environment for design and
- higher learning and creating a digital resource database on design.

Therefore, the e-Kalpa term is related to the digital learning environment for design.

Hence, the correct option is (C).

38. Step 1: We start with the positive version of the number:

⇒ |-23| = 23

Step 2: Divide the number repeatedly by 2, keeping track of each remainder, until we get a quotient that is equal to zero:

⇒ dividend ÷ divisor = quotient + remainder

⇒ 23 ÷ 2 = 11 + 1;

⇒ 11 ÷ 2 = 5 + 1;

⇒ 5 ÷ 2 = 2 + 1;

⇒ 2 ÷ 2 = 1 + 0;

⇒ 1 ÷ 2 = 0 + 1;

Now we got the quotient 0.

Step 3: Construct the base 2 representation of the positive number, by taking all the remainders starting from the bottom of the list in step 2.

⇒ $23_{(10)} = 10111_{(2)}$

Step 4: Determine the signed binary number bit length:

The base 2 number's actual length, in bits: 5.

A signed binary's bit length must be equal to a power of 2, as of:

21 = 2; 22 = 4; 23 = 8; 24 = 16; 25 = 32; 26 = 64; ...

First bit (the leftmost) indicates the sign,

1 = negative, 0 = positive.

The least number that is a power of 2 and is larger than the actual length so that the first bit (leftmost) could be zero is: 8.

Step 5: Positive binary computer representation on 8 bits - if needed, add extra 0s in front (to the left) of the base 2 number, up to the required length:

⇒ $23_{(10)}$ = 00010111

Step 6: To get the negative integer number representation on 8 bits, signed binary one's complement, replace all the bits on 0 with 1s and all the bits set on 1 with 0s (reversing the digits):

⇒ !(00010111) = 11101000

Step 7: To get the negative integer number representation on 8 bits, signed binary two's complement, add 1 to the number calculated above in step 6:

⇒ 11101000 + 1 = 11101001

Therefore, Number -23, a signed integer, converted from decimal system (base 10) to a signed binary two's complement representation is $-23_{(10)}$ = 11101001

Hence, the correct option is (B).

39. e-Shodh Sindhu provides access to scholarly articles, e-journals and e-books at higher education level. The MHRD, Government of India has formed e-ShodhSindhu merging three consortia initiatives namely UGC-INFONET Digital Library Consortium, NLIST, and INDEST-AICTE Consortium.

Hence, the correct option is (C).

40. "Shruti Drishti" is an Integrated Text-to-Speech [TTS] & Text-to-Braille [TTB] System for the Visually Impaired using the Information Extraction and Retrieval techniques.

Shruti Drishti is a web page browser developed for visually impaired users is considered to provide a user-friendly environment.

Hence, the correct option is (C).

41. Given:

Ratio of a and b number is = 3 : 7

Calculation:

Let the ratio be x

So, numbers a and b are 3x and 7x respectively.

According to the question,

$$\Rightarrow \frac{(3x+9)}{(7x+9)} = \frac{9}{17}$$

⇒ 17 × (3x + 9) = 9 × (7x + 9)

⇒ 51x + 153 = 63x + 81

⇒ 51x - 63x = 81 - 153

⇒ -12x = -72

⇒ x = 6

So, a = 3x = 3 × 6 = 18

⇒ b = 7x = 7 × 6 = 42

∴ Number a and b are 18 and 42

Hence, the correct option is (D).

42. Given:

Company	Number of employees	Male : female
N	900	4 : 1
P	1400	9 : 5

No. of male employees in company N = $\frac{4}{5} \times 900 = 720$

No. of male employees in company M = $\frac{9}{14} \times 1400 = 900$

∴ No. of male employees in company N and company P

= $720 + 900 = 1620$

Hence, the correct option is (A).

43. Given:

Total employees in company M $= 700$

Male to female ratio in company M $= 15:5$

Calculation:

Sum of ratios $= 15 + 5 = 20$

No. of female employees in company M $= \frac{5}{20} \times 700 = 175$

∴ No. of female employees in company M $= 175$

Hence, the correct option is (A).

44. Given:

Company	Number of employees
L	500
M	700
N	900
O	1200
P	1400

Total no. of employees in 5 companies $= 500 + 700 + 900 + 1200 + 1400 = 4700$

∴ Required average $= \frac{4700}{5} = 940$

Hence, the correct option is (B).

45. Given:

Male to female ratio in company O $= 13:12$

Calculation:

Sum of ratios $= 13 + 12 = 25$

Required percentage $= \frac{12}{25} \times 100 = 48\%$

∴ Required percentage is 48%.

Hence, the correct option is (C).

46. Given:

Company	Number of employees	Male : Female
L	500	12 : 8
P	1400	9 : 5

Calculation:

No. of females in company P $= \frac{5}{14} \times 1400 = 500$

No. of females in company L $= \frac{8}{20} \times 500 = 200$

∴ Required ratio $= \frac{500}{200} = 5:2$

Hence, the correct option is (A).

47. The pattern of the given series can be explained as:

100 ÷ 2 + 2 = 52

52 ÷ 2 + 2 = 28

28 ÷ 2 + 2 = 16

16 ÷ 2 + 2 = 10

10 ÷ 2 + 2 = 7

∴ The value of ? is 52.

Hence, the correct option is (A).

48. The least possible Venn diagram for the given statements is as follows:

Conclusions:

I. All diamond are club → False (as only few diamond are club i.e. some diamond must not be club)

II. Some spades are club → False (It is possible but not definite)

So, neither I nor II follows.

Hence, the correct option is (D).

49. Carbon dioxide, methane, and water vapour are the most important greenhouse gases and oxygen is not a GHG.

A Greenhouse gas (GHG) is a gas that absorbs and emits radiant energy within the thermal infrared range. Some other gases such as surface-level ozone, nitrous oxides, and fluorinated gases also trap infrared radiation.

Kyoto Protocol:

- Kyoto Protocol is an international agreement that aimed to reduce Carbon dioxide emissions and the presence of Greenhouse Gases (GHG) in the atmosphere.
- It was adopted in Kyoto, Japan on 11th December 1997. and became international law on 16 February 2005.

Hence, the correct option is (A).

50. A teacher proposes to find out the effect of praise and encouragement during a teaching learning session based on Skinner's theory of reinforcement. It belong to applied research.

Applied research:

- It discovers ways of applying principles and theories to solve social problems.
- Applied research refers to scientific study and research that seeks to solve practical problems.
- This type of research plays an important role in solving everyday problems that often have an impact on life, work, health, and overall well-being.

Hence, the correct option is (D).

Mock Test 14

Ques (1-5):Direction: Read the given passage carefully and select the best answer to each question out of the four given alternatives.

Patty was the type of pigeon who always had a sense of adventure and an active curiosity. She lived in a brick hole near the top of a building near Union Station, in Washington D.C.

Patty loved watching the trains come in and go out of the station. She loved the clickety-clack sound of the trains as they picked up speed going down the train track. And she loved the loud whistle that the train made.

Just before the train would blow its whistle, Patty would throw back her head and pretend as if the train's glorious whistle sound was coming directly from her own beak. Her friends looked at her a little strange when she did this, but those poor pigeons had no idea what it's like to ride a train.

Patty knew almost everything there is to know about trains since she once took the Amtrak train all the way to Boston. Actually, that's not totally true. She first took the train to Philadelphia, and then caught the second train to Boston.

First, fly down to the train tracks and pretend as if you're just pecking around for sandwich crumbs. Act as if you're just a regular pigeon looking for the odd scrap of food.

Then make your way over to the doorway of one of the cars of the train. All the while, pretend as if it is the furthest thing on your mind to hop onto a train.

When you get near to one of the doorways to the train, check to see that there aren't any conductors too close to you. Then just at the moment when someone is getting on or getting off the train, pretend as if you're startled and fly up into the air while screeching just a bit.

The hurried traveller may take notice of you for a second, but you can be sure that they will be quickly on their way. Then when you're up in the air near the doorway to the train car, pretend as if you accidentally land on the top step of the doorway of the train car.

Then pretend as if your sense of curiosity is so strong that you need to take a quick peek inside the train car. Waddle a little bit forward in the way that they tell you to do in the Pigeon's Acting Book. Then you can duck underneath one of the first seats you come to, put your head underneath your wing, and then snooze all the way until the train has completely left the station.

It's important that you not engage in regular pigeon clucking when you're hiding underneath the train seat. If the man in the seat above you is carrying on and on in the most boring way imaginable, resist the temptation to cluck. And if the kids in the seats across the aisle always seem to be making a big fuss about everything, resist the temptation to cluck.

Q.1 Why does Patty the pigeon throw back her head and pretend as if the train's glorious whistle sound was coming directly from her own beak?

A. Because she had traveled on a train already

B. Because she knows how to make that sound

C. Because she wants to show off her skills to her friends

D. None of these

Q.2 What did Patty suggest to not look suspicious at all?

A. Fly right into the train

B. Cluck in the train

C. Pretend to peck around for sandwich crumbs

D. None of these

Q.3 What is antonym of the given word?

Pretend

A. Profess **B.** Affect

C. Genuine **D.** None of these

Q.4 What is the meaning of the term 'cluck'?

A. Make a short, low sound

B. To poke with a beak

C. To squeak

D. None of these

Q.5 What did the pigeon suggest to not get noticed while travelling in the train?

A. One should not fly

B. One should not go after fallen sandwich crumbs

C. One should refrain from the usual clucking

D. All of these

Q.6 BOD test is made for measuring which of the following pollutions?

A. Noise pollution **B.** Water pollution

C. Soil Pollution **D.** Air pollution

Q.7 Which of the following programs of the Ministry of Human Resource and Development promotes life skill training among young people?

A. Samgra Shiksha

B. Adolescence Education Programme

C. Operation Blackboard

D. Swayam Prabha

Q.8 Which of the anthropogenic activity accounts for more than $\frac{2}{3}rd$ of global water consumption?

A. Agriculture

B. Hydropower generation

C. Industry

D. Domestic and Municipal usage

Q.9 Chlorofluorocarbons are replacing with less harmful compounds such as:

A. Hyloalkene
B. Hydrocarbons
C. Dichlorodifluoromethane
D. Difluoroethane

Q.10 Which of the following phenomena is not a natural hazard?
A. Chemical contamination
B. Landslide
C. Wildfire
D. Lightning

Q.11 Effective communication reduces pre-imagined ______.
A. Non-alignment **B.** Domination
C. Passivity **D.** Understanding

Q.12 Most often, the teacher-student communication is:
A. Spurious **B.** Critical
C. Utilitarian **D.** Confrontational

Q.13 What are the barriers to effective communication?
A. Moralising, being judgemental and comments of consolation
B. Dialogue, summary and self-review
C. Use of simple words, cool reaction and defensive attitude
D. Personal statements, eye contact and simple narration

Q.14 Classroom communication is the basis of:
A. Social identity **B.** External inanities
C. Biased passivity **D.** Group aggression

Q.15 Which of the following is/are correct in respect of non-verbal communication?
I. It helps illiterate people to communicate with others easily.
II. In this communication people can repeat the verbal messages according to their need.
III. In this communication there is a great possibility in distortion of information.
Codes:
A. Only I **B.** I and II
C. II and III **D.** All of these

Q.16 Which of the following has been ranked the best college in the country (2017) as per the National Institutional Ranking Framework (NIRF)?
[UGC NET Sociology, 2017]
A. Miranda House, Delhi
B. St. Stephen's College, Delhi
C. Fergusson College, Pune
D. Maharaja's College, Mysore

Q.17 The grounds on which discrimination in admission to educational institutions is constitutionally prohibited are?
1. Religion
2. Sex
3. Place of birth
4. Nationality

Select the correct answer from the codes given below:
A. 2, 3 and 4 **B.** 1, 2 and 3
C. 1, 2 and 4 **D.** 1, 2, 3 and 4

Q.18 Universities or Higher Education Institutions like to get accredited by NAAC because:
A. Degrees get accepted in the academic world
B. Status of the institution is established
C. Get relative placement in academic world
D. Strengths of university get streamlined

Q.19 Direction: Find the missing number in place of the question mark (?) in the given series.
2,7,28,63,126,?
A. 215 **B.** 245 **C.** 276 **D.** 296

Q.20 Rita traveled 35 Km from a point towards South and then turned left and traveled 30 Km and finally turned left again and traveled 35 Km. In which direction is she from the starting point?
A. East **B.** West **C.** North **D.** South

Q.21 The average of 35 raw scores is 18. The average of the first seventeen of them is 14 and that of the last seventeen is 20. Find the eighteenth raw score.
A. 42 **B.** 46 **C.** 52 **D.** 56

Q.22 In a class of 35 students, Ram is placed 7th from the bottom whereas Kishan is placed 9th from the top. Divya is placed exactly in between the two. What is the difference in the positions of Ram and Divya?
A. 9 **B.** 10 **C.** 11 **D.** 13

Q.23 If ACE = 18 and BOX = 82, then KEY = ?
A. 88 **B.** 84 **C.** 89 **D.** 82

Q.24 A compound proposition that is neither a tautology nor a contradiction is called a ________.
A. Condition **B.** Equivalence
C. Contingency **D.** Inference

Q.25 Direction: Choose the correct alternative form the given one that will complete the series.
GJR, ILT, KNV,?
A. MPX **B.** MKX **C.** MON **D.** MKY

Q.26 Direction: In a certain flight crew, the positions of the pilot, copilot and flight engineer are held by Mr. Ajit, Mr. Bhavesh and Mr. Chirag, though not necessarily in that order. The following statements are true for all the three:
1. The copilot is the only child and earns the least.
2. Chirag is married to Bhavesh's sister and earns more than the pilot.

Who is the copilot?
A. Chirag
B. Either Bhavesh or Chirag
C. Ajit
D. Bhavesh

Q.27 Structure of logical argument is based on:

A. Material truth
B. Formal Validity
C. Linguistic expression
D. Aptness of examples

Q.28 Which of the following is the highest level of cognitive ability?

A. Knowing
B. Understanding
C. Analysing
D. Evaluating

Q.29 If the majority of students in your class are weak you should:

A. Not care about the intelligent students
B. Keep your speed of teaching fast so that students comprehension level may increase
C. Keep your teaching slow
D. Keep your teaching slow along with some extra guidance to bright pupils

Q.30 Arrange the following teaching process in order:

(i) Relating the present knowledge with the previous knowledge
(ii) Evaluation
(iii) Reteaching
(iv) Formulating objectives
(v) Presentation of materials

A. (i), (ii), (iii), (iv)
B. (ii), (i), (iii), (iv), (v)
C. (v), (iv), (iii), (i), (ii)
D. (iv), (i), (v), (ii), (iii)

Q.31 Which of the following indicates the concept of Zone of Proximal development (ZPD) as suggested by psychologist Lev Vygotsky?

A. A learner's brain develops faster in childhood.
B. A learner learns effectively when its is supported with real life examples.
C. What a learner can do with help and without help.
D. Friends interaction is very important for the proper development of the child.

Q.32 Given below are two statements – one is labelled as Assertion (A) and the other is labelled as Reason (R).

Assertion (A): If a teacher wants to improve his or her abilities as an effective classroom communicator, he or she should first understand the students.

Reason (R): The ability to understand students and intended listening are disjointed propositions.

In light of the above two statements, choose the correct option from the following:

A. Both (A) and (R) are true and (R) is the correct explanation of (A)
B. Both (A) and (R) are true, but (R) is not the correct explanation of (A)
C. (A) is true, but (R) is false
D. (A) is false, but (R) is true

Ques (33-37):Direction: These are based on the tabulated data given below.

A company has 20 employees with their age (in years) and salary (in thousand rupees per month) mentioned against each of them:

S.No.	Age (in a year)	Salary (in thousand rupees per month)	S.NO.	Age (in a year)	Salary (in thousand rupees per month)
1.	44	35	11.	33	30
2.	32	20	12.	31	35
3.	54	45	13.	30	35
4.	42	35	14.	37	40
5.	31	20	15.	44	45
6.	53	60	16.	36	35
7.	42	50	17.	34	35
8.	51	55	18.	49	50
9.	34	25	19.	43	45
10.	41	30	20.	45	50

Q.33 Classify the data of age of each employee in a class interval of 5 years. Which class interval of 5 years has the maximum average salary?

A. $35-40$ years
B. $40-45$ years
C. $45-50$ years
D. $50-55$ years

Q.34 What is the frequency $(\%)$ in the class interval of $30-35$ years?

A. 20%
B. 25%
C. 30%
D. 35%

Q.35 What is the average age of the employees?

A. 40.3 years
B. 38.6 years
C. 47.2 years
D. 45.3 years

Q.36 What is the fraction $(\%)$ of employees getting salary ≥ 40000 per month?

A. 45%
B. 50%
C. 35%
D. 32%

Q.37 What is the average salary (in thousand per month) in the age group $40-50$ years?

A. 35
B. 42.5
C. 40.5
D. 36.5

Q.38 Objectivity in research implies:

A. The correct judgement of truth
B. Findings consistent with reality
C. Agreement in results
D. Methodological sophistication

Q.39 The formulation of a research problem can be compared to:

[UGC NET Home Science, 2019]

A. Laying the foundation of a building
B. Building the walls of a home
C. Painting the doors of a building
D. Constructing the ceiling of a house

Q.40 In doing action research what is the usual sequence of steps?

A. Reflect, observe, plan, act
B. Plan, act, observe, reflect

C. Plan, reflect, observe, act

D. Act, observe, plan, reflect

Q.41 The scope of 'creativity' and 'imagination' is largest in which of the following steps of research?

A. Defining and deciding the procedures for sampling

B. Identifying and defining the research problem

C. Data analysis using quantitative methods and interpretation

D. Hypothesis making and hypothesis testing

Q.42 A research problem is primarily chosen depending upon:

A. Its relevance

B. Available

C. Interest of the researcher

D. Availability of literature

Q.43 The full form of FTP is:

A. File Transfer Protocol

B. File Transfer Program

C. File Transfer Property

D. File Transfer Problem

Q.44 Which social media platform has lauched GOAL- digital skilling initiative for girls?

A. Instagram **B.** Snapchat

C. Facebook **D.** Twitter

Q.45 The main task of educational computer is:

A. Scoring the answers

B. Preserve the information

C. Analysis of data

D. All of these

Q.46 When you restart your computer after a software installation is basically comes under:

A. Cold booting

B. Arithmetic operation

C. Warm booting

D. Refreshing

Q.47 What is bit rate?

[UGC NET Sociology, 2020]

A. Number of bits stored in computer

B. Number of bits per second that can be transmitted over a network

C. Number of bits per hour stored in a computer over a network

D. Binary digit converted to hexa decimal number

Q.48 What is the basic concern of Rashtriya Uchchatar Shiksha Abhiyan?

A. To get over low enrolment in higher education

B. To improve achievement level of students in university exams

C. To improve the facilities for girls in colleges and universities

D. To provide NET qualified teachers to universities and colleges

Q.49 Rashtriya Uchchatar Shiksha Abhiyan (RUSA) is to fund the states for higher education. What is the ratio of funds between Central and State governments?

A. 75% Centre : 25% States Governments

B. 65% Centre : 35% States Governments

C. 100% Centre

D. 78% Centre : 22% States Governments

Q.50 The average age of the class is 20 years and one new student joined the class, then the average age of the class is increased by 1 year. If the initial number of students from the class is 28, what is the age of the new student?

A. 36 years **B.** 49 years **C.** 56 years **D.** 64 years

// Smart Answer Sheet //

Correct — Indicates percentage of students who answered questions correctly.

Skipped — Indicates percentage of students who skipped questions.

Q.	Ans.	Correct	Skipped
1	A	43.52 %	1.22 %
2	C	61.68 %	1.53 %
3	C	57.16 %	1.86 %
4	A	40.84 %	1.05 %
5	C	49.11 %	1.81 %
6	B	77.65 %	0.0 %
7	B	87.27 %	0.0 %
8	A	61.92 %	1.13 %
9	B	89.26 %	0.0 %
10	A	82.57 %	0.0 %
11	D	83.72 %	0.0 %
12	C	79.24 %	0.0 %
13	A	89.96 %	0.0 %
14	A	47.16 %	1.14 %
15	D	86.81 %	0.0 %
16	A	53.06 %	1.83 %
17	B	60.98 %	1.07 %
18	D	54.7 %	1.87 %
19	A	43.48 %	1.32 %
20	A	60.06 %	1.25 %
21	C	66.46 %	1.52 %
22	B	57.94 %	1.89 %
23	D	83.2 %	0.0 %
24	C	59.29 %	1.65 %
25	A	46.25 %	1.81 %
26	C	41.36 %	1.24 %
27	B	47.71 %	1.41 %
28	D	84.37 %	0.0 %
29	D	49.29 %	1.6 %
30	D	16.15 %	4.58 %
31	C	41.04 %	1.73 %
32	C	16.17 %	4.5 %
33	D	45.17 %	1.27 %
34	D	78.16 %	0.0 %
35	A	76.59 %	0.0 %
36	A	65.51 %	1.43 %
37	B	78.48 %	0.0 %
38	B	83.61 %	0.0 %
39	A	24.4 %	3.93 %
40	B	46.97 %	1.97 %
41	D	52.52 %	1.09 %
42	A	54.1 %	1.61 %
43	A	86.11 %	0.0 %
44	C	63.42 %	1.55 %
45	D	76.14 %	0.0 %
46	C	50.98 %	1.23 %
47	B	76.55 %	0.0 %
48	A	44.29 %	1.99 %
49	B	47.26 %	1.09 %
50	B	59.22 %	1.48 %

Performance Analysis	
Avg. Score (%)	63.0%
Toppers Score (%)	75.0%
Your Score	

//Hints and Solutions//

1. It is clearly stated in the passage that,

"Patty knew almost everything there is to know about trains since she once took the Amtrak train all the way to Boston."

Hence, the correct option is (A).

2. It is clearly stated in the passage that,

"First, fly down to the train tracks and pretend as if you're just pecking around for sandwich crumbs. Act as if you're just a regular pigeon looking for the odd scrap of food"

Hence, the correct option is (C).

3. Pretend means 'behave so as to make it appear that something is the case when in fact it is not'.

Genuine means 'authentic'.

Meaning of other words:

Profess means 'to claim, often falsely, that one has a quality or feeling'.

Pose means 'to present or constitute'.

Hence, the correct option is (C).

4. According to the passage, the word 'cluck' means 'to make a small, low sound'.

"It's important that you don't regularly clucklike pigeons when they're hiding under a train seat."

Hence, the correct option is (A).

5. It is clearly stated in the passage that,

"It's important that you not engage in regular pigeon clucking when you're hiding underneath the train seat. If the man in the seat above you is carrying on and on in the most boring way imaginable, resist the temptation to cluck. And if the kids in the seats across the aisle always seem to be making a big fuss about everything, resist the temptation to cluck."

Hence, the correct option is (C).

6. Biochemical oxygen demand (BOD) is a test to measure how much organic pollution is in water. The lower the BOD level in the water, the healthier would be the water.

BOD is based on the principle that if sufficient oxygen is available, aerobic biological decomposition (i.e., stabilization of organic waste) by microorganisms will continue until all waste is consumed.

Hence, the correct option is (B).

7. The Adolescent Education Program of the Ministry of Human Resource and Development promotes life skills training among young people.

The Adolescence Education Programme (AEP) is an important initiative that aims to empower young people with accurate, age-appropriate, and culturally relevant information, promote healthy attitudes and develop skills to enable them to respond to real-life situations in positive and responsible ways.

Hence, the correct option is (B).

8. Worldwide, agriculture accounts for around 67% of all water consumption, compared to 23% for industry and 10% for domestic use.

In most regions of the world, over 70% of fresh water is used for agriculture. By 2050, feeding a planet of 9 billion people will require an estimated 50% increase in agricultural production and a 15% increase in water withdrawals.

Hence, the correct option is (A).

9. Two of the chemical classes under consideration for replacing CFCs are hydrochlorofluorocarbons (HCFCs) and hydrofluorocarbons (HFCs). HCFCs contribute to the destruction of stratospheric ozone, but to a much lesser extent than CFCs. HCFCs are less stable than CFCs because HCFC molecules contain carbon-hydrogen bonds.

Hence, the correct option is (B).

10. Chemical contaminants are chemicals toxic to plants and animals in waterways. The phrase 'chemical contamination' is used to indicate situations where chemicals are either present where they shouldn't be, or are at higher concentrations than they would naturally have occurred.

Hence, the correct option is (A).

11. Effective communication reduces pre-imagined Understanding.

Effective communication is a basic prerequisite for the attainment of organizational goals. No organization, no group can exist without communication. Coordination of work is impossible and the organization will collapse for lack of communication.

Hence, the correct option is (D).

12. Teacher-student communication is Utilitarian. Utilitarian is the practice which states that best action is the one that maximizes utility, which produces the well being for the greater number of people.

Hence, the correct option is (C).

13. 'Moralising, being judgemental and comments of consolation' are the barriers to effective communication.

Barriers to Effective Communication are:

Anything that prevents understanding of the information leading to failure of the communication process is termed as barriers. Good communication skills are mutual respect skills. You show respect for the other person by listening fully and demonstrating that you get what that person means and you respect yourself when you assert or give your legitimate self-interest without aggression. To have complete communication, each person must both "get" and "give." Anything which blocks the meaning of communication is a barrier to communication.

The following are the conversational bad habits that often interfere with effective communication. These usually fall into one of three categories: judging, sending solutions, or avoiding the other person's concerns. Some common examples follow:

1. CRITICIZING/BLAMING "Well, you brought that on yourself."
2. ORDERING "Go fix that right now."
3. MORALIZING "You ought to apologize to her."
4. UNSOLICITED ADVISING "If I were you, this is what I would do..."
5. REASSURING: "You have the tools to handle this. You'll get over it."
6. CONSOLING: "I feel sorry for you".

Hence, the correct option is (A).

14. Classroom communication is the basis of social identity.

The nature and planning of classroom communication and also the various measures adopted for creating a conducive learning environment are:

- Classroom communication is the basis of social identity. Teaching is a social activity that involves both the teacher and the learners. It is therefore important, that two-way communication exists between them in order to trigger learning.
- Moreover, direct communication between a teacher and learners allows the teacher to get immediate feedback that can help him/her gauge learners', understanding of what has been taught. Based on such feedback the teacher can improve his/her communication.
- Teachers inculcate proper values among the students to enable them to face the economic, social, and cultural challenges lying ahead, and all these calls upon the skills of communication of the teacher.
- Thus pedagogy, social interaction, management, and technology comprise crucial activities of a teacher and the role of communication is paramount in all these activities.

Hence, the correct option is (A).

15. Communication is the transfer of information from one person to another, whether or not it elicits confidence. But the information transferred must be understandable to the receiver – G.G. Brown.

Non-Verbal Communication:

- Nonverbal communication refers to all the other ways, other than words, which are used in communicating.
- More specifically, it encompasses the symbolic messages, which are expressed through variation in intonation, vocally produced noises, body posture, gestures, and facial expressions. Anytime an individual speaks, he is not confined to the mere emission of words. In fact, he conveys plenty of meanings with the aid of nonverbal cues.
- The best technique to relay vital information to illiterate people is with the help of nonverbal symbols.
- Examples: Bottles or containers containing images of skulls or crossbones can indicate to uninformed persons that the products are likely to cause harm. Similarly, some companies use films to explain complex processes to people, who may not be well versed in oral communication.
- When communicating, nonverbal messages can interact with verbal messages in six ways: repeating, conflicting, complementing, substituting, regulating, and accenting/ moderating.
- Gestures Repeat Words. Example: (i) Saying no, then shaking head afterward; (ii) Asking for help and then, after a short delay during which they do not respond, raising eyebrows and saying 'mm?'
- Since non-verbal communication uses gestures, facial expressions, eye contact, touch, sign, sound, paralanguage, etc. for communicating with others, there is a great possibility of distortion of information in non-verbal communication. Example: In some countries such as Turkey or the Arabic-speaking Middle East, handshakes are not as firm as in the West. Consequently, a grip that is too firm is rude.

Hence, the correct option is (D).

16. The National Institutional Ranking Framework (NIRF) rankings, Miranda House in Delhi has been adjudged the best college in the country. Miranda House (MH) is constituent college for women at the University of Delhi in India.

Hence, the correct option is (A).

17. The grounds on which discrimination in admission to educational institutions is constitutionally prohibited are a religion B Sex C Place of birth D nationality.

Article 29(2) states: "No citizen shall be denied admission into any educational institution maintained by the State or receiving aid out of State funds on grounds only of religion, race, caste, language or any of them." Article 29(2) deals with a particular topic, viz., admission to educational institutions.

Hence, the correct option is (B).

18. Universities or Higher Education Institutions like to get accredited by NAAC because strengths of university get streamlined.

National Assessment and Accreditation Council (NAAC):

- It is an autonomous (Unstatutory body) of the University Grant Commission.
- It conducts assessment and accreditation of Higher Educational Institutions (HEI) such as colleges, universities, or other recognized institutions to derive an understanding of the 'Quality Status' of the institution.

Hence, the correct option is (D).

19. Logic:

$$(1^3 + 1) = 2$$

$$(2^3 - 1) = 7$$

$$(3^3 + 1) = 28$$

$(4^3 - 1) = 63$

$(5^3 + 1) = 126$

$(6^3 - 1) = 215$

So, the next term of series will be 215.

Hence, the correct option is (A).

20. The movement of Rita is shown in the figure below.

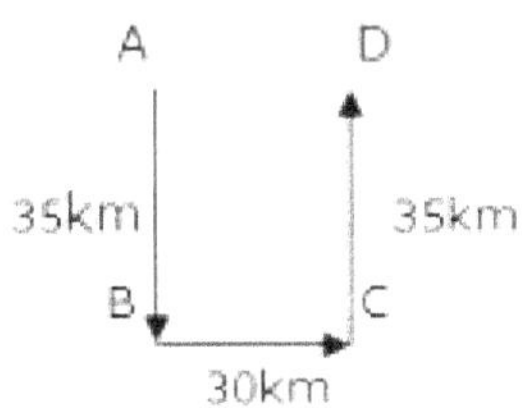

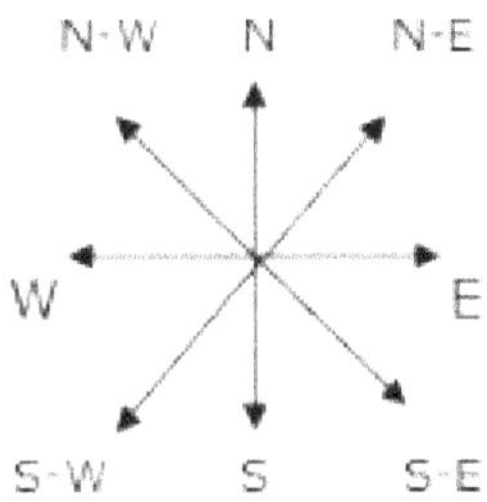

Rita is in the east direction from the starting point.

Hence, the correct option is (A).

21. Given,

Average of 35 raw scores is 18.

Sum of 35 raw scores $= 35 \times 18 = 630$ ....(i)

Average of first seventeen raw scores $= 14$

Sum of first seventeen raw scores $= 17 \times 14 = 238$ ....(ii)

Average of last seventeen raw scores $= 20$

Sum of last seventeen raw scores $= 17 \times 20 = 340$ ....(iii)

From (i), (ii) and (iii)

Eighteenth raw score $= [$ sum of 35 raw scores $-($ sum of first seventeen raw scores $+$ sum of last seventeen raw scores)]

Eighteenth raw score $= [630 - (238 + 340)]$

Eighteenth raw score $= 52$

The eighteenth raw score is 52.

Hence, the correct option is (C).

22. Given,

Total students $= 35$

Ram is $= 7$th from the bottom, Kishan is 9 th from top and Divya is exactly between Kishan and Ram

n position from bottom $=$ (Total $+1 - n)$ position from top

Ram $= 7$th from bottom $= (35 + 1 - 7)$ the from top $= 29$ th from top

Kishan $= 9$th from top

Divya is placed exactly in between Ram and Kishan.

Total students between Kishan and Ram $= 35 - (9 + 7) = 35 - 16 = 19$

Thus,

Divya's position from Kishan $= \frac{19+1}{2} = \frac{20}{2} = 10$

Divya's position from top $= 9 + 10 = 19$

So, differences in the positions of Ram and Divya $= 29 - 19 = 10$ i.e total 10 seats.

∴ Differences in the positions of Ram and Divya is of 10 seats.

Hence, the correct option is (B).

23.

Alphabets	A	B	C	D	E	F	G	H	I	J	K	L	M
Positional Value	1	2	3	4	5	6	7	8	9	10	11	12	13
Alphabets	N	O	P	Q	R	S	T	U	V	W	X	Y	Z
Positional Value	14	15	16	17	18	19	20	21	22	23	24	25	26

The logic followed is:
ACE → (1 × 2) + (3 × 2) + (5 × 2) = 2 + 6 + 10 = 18;
BOX → (2 × 2) + (15 × 2) + (24 × 2) = 4 + 30 + 48 = 82;
Thus, KEY → (11 × 2) + (5 × 2) + (25 × 2) = 22 + 10 + 50 = 82;
Hence, the correct option is (D).

24. A compound proposition that is neither a tautology nor a contradiction is called a contingency. Definition (Logical equivalence) Compound propositions p and q are called logically equivalent if p ↔ q is a tautology.

Hence, the correct option is (C).

25. The pattern is as follows,

$G \quad J \quad R$

$\downarrow +2 \quad \downarrow +2 \quad \downarrow +2$

$$\begin{array}{ccc} I & T & L \\ \downarrow +2 & \downarrow +2 & \downarrow +2 \\ K & N & V \\ \downarrow +2 & \downarrow +2 & \downarrow +2 \\ M & P & X \end{array}$$

So, the next term is MPX.

Hence, the correct option is (A).

26. Copilot is the only child and earns the least ⇒ The income of Copilot is less than the income of flight engineer and income of pilot (a)

Chirag is married to Bhavesh's sister and earns more than the pilot ⇒ Both are adult and income of Chirag is greater than Pilot, hence, Chirag is the Flight Engineer (b)

Considering the equations (a) and (b) If Chirag and Bhavesh are adults and earns more than the copilot then, obviously Ajit is the Child and copilot here.

Hence, the correct option is (C).

27. The structure of the logical argument is based on Formal Validity. A logical argument is termed formally valid if it has structural self-consistency, i.e. if when the operands between premises are all true, the derived conclusion is always also true. An argument is a connected series of statements that create a logical, clear, and defined statement. There are three stages to creating a logical argument: Premise, inference, and conclusion.

Hence, the correct option is (B).

28. Evaluation is concerned with the ability to judge the value of material for a given purpose. The judgments are on the basis of specific criteria which may be either internal criteria (organization) or external criteria (relevance to the purpose). Cognitive Ability is the ability of an individual to perform the different mental activities mostly linked with learning and problem-solving. So, Evaluation is the highest level of cognitive ability.

Hence, the correct option is (D).

29. If the majority of students in your class are weak the teacher should keep your teaching slow along with some extra guidance to bright pupils as:

- Every student differs from others in psychological aspects such as intelligence, personality, etc.
- Every child has a different pace of learning and a single method cannot be applicable to all children.
- Extra guidance to bright people will not let them bore and will keep them busy in constructing knowledge

Keeping teaching slow along with some extra guidance to bright pupils will help the teacher in:

- Emphasizing the active involvement of all learners.
- Meeting the diverse learning needs of every learner.
- Assisting students with proper guidance in the right way.

So, it could be concluded that If the majority of students in your class are weak the teacher should keep your teaching slow along with some extra guidance to bright pupils.

Hence, the correct option is (D).

30. Teaching process in order:

(iv) Formulating objectives

(i) Relating the present knowledge with the previous knowledge

(v) Presentation of materials

(ii) Evaluation

(iii) Reteaching

Hence, the correct option is (D).

31. The zone of proximal development (sometimes abbreviated ZPD), is the difference between what a learner can do without help and what he or she can do with help. It is a concept developed by Soviet psychologist and social constructivist Lev Vygotsky (1896 - 1934). Vygotsky also described the ZPD as the difference between the actual development level as determined by individual problem solving and the level of potential development as determined through problem-solving under adult guidance or collaboration with more knowledgeable peers.

Hence, the correct option is (C).

32. This assertion is true but the reason is false. For effective teaching, a teacher should have good knowledge of teaching models and should choose the appropriate model, keeping in mind the needs of students and the subject. These models help in boosting interest, creativity, motivation, and innovations. The different types of models are- Social interaction models, Behaviour altering models, Personal basis models, Information processing models.

Hence, the correct option is (C).

33. In $35-40$ years:

Average salary $=\frac{(40+35)}{2}=37{,}500$ per month

In $40-45$ years:

Average salary $=\frac{35+35+50+30+45+45}{6}$

$=\frac{240}{6}=40000$ per month

In $45-50$ years:

Average salary $=\frac{50+50}{2}$

$=\frac{100}{2}=50{,}000$ per month

In $50-55$years:

Average salary $=\frac{45+60+55}{3}=53300$ per month

Therefore, people in the $50-55$ class interval have the maximum average salary.

Hence, the correct option (D).

34. According to the data given above there are 7 employees in the age group $30-35$ respectively.

frequency $(\%)=\frac{7}{20}\times 100=35\%$

Hence, the correct option is (D).

35. Average

$$=\frac{44+32+54+42+31+53+42+51+34+41+33+31+30+37+44+36+34+49+43+45}{20}$$

$$=\frac{806}{20}=40.3$$

Hence, the correct option is (A).

36. The fraction $(\%)$ of employees getting salary ≥ 40000 per month:

$(\%)$ of employees getting $(\geq 40000)=\frac{9}{20}\times 100=45\%$

Hence, the correct option is (A).

37. Average salary $=\frac{35+35+50+30+45+45+50+50}{8}=\frac{340}{8}$

$=42500$ per month

Hence, the correct option is (B).

38. Objectivity in research implies findings consistent with reality.

Research is a careful investigation to find new facts. It constitutes two words, 'Re' and 'Search' which means investigate again to an already existing fact/reality.

The objectives of the research are as follows:

- To get an answer to a question
- To get familiar with a new phenomenon
- Review and synthesize the existing knowledge
- To explore knowledge
- To find out the solution to a problem
- To investigate an existing problem
- To generate new methods, plan, system, etc

Hence, the correct option is (B).

39. The formulation of a research problem can be compared to laying the foundation of a building.

Formulation of Research Problem and its Importance:

- The first thing after undertaking a study is to identify and determine the problem to study. Any question that the researcher wants to be answered or investigate is called a research problem.
- A research problem can be compared to the foundation of a building. The type and design of the building are dependent upon the foundation. A strong foundation will result in a strong building.
- Identifying a research problem is of utmost importance as the issue identified in a particular setting is what guides and motivates the need for conducting the research, it lays the foundation of an entire project. If the foundation is shaky, the entire project is doomed to failure.
- So, the research problem serves as the foundation of a research study, if it is well formulated, you can expect a good study to follow.

Hence, the correct option is (A).

40. In doing action research the usual sequence of steps is Plan, act, observe, reflect.

Action Research: Action Research refers to the application of research to educational problems in particular classroom settings. Its primary aim is to improve practice. It encourages change in the educational system and thereby fosters a democratic approach towards education. It positions teachers and other educators as learners who seek to narrow the gap between the practice and their vision of education. It encourages educators to reflect on their practices. Subsequently, it promotes the process of testing new ideas.

Hence, the correct option is (B).

41. The scope of 'creativity' and 'imagination' is largest in hypothesis making and hypothesis testing steps of research.

Creativity' and Imagination in research: Creativity and imagination in research refer to the capacity of the researcher to be curious and open-minded immersing him in the complexity of a place or people. The scope of 'creativity' and 'imagination' is largest in hypothesis making and hypothesis testing i.e. while exploring and investigating a topic beyond what is given, creating an unimagined future together with organization and/or communities. It is about moving away from logic and promoting a variety of rich meanings and knowledge related to the topic being investigated. There is a combination of design approaches with an epistemology of social construction that can offer new possibilities in framing, reframing, and doing research that value and endorse creativity and imagination.

Hence, the correct option is (D).

42. A research problem is primarily chosen depending upon its relevance.

Research problem: A research problem is defined as an area of concern that requires a meaningful understanding of a specific topic, a condition, a contradiction, or difficulty. A research problem means finding answers to questions or strengthening existing findings to bridge the knowledge gap to solve problems.

Characteristics of a research problem:

- Covers the essential needs or issues
- The problem is stated logically and clearly

- The research is based on actual facts and evidence (non-hypothetical)
- The research problem generates and encourages research questions
- Sufficient data can be obtained
- The problem has an unsatisfactory answer or is a new problem

Hence, the correct option is (A).

43. The full form of FTP is file transfer protocol. File transfer protocol is a standard protocol which is used to transfer computer files from one place to another. FTP is a client-server protocol where a client will ask for a file, and a local or remote server will provide it. The end-users machine is typically called the local host machine, which is connected via the internet to the remote host - which is the second machine running the FTP software.

Hence, the correct option is (A).

44. Facebook has launched an initiative named GOAL (Going Online As Leaders) that is a digital skilling and mentorship initiative. The initiative will train young girls from 5 states- West Bengal, Maharashtra, Jharkhand, Odisha and Madhya Pradesh. The focus area of training will be digital literacy, life skills, leadership and entrepreneurship.

Hence, the correct option is (C).

45. The computer has the potential to solve many educational problems. The use of computers in education can be categorized into two categories.

Administrative use:

- Office use for typing, emailing, etc.
- In the library, computers are used for retrieval of bibliography information, cataloguing, searching for books, etc.
- For tasks such as student fees records, employees' salary records, making a budget, etc.
- Making time table, scoring and grading, storing student's and staff's data, maintenance of attendance, processing and analysing results, evaluation of answer sheet.

Instructional use:

- Audio-Visual guides in the teaching process for viable learning.
- Make the content presentable for students and easier to understand.
- Possible to teach those students or learners that are located in remote or far places.

Hence, the correct option is (D).

46. When the system is already running and needs to be restarted or rebooted, it is called warm booting. Warm booting is faster than cold booting because BIOS is not reloaded. For example, booting after the installation of software

Hence, the correct option is (C).

47. Number of bits per second that can be transmitted over a network is known as bit rate. Bit rate refers to the rate at which data is processed or transferred. It is usually measured in seconds, ranging from bps for smaller values to kbps and mbps. Bit rate is also known as bitrate or data rate.

Hence, the correct option is (B).

48. Rashtriya Uchchatar Shiksha Abhiyan, commonly known as RUSA, is a centrally sponsored scheme of the Indian government for the development of higher education in India.

It is a holistic scheme of development for higher education in India initiated in 2013 by the Ministry of Human Resource Development, Government of India. The main objective of RUSA is to improve the overall quality of higher education by establishing facilitative institutions in underserved areas of the country thereby increasing the enrolment in higher education. The portal is a one-stop for the States' Higher Education Plans, the decision of the States' Higher Education Councils.

It focuses to ensure equity in higher education by promoting the inclusion of women, tribals, minorities, differently-abled persons, socially disadvantaged and economically weaker sections, etc.

Therefore, from the above explanation, we can conclude that the basic concern of Rashtriya Uchchatar Shiksha Abhiyan is to get over low enrolment in higher education.

Hence, the correct option is (A).

49. Rashtriya Uchchatar Shiksha Abhiyan (RUSA) is to fund the states for higher education. the ratio of funds between Central and State governments is 65% Centre : 35% States Governments.

RUSA or Rashtriya Uchchatar Shiksha Abhiyan was launched in 2013. It is a Centrally Sponsored Scheme (C.S.S.)

The aim is to provide strategic funding to the eligible state Higher Educational Institutions. This program is administered by the Ministry of Human Resource Development as a nodal agency.

The budget targets participating States, reviews/ analyzes them, and then gives approvals and makes disbursements are part of this program. The vision is to attain higher levels of access, equity, and excellence in the State higher education system with greater efficiency, transparency, accountability, and responsiveness.

Hence, the correct option is (B).

50. Given,

The number of students in class initially = 28

The average age of class = 20

If one student joined in class average age increases by \(1 year.

After one student joins in class the number of students = 29

The average age of class $= 21$

The total age of 28 students = 28×20

$= 560$

The total age of 29 students = 29×21

$= 609$

The age of new student = The total age of 29 students - the total age of 28 students

The age of new student $= 609 - 560$

$= 49$

∴ The age of the new student is 49.

Hence, the correct option is (B).

Mock Test 15

Ques (1-5):Direction: Read the passage carefully and answer the question that follows.

In the narrowest sense, price is the amount of money charged for a product or a service. More broadly, price is the sum of all the values that customers give up to gain the benefits of having or using a product or service. Historically, price has been the major factor affecting buyer choice. In recent decades, however, nonprice factors have gained increasing importance. Even so, the price remains one of the most important elements that determine a firm's market share and profitability.

Price is the only element in the marketing mix that produces revenue; all other elements present costs. Price is also one of the most flexible marketing mix elements. Unlike product features and channel commitments, prices can be changed quickly. At the same time, pricing is the number one problem facing many marketing executives, and many companies do not handle pricing well. So we managers view pricing as a big headache, preferring instead to focus on other marketing mix elements. However, smart managers treat pricing as a key strategic tool for creating and capturing customer value. Prices have a direct impact on a firm's bottom line. A small percentage improvement in price can generate a large percentage increase in profitability. More important, as part of a company's overall value proposition, price plays a key role in creating customer value and building customer relationships. "Instead of running away from pricing," says an expert, "savvy marketers are embracing it".

The price the company charges will fall somewhere between one that is too low to produce a profit and one that is too high to produce any demand. It summarizes the major considerations in setting the price. Customer perceptions of the product's value set the ceiling for prices. If customers perceive that the product's price is greater than its value, they will not buy the product. Likewise, product costs set the floor for prices. If the company prices the product below its costs, the company's profits will suffer. In setting its price between those two extremes, the company must consider several external and internal factors, including competitors' strategies and prices, the overall marketing strategy and mix, and the nature of the market and demand.

Q.1 Historically price was considered important because:

A. Sellers were always benefitted
B. Money was charged for product or service
C. It provided option for buyers
D. It promoted non-price factors

Q.2 Why is the price different from other elements in the marketing mix?

A. It offsets cost
B. It generates revenue
C. It is rigid in character
D. It ensures channel commitment

Q.3 What is the perception of smart managers regarding pricing?

A. It is a strategic tool for consumer value
B. It invites issues
C. It is better to focus on other elements in the marketing mix
D. It is of indirect value to the firm

Q.4 Which of the following is the major determinant of pricing for product or service?

A. High demand
B. Low demand
C. Customer's value perception
D. Company's quest for high profitability

Q.5 What are the other factors influencing or setting the price for products or services?

a. Competitors' strategies
b. Over-all marketing mix
c. Type of market
d. Pricing from one extreme to the other
e. Predators pricing strategies

Choose the correct answer from the options given below:

A. a, d and e only **B.** a, b and c only
C. c, d and e only **D.** b, c and d only

Ques (6-10):Direction: Read the following table carefully and answer the following questions:

Table shows the stock of 3 different watches of 4 different brands in the store (in Hundred).

Types/Stock(in Hundred)	Titan	Sonata	Fossil	Timex
Analog	60	45	50	30
Digital	70	50	40	25
Automatic	55	35	65	35

Q.6 What is the average stock available of three types of watches.

A. 18456.67 **B.** 17634.33
C. 18666.67 **D.** 17569.33

Q.7 Stock of Analog Titan watch is approximately what percent of the total stock of Analog watches?

A. 37.5% **B.** 39.41% **C.** 32.43% **D.** 41.56%

Q.8 What is the ratio between available stock of Timex and Titan watches.

A. 18 : 35 **B.** 2 : 1 **C.** 18 : 37 **D.** 37 : 18

Q.9 Stock of Sonata watches is approximately what percent less than the stock of Fossil watches of three types?

A. 11% **B.** 14% **C.** 21% **D.** 16%

Q.10 Find the difference between the stocks of Automatic and Digital watches of four brands.

A. 750 **B.** 500 **C.** 240 **D.** 450

Q.11 Communication with oneself is known as:

A. Organisational Communication
B. Grapewine Communication
C. Interpersonal Communication
D. Intrapersonal Communication

Q.12 Classroom communication is normally considered as:

A. Effective **B.** Affective
C. Cognitive **D.** Non-selective

Q.13 Which of the following come under the mandate of the University Grants Commission (UGC)?

(A) Promotion and coordination of University education.

(B) Determining and monitoring standards of teaching, examination, and research in Universities.

(C) Organising continuous professional development programs for college and university teachers.

(D) Framing regulations on minimum standards of education.

(E) Disbursing and regulating grants to the universities and colleges.

Choose the correct answer from the options given below :

A. (A), (B), (C), (D) only
B. (B), (C), (D), (E) only
C. (A), (C), (D), (E) only
D. (A), (B), (D), (E) only

Q.14 What is the proposed name of national teacher education frame work 2021?

A. National Council for Teacher Education, NCTE 2021
B. National Professional Standards for Teachers, NPST 2021
C. National Curriculum Framework for Teacher Education, NCFTE 2021
D. Professional Standard Setting Body, PSSB 2021

Q.15 Who among the following is responsible for preparing National Curriculum Framework for School Education (NCFSE)?

A. NCERT **B.** IITs **C.** AICTE **D.** SAFAL

Q.16 NEP gave a new direction for the overall improvements of the evaluation system called _______

A. CEC **B.** PARAKH
C. DIKSHA **D.** AICTE

Q.17 'Gyan Vijnan Vimuktaye' is the motto of:

A. IGNOU
B. Jana Vijnana Aayog
C. University of Mysuru
D. UGC

Q.18 Men and women may have different reproductive strategies but neither can be considered inferior or superior to the other, any more than a bird's wings can be considered superior or inferior to a fish's fins. What type of argument it is?

A. Biological **B.** Physiological
C. Analogical **D.** Hypothetical

Q.19 When in a group of propositions, one proposition is claimed to follow from the others, that group of propositions is called?

A. An argument
B. A valid argument
C. An explanation
D. An invalid argument

Q.20 Which of the following set of statements reflects the basic characteristics of teaching?

(i) Teaching is the same as training.

(ii) There is no difference between instruction and conditioning when we teach.

(iii) Teaching is related to learning.

(iv) Teaching is a 'task' word while learning is an 'achievement' word.

(v) Teaching means giving information.

(vi) One may teach without learning taking place.

Choose the correct option from the given code:

A. (i), (ii) and (iii) **B.** (iii), (iv) and (vi)
C. (ii), (iii) and (v) **D.** (i), (iv) and (vi)

Q.21 The teacher's primary responsibility lies in:

A. Planning educational experiences
B. Implementing administrative policies
C. Experimenting with teaching techniques
D. Promoting human relations with parents

Q.22 Which of the following protocol is designed to protect the ozone layer by phasing out substances responsible for ozone depletion?

A. Nagoya Protocol
B. Bretton Woods Conference
C. Kyoto Protocol
D. Montreal Protocol

Q.23 The most harmful type of environmental pollutants are:

A. Human organic wastes
B. Wastes from faecal matter
C. Non-biodegradable chemicals
D. Natural nutrients present in excess

Q.24 Which one of the following green house gases has the shortest residence time in the atmosphere?

A. Chlorofluorocarbon **B.** Carbon dioxide
C. Methane **D.** Nitrous oxide

Q.25 India launched National Green Tribunal to make polluters pay damages, in the year:

A. 2008 **B.** 2009 **C.** 2010 **D.** 2011

Q.26 Which of the following is the renewable source of energy?

A. Oil **B.** Natural Gas
C. Solar **D.** Coal

Q.27 The research aims at understanding reality, discovering new knowledge and inventions for, development in the society and research ethics certainly can restrain researchers. Considering all aspects it is amicably decided that researchers:

A. Will have complete freedom for research
B. Will not conduct studies involving risks to human beings
C. Will follow some code of research ethics

D. Will decide themselves research ethics

Q.28 Which one of the following NOT support practice of ethics in research?

A. Restricting access to participants identification

B. Revealing information of participant only with written consent

C. Disclosing the data subsets

D. Restricting access to data instruments where the participant is identified

Q.29 Identify the unethical practice of a researcher from the following:

A. Avoiding Plagiarism

B. Avoiding Duplication

C. Avoiding Reliable Information

D. Avoiding Manipulation

Q.30 Research journals with a high ______ are commonly considered to be more important than those with lower ones.

A. Eigen factor **B.** h-index

C. Impact factor **D.** i10 score

Q.31 Match list-1 with list-2 and select the correct code for the answer.

List-1 (Fallacies)		List-2 (explanation)	
a.	Fallacies of Presupposition	i)	At the point when the premises in an argument don't give a significant reason for accepting the truth of the conclusion.
b.	Fallacies of Relevance	ii)	Because they are based on unwanted assumptions.
c.	Fallacies of Denying the Antecedent	iii)	By denying the antecedent of a conditional proposition can not deny the consequent

A. a-i, b-ii, c-iii **B.** a-ii, b-iii, c-i

C. a-ii, b-i, c-iii **D.** a-i, b-iii, c-ii

Q.32 The statement "the study, design, development, implementation, support or management of computer-based information systems, particularly software applications and computer hardware" refers to

A. Information Technology (IT)

B. Information and Collaborative Technology (ICT)

C. Information and Data Technology (IDT)

D. Artificial Intelligence (AI)

Q.33 A small text file stored on the user's computer by some websites in order to recognize and keep track of user's preferences is called:

A. Log **B.** Report **C.** Cookie **D.** History

Q.34 The following list indicates different types of computer networks. Arrange them in ascending order on the basis of geographical space implied.

A. LAN < WAN < MAN

B. WAN < LAN > MAN

C. MAN > LAN < WAN

D. LAN < MAN < WAN

Q.35 A small text file stored on user's computer by some websites in order to recognize and keep track of user's preferences is called:

A. Log **B.** Report **C.** Cookie **D.** History

Q.36 ______denotes an error in a computer program:

A. Bit **B.** Bug **C.** Spam **D.** Virus

Q.37 For effective teaching which of the following is a key behaviour?

A. Encouraging students to elaborate their own answer or that of other students

B. Summarizing what was told by a student

C. The teacher gives comments for the purpose of organizing what is to come

D. Making ideas clear to learners who may be at different levels of understanding

Q.38 Identify the characteristics and basic requirements of reflective level teaching in the following list of statements:

(a) Teacher presents the information and ideas systematically to help recall them when needed

(b) Teacher conducts drills and exercises to fix up the ideas in the minds of students.

(c) Issues are raised and discussed with a view to sift the potential rational solution of problems.

(d) Teacher asks students to give examples and parallel ideas.

(e) Academic sessions are conducted in a dialogic mode to explore and explain the basis of arguments.

Choose the correct answer from the options given below:

A. (a) and (b) only **B.** (c) and (d) only

C. (c) and (e) only **D.** (d) and (e) only

Q.39 Given below are two statements:

Statement I: Measurement is a set of rules for assigning numbers to represent objects, traits, attributes and behaviours.

Statement II: A test is a procedure in which a sample of an individual's behaviour is obtained, evaluated and scored using standardized procedures.

In the light of the above statements, choose the correct answer from the options given below:

A. Both Statement I and Statement II are true

B. Both Statement I and Statement II are false

C. Statement I is correct but Statement II is false

D. Statement I is incorrect but Statement II is true

Q.40 Given below are two statements- one is labelled as Assertion (A) and the other is labelled as Reason (R).

Assertion (A): For the impact of communication, the individual students must be considered as a product of a common cause.

Reason (R): Effective teachers normally attempt to identify the general characteristics of learners to communicate with them.

In the light of the above two statements choose the correct answer from the options given below.

A. Both A and R are true and R is the correct explanation of A

B. Both A and R are true but R is not the correct explanation of A

C. A is true, but R is false

D. A is false, but R is true

Q.41 'Non-content behaviours such as rate of speaking, loudness, tendency to interrupt and pronunciation peculiarities' are referred to as _____ behaviour.

A. Extra-personal **B.** Animated
C. Extra-linguistic **D.** Involuntary

Q.42 Given below are two statements - one is labelled as Assertion (A) and the other as Reason (R).

Assertion (A): Skills of oration coupled with wit and humour make classroom communication compelling.

Reason (R): Rhetorical interventions do not make classroom communication purposeful.

Select the correct option based on the above two statements.

A. Both (A) and (R) are true and (R) is the correct explanation of (A)
B. Both (A) and (R) are true and (R) is not the correct explanation of (A)
C. (A) is true but (R) is false
D. (A) is false but (R) is true

Q.43 Rashmi covered a distance at some speed. If she had moved 6 kmph faster, she would have taken 30 minutes less. If she had moved 5 kmph slower, she would have taken 30 minutes more. What is the distance in km?

A. 330 km **B.** 300 km **C.** 490 km **D.** 640 km

Q.44 Given below are two statements:

Statement I: An article of Rs. 500 sold for Rs. 400 earned a loss of 5%.

Statement II: To earn 8% profit, an article of Rs. 600 sold for Rs. 648.

Select the correct option based on the above two statements.

A. Both statements I and statement II are true
B. Both statements I and statement II are false
C. Statement I is true but statement II is false
D. Statement I is false but Statement II is true

Q.45 Given below are two statements:

Statement I: 300 m long train crosses a platform of the same length in 30 seconds. Speed of train 10 m/sec.

Statement II: The average speed is the mean speed.

In light of the above statements, choose the correct option given below.

A. Both statements I and statement II are true.
B. Both statements I and statement II are false.
C. Statement I is true but statement II is false.
D. Statement I is false but Statement II is true.

Q.46 Nishu has six and a half dozen chocolates. She gave $\frac{1}{6}$ of these to Ravi, $\frac{1}{13}$ of these to Rahul and one half of these to her other friends. The number of chocolate left with her is:

A. 27 **B.** 32 **C.** 20 **D.** 26

Q.47 On selling the scooter for Rs. 3440, Ranvijay loses 14%. If he wanted to gain 14%, for how much should he have sold the scooter?

A. Rs. 4560 **B.** Rs. 5460 **C.** Rs. 3450 **D.** Rs. 4450

Q.48 Direction: In the question below is given a statement followed by two conclusions numbered I and II. You have to assume everything in the statement to be true, then consider the two conclusions together and decide which of them logically follows beyond a reasonable doubt from the information given in the statement.

Statement:

Time and Tide waits for none.

Conclusions:

I. Regardless of our actions, time will pass anyway so how we use it does not matter.

II. Time is very precious so we must utilize it very well.

A. Only conclusion I follows
B. Neither conclusion I nor conclusion II follows
C. Either conclusion I or conclusion II follows
D. Both conclusion I and conclusion II follow

Q.49 Inductive argument proceeds from:

A. Particulars to Particulars
B. Particulars to Universals
C. Universals to Particulars
D. Universals to Universals

Q.50 Given below are two premises (a and b). From those two premises, four conclusions (i), (ii), (iii) and (iv) are drawn. Select the code that states the conclusion/conclusions drawn validly (taking the premises singularly or jointly).

Premises:

(a) All bats are mammals.

(b) No birds are bats.

Conclusions:

(i) No birds are mammals.

(ii) Some birds are not mammals.

(iii) No bats are birds.

(iv) All mammals are bats.

A. (i) only **B.** (i) and (ii) only
C. (iii) only **D.** (iii) and (iv) only

// Smart Answer Sheet //

Correct — Indicates percentage of students who answered questions correctly.

Skipped — Indicates percentage of students who skipped questions.

Q.	Ans.	Correct	Skipped
1	C	40.6 %	1.36 %
2	B	47.74 %	1.22 %
3	A	44.97 %	1.64 %
4	D	47.97 %	1.07 %
5	B	42.52 %	1.69 %
6	C	53.64 %	1.63 %
7	C	42.26 %	1.99 %
8	C	40.64 %	1.52 %
9	D	67.62 %	1.54 %
10	B	62.86 %	1.94 %
11	D	88.64 %	0.0 %
12	C	44.98 %	1.97 %
13	D	68.6 %	1.07 %
14	C	53.61 %	1.17 %
15	A	20.93 %	3.64 %
16	B	43.2 %	1.07 %
17	D	56.42 %	1.28 %
18	C	81.45 %	0.0 %
19	A	78.12 %	0.0 %
20	B	11.06 %	3.49 %
21	A	40.93 %	1.72 %
22	D	61.46 %	1.8 %
23	C	81.58 %	0.0 %
24	C	41.26 %	1.25 %
25	C	32.08 %	4.14 %
26	C	51.75 %	1.13 %
27	C	47.42 %	1.84 %
28	C	61.43 %	1.09 %
29	C	64.07 %	1.44 %
30	C	57.58 %	1.38 %
31	C	24.48 %	4.24 %
32	A	88.9 %	0.0 %
33	C	55.53 %	1.03 %
34	D	40.96 %	1.82 %
35	C	57.65 %	1.56 %
36	B	89.34 %	0.0 %
37	D	43.03 %	1.67 %
38	C	23.78 %	3.39 %
39	A	58.37 %	1.79 %
40	A	59.48 %	1.05 %
41	C	59.42 %	1.64 %
42	C	29.51 %	3.07 %
43	A	47.67 %	1.32 %
44	D	59.85 %	1.55 %
45	B	44.42 %	1.48 %
46	C	54.71 %	1.12 %
47	A	60.87 %	1.63 %
48	C	50.84 %	1.96 %
49	B	49.3 %	1.98 %
50	C	66.35 %	1.54 %

Performance Analysis	
Avg. Score (%)	49.0%
Toppers Score (%)	70.0%
Your Score	

//Hints and Solutions//

1. The third sentence of the passage says - "Historically, the price has been the major factor affecting buyer choice."

If we carefully go through the entire paragraph, this is the only sentence where the historical significance of price is mentioned.

In this regard, no other option given has been mentioned related to why the price was historically important according to the passage.

Hence, the correct option is (C).

2. The sixth sentence of the passage (or the first sentence of the second paragraph) says - "Price is the only element in the marketing mix that produces revenue; all other elements present costs."

No other option given is mentioned in the passage.

Hence, the correct option is (B).

3. The eleventh sentence of the passage (or the sixth sentence of the second paragraph) says - "However, smart managers treat pricing as a key strategic tool for creating and capturing customer value."

No other option serves as a suitable answer according to the passage.

Hence, the correct option is (A).

4. The seventeenth and eighteenth sentences of the passage (or the first and second sentences of the third paragraph) say - "The price the company charges will fall somewhere between one that is too low to produce a profit and one that is too high to produce any demand. It summarizes the major considerations in setting the price."

If we try to understand the above sentence, we can easily see that if the price goes lower than what produces a profit, it will not be an acceptable price to the company

Also, we can infer that if the price is too high to generate any demand, the sales will not happen and again, the profits will suffer. Hence such a price is also unacceptable to the company

Thus in both the cases of the upper and the lower limits of the price, it is the profits that are the major factor.

Hence, the correct option is (D).

5. "In setting its price between those two extremes, the company must consider several external and internal factors, including competitors' strategies and prices, the overall marketing strategy and mix, and the nature of the market and demand."

Only a, b and c represent the other factors considered in determining the price (as they match with the boldened parts above).

Hence, the correct option is (B).

6. From the table we can say that,

Total stock available of Analog watch = 6000 + 4500 + 5000 + 3000 = 18500

Total stock available of Digital watch = 7000 + 5000 + 4000 + 2500 = 18500

Total stock available of Automatic watch = 5500 + 3500 + 6500 + 3500 = 19000

∴ Required average = $\frac{18500+18500+19000}{3} = 18666.67$

Hence, the correct option is (C).

7. From the table we can say that,

Total stock available of Analog watch = 6000 + 4500 + 5000 + 3000 = 18500

Stock of Analog Titan watches = 6000

∴ Required percentage = $\frac{6000}{18500} \times 100 = 32.43\%$

Hence, the correct option is (C).

8. From the table we can say that,

Total stock of Titan watches = 6000 + 7000 + 5500 = 18500

Total stock of Timex watches = 3000 + 2500 + 3500 = 9000

∴ Required ratio = 9000 : 18500

= 18 : 37

Hence, the correct option is (C).

9. From the table we can say that,

Total stock of Sonata watches = 4500 + 5000 + 3500 = 13000

Total stock of Fossil watches = 5000 + 4000 + 6500 = 15500

∴ Required percentage = $\frac{15500-13000}{15500} \times 100$

⇒ 16.12% ≈ 16%

Hence, the correct option is (D).

10. From the table we can say that,

Total stock available of Digital watch = 7000 + 5000 + 4000 + 2500 = 18500

Total stock available of Automatic watch = 5500 + 3500 + 6500 + 3500 = 19000

∴ Required difference = 19000 – 18500 = 500

Hence, the correct option is (B).

11. Communication with oneself is known as Intrapersonal Communication. Communication is simply the act of transferring information from one place, person or group to another.

Intrapersonal communication: It can be defined as communication with one's self, and that may include selftalk, acts of imagination and visualization, and even recall and memory.

Organizational Communication: It refers to the forms and channels of communication among the members of an organization. It can be formal or informal and flow in varied hierarchy structures within the industrial premises.

Grapevine communication: It is informal workplace dialogue in its purest form: it is characterized by conversations between employees and superiors that do not follow any prescribed structure or rule-based system. Grapevine communication spreads rapidly and likely touches each person throughout the organization.

Interpersonal communication: It is the process of exchange of information, ideas and feelings between two or more people through verbal or non-verbal methods. It often includes the face-to-face exchange of information, in a form of voice, facial expressions, body language and gestures.

Hence, the correct option is (D).

12. Classroom communication is normally considered as cognitive.

Classroom communication- Communication within the classroom is important in order for students to learn effectively and should be put in place from an early stage of learning. Non-verbal communication refers to communicating without words through body language, gestures, facial expressions, the tone and pitch of the voice, and posture.

Hence, the correct option is (C).

13. UGC stands for University Grants Commission is a statutory organization in India.

UGC was set up by the Union of Government In 1956. UGC has power and holds the authority to approve the universities in India. Before providing university authority, the UGC team checked university educational standards.

The main function of the UGC is to allocate funding to its funded institutions and to offer impartial and respected expert advice to the Government on the strategic development and resource requirements of higher education.

Hence, the correct option is (D).

14. The National Education Policy has made suggestions for stopping the harmful practice of excessive teacher transfers and recommended that it will be conducted through an online computerized system that ensures transparency.

By 2021, a new and comprehensive National Curriculum Framework for Teacher Education, NCFTE 2021, will be formulated by the NCTE in consultation with NCERT. The NCFTE will thereafter be revised once every 5-10 years by reflecting the changes in revised NCFs as well as emerging needs in teacher education.

Hence, the correct option is (C).

15. The formulation of a new and comprehensive National Curricular Framework for School Education, NCFSE 2020-21, will be undertaken by the NCERT.

It is based on the principles of this National Education Policy 2020, frontline curriculum needs, and after discussions with all stakeholders including State Governments, Ministries, relevant Departments of the Central Government, and other expert bodies, and will be made available in all regional languages.

Hence, the correct option is (A).

16. PARAKH stands for Performance Assessment, Review, and Analysis of Knowledge for Holistic Development.

The National Assessment Center attempt to established to improve the overall evaluation system.

Prime Minister emphasized providing quality and industry-related education. He mentioned that when education is imparted in relation to the surrounding environment, the student can develop practical knowledge.

Hence, the correct option is (B).

17. The motto of the UGC is Gyan Vigyan Vimuktaye which means that knowledge liberates.

University Grants Commission of India which is a governing body or a statutory committee for the Indian nation. That has been formulated by the Indian Union Government in accordance with the UGC Act 1956 of the Human Resource Development Ministry.

It's required to coordinate and maintain the different standards of education within India by different academic institutions within the country. Hence this is why the word UGC is often heard whenever one talks of a university imparting quality.

In other words, UGC has become the face of recognized education because if any university has been accredited or affiliated by the University Grants Commission UGC then that means that all the education, the degrees as well as the courses imparted to the students and the people are well under constant monitoring and are also regularly checked by the committee for any errors or loopholes in the effective and efficient management, merit selection or examination systems and other operations of the institution.

Hence people mostly go for those universities which are affiliated with the UGC which means that they will surely receive quality as well as recognized education from there through innovative facilities at all times.

Hence, the correct option is (D).

18. The above-mentioned argument is an analogical argument. Analogical arguments are a form of Induction where a conclusion is derived from a comparison of similarities between two or more cases.

Hence, the correct option is (C).

19. When in a group of propositions, one proposition is claimed to follow from the others, that group of propositions is called an Argument. An argument is a main idea or thesis presented in a text, and for which the author will present evidence throughout the text.

Hence, the correct option is (A).

20. As we all know that teaching is a process where a teacher imparts his/her knowledge to the students in order to make students learn.

Teaching is related to learning here is the correct alternative because all the teaching is related to learning. Teaching can be acquired only by learning and teaching can be done to make the students learn.

Teaching is a 'task' word while learning is an 'achievement' word – this statement is also correct because teaching is a task and it can be performed in order to make the student learn and improve their behaviour while learning is an achievement because an individual or students acquire a number of behaviour and knowledge in order to modify their behaviour so it is an achievement for the student.

One may teach without learning taking place- This statement also corrects because teaching may occur without the learning takes place. It is the work of a teacher to teach but learning depends upon the students if they are not ready to acquire knowledge then learning cannot happen.

Hence, the correct option is (B).

21. The teacher's primary responsibility lies in planning educational experiences. A teacher plans many things for teaching-learning.

The teacher is a pillar in the teaching-learning process. In the present context, a teacher is not merely a disseminator of knowledge, rather plays a variety of roles. Due to the paradigm shift in the teaching-learning process, the teacher's role has become more challenging due to increasing expectations. To match those expectations, the teacher has to play diverse roles like a planner, facilitator, co-creator of knowledge, leader in the classroom and outside the classroom, manager, counselor, and apart from that, a true human being.

Hence, the correct option is (A).

22. Montreal protocol is designed to protect the ozone layer by phasing out substances responsible for ozone depletion.

The Montreal Protocol is an international treaty designed to protect the ozone layer by phasing out the production of numerous substances that are responsible for ozone-layer depletion.

It was decided on 16 September 1987 and came into force on 16 September 1989.

The main objective of the protocol is to phase out the production and consumption of compounds that deplete ozone in the stratosphere such as chlorofluorocarbons (CFCs), halons, methyl chloroform, and carbon tetrachloride.

Hence, the correct option is (D).

23. A pollutant is a physical agent that adversely affects the environment if its presence exceeds the desirable level. Pollutants may emerge in different forms such as solid waste, heat, radioactive waste, or gaseous pollutants like carbon monoxide, sulphur dioxide, nitrogen oxides, and so forth. Pollution caused by these agents takes different forms. For example, air or water pollution.

'Environmental pollutant' means any solid, liquid, or gaseous substances present in such concentration as may be, or tend to be injurious to the environment.

Non-biodegradable wastes: One of the side effects of developing civilization can be observed in the form of the presence of non-biodegradable material which cannot be broken down into simple, harmless substance by the action of bacteria. They are lethal to the land where they are dumped and last for centuries, burning of them release poisonous gases injurious to human and animal health in various possible ways. The entry of such substances pollute water bodies because of their non-depleting nature they occupy space in water bodies and consumed by animals causing severe health condition and death. Polythene, plastic is some deadly non-biodegradable waste.

Human Organic wastes: Human organic waste refers to the waste products of the human digestive system and human metabolism. Human excreta is used as fertilizer in farming.

Wastes from faecal matter: The safe disposal of Wastes from faecal matter is of paramount importance for the health and welfare of populations living in low-income countries as well as the prevention of pollution to the surrounding environment. However, if disposed of safely can be used in the production of Biogas, is generated through the bacterial breakdown of faecal matter, and any other organic matter, in an oxygen-free (anaerobic) system.

Natural nutrients present in excess: Nutrient pollution is the process where too many nutrients, mainly nitrogen and phosphorus, are added to bodies of water and can act like fertilizer, causing excessive growth of algae.

Hence, the correct option is (C).

24. Methane is the green house gas that has the shortest residence time in the atmosphere.

A greenhouse gas is a gas that absorbs and emits radiant energy within the thermal infrared range, causing the greenhouse effect. The primary greenhouse gases in Earth's atmosphere are water vapor (H_2O), carbon dioxide (CO_2), methane (CH_4), nitrous oxide (N_2O), and ozone (O_3).

Hence, the correct option is (C).

25. India launched National Green Tribunal to make polluters pay damages, in the year 2010.

The National Green Tribunal (NGT) is a statutory body that was established in 2010 by the National Green Tribunal Act. It was set up to handle cases and speed up the cases related to environmental issues. The Tribunal has the mandate to dispose of applications and petitions within a period of six months. India is the third country in the world – after Australia and New Zealand – to set up such a body to deal with environmental cases.

Hence, the correct option is (C).

26. Solar is the renewable source of energy.

A natural resource is given by nature and can be used as a source of energy. A renewable natural source of energy is one that can be renewed, or replenished in a reasonable amount of time, once it has been used.

Hence, the correct option is (C).

27. The research aims at understanding reality, discovering new knowledge and inventions for, development in the society, and research ethics certainly can restrain researchers. Considering all aspects it is amicably decided that researchers will follow some code of research ethics.

These are based on six key principles of ethical research that should be addressed whenever applicable:

1. Research should aim to maximize the benefit for individuals and society and minimize risk and harm.
2. The rights and dignity of individuals and groups should be respected.
3. Wherever possible, participation should be voluntary and appropriately informed.
4. Research should be conducted with integrity and transparency.
5. Lines of responsibility and accountability should be clearly defined.
6. Independence of research should be maintained and where conflicts of interest cannot be avoided they should be made explicit.

Hence, the correct option is (C).

28. Disclosing the data subsets is not the support practice of ethics in research.

Ethics are the principle or guidelines that help us to uphold the things we value. Research ethics concerns with issues related to what is appropriate in the conduct of research.

Hence, the correct option is (C).

29. Among the options stated above, the unethical practice of a researcher is avoiding Reliable Information.

Research ethics:

- It is a guideline for the responsible conducts of a research
- It related to the ethical principles of social responsibility
- There are three types of ethics, metaethics, normative ethics, and applied ethics
- Ethics always help us to identify right or wrong, differentiate good or bad

Avoiding Plagiarism, Avoiding Duplication, Avoiding Manipulation all are ethical in nature but Avoiding Reliable Information is unethical in nature.

Hence, the correct option is (C).

30. Research journals with a high impact factor are commonly considered to be more important than those with lower ones. The impact factor is commonly used to evaluate the relative importance of a journal within its field and to measure the frequency with which the "average article" in a journal has been cited in a particular time period.

Hence, the correct option is (C).

31. Correct match:

List-1 (Fallacies)		**List-2 (explanation)**	
a.	Fallacies of Presupposition	ii)	Because they are based on unwanted assumptions.
b.	Fallacies of Relevance	i)	At the point when the premises in an argument don't give a significant reason for accepting the truth of the conclusion.
c.	Fallacies of Denying the Antecedent	iii)	By denying the antecedent of a conditional proposition can not deny the consequent

Fallacies of presupposition: Some arguments are fallacies because they are based on unwanted assumptions. In these arguments, the error arises out of an implicit supposition of some other proposition whose truth is uncertain or questionable.

Fallacies of Relevance: When the premises are not relevant to the conclusion the fallacy of relevance is committed. This fallacy has many forms, appeal to force, appeal to pity, appeal to people, appeal to authority.

Fallacies of denying the antecedent: The fallacy consists in proceeding to argue by denying the antecedent of a conditional proposition.

Hence, the correct option is (C).

32. Information technology (IT) refers to everything that businesses use computers for. Information technology is building communications networks for a company, safeguarding data and information, creating and administering databases, helping employees troubleshoot problems with their computers or mobile devices, or doing a range of other work to ensure the efficiency and security of business information systems.

Hence, the correct option is (A).

33. A small text file stored on a user's computer by some websites in order to recognize and keep track of a user's preferences is called a cookie. The cookie stores some data that might be specific to a particular client. A small text file (up to 4KB) created by a website that is stored in the user's computer either temporarily for that session only or permanently on the hard disk (persistent cookie). Cookies provide a way for the website to recognize you and keep track of your preferences.

Hence, the correct option is (C).

34. Ascending order on the basis of geographical space is LAN < MAN < WAN.

Local Area Network (LAN): A local area network connects computers that are in the same building. A network spread over a few kilometres also comes under LAN. The LAN is usually realized using Ethernet technology or token ring technology. Fiber Distributed Data Interface (FDDI) is also becoming popular. The transmission rate varies from 10 Million bits per second to 1-gigabits per second (10Mbps-1Gbps).

Metropolitan Area Network (MAN): A Metropolitan Area Network (MAN) is basically a bigger version of LAN and normally uses similar technology. It might cover a group of nearby corporate offices or it can be in a city. It can be a private or public network.

Wide Area Network (WAN): A wide area network connects computers in different cities or countries. The network to connect computers that are thousands of miles apart is not built by an organization. Instead, the organization uses leased telephone lines. It is owned and managed collectively by many cooperating organizations.

Hence, the correct option is (D).

35. A small text file stored on a user's computer by some websites in order to recognize and keep track of user's preferences is called a cookie. Cookie store some data that might be specific to a particular client.

Hence, the correct option is (C).

36. The bug is a term used in computer science to denote an error in a particular program that is used to run a software.

Hence, the correct option is (B).

37. Effective teaching includes teacher behaviour, teacher knowledge regarding the subject matter, teacher beliefs, and teachers' dedication towards improving their students. Here effective teaching is defined as the ability to improve student achievements. For effective teaching, it is necessary to make ideas clear to learners who may be at a different level of understanding.

Factors that contribute to Effective Teaching are:

- Teaching-learning challenges effectively fulfilled by the teacher
- Previous experiences
- Socio-cultural factor
- Skills required
- Knowledge of the teacher
- Aptitude
- Maturity
- Self-concept
- Personal beliefs/value system
- Skills and training received
- Coping strategies
- Providing students with feedback
- Checking the understanding of the student by asking questions
- Being flexible with the learning pattern and pace of learning of the students

Therefore for effective teaching, it is necessary to make ideas clear to learners who may be at a different level of understanding.

Hence, the correct option is (D).

38. Morris L. Bigge defines reflection as, "careful, critical examination of an idea or supposed article of knowledge in the light of testing evidence which supports it and the further conclusions towards which it points.

Reflective level teaching does not depend upon the memorization, understanding of concepts, and their application only; it demands the use of higher mental processes such as reasoning, thinking, analyzing concepts, imagination, ideas and thoughts; and other bodies of knowledge critically, finding out the facts. Reflective level teaching-learning comprises the highest level of learning by the learner to develop new insight to solve problems, to explore the field of knowledge, to discover, to test, and retest the achieved facts, to understand and present generalizations in the light of the new evidence.

It also means thinking deeply about something. The reflective level of teaching is considered to be the highest level at which teaching is carried out. It is highly thoughtful and useful. A student can attain this level only after going through memory level and understanding level This level is also known as the introspective level. Reflecting on something means giving careful thought to something over a period of time

Teaching at the reflective level enables the students to solve the real problems of life. At this level, the student is made to face a real problematic situation. The student by understanding the situation and using his critical abilities succeeds in solving the problem. At this level, the emphasis is laid on identifying the problem, defining it, and finding a solution to it. The student's original thinking and creative abilities develop at this level.

Hence, the correct option is (C).

39. Both Statement I and Statement II are true.

Measurement is the process of systematically assigning numbers to objects and their properties to facilitate the use of mathematics in studying and describing objects and their relationships.

Some types of measurement are fairly concrete: for instance, measuring a person's weight in pounds or kilograms or his height in feet and inches or in meters. Measurement is not limited to physical qualities such as height and weight. Tests to measure abstract constructs such as intelligence or scholastic aptitude are commonly used in education and psychology, and the field of psychometrics is largely concerned with the development and refinement of methods to study these types of constructs. Scales of measurement refer to ways in which variables/numbers are defined and categorized.

Each scale of measurement has certain properties which in turn determines the appropriateness for use of certain statistical analyses. The four scales of measurement are nominal, ordinal, interval, and ratio. Thus, the statement I is correct.

A test is a device or procedure in which a sample of an individual's behaviour is obtained, evaluated, and scored using standardized procedures. A test provides a mechanism for making quantitative decisions about a process or processes. The intent is to determine whether there is enough evidence to "reject" a conjecture or hypothesis about the process. The conjecture is called the null hypothesis.

Not rejecting may be a good result if we want to continue to act as if we "believe" the null hypothesis is true. Or it may be a disappointing result, possibly indicating we may not yet have enough data to "prove" something by rejecting the null hypothesis. Thus, statement II is correct.

Hence, the correct option is (A).

40. Communication is defined as a process where ideas, thoughts, facts, and information is shared from one person to another. Communication is an important part of the teaching-learning process.

Effective communication involves knowing how to listen attentively. It's the ability to offer empathy, open-mindedness, and helpful feedback based on what you hear.

Communication skills are most vital for interactions with students because the act of teaching itself requires them.

As a teacher, you are responsible for comprehending and breaking down complex information, conveying this information clearly to your students (both verbally and in written resources), presenting in a manner that sustains their attention, and listening to and resolving their questions or problems.

For imparting communication, each student must be considered as a product of a common cause and the teacher should identify the characteristics of the learner. The teacher communicates in a lucid way so that there is no communication barrier and the student understands the concept easily. Thus, both A and R are true and R is the correct explanation of A.

Hence, the correct option is (A).

41. Communication refers to the exchange of information from one person to another. Effective communication occurs only when the receiver understands the exact information that the sender intended to transmit. Communication can be broadly classified as verbal and non-verbal.

Non-verbal Communication: It refers to the body movements or body language consisting of motor expressions that may originate in various parts of the body. Facial expressions convey a wide range of emotions such as fear, anger, surprise, etc. Non-verbal messages serve to repeat, contradict or substitute a verbal message.

They are divided into:

Spatial Behaviour: It refers to the distinct patterns in the way people use the space that immediately surrounds them when interacting with others. For example, people move towards or away from a person they maintain closeness or distance.

Extralinguistic Behaviour: The non-content aspects of behaviour include temporal (such as rate of speaking, rhythm), interaction (such as the tendency to interrupt or dominate) or verbal stylistic (such as pronunciation peculiarities, dialect etc.) are referred to as extralinguistic behaviour or paralanguage.

For example, a vocal characteristic such as pitch accurately measures emotional states. People express passive emotions such as sadness through slow speech, lower volume and pitch; active emotions such as anger by fast, loud and high-pitched speech.

Linguistic Behaviour: It refers to the manifest content of speech and the various attributes of verbal communication.

Hence, the correct option is (C).

42. Assertion (A) is true but Reason (R) is false.

Oration and humour in classroom communication:

The core purpose of communication is to elicit a change in perceptions, understanding, or behavior in the receiver; this is particularly true of communication with the students in the classroom.

The Ancient Greeks developed the art of oratory over 2000 years ago. In classical Greece and Rome, the main component was rhetoric (that is, composition and delivery of speeches), and was an important skill in public and private life. Good orators are able to change the emotions of their listeners, not just inform them.

Humour, as we notice, has immense importance in communication. It brings teacher-student together, breaks the ice and barriers between people, and enlivens the atmosphere. It encourages us to think more and get creative.

A good, clean joke can even enhance creativity and produce fresh, vibrant ideas.

Anything presented in a humorous manner seems more interesting and inviting.

Rhetorical intervention:

Rhetoric refers to the study and use of written, spoken, and visual language.

Rhetoric began 2500 years ago as the study of the forms of communication and argument essential to public, political, and legal life in Ancient Greece.

Rhetorical Communication: Rhetorica: the communicator gives thought to the intended message and stimulates the receiver in a manner designed to achieve a specific result. • Rhetorical communication is simply a way to win over an audience.

It investigates how language is used to organize and maintain social groups, construct meanings and identities, coordinate behavior, mediate power, produce change, and create knowledge.

Hence, the correct option is (C).

43. Given,

When Rashmi moves 6 kmph faster, She takes 30 minutes less.

When Rashmi moves 5 kmph slower, She takes 30 minutes more.

Distance = $\frac{(\text{Speed 1} \times \text{Speed 2})}{(\text{Difference in the speed})} \times$ Difference in time

Let the original speed be S.

Now, according to the question,

$\frac{S(S+6)}{6} \times \frac{1}{2} = \frac{S(S-5)}{5} \times \frac{1}{2}$

$\Rightarrow 6(S-5) = 5(S+6)$

$\Rightarrow 6S - 30 = 5S + 30$

$\Rightarrow S = 60$ kmph

Now, Distance $= \frac{S(S+6)}{6} \times \frac{1}{2}$

$= \frac{60(60+6)}{6} \times \frac{1}{2}$

$= 330$ km

$\therefore$ The distance is 330 km.

Hence, the correct option is (A).

44. Statement I is false but Statement II is true.

Statement I:

Loss% = $\frac{\text{Loss}}{\text{Cost price}} \times 100$

Loss% = $\frac{(500-400)}{500} \times 100$

Loss% $= 20\%$

Loss% in this transaction is 20% but according to the question, it is 5%. This statement is false.

Statement II:

Profit% = $\frac{\text{Profit}}{\text{Cost price}} \times 100$

Profit% $= \frac{(648-600)}{600} \times 100$

Profit% $= 8\%$

Profit% in this transaction is 5% and according to the question, it is 5%. This statement is true.

Hence, the correct option is (D).

45. Statement I:

Length of train = 300 m

Length of platform = 300 m

Total distance = 300 m + 300 m = 600 m

Time = 30 seconds

Speed = $\frac{\text{Total distance}}{\text{Time}}$

Speed = $\frac{600 \text{ m}}{30 \text{ seconds}}$

Speed= 20 m\second

Statement II:

The average speed is the total distance travelled by the object in a particular time interval.

Conclusion:

In the statement I speed of the train is 20 m/seconds but it is given 10 m/seconds. So, it is an incorrect statement.

In statement II:

The average speed is (Total distance)/(Total time) but it is given the mean of speeds. So, it is an incorrect statement.

Hence, the correct option is (B).

46. Given:

Nishu has chocolates $= 6\frac{1}{2}$ dozens

Nishu gave chocolates to Ravi $= \frac{1}{6}$ of $6\frac{1}{2}$ dozens

Nishu gave chocolates to Rahul $= \frac{1}{13}$ of $6\frac{1}{2}$ dozens

Half of the chocolates given to her friends $= \frac{1}{2}$ of $6\frac{1}{2}$ dozens

$6\frac{1}{2}$ dozens $= \left(\frac{13}{2}\right) \times 12$

$13 \times 6 = 78$ chocolates

The number of chocolates given to Ravi $= \left(\frac{1}{6}\right) \times 6\frac{1}{2}$ dozens

$\Rightarrow 78 \times \frac{1}{6} = 13$ chocolates

The number of chocolates given to Rahul= $\left(\frac{1}{13}\right) \times 6\frac{1}{2}$ dozens

$\Rightarrow 78 \times \frac{1}{13} = 6$ chocolates

The number of chocolates given to her friends $= \left(\frac{1}{2}\right)$ of 78

$\Rightarrow \left(\frac{1}{2}\right) \times 78 = 39$

The number of chocolates given to friends, Ravi and Rahul $=$ $39 + 6 + 13$

$= 58$

The number of chocolates left with her = Total chocolates - The number of chocolates given to other friends, Ravi and Rahul

$\Rightarrow 78 - 58 = 20$

$\therefore$ The number of chocolates left with her is 20.

Hence, the correct option is (C).

47. Given:

Selling Price of scooter $=$ Rs. 3440

Loss $\% = 14\%$

Gain $\% = 14\%$ $\text{S.P} = \frac{\text{C.P} \times (100-L\%)}{100}$

$\text{S.P} = \frac{\text{C.P} \times (100+P\%)}{100}$

Where,

S.P $\rightarrow$ Selling price

C.P $\rightarrow$ Cost price

$\text{L}\% \rightarrow \text{Loss } \%$

$\text{P}\% \rightarrow \text{Profit } \%$

Selling Price of scooter $=$ Rs. 3440

Loss $\% = 14\%$

Let the C.P. be x.

∴ Required equation:

$$\Rightarrow x \times \frac{86}{100} = 3440$$

$$\Rightarrow x = 3440 \times \frac{100}{86}$$

$$\Rightarrow x = \text{Rs. } 4000$$

$$\text{Gain } \% = 14\%$$

The new S.P $= 4000 \times \frac{114}{100}$

$= 40 \times 114$

$=$ Rs. 4560

∴ The new S.P of the scooter is Rs. 4560.

Hence, the correct option is (A).

48. Statement: Time and Tide wait for none.

We must forget the fact that the statement is a proverb and evaluate it in its own merit.

There are two ways of interpreting the statement depending on how one looks at it.

Conclusions:

A materialistic or an optimistic person interprets the meaning of the statement as Conclusion II.

An aesthetic or a pessimistic person could interpret the meaning of the statement as Conclusion I.

Both have merits when looked at from their own point of view and we cannot say one is definitely better than the other.

The truth, though, is only one of these opposing views can be true.

Hence, the correct option is (C).

49. Inductive argument proceeds from particulars to Universals.

Inductive Argument: It observes some common patterns among the premises and conclusion and that observed pattern will hold in general according to the argument. Proceeds from particular to general/universal.

Example: The chair in the bedroom is red. The chair in the living room is red.

Therefore, all the chairs in the house are red.

Hence, the correct option is (B).

50. The least possible Venn diagram is:

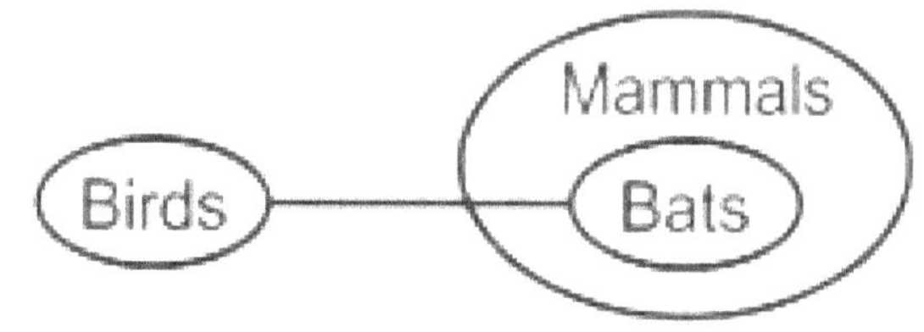

(i) No birds are mammals. → False (It can be possible, but it is not definite)

(ii) Some birds are not mammals. → False (It can be possible, but it is not definite)

(iii) No bats are birds. → True (It is definite)

(iv) All mammals are bats. → False (It can be possible, but it is not definite)

Hence, the correct option is (C).

Mock Test 16

Ques (1-5):Direction: Read the following passage carefully and answer questions:

Traditional Indian Values must be viewed both from the angle of the individual and from that of the geographically delimited agglomeration of peoples or groups enjoying a common system of leadership which we call the 'State'. The Indian 'State's' special feature is the peaceful, or perhaps mostly peaceful, co-existence of social groups of various historical provenances which mutually adhere in a geographical, economic, and political sense, without ever assimilating to each other in social terms, in ways of thinking, or even in language. Modern Indian law will determine certain rules, especially in relation to the regime of the family, upon the basis of how the loin-cloth is tied, or how the turban is worn, for this may identify the litigants as members of a regional group, and therefore as participants in its traditional law, though their ancestors left the region three or four centuries earlier. The use of the word 'State' above must not mislead us. There was no such thing as a conflict between the individual and the State, atleast before foreign governments became established, just as there was no concept of state 'sovereignty' or of any church-and-state dichotomy. Modern Indian 'secularism' has an admittedly peculiar feature : It requires the state to make a fair distribution of attention and support amongst all religions. These blessed aspects of India's famed tolerance (Indian kings so rarely persecuted religious groups that the exceptions prove the rule) at once struck Portuguese and other European visitors to the West Coast of India in the sixteenth century, and the impression made upon them in this and other ways gave rise, at one remove, to the basic constitution of Thomas More's Utopia. There is little about modern India that strikes one at once as Utopian : but the insistence upon the inculcation of norms, and the absence of bigotry and institutionalized exploitation of human or natural resources, are two very different features which link the realities of India and her tradition with the essence of all Utopians.

Q.1 What is the striking feature of modern India?

A. A replica of Utopian StateUniform laws
B. Uniform laws
C. Adherence to traditional values
D. Absence of Bigotry

Q.2 The basic construction of Thomas More's Utopia was inspired by:

A. Indian tradition of religious tolerance
B. Persecution of religious groups by Indian rulers
C. Social inequality in India
D. European perception of Indian State

Q.3 Which one is the peculiar feature of modern Indian 'Secularism'?

A. No discrimination on religious considerations
B. Total indifference to religion
C. No space for social identity
D. Disregard for social law

Q.4 The author uses the word 'State' to highlight:

A. Antagonistic relationship between the state and the individual throughout the period of history
B. Absence of conflict between the state and the individuals upto a point in time
C. The concept of state sovereignty and dependence on religion
D. Dependence on religion.

Q.5 Which of the following is a special feature of the Indian State?

A. Peaceful co-existence of people under a common system of leadership
B. Peaceful co-existence of social groups of different historical provenances attached to each other in a geographical, economic and political sense
C. Social integration of all groups
D. Cultural assimilation of all social groups

Ques (6-10):Direction: Read the following table carefully and answer the following questions.

The following table shows the five types of books sold in three months.

Subject (No. of books)	January	February	March
English	80	40	60
Hindi	60	20	90
Marathi	50	10	80
Sanskrit	70	30	100
History	40	35	70

Q.6 The number of English books in three months is approximately what percent less than the number of Sanskrit books?

A. 25% **B.** 15% **C.** 20% **D.** 10%

Q.7 The number of Hindi books sold in March is approximately what percent of the total number of books sold in March?

A. 11% **B.** 19% **C.** 15% **D.** 22.5%

Q.8 Find the ratio between the number of books sold in January and February.

A. 9 : 8 **B.** 9 : 14 **C.** 15 : 8 **D.** 20 : 9

Q.9 Find the difference between the number of History books sold in three months and the number of Marathi books in three months.

A. 10 **B.** 15 **C.** 5 **D.** 8

Q.10 Find the average number of books sold in March.

A. 80 **B.** 55 **C.** 50 **D.** 60

Q.11 _______ means the ownership of several businesses one of which a media business.

A. Chain ownership
B. Joint Stock ownership
C. Conglomerate ownership
D. Business ownership

Q.12 The term 'Yellow journalism' refers to:

A. Sensational news about terrorism and violence
B. Sensationalism and exaggeration to attract readers/viewers
C. Sensational news about arts and culture
D. Sensational newsprints in yellow paper

Q.13 Imagine you are working in an educational institution where people are of equal status. Which method of communication is best suited and normally employed in such a context?

A. Horizonatal Communication
B. Vertical communication
C. Corporate communication
D. Cross communication

Q.14 Information overload in a classroom environment by a teacher will lead to:

A. High-level participation
B. Semantic precision
C. Effective impression
D. Delayed feedback

Q.15 As we move from interpersonal to mass communication:

A. messages become less structured and feedback becomes more instantaneous
B. messages become less structured and feedback becomes less instantaneous
C. messages become more structured and feedback becomes more instantaneous
D. messages become more structured and feedback becomes less instantaneous

Q.16 The Pancha Kosh Theory of Education was elaborated by:

A. Swami Vivekananda
B. Patanjali
C. Mahatma Gandhi
D. Aurobindo

Q.17 In the following table, Set-I mentions an apex level institution in India while Set-II indicates their establishment date. Match the two sets and give your answer.

Set - I	Set - II
(a) University Grants Commission (UGC)	(i) 1995
(b) All India Council of Technical Education (AICTE)	(ii) 1956
(c) National Council of Teacher Education (NCTE)	(iii) 1994
(d) National Assessment and Accreditation Council (NAAC)	(iv) 1945

A. a-i, b-iv, c-iii, d-ii **B.** a-ii, b-iv, c-i, d-iii
C. a-ii, b-i, c-iii, d-iv **D.** a-i, b-iv, c-ii, d-iii

Q.18 The total number of Deemed Universities in India till 2020 was:

A. 125 **B.** 99 **C.** 69 **D.** 97

Q.19 The average of 50 numbers is 38. If the numbers 45 and 55 are discarded, then the average of the remaining numbers is:

A. 36.5 **B.** 37 **C.** 37.5 **D.** 37.52

Q.20 In certain code MATHURA is coded as JXQEROX. The code of HOTELS will be:

A. LEQIBP **B.** ELQBIP **C.** LEBIQP **D.** ELIPQB

Q.21 One day Prakash left home and walked 10 km towards south, turned right and walked 5 km, turned right and walked 10 km and turned left and walked 10 km. How many km will have to walk to reach his home straight?

A. 10 **B.** 20 **C.** 15 **D.** 3

Q.22 Pointing towards a person in a photograph, Anjali said, "He is the only son of the father of my sister's brother." How is that person is related to Anjali?

A. Father **B.** Mother **C.** Brother **D.** Uncle

Q.23 In an examination, 52% of candidates failed in English and 42% failed in Mathematics. If 17% of candidates failed in both English and Mathematics, what percentage of candidates passed in both the subjects?

A. 23% **B.** 18% **C.** 21% **D.** 25%

Q.24 If the code of ALLAHABAD is DPQGOIKKO, then the code of BENGULURU will be

A. ESBTBDIMF **B.** MBDBFEIST
C. EISMBTDBF **D.** ESBDFBTMI

Q.25 Identify the type of reasoning shown in the following statements.

Statement 1: We see smoke coming out of the hills.

Statement 2: Wherever there is smoke, there is always a fire.

Conclusion: Therefore, hills have fire.

A. Pratyaksha pramana (Perception)
B. Upmana (Comparison)
C. Anumana (Fallacy)
D. Vyapti (Invariable relations)

Q.26 Direction: Select the option that is related to the third number in the same way as the second number is related to the first number.

8 : 514 : : 11 : ?

A. 1333 **B.** 123 **C.** 113 **D.** 1331

Q.27 Direction: Select the related letters/numbers from the given alternatives.

CARD : 18 : : SORT : ?

A. 1 **B.** 6 **C.** 4 **D.** 5

Q.28 Direction: Statement is given followed by two inferences I and II. You have to consider the statement to be true even if it seems to be at variance from commonly known facts. You have to decide which of the given inferences, if any, follow from the given statement?

Statement: It is really mocking for the largest democratic country to retain the tag of developing nations for so long.

Inferences:

I. India yet has to become a developed nation.

II. Unless we change our perception India cannot become developed.

A. Only inference I follows
B. Only inference II follows
C. Both I and II follow
D. Either I or II follows

Q.29 Which of the following steps are required to design a questionnaire?

(1) Writing primary and secondary aims of the study.
(2) Review of the current literature.
(3) Prepare a draft of the questionnaire.
(4) Revision of the draft.

Select the correct answer from the codes given below:

A. 1, 2 and 3 **B.** 1, 3 and 4
C. 2, 3 and 4 **D.** 1, 2, 3 and 4

Q.30 Arrange the following steps of teaching in a logical order.

(i) Diagnosis of the learner
(ii) Fixing goals and content
(iii) Actions and Reactions
(iv) Feedback to teaching
(v) Decision about the strategy
(vi) Appropriate testing devices

A. (iii)-(i)-(iv)-(ii)-(v)-(vi)
B. (ii)-(v)-(i)-(iii)-(vi)-(iv)
C. (ii)-(i)-(v)-(vi)-(iv)-(iii)
D. (i)-(v)-(vi)-(ii)-(iii)-(iv)

Q.31 Instructional aids are used by the teacher by

A. Glorify the class **B.** Attract the students
C. Clarify the concepts **D.** Ensure discipline

Q.32 From the list of evaluation procedures given below to identify those which will be called 'formative evaluation'. Indicate your answer by choosing from the code:

(1) A teacher awards grades to students after having transacted the course work.
(2) During interaction with students in the classroom, the teacher provides corrective feedback.
(3) The teacher gives marks to students on a unit test.
(4) The teacher clarifies the doubts of students in the class itself.
(5) The overall performance of students is reported to parents at every three months interval.
(6) The learner's motivation is raised by the teacher through a question-answer session.

Code:

A. 1, 2 and 3 **B.** 2, 3 and 4
C. 1, 3 and 5 **D.** 2, 4 and 6

Q.33 Which of the following factors does not impact teaching?

A. Teacher's knowledge
B. Classroom activities that encourage learning
C. Socio-economic background of teachers and students
D. Learning through experience

Q.34 Biomagnification means increase in the______.

A. concentration of pollutants in living organisms
B. number of species
C. size of living organisms
D. biomass

Q.35 The Deccan Thorn Forests covers which of the following states in India?

A. Maharashtra **B.** Andhra Pradesh
C. Karnataka **D.** All of them

Q.36 The Earth Summit of 1992 at Rio de Janeiro resulted into a Convention on Biodiversity, which came into force on:

A. 5 June, 1992 **B.** 19 December, 1993
C. 29 December, 1993 **D.** 1 April, 2000

Q.37 The President can be removed from office by a process of impeachment for 'violation of the Constitution'. Consider the following statements in this regard:

1) Constitution does not define the meaning of the phrase 'violation of the Constitution'.
2) The impeachment charges to be initiated, should be signed by 100 MPs in case of lok sabha and 50 MPs in case of Rajya Sabha.
3) The impeachment is a quasi-judicial procedure in the Parliament.

Select the correct answer using the code given below:

A. 1 and 2 only **B.** 1 and 3 only
C. 2 and 3 only **D.** 1, 2 and 3

Q.38 The principal of a school conducts an interview session of teachers and students with a view to exploring the possibility of their enhanced anticipation in school programmes. This endeavour may be related to which type of research?

A. Evaluation Research
B. Fundamental Research
C. Action Research
D. Applied Research

Q.39 The ability to see and size up the situation creatively is most relevant at which stage of research?

A. At the stage of identifying and defining a research problem.
B. In determining the research design and its execution.
C. In formulating research hypotheses and procedures for testing them.
D. In deciding and identifying the sampling procedures to ensure their representative character.

Q.40 In order to augment the accuracy of the study the researcher -

A. Should increase the size of his sample
B. Should be honest and unbiased

C. Should keep the variance high
D. All of these

Q.41 In case the population of the research is heterogeneous in nature which of the following sampling techniques will ensure optimum representativeness of sample units?
A. Simple random sampling
B. Stratified random sampling
C. Cluster sampling
D. Systematic sampling

Q.42 The review of the related study is important while undertaking research because-
A. It avoids repetition or duplication
B. It helps in understanding the gaps
C. It helps the researcher not to draw illogical conclusions
D. All of the above

Q.43 Which of the following are the basic rules of APA style of referencing format?
(a) Italicize titles of shorter works such as journal articles or essays
(b) Invert authors' names (last name first)
(c) Italicize titles of longer works like books and journals
(d) Alphabetically index reference list
Select the correct answer from the codes given below:
A. (a) and (b) **B.** (b), (c) and (d)
C. (c) and (d) **D.** (a), (b), (c) and (d)

Q.44 Which of the following is an instant messaging application?
1. WhatsApp
2. Google Talk
3. Viber

Select the correct answer from the codes given below:
A. 1 and 2 only **B.** 2 and 3 only
C. 1 only **D.** 1, 2 and 3

Q.45 Cloud computing has the following distinct characteristics :
(a) The service is hosted on the internet.
(b) It is made available by a service provider.
(c) It computes and predicts rain when the weather is cloudy.
(d) The service is fully managed by the provider.
Choose the correct answer from the options given below :
A. (a), (b) only **B.** (a), (b), (c) only
C. (a), (d) only **D.** (a), (b), (d) only

Q.46 The full form TKDL is:
A. Traditional knack digital library
B. Traditional knowledge digital library
C. Transfer knowledge desktop literature
D. Transfer knowledge digital library

Q.47 Which of the following statements is/are correct with respect to Internet and Intranet?
i. The number of users in Intranet is limited.
ii. Internet is a wide network of computers & open to all.
iii. Intranet uses internet protocols such as TCP/IP and FTP.
iv. Internet is safer than Intranet.
A. (i), (ii) and (iii) only
B. (ii), (iii) and (iv) only
C. (i) and (iv) only
D. All of the above

Q.48 Which one of the following factors is a deterrent for the students to do well in higher education?
A. Political orientation
B. Academic strategies
C. Comprehension ability
D. Academic discourse

Q.49 The Tenth Five Year Plan approach paper on higher education focussed on:
A. Internationalisation **B.** Ruralisation
C. Universalisation **D.** ICT orientation

Q.50 Polar Stratospheric Clouds are associated with which of the following environmental issues?
A. Flash floods
B. Acid rain
C. Ozone layer depletion
D. Photo-chemical smog

// Smart Answer Sheet //

Correct Indicates percentage of students who answered questions correctly.

Skipped Indicates percentage of students who skipped questions.

Q.	Ans.	Correct	Skipped
1	D	50.19 %	1.43 %
2	A	66.62 %	1.17 %
3	A	54.49 %	1.01 %
4	B	64.47 %	1.05 %
5	B	69.07 %	1.31 %
6	D	68.51 %	1.96 %
7	D	63.81 %	1.02 %
8	D	88.55 %	0.0 %
9	C	88.63 %	0.0 %
10	A	49.55 %	1.82 %

Q.	Ans.	Correct	Skipped
11	C	51.22 %	1.33 %
12	B	45.27 %	1.68 %
13	A	22.46 %	4.53 %
14	D	65.17 %	1.57 %
15	D	12.27 %	3.85 %
16	A	15.74 %	3.85 %
17	B	17.42 %	4.37 %
18	A	50.32 %	1.94 %
19	C	79.2 %	0.0 %
20	B	77.23 %	0.0 %

Q.	Ans.	Correct	Skipped
21	C	53.44 %	1.39 %
22	C	40.21 %	1.65 %
23	A	63.94 %	1.07 %
24	C	79.11 %	0.0 %
25	C	79.26 %	0.0 %
26	A	42.65 %	1.53 %
27	C	60.01 %	1.14 %
28	A	61.82 %	1.08 %
29	D	65.31 %	1.39 %
30	B	60.16 %	1.41 %

Q.	Ans.	Correct	Skipped
31	C	66.09 %	1.85 %
32	D	41.51 %	1.12 %
33	C	55.31 %	1.43 %
34	A	28.64 %	3.68 %
35	D	61.32 %	1.18 %
36	A	30.31 %	4.85 %
37	B	89.41 %	0.0 %
38	C	45.62 %	1.46 %
39	C	50.36 %	1.76 %
40	D	87.32 %	0.0 %

Q.	Ans.	Correct	Skipped
41	B	55.11 %	1.6 %
42	D	85.28 %	0.0 %
43	B	54.16 %	1.23 %
44	D	32.21 %	4.17 %
45	D	69.73 %	1.47 %
46	B	41.5 %	1.87 %
47	A	10.76 %	4.8 %
48	A	47.93 %	1.83 %
49	D	89.1 %	0.0 %
50	C	77.13 %	0.0 %

Performance Analysis	
Avg. Score (%)	55.0%
Toppers Score (%)	57.0%
Your Score	

//Hints and Solutions//

1. Absence of Bigotry is the striking feature of modern India.

In the last paragraph of the passage, the author talks about features of modern India that have the essence of Utopia.

He says there is not much that can strike someone as utopian about Modern India.

However, he points two different features that link India with the essence of all Utopians, which are 'inculcation of norms, and the absence of bigotry and institutionalized exploitation of human or natural resources.'

Hence, the correct option is (D).

2. The author is trying to emphasize the roots of religious tolerance in India and comparing it with Modern Indian secularism.

He believes the aspect of religious tolerance made its impact on the colonizers namely Portuguese and other European visitors.

This impression also inspired the famous socio-political satire Utopia by noted humanist writer Thomas More.

So, we can infer from the above given points that the correct answer will be 'Indian tradition of religious tolerance.'

Hence, the correct option is (A).

3. Peculiar means something that belongs to only one person or place or something unique or odd.

The author of the passage talks about the aspect of religious tolerance in India.

He clearly states in the passage that, 'Modern Indian 'secularism' has an admittedly peculiar feature: It requires the state to make a fair distribution of attention and support amongst all religions.'

From all the options 'Fair distribution of attention and support amongst all religions' clearly matches with option (A) i.e No discrimination on religious considerations.

Thus, from above points we can infer that the peculiar feature of modern Indian 'Secularism' that the author talks about is no discrimination on religious considerations.

Hence, the correct option is (A).

4. This is obvious from the first line of the paragraph which explains "Traditional Indian values must both be viewed from the angle of an individual and from that of a geographically delimited agglomeration of peoples or groups enjoying a common system of leadership which we call as State"

Since the author is comparing the traditional and modern India, he's defining what modern terms meant in past.

The author states, 'There was no such thing as a conflict between the individual and the State, atleast before foreign governments became established.'

Since, the option that correctly expresses the above given statement of passage is option (B).

Hence, the correct option is (B).

5. In the second line of the passage, author clearly states the special feature of the Indian state.

'State's' special feature is the peaceful, or perhaps mostly peaceful, co-existence of social groups of various historical provenances which mutually adhere in a geographical, economic, and political sense'.

Hence, the correct option is (B).

6. Given:

Total number of English books sold in three months = 80 + 40 + 60 = 180

Total number of Sanskrit books sold in three months = 70 + 30 + 100 = 200

Required percentage = $\frac{200-180}{200}$

Required percentage = $\frac{20}{200}$

= 10% Less

Hence, the correct option is (D).

7. Given:

Total number of books sold in March = 60 + 90 + 80 + 100 + 70

= 400

Total number of Hindi books in March = 90

Required percentage = $\frac{90}{400} \times 100$

= 22.5%

Hence, the correct option is (D).

8. Given:

Total number of books sold in January = 80 + 60 + 50 + 70 + 40

= 300

Total number of bools sold in February = 40 + 20 + 10 + 30 + 35

= 135

Required ratio = 300 : 135

= 20 : 9

Hence, the correct option is (D).

9. Total number of Marathi books sold in three months = 50 + 10 + 80 = 140

Total number of History books sold in three months = 40 + 35 + 70 = 145

Required difference = 145 - 140 = 5

Hence, the correct option is (C).

10. Given:

Total number of books sold in March = 60 + 90 + 80 + 100 + 70 = 400

Required average = $\frac{400}{5}$ = 80

Hence, the correct option is (A).

11. Conglomerate ownership means the ownership of several businesses one of which a media business.

In a conglomerate, there is the interlocking of directorships. Their main business will be a high-profit industry, but they run a media company for prestige or to exercise social and political influence on decision-makers in the private or public sector and in the government of the day. Such a conglomeration may not always support an unbiased or dispassionate presentation of events, issues and personalities.

Hence, the correct option is (C).

12. Yellow journalism refers to sensationalism and exaggeration to attract readers/viewers. It is the type of journalism that does not report complete real news, instead of that, it exaggerates the real issue.

Hence, the correct option is (B).

13. Horizontal communication is the transmission of information between people, divisions, departments or units within the same level of the organizational hierarchy. You can distinguish it from vertical communication, which is the transmission of information between different levels of the organizational hierarchy.

Hence, the correct option is (A).

14. Information overload in a classroom environment by a teacher will lead to delayed feedback.

The actual response of the students to the lesson communicated to him/her is known as 'feedback'. If the communication is overloaded with information, it may affect the entire communication process negatively as an excessive amount of information conveyed might make it difficult for the students to grasp the content completely which might, in turn, result in delayed feedback from the students.

Hence, the correct option is (D).

15. As we move from interpersonal to mass communication messages become more structured and feedback becomes less instantaneous.

Interpersonal communication is immediate and dynamic but less emphasis is given to the presentation part. At the same time, the attractiveness of mass communication depends on the structure and presentation of the massage but feedback receives late.

Hence, the correct option is (D).

16. The Pancha Kosh Theory of Education was elaborated by Swani Vivekanand.

The Panchkosh are commonly referred to as five hierarchical levels of energy in the body. It is a certain discipline which is based on the ancient texts of Indian Philosophy. 'Panch' stands for five and word 'Kosha' means sheath or shell. Therefore, Panchkosh means five sheaths which reside in human body. They are :

- Annamay Kosha or The Food Sheath
- Pranamay Kosha or The Energy Sheath
- Manomany Kosha or The Mental Sheath
- Vigyanmay Kosha or The Intellectual Sheath
- Anandmay Kosha or The Bliss Sheath

Hence, the correct option is (A).

17. The correct combination is - a-ii, b-iv, c-i, d-iii

UGC (University Grants Commission) was established in the year 1956 as a statutory body through the Parliament Act for coordinating and maintaining the higher education standards in India.

AICTE (All India Council for Technical Education) was established in the year 1945 as an advisory body & as a statutory body through the Parliament Act for planning and development of technical education in India.

NCTE (National Council for Teacher Education) was established in the year 1995 to undertake and maintain the procedures and processes in the Indian Education System.

NAAC (National Assessment and Accreditation Council) was established in the year 1994 with the motive to evaluate the performances of universities and colleges in India.

Hence, the correct option is (B).

18. The total number of Deemed Universities in India till 2020 was 125.

Deemed university, is an accreditation granted to higher educational institutions in India, conferring the status of a university. It is granted by the Department of Higher Education.

Hence, the correct option is (A).

19. Given,

Average of 50 numbers $= 38$

Then, sum of 50 numbers $= 38 \times 50 = 1900$

If two number 45 and 55 are discarded

Then, sum of remaining 48 numbers $= 1900 - (45 + 55)$

$= 1800$

$\therefore$ Required average $= \left(\frac{1800}{48}\right)$

$= 37.5$

Hence, the correct option is (C).

20.

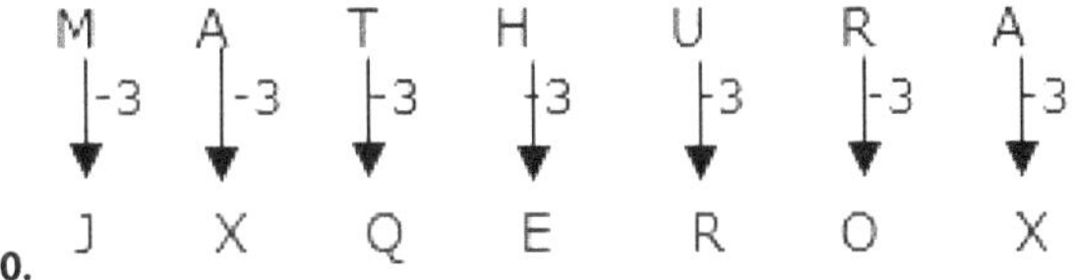

Here in MATHURA,

Place value of M=13 and place value of J=10 so the difference in place value is 3.

Place value of A=1 and place value of X=24 so the difference in place value is 3.

Therefore, the fixed pattern is followed in which coded letter place value is 3 less.

Code of HOTELS is,

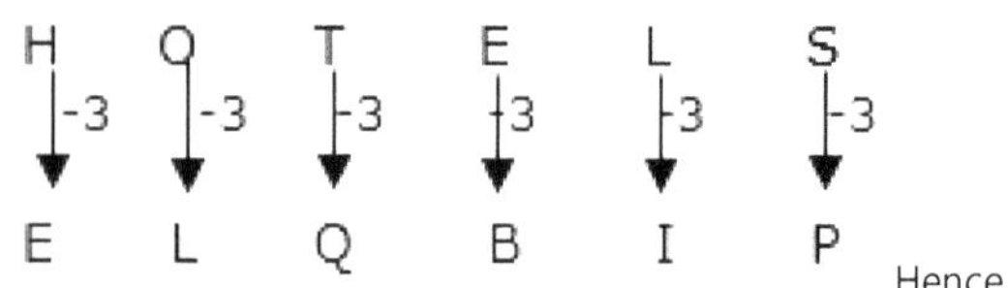

Hence, the correct option is (B).

21.

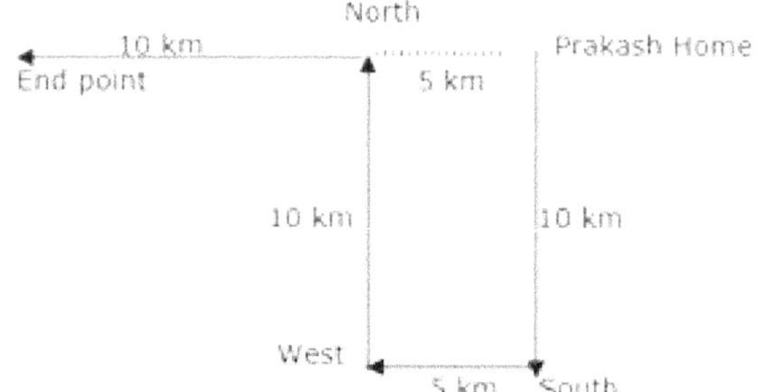

From the above figure, it is clear that Prakash has to walk 15 km to reach his home straight.

Hence, the correct option is (C).

22. Relation's given in the question may be analysed as follows:

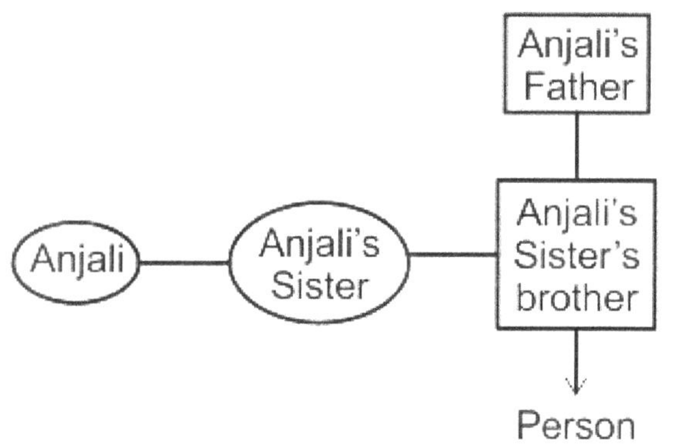

Sister's brother - brother;

Brother's father - father;

Father's son - brother;

So, he is Anjali's Brother.

Hence, the correct option is (C).

23. Given that 52% of candidates failed in English, 42 % failed in mathematics and 17% failed in both subjects.

Let,

n(A)=52%

n(B)=42%

Thus the number of students who failed in one or both subjects =(52+42-17)%

= 77%

Therefore, pass percentage = 23%

Hence, the correct option is (A).

24. A + 3 = D

L + 4 = P

L + 5 = Q

A + 6 = G

H + 7 = O

A + 8 = I

B + 9 = K

A + 10 = K

D + 11 = O

So, code of BENGULURU will be:

B + 3 = E

E + 4 = I

N + 5 = S

G + 6 = M

U + 7 = B

L + 8 = T

U + 9 = D

R + 10 = B

U + 11 = F

So, code of BENGULURU will be EISMBTDBF.

Hence, the correct option is (C).

25. Anumana (Fallacy) is a method by which knowledge is derived from another knowledge. On the basis of our perceptual knowledge, we know that wherever there is smoke there is fire (the opposite might not be true). After knowing the invariable relation between the two we can logically deduce the presence of fire whenever we see smoke. This is anumana.

Hence, the correct option is (C).

26. Given:

8 : 514 : : 11 : ?

The pattern followed here is,

8 is related to 514 as:

$8^3 + 2 = 512 + 2$

= 514

Similarly,

$11^3 + 2 = 1331 + 2$

= 1333

⇒ 8 : 514 : : 11 : 1333

Hence, the correct option is (A).

27. The pattern followed here is:

Take the sum of (first and second letter) and (third and fourth letter), then subtract both sums.

C = 3, A = 1, 3 + 1 = 4

R = 18, D = 4, 18 + 4 = 22

22 – 4 = 18

Same pattern will be followed for 'SORT : ?'.

S = 19, O = 15, 19 + 15 = 34

R = 18, T = 20, 18 + 20 = 38

38 – 34 = 4

Hence, the correct option is (C).

28. The statement suggests that despite being the largest democracy in the world, India is still classified as a developing country.

From the statement, it can be deduced that India is progressive and has yet to become a developed nation. Therefore, the inference I follows.

But since the statement does not discuss the parameters of development and the criteria to assess development. We cannot deduce that a change in perception will help India become developed. Therefore, inference II does not follow.

Hence, the correct option is (A).

29. The steps which are required to design a questionnaire includes the aim of the study i.e. writing the primary and secondary aims of the study, to prepare a draft of the questionnaire in which a number of questions will be asked related to the topic, review the literature so as to frame the relevant questions and revision of the draft for making it error-free.

Hence, the correct option is (D).

30. The correct sequence of teaching is:

Fixing goals and content-Decision about strategy- Diagnosis of the learner- Actions and Reactions - Appropriate testing devices - Feedback to teaching.

Therefore the correct order is: (ii)-(v)-(i)-(iii)-(vi)-(iv).

Hence, the correct option is (B).

31. When any teacher wants to clarify the basics and concepts about a particular topic then they use instructional aids. Instructional aids are devices that assist an instructor in the teaching-learning process. Instructional aids are not self-supporting; they support, supplement, or reinforce what is being taught.

Hence, the correct option is (C).

32. Formative evaluation helps students in the following ways:

1. It provides constant feedback to both teacher and student concerning learning successes and failure while instruction is in process.

2. It often happens during the course of instruction. The teacher clarifies the doubts of students in the class itself.

3. Feedback to candidates reinforces successful learning and locates the particular learning errors that need correction.

4. The teacher raises the learner's motivation through a question-answer session.

Therefore, 2,4 and 6 are the correct answers.

Hence, the correct option is (D).

33. The Socio-economic background of teachers and students has nothing to do with the impact on enhancing the knowledge of the student. Teacher's knowledge, Classroom activities, and learning through experience will have a positive impact on teaching, as it will help in improving the knowledge of students.

Hence, the correct option is (C).

34. Biomagnification means increase in the concentration of pollutants in living organisms. Biomagnification is the build up of toxins in a food chain.

A Real-Life Example of Biomagnification: When a marsh is sprayed to control mosquitoes, it releases a trace amount of DDT. When mixed with water, it accumulates in the cell of various aquatic organisms. Once feeders up the food chain, such as clams and fishes, eat these organisms, they consume that DDT.

Hence, the correct option is (A).

35. The Deccan Thorn Forests cover the arid region extending across Maharashtra, Tamil Nadu, Andhra Pradesh, Karnataka and Telangana.

The Deccan thorn scrub forests are a xeric shrubland ecoregion of south India and northern Sri Lanka. Historically this area was covered by tropical dry deciduous forest, but this only remains in isolated fragments. The vegetation now consists of mainly of southern tropical thorn scrub type forests.

Hence, the correct option is (D).

36. The Earth Summit of 1992 at Rio de Janeiro resulted into a Convention on Biodiversity, which came into force on 5 June, 1992.

The United Nations Conference on Environment and Development (UNCED), also known as the Rio de Janeiro Earth Summit, the Rio Summit, the Rio Conference, and the Earth Summit, was a major United Nations conference held in Rio de Janeiro from 3 to 14 June in 1992.

Hence, the correct option is (A).

37. Only 1 and 3 are the correct statements.

- Constitution does not define the meaning of the phrase 'violation of the Constitution'.

- The impeachment charges to be initiated, should be signed by 25% members of the house where president gets opportunity to represent his side.

The Constitution gives Congress the authority to impeach and remove "The President, Vice President, and all civil Officers of the United States" upon a determination that such officers have engaged in treason, bribery, or other high crimes and misdemeanors.

Hence, the correct option is (B).

38. The principal of a school conducts an interview session of teachers and students with a view to exploring the possibility of their enhanced anticipation in school programmes. This endeavour is related to Action Research.

Action research is an inquiry or research which is related to the focused efforts to improve or enhance the quality and the performance of a particular organization.

Hence, the correct option is (C).

39. The ability to see and size up the situation creatively is most relevant stage of research in formulating research hypotheses and procedures for testing them.

Research is a systematic inquiry towards understanding a complex social phenomenon or a process. Based on the research problem, the selection of research methods by the researcher may vary. The research process consists of a series of actions and steps needed for conducting scientific research, if the researcher follows certain steps in conducting the research, the work can be carried out smoothly with the least difficulty.

Stages of Research:

1. Formulation of Research Problem
2. Preparing Research Design
3. Developing Data Collection Instrument (Research Instrument)
4. Selecting Samples Types of samples
5. Writing a Research Proposal Main elements
6. Collecting Data
7. Processing and Analyzing Data
8. Writing a Research Report

Hence, the correct option is (C).

40. In order to augment the accuracy of the study the researcher should increase the size of his sample, should be honest and unbiased and should keep the variance high.

Hence, the correct option is (D).

41. In case the population of the research is heterogeneous in nature 'Stratified random sampling' techniques will ensure optimum representativeness of sample units.

There are many different characteristics that may call for the use of stratified sampling.

- It is a type of random sampling in which the population is first divided into two or more strata or subgroups before the sampling process begins.
- The sampling units of stratum are similar in each other and different from the members of another stratum in the characteristics that we are measuring.

Hence, the correct option is (B).

42. The review of the related study is important while undertaking research because it avoids repetition or duplication, it helps in understanding the gaps and it helps the researcher not to draw illogical conclusions.

Hence, the correct option is (D).

43. The basic rules of APA style of referencing format are:

- Invert authors' names (last name first)
- Italicize titles of longer works like books and journals
- Alphabetically index reference list

APA (American Psychological Association) style of referencing format includes the inverting authors' names (last name first), to italicize the titles of longer works like books and journals and alphabetically index reference list. In the APA style of referencing format, we never italicize the titles of the essay part.

Hence, the correct option is (B).

44. Whatsapp, Google talk and Viber all are instant messaging applications. Instant messaging (IM) technology is a type of online chat that offers a real-time transmission of texts over the internet.

Hence, the correct option is (D).

45. Cloud computing service is hosted on the internet, made available by a service provider and fully managed by the provider.

Cloud Computing: Cloud computing is an emerging trend in the field of information technology, where computer-based services are delivered over the Internet or the cloud, and it is accessible to the user from anywhere using any device. The services comprise software, hardware (servers), databases, storage, etc. These resources are provided by companies called cloud service providers and usually charge on a pay per use basis, like the way we pay for electricity usage. Cloud computing is an infrastructure and software model that enables ubiquitous access to shared pools of storage, networks, servers, and applications. It allows for data processing to be done on a privately-owned cloud or a third-party server. This creates maximum speed and reliability. But the greatest benefit is its ease of installation, low maintenance, and scalability. This way it grows with your needs.

We already use cloud services while storing our pictures and files as backups on the Internet or host a website on the Internet. Through cloud computing, a user can run a bigger application or process a large amount of data without having the required storage or processing power on their personal computer as long as they are connected to the Internet. Besides other numerous features, cloud computing offers cost-effective, on-demand resources. A user can avail of need-based resources from the cloud at a very reasonable cost.

Examples Of Cloud Storage: Dropbox, Gmail, Facebook

Examples Of Marketing Cloud Platforms: Maropost For Marketing, Hubspot, Adobe Marketing Cloud.

Examples Of Cloud Computing In Education: SlideRocket, Ratatype, Amazon Web Services.

Examples Of Cloud Computing In Healthcare: ClearDATA, Dell's Secure Healthcare Cloud, IBM Cloud.

Hence, the correct option is (D).

46. The full form TKDL is the Traditional Knowledge Digital Library.

The TKDL initiative preserves the country's traditional knowledge through digitalisation and aims to prevent the misappropriation of India's traditional medicine knowledge through patenting worldwide.

Hence, the correct option is (B).

47. (i), (ii) & (iii) are true.

The number of users in Intranet is limited. Intranet is safer than the Internet. Intranet uses internet protocols such as TCP/IP and FTP.

Internet is a wide network of computers & open to all.

Hence, the correct option is (A).

48. Political orientation factors is a deterrent for the students to do well in higher education. Several factors can negatively impact student learning in higher educational institutions. One of the most prominent factors in today's times is the campus politics and political ideologies.

Political Orientation and Higher Education:

- Political orientation refers to the orientation that characteristics the thinking of a group or nation.
- Higher learning institutions usually have a student's council for the representation of students before the administrative unit.
- These unions might have varying political orientations that may interfere with the proper functioning of an institution.

Hence, the correct option is (A).

49. The Tenth Five Year Plan approach paper on higher education focussed on ICT orientation. From 1947 to 2017, the Indian economy was premised on the concept of planning. This was carried through the Five-Year Plans, developed, executed, and monitored by the Planning Commission (1951-2014) and the NITI Aayog (2015-2017).

The plan focuses on increasing access, quality, adoption of state-specific curriculum modification, vocationalisation, and networking on the use of information technology. The plan also focuses on distant education, a convergence of formal, non-formal, distant, and IT education institutions.

Hence, the correct option is (D).

50. Polar Stratospheric Clouds are associated with ozone layer depletion environmental issues.

Polar stratospheric clouds (PSCs), also known as nacreous clouds from nacre, or mother of pearl, due to their iridescence (change of colours), are clouds in the winter polar stratosphere. PSCs are wave clouds. They are often found downwind of mountain ranges, which can induce gravity waves in the lower stratosphere.

Hence, the correct option is (C).

Mock Test 17

Ques (1-5):Direction: Read the passage, carefully and choose the best answer to each question out of the four alternatives.

India is facing the challenge of sustaining its rapid economic growth while dealing with the global threat of climate change. This threat emanates from accumulated greenhouse gas emissions, generated through long-term industrial growth and high consumption lifestyles. Presently, India is among the top 10 emitters of Greenhouse Gases (GHG) in the world. However, it is in India's interest to ensure that the world moves towards a low carbon future. With changes in key climate variables, namely temperature, precipitation, and humidity, crucial sectors like agriculture and rural development are likely to be affected in a major way. As a developing country, India is closely tied to natural resources and agriculture, and water and forestry are climate-sensitive.

To combat climate change, India's National Action Plan for Climate Change (NAPCC) aims to achieve national growth objectives, along with enhancing ecological sustainability that leads to further mitigation of greenhouse gas emissions. NAPCC endeavours to deploy appropriate technologies, for both adaptation and mitigation of greenhouse gases and to promote sustainable development. NAPCC also plans to extend international cooperation for research, development, sharing, and transfer of technologies enabled by additional funding. India is a member of the United Nations Framework Convention and intends to cooperate with the-same on Climate Change. The United Nations Framework Convention on Climate Change (UNFCCC) is an international environmental treaty produced at the United Nations Conference on Environment and Development (UNCED) and is informally known as the Earth Summit. The objective of the treaty is to stabilise greenhouse gas concentrations in the atmosphere at a level that would prevent dangerous anthropogenic interference with the climate system.

Q.1 Suggest an appropriate title for the passage:

A. India and the global threat of climate change
B. National Action Plan for Climate Change
C. Role of United nations in Global warming
D. Environmental pollution

Q.2 What inference can we draw from this passage?

A. Climate change is a global threat and the entire world must work together to tackle this issue.
B. Developed countries are putting all the blames on developing countries for releasing excess carbon dioxide.
C. To promote sustainable development, the world needs a clean atmosphere.
D. The United Nations Framework Convention on Climate Change (UNFCCC) is an international environment treaty but the member nations are not serious about this treaty.

Q.3 Which sector of a developing country is the most vulnerable due to climate change?

A. Climate change is only dangerous for developed country.
B. The sector of agriculture and rural development.
C. The sector of Sustainable development is the most vulnerable.
D. The sector of the Industrial development.

Q.4 Why National action plan was necessary?

A. To control greenhouse gas emissions.
B. To save the natural resources of India.
C. To eradicate poverty from India.
D. To counter The United Nations Framework Convention on Climate Change (UNFCCC).

Q.5 Why it is difficult for India to sustain it's economic growth in the long run?

A. The threat of climate change is blocking the rapid economic progress of India.
B. International treaties on climate change prohibit India from making rapid economic progress.
C. India's National Action Plan for Climate Change (NAPCC) aims to restrict rapid economic and industrial growth.
D. India falls in a climate sensitive zone. So, it can't sustain it's economic growth for too long.

Q.6 Identify the correct sequence of countries in decreasing order of their contribution to global carbon dioxide emissions:

A. USA
B. China
C. Russia
D. India
E. Japan

Choose the correct answer from the option given below:

A. A, B, D, C, E   **B.** B, A, D, C, E
C. B, A, D, E, C   **D.** A, B, D, E, C

Q.7 Which of the following Acts gives rights to citizens to file cases against violation of environmental norms?

A. Environment (Protection) Act
B. Air Pollution Act
C. Water Pollution Act
D. Forest Act

Q.8 Climate change has implications for-

i. soil moisture
ii. forest fires
iii. biodiversity
iv. groundwater

Identify the correct combination according to the code:

A. i and iii   **B.** i, ii, and iii
C. i, iii, and iv   **D.** i, ii, iii, and iv

Q.9 Direction: Given below are two statements – one is labelled as Assertion (A) and the other is labelled as Reason (R).

Assertion (A): In the world as a whole, the environment has degraded during the past several decades.

Reason (R): The population of the world has been growing significantly.

A. (A) is correct, (R) is correct and (R) is the correct explanation of (A).
B. (A) is correct, (R) is correct and (R) is not the correct explanation of (A).
C. (A) is correct, but (R) is false.
D. (A) is false, but (R) is correct.

Q.10 The constituents of photochemical smog responsible for eye irritation are-

A. SO_2 and O_3 **B.** SO_2 and NO_2
C. HCHO and PAN **D.** SO_2 and SPM

Q.11 Which of the following bodies/units in a University has a statutory function to perform?

A. Board of Management
B. Finance Committee
C. Research Degree Committee'
D. Board of Studies

Q.12 Which of the following statement correctly describe the functions/status of the National Institute of Educational Planning and Administration deemed to be University?

Code:

(a) Capacity building and research in planning and management of education

(b) Educational planning and administration

(c) Fully maintained by the Government of India like any Central University

(d) A Statutory Institute of Educational Planning and Administration

Select the correct answer from the code given below:

A. (a) and (b) **B.** (b) and (d)
C. (a) and (d) **D.** (a) and (c)

Q.13 In the context of a School/University which of the following aspects of environment determine the academic ethos?

A. Patterns of human relations as evident in workplace
B. Latest lab equipment
C. Attractive physical campus
D. Well – equipped lecture halls

Q.14 Which one of the following is considered as the third dimension of higher education in India?

A. Teaching **B.** Research
C. Extension **D.** Training

Q.15 When verbal and non-verbal messages are contradictory, it is that most people believe in:

A. Indeterminate messages
B. Verbal messages
C. Non-verbal messages
D. Aggressive messages

Q.16 The rhetorical approach in classroom communication considers teachers as _______ agents of students.

A. Non-official **B.** Official
C. Influencing **D.** Academic

Q.17 In communication, the language is:

A. The verbal code
B. Intrapersonal
C. The symbolic code
D. The non-verbal code

Q.18 Communication will be effective if it is:

A. Delivered slowly and clearly
B. Delivered using appropriate media
C. Received as intended by the sender
D. Received immediately

Q.19 If the day of 26th August in a year is Thursday, then the number of Sundays in that month is:

A. 3 **B.** 5 **C.** 4 **D.** 6

Q.20 The next term in the series:

B2E, D5H, F12K, H27N, _____is:

A. J561 **B.** I62Q **C.** Q62J **D.** J58Q

Q.21 A rational number has its denominator greater than its numerator by 6. If the numerator is increased by 4 and the denominator is decreased by 8, the number becomes $\frac{5}{3}$. What is the original rational number?

A. $\frac{11}{17}$ **B.** $\frac{5}{17}$ **C.** $\frac{7}{13}$ **D.** $\frac{13}{19}$

Q.22 The proportions "All Indians eat rice" and "Some Indians eat rice" are an example of:

A. Subalternation **B.** Contraries
C. Contradictions **D.** Sub contraries

Q.23 Direction: Out of the given four options which one does not belong to the class of other three?

Neurologist, Cardiologist, Alchemist, Gynecologist

A. Gynecologist **B.** Cardiologist
C. Alchemist **D.** Neurologist

Q.24 Direction: Given below are two statements, read these statements and give the answer carefully.

Statement I: Buddhism accepts Upamana as an independent source of valid knowledge.

Statement II: In Upamana, knowledge of an object is determined by perception and testimony.

A. Both Statement I and Statement II are true.
B. Both Statement I and Statement II are false.
C. Statement I is true but Statement II is false.
D. Statement I is false but Statement II is true.

Q.25 Find the value of X in the given series.

121, 120, 124, 115, 131, X

A. 122 **B.** 106 **C.** 98 **D.** 108

Q.26 If the term HJLN is converted into ILOR, then by the same principle what could be the correct alternative for the term DFHJ?

A. FHJN **B.** EHKN **C.** EGIL **D.** FHNJ

Q.27 To communicate effectively with students, teachers should not use which of the following methods?

(a) Affinity-seeking strategies

(b) Immediacy behaviours

(c) Humor

(d) Collaborative filters

(e) Technical words

(f) Ambiguous statement

A. (a) and (f) only **B.** (a), (b) and (c)
C. (a), (c) and (d) **D.** (d), (e) and (f)

Q.28 In the following table, Set-1 mentions an apex level institution in India while Set-2 indicates their establishment date. Match the two sets and give your answer.

Set-1	Set-2
(a) University Grants Commission (UGC)	(i) 1995
(b) All India Council of Technical Education (AICTE)	(ii) 1956
(c) National Council of Teacher Education (NCTE)	(iii) 1994
(d) National Assessment and Accreditation Council (NAAC)	(iv) 1945

A. (a)-(i), (b)-(iv), (c)-(iii), (d)-(ii)
B. (a)-(ii), (b)-(iv), (c)-(i), (d)-(iii)
C. (a)-(ii), (b)-(i), (c)-(iii), (d)-(iv)
D. (a)-(i), (b)-(iv), (c)-(ii), (d)-(iii)

Q.29 Match the following combination of evaluation approaches with their correct meaning correctly.

List-I	List-II
(i) Formative Evaluation	(a) Evaluation carried at the end of the course
(ii) Criteria-Referenced Evaluation	(b) Evaluation of individual performance in comparison to others
(iii) Summative Evaluation	(c) Evaluation against specific standards
(iv) Norm-Referenced Evaluation	(d) Evaluation carried throughout the course

A. (i)-(a), (ii)-(c), (iii)-(d), (iv)-(b)
B. (i)-(d), (ii)-(c), (iii)-(a), (iv)-(b)
C. (i)-(a), (ii)-(b), (iii)-(d), (iv)-(c)
D. (i)-(d), (ii)-(b), (iii)-(a), (iv)-(c)

Ques (30-34):Direction: Following data shows the number of people (in thousand) from different age group who likes 7 different kind of music in a city.

Music	Age Group		
	15-20	**21-30**	**>30**
Classical	6	4	17
Pop	7	5	5
Rock	6	12	14
Jazz	1	4	11
Blues	2	3	15
Hip-Hop	9	3	4
Ambient	2	2	2
Total	33	33	68

Q.30 Which kind of music people like most?

A. Classical **B.** Pop **C.** Rock **D.** Blues

Q.31 People from which age group like hip-hop the most?

A. $15-20$ **B.** $21-30$
C. >30 **D.** None of these

Q.32 The ratio of number of people who like Rock to that who likes Jazz is:

A. $4:3$ **B.** $3:1$ **C.** $5:3$ **D.** $2:1$

Q.33 What is the average number of people from an age group who likes classical?.

A. 9000 **B.** 7500 **C.** 12000 **D.** 14500

Q.34 What percent of people from age group $21-30$ likes pop or hip-hop or blues?

A. 33% **B.** $33\frac{1}{3}\%$ **C.** 13% **D.** 25%

Q.35 The format of thesis writing is the same as in-

A. Preparation of a research paper/article
B. Writing of seminar presentation
C. A research dissertation
D. Presenting a workshop / conference paper

Q.36 According to Nyaya Sutra, which of the following is/are the kind of Hetvabhasa according to Indian Logic?

(i) Savyabhichara

(ii) Viruddha

(iii) Badhita

(iv) Prakaranasama

A. (i), (iii) and (iv) only
B. (ii) ,(iii) and (iv) only
C. (i) , (ii) and (iii) only
D. All of the above

Q.37 Which of these is true about ethnography?

a) Ethnography studies a group or culture of a group.

b) Participant's observation can be included while doing ethnography.

c) Ethnography as a method is appropriate for qualitative research as well as quantitative research.

d) It is not a holistic study.

e) It emerged as an important method in anthropology for studying the culture of 'other' subjects.

A. a, b, c and e **B.** b, c, d and e
C. a, b, d **D.** a, b, e

Q.38 _____is the mechanical/electronic conversion of images of handwritten, typed, or printed text into machine-encoded text.

A. Digitizer
B. Optical Mark Reader
C. Optical Character Recognition
D. Bar Code Reader

Q.39 What is the minimum limit for RTGS transfer system?

A. 1 lakh **B.** 2 lakhs **C.** 5 lakhs **D.** 10 lakhs

Q.40 An ASCII is a character-encoding scheme that is employed by personal computers in order to represent various characters, numbers, and control keys that the computer user selects on the keyboard. ASCII is an acronym for:

A. American Standard Code for Information Interchange
B. American Standard Code for Intelligent Information
C. American Standard Code for Information Integrity
D. American Standard Code for Isolated Information

Q.41 In a computer, if 8 bits are used to specify the address in memory, the total number of addresses will be:

A. 256 **B.** 8 **C.** 216 **D.** 512

Q.42 Which of the following are audio file formats?

(a) .wav
(b) .aac
(c) .wmv
(d) .flv

A. (a) and (d) **B.** (b) and (c)
C. (a) and (b) **D.** (c) and (d)

Q.43 Genuine communication cannot be planned because:

A. many channels need to be utilized
B. it is difficult to stick to the pre-decided topic
C. language is a very poor medium of expression
D. the cycle of messages depends on spontaneous, verbal and non-verbal feedback chain

Q.44 Continuous and Comprehensive Evaluation mainly aims at promoting:

A. Competition among children
B. Competition among teachers
C. Academic excellence among children
D. Inclusive education

Q.45 The objective of evaluation is to ________.

A. disclose the teacher's needs
B. serve as a method of improvement
C. set competition among the students
D. test a particular activity of the students

Q.46 A fraction is such that when 7 is added to the numerator then its value is 1, again when 2 is added to the denominator then the value is $\frac{1}{2}$. The fraction is:

A. $\frac{13}{21}$ **B.** $\frac{13}{18}$ **C.** $\frac{9}{16}$ **D.** $\frac{18}{21}$

Q.47 A research paper:

A. is a compilation of information on a topic.
B. contains original research as deemed by the author.
C. contains peer-reviewed original research or evaluation of research conducted by others.
D. can published in more than one journal.

Q.48 Which of the following are NOT sources of secondary data?

a) Interview
b) Questionnaire
c) Observation
d) Unpublished thesis
e) Annual report

Choose the correct option from the following:

A. a, d and e **B.** b, c and d
C. c, d and e **D.** a, b and c

Q.49 The key to effective listening by students in a classroom is ________.

A. Sympathy towards the teacher
B. Interest in informal education
C. Empathetic learning
D. Desire to memorize

Q.50 The average height of A, B and C is 125 cm. If the average height of B and C is 100 cm. Find the height of A.

A. 175 cm **B.** 150 cm **C.** 160 cm **D.** 135 cm

// Smart Answer Sheet //

Correct Indicates percentage of students who answered questions correctly.

Skipped Indicates percentage of students who skipped questions.

Q.	Ans.	Correct	Skipped
1	A	56.01 %	1.8 %
2	A	61.79 %	2.0 %
3	B	56.61 %	1.18 %
4	A	65.61 %	1.52 %
5	A	46.17 %	1.05 %
6	B	66.54 %	1.36 %
7	A	48.25 %	1.84 %
8	B	59.99 %	1.75 %
9	B	43.88 %	1.09 %
10	C	58.38 %	1.3 %

Q.	Ans.	Correct	Skipped
11	A	32.43 %	4.63 %
12	D	49.02 %	1.91 %
13	A	21.13 %	4.03 %
14	C	15.29 %	4.06 %
15	C	47.87 %	1.1 %
16	C	58.54 %	1.44 %
17	A	77.63 %	0.0 %
18	C	66.03 %	1.03 %
19	B	61.16 %	1.58 %
20	D	77.44 %	0.0 %

Q.	Ans.	Correct	Skipped
21	A	53.06 %	1.17 %
22	A	62.09 %	1.72 %
23	C	88.9 %	0.0 %
24	B	48.33 %	1.21 %
25	B	88.58 %	0.0 %
26	B	81.59 %	0.0 %
27	D	52.41 %	1.55 %
28	B	62.28 %	1.72 %
29	B	52.76 %	1.47 %
30	C	49.97 %	1.31 %

Q.	Ans.	Correct	Skipped
31	A	76.02 %	0.0 %
32	D	85.64 %	0.0 %
33	A	81.12 %	0.0 %
34	B	81.56 %	0.0 %
35	C	44.78 %	1.72 %
36	D	27.32 %	4.67 %
37	D	40.41 %	1.56 %
38	C	51.2 %	1.88 %
39	B	83.28 %	0.0 %
40	A	63.08 %	1.53 %

Q.	Ans.	Correct	Skipped
41	A	59.66 %	1.68 %
42	C	87.01 %	0.0 %
43	D	62.73 %	1.28 %
44	D	42.02 %	1.9 %
45	B	76.75 %	0.0 %
46	C	23.76 %	4.53 %
47	C	20.17 %	3.33 %
48	D	50.8 %	1.65 %
49	C	50.53 %	1.53 %
50	A	45.51 %	1.82 %

Performance Analysis	
Avg. Score (%)	71.0%
Toppers Score (%)	71.0%
Your Score	

//Hints and Solutions//

1. The correct answer is 'India and the global threat of climate change'.

This passage talks about the threat of climate change globally in general and specifically in India and it also mentions the steps taken by India to counter this global threat.

This passage mentions the efforts of the international community like the United Nations to tackle the threat of Climate change.

It also mentions that India being a developing country is more likely to suffer as compared to developed countries because agriculture is a crucial sector.

The author talks about the role of the United Nations, the role of the National Action plan for climate change but the central idea is always 'the global threat of climate change'.

So, If I put 'India and the global threat of climate change' as the heading of the passage then I can surely put 'National Action Plan for Climate Change' and 'Role of United Nations in Global warming' as the sub-headings.

It is in India's interest to ensure that the world moves towards a low carbon future. So, 'India' should be a part of the title of this passage.

Hence, the correct option is (A).

2. The correct answer is 'Climate change is a global threat and the entire world must work together to tackle this issue'.

In the first paragraph, the author says that the world should move together to reduce the emission of Carbon dioxide and the author also strongly puts forward the commitment of India towards this cause.

In the 2nd paragraph, the author describes the commitment of the international community in the form of 'The United Nations Framework Convention on Climate Change (UNFCCC)' of which India is also a member.

The author tries to portray as to how India and the International community must work together to counter the menace of climate change.

Hence, the correct option is (A).

3. The correct answer is 'The sector of Agriculture and rural development'.

India is largely dependent on agriculture and for any developing country, this sector is very important for the growth of the country.

In the 4th and the 5th line of the passage, we can note that with changes in key climate variables, namely temperature, precipitation, and humidity, crucial sectors like agriculture and rural development are likely to be affected in a major way. As a developing country, India is closely tied to natural resources.

Water is a very important natural resource for agriculture and it is important to note that water is climate-sensitive. In a developing country like India, farmers are largely dependent on natural rainfall which gets directly affected by climate change.

Hence, the correct option is (B).

4. The correct answer is 'To control greenhouse gas emissions'.

In the 7th and 8th line of the passage, we can note that - To combat climate change, India's National Action Plan for Climate Change (NAPCC) aims to achieve national growth objectives, along with enhancing ecological sustainability that leads to further mitigation of greenhouse gas emissions.

NAPCC endeavours to deploy appropriate technologies, for both adaptation and mitigation of greenhouse gases and to promote sustainable development.

Mitigation(Noun): the action of reducing the severity, seriousness, or painfulness of something.

NAPCC is not formed to counter The United Nations Framework Convention on Climate Change (UNFCCC), rather NAPCC and UNFCCC work together to wards achieving a common objective i.e. mitigation of greenhouse gases.

Option (B), Option (C) and Option (D) have nothing to do with the objective of NAPCC.

Hence, the correct option is (A).

5. The correct answer is 'The threat of climate change is blocking the rapid economic progress of India'.

In the Ist and 2nd line of the passage, we can note that - India is making rapid economic progress but it is facing the challenge of sustaining this economic growth while dealing with the global threat of climate change.

The reason for this threat is accumulated greenhouse gas emissions, generated through long-term industrial growth and high consumption lifestyles.

Presently, India is among the top 10 emitters of Greenhouse Gases in the world, so there is a lot of pressure from the international community to reduce the emission of Carbon dioxide.

Option (B), Option (C) and Option (D) are irrelevant to the economic growth of India.

Hence, the correct option is (A).

6. According to World Green House Gas Emission Data, the correct sequence of countries in decreasing order of their contribution to global carbon dioxide emissions is China, USA, India, Russia, Japan.

Country	CO_2 Emission (billion metric ton)	Global share
China	9.43	27.8%
USA	5.15	15.2%
India	2.48	7.3%
Russia	1.55	4.6%
Japan	1.15	3.4%

Hence, the correct option is (B).

7. Environment (Protection) Act gives rights to citizens to file cases against violations of environmental norms.

Environment Protection Act, 1986 (EPA):

- Environment Protection Act, 1986 is an Act of the Parliament of India.
- In the wake of the Bhopal gas Tragedy or Bhopal Disaster, the Government of India enacted the Environment Protection Act of 1986 under Article 253 of the Constitution.
- Passed in March 1986, it came into force on 19 November 1986.
- It has 26 sections and 4 chapters.
- The purpose of the Act is to implement the decisions of the United Nations Conference on the Human Environment.
- They relate to the protection and improvement of the human environment and the prevention of hazards to human beings, other living creatures, plants, and property.
- The Act is an "umbrella" legislation designed to provide a framework for central government coordination of the activities of various central and state authorities established under previous laws, such as the Water Act and the Air Act.

Hence, the correct option is (A).

8. Climate change includes both global warming driven by human emissions of greenhouse gases and the resulting large-scale shifts in weather patterns. Global climate change has already had observable effects on the environment. Glaciers have shrunk, ice on rivers and lakes is breaking up earlier, plant and animal ranges have shifted and trees are flowering sooner. Effects that scientists had predicted in the past would result from global climate change are now occurring: loss of sea ice, accelerated sea-level rise, and longer, more intense heat waves.

Climate change has definitely impacted the following:

- Soil moisture: seems to be more important for modern human societies than ever before to meet the global demands for food and fiber for the increasing population from limited soil resources.
- Forest fires have been increasing dramatically, as global warming is leading to longer, harsher droughts and more extreme weather events.

Climate change and groundwater:

- There is no direct link between climate change and groundwater.
- When the temperature of the atmosphere is increasing due to global warming it does not affect groundwater.
- Groundwater is under the ground, it has no direct contact with the atmosphere hence increase in temperature will not lead to its evaporation.

Climate change has no direct impact on groundwater.

Hence, the correct option is (B).

9. Environmental degradation:

- Environmental degradation is the deterioration of the environment through depletion of resources such as air, water, and soil; the destruction of ecosystems; habitat destruction; the extinction of wildlife; and pollution.
- The primary cause of environmental degradation is human disturbance.
- Environmental changes are based on factors like urbanization, population, and economic growth, increase in energy consumption, and agricultural intensification. The degradation has adverse impacts on humans, plants, animals, and microorganisms.
- The population of the world, now somewhat in excess of three billion persons, is growing at about two percent a year, or faster than at any other period in man's history.

The assertion is true that in the world as a whole, the environment has degraded during the past several decades.

The reason is also true that the population of the world has been growing significantly.

Both the statements are true but since the reason is not significantly related to the assertion therefore the answer becomes Option (B) which is Both (A) and (R) are correct and (R) is not the correct explanation of (A).

Hence, the correct option is (B).

10. Natural smog is actually a result of large amounts of coal burning and mixing with atmospheric smoke and sulfur dioxide.

SMOG = Smoke + Fog

Photochemical Smog:

- Photochemical smog is a type of smog produced when ultraviolet light from the sun reacts with nitrogen oxides in the atmosphere.
- It is visible as a brown haze, and is most prominent during the morning and afternoon, especially in densely populated, warm cities.
- The largest contributor is automobiles, while coal-fired power plants and some other power plants also produce the necessary pollutants to facilitate their production.
- Nitric oxide (NO) and nitrogen dioxide (NO_2) are emitted from the combustion of fossil fuels, along with being naturally emitted from things such as volcanos and forest fires.
- When exposed to ultraviolet radiation, NO_2 goes through a complex series of reactions with hydrocarbons to produce the components of photochemical smog—a mixture of ozone, nitric acid, aldehydes, Peroxyacyl nitrates (PANs), and other secondary pollutants.
- Photochemical smog has many adverse effects. When combined with hydrocarbons, the chemicals contained within it form molecules that cause eye irritation.

HCHO- Formaldehyde or methanol is a colorless, flammable gas with a chemical formula of HCHO. It is classified as an aldehyde and is a part of the formyl group.

PAN- Peroxyacetyl nitrate, or PAN, is an oxidant that is more stable than ozone.

Hence, the correct option is (C).

11. Universities established under Acts of Parliament and state legislatures are generally known as Central Universities and State Universities respectively. The pattern and structure of governance of most of these universities are similar; the management responsibility vesting with an Executive Council (also known as syndicate or Board of Management).

Board of Management:

The Board of Management is the principal organ of management in the university. Being the highest executive authority of the university, it should be a compact body capable of functioning with the unity of purpose.

The prime concern in determining its size and composition is that it should be an instrument to run the university effectively and to see that the larger objectives and purposes for which the university is supported by public funds are fulfilled. That is why it is suggested that the syndicate/executive council should be a compact, rather than the too large body and that it should be a homogenous rather than & broadly representative body, enabling it to make and implement well-considered decisions promptly and to handle the crisis effectively.

Hence, the correct option is (A).

12. The National University of Educational Planning and Administration (NUEPA), also known as the National Institute of Educational Planning and Administration (NIEPA):

The National Institute of Educational Planning and Administration (NIEPA), (Deemed to be University) established by the Ministry of Human Resource Development, Government of India.

It is a premier organization dealing with capacity building and research in the planning and management of education not only in India but also in South Asia.

In recognition of the pioneering work done by the organization in the field of educational planning and administration, the Government of India has empowered it to award its own degrees by way of conferring it the status of Deemed to be University in August 2006. Like any Central University, NIEPA is fully maintained by the Government of India.

Its vision is to evolve a humane learning society through the advancement of knowledge.

Its mission is to become a centre of excellence in educational policy, planning and management by promoting advanced level teaching, research and capacity building in national and global contexts.

Hence, the correct option is (D).

13. In the context of a School/University Patterns of human relations as evident in workplace aspects of environment determine the academic ethos.

The environment may be described as a composite of natural conditions, circumstances and influences, and socio-cultural contexts in which an organism is situated. Interactions between human beings and the environment operate in a dynamic fashion and throughout life. The environment is more of an external force with which humans interact and get influenced in the course of time.

Hence, the correct option is (A).

14. The Kothari Commission the India Education Commission in 1964 comprehensively examined and reviewed the entire educational system and emphasized 'Extension as the third dimension of higher education'. It introduced the trinity of Teaching, Research & Extension in higher education.

Hence, the correct option is (C).

15. When verbal and non-verbal messages are contradictory, most people believe in non-verbal messages because actions and gestures speak louder than words. People pay more attention to eye-contacts, voice tone, facial expression, etc.

Hence, the correct option is (C).

16. The rhetorical approach in classroom communication considers teachers as influencing agents of students. It is the teacher who regulates his class upon the basis of his knowledge and that knowledge can only be delivered through the interaction between the teacher and students.

Hence, the correct option is (C).

17. In communication, the language is the verbal code.

A verbal code is a set of rules about the use of words in the creation of messages. Words can obviously be either spoken or written. Verbal codes, then, include both oral (spoken) language and non-oral (written) language.

Hence, the correct option is (A).

18. The idea of communication is the exchange of information from one point to another, such communication can only be termed as effective if the message/information send from the sender is received in the form and content by the receiver as intended by the sender.

Immediate response can not check the quality of the medium it can be an advantage but can not be a defining feature for effective communication. For example- If a person A talking to another person B in Spanish, when person B has no knowledge of Spanish is completely useless. No matter how immediate they received feedback because the message is not delivered effectively.

So, it is clear from the above points that Communication will be effective if it is received as intended by the sender.

Hence, the correct option is (C).

19. The number of Sundays in that month is 5.

If 26th August in a year is Thursday.

So, next Sunday on 29th August.

Therefore, the Sundays are on 29, 22,15, 8, 1.

The total number of Sundays is 5.

Hence, the correct option is (B).

20. Taking the first alphabet,

B+2=D, D+2=F, F+2=H, H+2=J

Taking the number,

2 × 2+1= 5, 5 × 2+2=12, 12 × 2+3=27, 27 × 2+4=58

Taking the last alphabet,

E+3=H, H+3=K, K+3=N, N+3=Q

So, the next term = J58Q
Hence, the correct option is (D).

21. Let the numerator of the rational number be x then its denominator be $x+6$.

Rational number $=\frac{\text{Numerator}}{\text{Denominator}}$

The original rational number $=\frac{x}{(x+6)}$

Now, $\frac{A}{Q}$

$\frac{(x+4)}{(x+6-8)}=\frac{5}{3}$

$\Rightarrow \frac{(x+4)}{(x-2)}=\frac{5}{3}$

$\Rightarrow 3(x+4)=5(x-2)$

$\Rightarrow 3x+12=5x-10$

$\Rightarrow 2x=22$

$x=11$

Numerator $=x$ and Denominator $=11+6=17$

∴ The original rational number is $\frac{11}{17}$.

Hence, the correct option is (A).

22. Sub alteration: Sub alternation is an immediate inference that is only made between A (All S are P) and I (Some S are P) categorical propositions and between E (Some S are P) and O (Some S are not P or originally, Not every S is P) categorical propositions of the traditional square of opposition and the original square of opposition. If the A proposition is true we may immediately infer that I is true.

- An example of a subalternation is "If all leopards are mammals, then some leopards are mammals."

Therefore, the proportions "All Indians eat rice" and "Some Indians eat rice" are an example of Subalternation.

Hence, the correct option is (A).

23. Gynecologist → A doctor who specializes in treating diseases of the female reproductive organs and providing well-woman health care that focuses primarily on the reproductive organs.

Cardiologist → A doctor who specializes in the study or treatment of heart diseases and heart abnormalities.

Alchemist → A person who transforms or creates something through a seemingly magical process.

Neurologist → A doctor who specializes in the anatomy, functions, and organic disorders of nerves and the nervous system.

All options except 'Alchemist' represents Doctors.

Hence, the correct option is (C).

24. Statement I: Buddhism accepts Upamana as an independent source of valid knowledge: False

Buddhism (Buddhist philosophy) does not accept comparison as an independent source of valid knowledge.

Statement II: In Upamana, knowledge of an object is determined by perception and testimony: False.

In upamana, knowledge of an object is determined by comparing it to other similar kinds of objects.

Thus, upamana is the knowledge of the relation between a name and the object it denotes by that name.

So, Both Statement I and Statement II are false.

Hence, the correct option is (B).

25. Series follows the following pattern:

121 – 1^2 = 120

120 + 2^2 = 124

124 – 3^2 = 115

115 + 4^2 = 131

131 – 5^2 = 106 = X

∴ The value of X in the given series is 106.

Hence, the correct option is (B).

26.

Alphabets	A	B	C	D	E	F	G	H	I	J	K	L	M
Positional Value	1	2	3	4	5	6	7	8	9	10	11	12	13
Alphabets	N	O	P	Q	R	S	T	U	V	W	X	Y	Z
Positional Value	14	15	16	17	18	19	20	21	22	23	24	25	26

According to the alphabetical positions of the letters,
H J L N
↓ +1 ↓ +2 ↓ +3 ↓ +4

I L O R
Similarly,
D F H J
$\downarrow +1 \quad \downarrow +2 \quad \downarrow +3 \quad \downarrow +4$
E H K N
Therefore, 'EHKN' is the correct answer.

Hence, the correct option is (B).

27. Collaborative filters, Technical words and Ambiguous statements must not be a part of effective communication because they affect the quality of communication.

Technical words are considered as jargons in business communication and ambiguous statement are those statements whose meaning is not clear.

When you make statements that are ambiguous, you confuse the reader and hinder the meaning of the text. However, sometimes ambiguity is used deliberately to add humour to a text.

Hence, the correct option is (D).

28. The correct match is (a)-(ii), (b)-(iv), (c)-(i), (d)-(iii).

UGC (University Grants Commission) was established in the year 1956 as a statutory body through the Parliament Act for coordinating and maintaining the higher education standards in India.

AICTE (All India Council for Technical Education) was established in the year 1945 as an advisory body & as a statutory body through the Parliament Act for planning and development of technical education in India.

NCTE (National Council for Teacher Education) was established in the year 1995 to undertake and maintain the procedures and processes in the Indian Education System.

NAAC (National Assessment and Accreditation Council) was established in the year 1994 with the motive to evaluate the performances of universities and colleges in India.

Hence, the correct option is (B).

29. The correct match is (i)-(d), (ii)-(c), (iii)-(a), (iv)-(b).

Formative Evaluation: Evaluation is carried throughout the course in the form of weekly assignments, discussion etc.

Summative Evaluation: Evaluation is carried at the end of the course in the form examinations.

Criteria-Referenced Evaluation: Evaluation is done against specific standards or criteria.

Norm-Referenced Evaluation: Evaluation of individual performance in comparison to others. It is to assess how a student performs in relation to other peers.

Hence, the correct option is (B).

30. Classical $= 6+4+17 = 27$

Pop $= 7+5+5 = 17$

Rock $= 6+12+14 = 32$ (Maximum)

Blues $= 2+3+15 = 20$

Hence, the correct option is (C).

31. Age group $15-20 \rightarrow 9$ thousand

Age group $21-30 \rightarrow 3$ thousand

Age group $>30 \rightarrow 4$ thousand.

So, age group $15-20$ are mostly like the hip- hop.

Hence, the correct option is (A).

32. People who like Rock $= 6+12+14 = 32$

People who like Jazz $= 1+4+11 = 16$

So, the required ratio who like Rock and who like Jazz $= \frac{32}{16} = \frac{2}{1}$

Therefore the ratio is $2:1$.

Hence, the correct option is (D).

33. The people who like the classical $= 6,4,17$

Required average $= \frac{6+4+17}{3}$

$= \frac{27}{3} = 9000$

Hence, the correct option is (A).

34. Total number of people in age group $21-30$ is 33 thousand.

And, the number of people who like age group is $5+3+3 = 11$ thousand.

So, required percent $= \frac{11}{33} \times 100$

$= 33\frac{1}{3}\%$

Hence, the correct option is (B).

35. The format of thesis writing is the same as in a research dissertation. The aim of the dissertation or thesis is to produce an original piece of work on a clearly defined topic.

Hence, the correct option is (C).

36. All of the above are the kind of Hetvabhasa.

Hetvabhasa, means that a Hetu (reason) which appears to be real or appropriate but in fact is not. According to the Nyaya Sutra, there are five kinds of Hetvbahasa:

- Savyabhichara (anaikanita)
- Badhita
- Asidha
- Viruddha
- Prakaranasama

Hence, the correct option is (D).

37. Statements a, b and e are true about ethnography.

Ethnography is a systematic study of people and culture.

It requires the researcher to immerse into the lives of individuals being studied, which is called Participant Observation.

Ethnographic studies are extremely important for a qualitative researcher for a detailed study of the cultural phenomenon.

The method was first introduced to the discipline of anthropology but later on, become popular in social sciences as well. Ethnography is a holistic study.

Hence, the correct option is (D).

38. Optical Character Recognition is the mechanical/electronic conversion of images of handwritten, typed, or printed text into machine-encoded text.

Digitizer- It converts the analog data into digital form.

Optical Mark Reader- This device reads the marks made in on paper forms as responses to questions or tick list prompts by a pencil/pen.

Optical Character Recognition- It is the mechanical/electronic conversion of images of handwritten, typed, or printed text into machine-encoded text.

Bar Code Reader- It can read and output printed barcodes to a computer.

Hence, the correct option is (C).

39. RTGS (Real Time Gross Settlement) is a funds transfer system where the transfer of money or securities takes place from one bank to another on a 'real-time' and on a 'gross' basis. The minimum limit for RTGS transfer is 2 Lakhs
Hence, the correct option is (B).

40. ASCII is an acronym for American Standard Code for Information Interchange.

ASCII codes represent text in computers, telecommunications equipment, and other devices. Most modern character-encoding schemes are based on ASCII, although they support many additional characters.
Hence, the correct option is (A).

41. In a computer, if 8 bits are used to specify the address in memory, the total number of addresses will be 2^{bits}

$= 2^8$

= 256 addresses.

Hence, the correct option is (A).

42. Audio file formats are: .wav and .aac:

(a) .wav – Waveform Audio File Format

(b) .aac – Advanced Audio Coding

(c) .wmv – Windows Media Video

(d) .flv – Flash Live Video

Hence, the correct option is (C).

43. Genuine communication cannot be planned because the cycle of messages depends on spontaneous, verbal and non-verbal feedback chain.

Genuine communication is the one, where honesty and credibility become the core of the message. In some cases, Genuine Communication and Effective Communication can be used interchangeably. Genuine communication cannot be planned as the process/ cycle of massages depends entirely on spontaneous, verbal, and non-verbal feedback chain.

Hence, the correct option is (D).

44. Continuous and Comprehensive Evaluation mainly aims at promoting Inclusive education.

Continuous and Comprehensive Evaluation, commonly know as 'CCE' has been introduced as a school-based system of evaluation by the CBSE in 2009 with the enactment of the Right to Education Act. CCE can be incorporated in the inclusive classroom while engaging in teaching through a variety of activities.

Hence, the correct option is (D).

45. The objective of evaluation is to serve as a method of improvement.

Evaluation is a systematic determination of a subject's merit, worth and significance, using criteria governed by a set of standards. Objectives of evaluation:

- To impart factual knowledge
- Solving shortcomings and diagnose the weakness to change it into strength.
- Predetermined aims and goals of achievement.
- To know the inherent and inbuild capacity of the learner and encourage them to learn and act more on self-improvement.

Hence, the correct option is (B).

46. Let, the fraction is $\left(\frac{x}{y}\right)$

7 is added to the numerator then its value is 1,

$\therefore \frac{x+7}{y} = 1$

$\Rightarrow x + 7 = y$ ....(1)

2 is added to the denominator then the value is $\frac{1}{2}$.

$\therefore \frac{x}{y+2} = \frac{1}{2}$

$\Rightarrow 2x = y + 2$

$\Rightarrow 2x - y = 2$ .....(2)

From (1) and (2)

$x + 7 = 2x - 2$

$\Rightarrow x = 9$

Putting this value in (1)

$y = 9 + 7 = 16$

$\therefore$ The fraction is $\frac{9}{16}$.

Hence, the correct option is (C).

47. A research paper contains peer-reviewed original research or evaluation of research conducted by others.

The term research paper refers to a scholarly article that contains the results of original research or an evaluation of research conducted by others. Most scholarly articles must undergo a process of peer review before they can be accepted for publication in an academic journal.

Hence, the correct option is (C).

48. Interview, Questionnaire and Observation are not sources of secondary data

Secondary data is data collected by someone other than the actual user. It means that the information is already available, and someone analyses it. The secondary data includes magazines, newspapers, books, journals, etc. It may be either published data or unpublished data.

Hence, the correct option is (D).

49. The key to effective listening by students in a classroom is empathetic learning.

Active listening, loosely defined, is paying attention to a speaker and listening to understand, not to respond. It also includes a complete focus on the speaker with minimal distractions out of respect and an intent to learn. Active learning promotes empathy in the students which help them to enrich their life in and outside the classroom.

Hence, the correct option is (C).

50. Given:

Average height of A, B and C $= 125$ cm

Average height of B and C $= 100$ cm

Formula used:

Average $= \frac{\text{Sum of all observations}}{\text{Number of observations}}$

$\frac{(A+B+C)}{3} = 125$

$A + B + C = 375$ ---- (1)

$\frac{(B+C)}{2} = 100$

$B + C = 200$ ---- (2)

From (1) and (2)

$A + 200 = 375$

$\Rightarrow A = 175$ cm

$\therefore$ A's height is 175 cm.

Hence, the correct option is (A).

Mock Test 18

Ques (1-5):Direction: Read the passage carefully and answer the question that follows:

Life Insurance in its modern form came to India from England in the year 1818. The Oriental Life Insurance Company started by Europeans in Calcutta was the first life insurance company on Indian soil. All the insurance companies established during that period were brought up with the purpose of looking after the needs of the European community and Indian natives were not being insured by these companies. However, later with the efforts of eminent people like Babu Muttylal Seal, foreign insurance companies started insuring Indian lives too. But Indian lives were being treated as sub standard lives and heavy extra premium were being charged upon them. The Bombay Mutual Life Assurance Society heralded the birth of the first Indian life insurance company in the year 1870 and covered Indian lives at normal rates. Starting as an Indian enterprise with highly patriotic motives, insurance companies came into existence to carry the message of insurance and social security through insurance to various sectors of society. In 1907, the Hindustan Co-operative Insurance Company took birth in one of the rooms of The Jorsanko', house of the great poet Rabindranath Tagore in Calcutta. The Indian Mercantile, General Assurance and Swadeshi Life (later Bombay Life) were some of the companies established during the same period. Prior to 1912, India had no legislation to regulate the insurance business. In the year 1912, Life Insurance Companies Act and Provident Fund Act were passed. The Life Insurance Companies Act 1912 made it necessary that the premium rate tables and periodical valuations of companies should be certified by an actuary. But the Act discriminated between foreign and Indian Companies on many accounts, putting Indian Companies at a disadvantage.

Q.1 The paragraph is about which of the following?

1. Genesis of insurance in India
2. Struggle of insurance business
3. Conflict of insurance business
4. Complications of insurance business

A. 1 **B.** 2 **C.** 3 **D.** 4

Q.2 Identify the correct statement from the following

1. Initially, insurance companies used to discriminate between Indian and European clients.
2. There was no discrimination in Indian and European clients by the insurance companies initially.
3. Indian clients were charged lower premium by the insurance companies in the beginning.
4. Indian insurance companies charged higher premium to Europeans at a later stage.

A. 1 **B.** 2 **C.** 3 **D.** 4

Q.3 Which one among the following grew along with insurance business in India?

1. Pension Fund
2. Provident Fund
3. Gratuity
4. Arbitrage

A. 1 **B.** 2 **C.** 3 **D.** 4

Q.4 The insurance business in India was started first by which one of the following?

1. Americans
2. Indian merchants
3. Europeans
4. Afro-Indians

A. 1 **B.** 2 **C.** 3 **D.** 4

Q.5 Which among the following was later renamed Bombay Life?

1. The Indian Mercantile General Assurance
2. The Oriental Life Insurance Company
3. National Insurance
4. Swadeshi Life

A. 1 **B.** 2 **C.** 3 **D.** 4

Ques (6-10):Direction: Given below in the table is the decadal data of Population and Electrical Power Production of a country.

Year	Population (million)	Electrical Power Production (GW)*
1951	20	10
1961	21	20
1971	24	25
1981	27	40
1991	30	50
2001	32	80
2011	35	100
		*1GW=1000 million watt

Q.6 Which decade registered the maximum growth rate (%) of the population?

A. 1961 – 1971 **B.** 1971 – 1981
C. 1991 – 2001 **D.** 2001 – 2011

Q.7 The average decadal growth rate (%) of the population is (approx.):

A. 12.21% **B.** 9.82% **C.** 6.73% **D.** 5%

Q.8 Based on the average decadal growth rate, what will be the population in the year 2021?

A. 40.34 million **B.** 38.44 million
C. 37.28 million **D.** 36.62 million

Q.9 In the year 1951, what was the power availability per person?

A. 100 watt **B.** 200 watt **C.** 400 watt **D.** 500 watt

Q.10 In which decade, the average power availability per person was maximum?

A. 1991 **B.** 2001 **C.** 2011 **D.** 1981

Q.11 Direction: In the following question, the Assertions (A) and Reason (R) have been put forward. Read both the statements carefully and choose the correct alternative from the following:

Assertion (A): The purpose of higher education is to promote critical and creative thinking abilities among students.

Reason (R): These abilities ensure job placements.

Choose the correct answer from the following code:

A. Both (A) and (R) are true and (R) is the correct explanation of (A)
B. Both (A) and (R) are true but (R) is not the correct explanation of (A)
C. (A) is true but (R) is false
D. (A) is false but (R) is true

Q.12 National Educational Alliance for Technology (NEAT) implementing agency is which among the following organizations?

A. University Grants Commission (UGC)
B. All India Council for Technical Education (AICTE)
C. Indian Space Research Organisation (ISRO)
D. NITI Aayog

Q.13 Which of the following are the demerits of globalization of higher education?

(a) Exposure to global curriculum

(b) Promotion of elitism in education

(c) Commodification of higher education

(d) Increase in the cost of education

Select the correct answer from the codes given below:

A. (a) and (d) **B.** (a), (c) and (d)
C. (b), (c) and (d) **D.** (a), (b), (c) and (d)

Q.14 Which of the following was ranked the best college in the country (2017) as per the National Institutional Ranking Framework (NIRF)?

A. Miranda House, Delhi
B. St. Stephen's College, Delhi
C. Fergusson College, Pune
D. Maharaja's College, Mysore

Q.15 The teaching in the universities of ancient India was controlled by board of eminent teachers. The affairs of which university were administered by the Board of Vikramsila University?

A. Jagaddala University
B. Valabhi University
C. Nalanda University
D. Odantapuri University

Q.16 In which of these problems, is the actual message lost in the abundance of transmitted information?

A. Under communication
B. Selecting perception
C. Over-communication
D. Filtering

Q.17 Direction: In the following question, the Assertions (A) and Reason (R) have been put forward. Read both the statements carefully and choose the correct alternative from the following:

Assertion (A): To communicate well in the classroom is a natural ability.

Reason (R): Effective teaching in the classroom demands knowledge of the communication process.

Code:

A. Both (A) and (R) are true, and (R) is the correct explanation of (A).
B. Both (A) and (R) are true, but (R) is not the correct explanation of (A).
C. (A) is true, but (R) is false.
D. (A) is false, but (R) is true.

Q.18 Which of the following is not an semantic barrier of communication?

A. Choice of word **B.** Cultural difference
C. Poor retention **D.** Spelling error

Q.19 Find the missing number (?) from the series:

3, 12, 39, 120, ?

A. 296 **B.** 275 **C.** 263 **D.** 363

Q.20 Direction: What will come at the place of question mark?

10, 100, 200, 310, ?

A. 430 **B.** 420 **C.** 410 **D.** 400

Q.21 A series is given, with one term missing. Choose the correct alternative from the given options that will complete the series.

XWV, TSR, PON, LKJ, ?

A. IJK **B.** DEF **C.** HGF **D.** LMO

Q.22 In a certain code, 'SURE' is written as '63', and 'GONE' is written as '41', then how will 'WIND' be written in the same code language?

A. 70 **B.** 62 **C.** 49 **D.** 50

Q.23 A tree has nine branches and on each branch there are nine nests. Each nest having nine birds and each bird needs nine grains to be fed. How many grains are needed?

A. 36 **B.** 4781 **C.** 6561 **D.** 7248

Q.24 Given below are three statements: a, b and c. From the given statements, four conclusions, I, II, III and IV are drawn. Select the correct option which states that conclusions logically follow from the given statements.

Statements:

a) Some chairs are tables.

b) Some tables are sofas.

c) All sofa is a bed.

Conclusions:

(i) Some beds are chairs.

(ii) Some tables are beds.

(iii) Some sofas are chairs.

(iv) All beds are sofas.

Code:

A. Only (4) follows
B. Only (2) follows
C. Only (1) and (2) follows
D. Only (1) and (4) follows

Q.25 A deductive argument is sound if it satisfies some conditions. Select the option which states these conditions.

(i) If the argument is valid.

(ii) Its premises are all true.

(iii) The argument may be valid or invalid.

A. (i) and (ii) only **B.** (iii) only
C. (ii) and (iii) only **D.** (ii) only

Q.26 Given below are two statements related to the Upanishadic tradition

Statement I: Paravidya means knowledge that transcends human experience

Statement II: Aparavidya means knowledge based on the human experience

In light of the above statements, choose the most appropriate answer from the options given below:

A. Both Statement I and Statement II are true
B. Both Statement I and Statement II are false
C. Statement I is true but Statement II is false
D. Statement I is false but Statement II is true

Q.27 From the list given below identify the learner characteristics which would facilitate the teaching-learning system to become effective.

(1) Prior experience of the learner

(2) Learner's family lineage

(3) Aptitude of the learner

(4) Learner's Stage of Development

(5) Lerner's food habits and hobbies

(6) Learner's religious affiliation

Choose the correct option:

A. 1, 3 and 4 **B.** 4, 5 and 6
C. 1, 4 and 5 **D.** 2, 3 and 6

Q.28 Which among the following is the best field of study to improve the ability of students to experiment and analyze?

A. Economics **B.** History
C. Science **D.** Languages

Q.29 Which of the following characteristic do not belong to an effective teacher/teaching. Identify the correct option .

A. A teacher is effective if he/she has full confidence in the subject
B. Teaching is always in a formal manner
C. Teaching is a continuous process
D. Teaching is an interaction between teacher and students

Q.30 Which among the following reflects best the quality of teaching in a classroom?

A. Through the use of many teaching aids in the classroom
B. Through full attendance in the classroom
C. Through the quality of questions asked by students in the classroom
D. Through observation of silence by the students in the classroom

Q.31 Which of the following pairs is not correctly matched?

A. Avalanche - Geological Hazard
B. Deforestation - Environmental hazard
C. Volcanic Eruption - Chemical Hazard
D. Cloudburst - Climatic Hazard

Q.32 Which among the following are emitted from a coal-based thermal power plant?

A. Carbon monoxide

B. Ozone

C. Sulphur dioxide

D. Methane

E. Particulate matter

Choose the correct answer from the options given below:

A. A, B, C and E only **B.** A, C and E only
C. A, B and C only **D.** A, C, D and E only

Q.33 Which of the following is not a Sustainable Development Goal?

A. Gender equity
B. Climate action
C. Protection of Ozone layer
D. Life below water

Q.34 Which of the following indoor plant helps to improve indoor air quality?

A. Areca Palm **B.** Lady Palm
C. Dragon Tree **D.** All of them

Q.35 Match List I with List II.

List I	**List II**
Emitted Pollutants	**Environmental Impact**
A. Carbon dioxide	I. Formation of acid rain
B. Carbon monoxide	II. Toxic and are carcinogenic
C. Nitrogen oxides	III. Toxic and can cause respiratory diseases
D. Benzene and hydrocarbon	IV. Contribution to global warming as a Greenhouse gas

Choose the Correct Answer from the option given below:

A. A - IV, B - III, C - I, D - II
B. A - IV, B - II, C - I, D - III
C. A - IV, B - II, C - III, D - I
D. A - I, B - III, C - II, D - IV

Q.36 Which of the following is not a type of research?

A. Exploratory **B.** Explanatory
C. Applied **D.** Variable

Q.37 Direction: Which of the following statements regarding the meaning of research are correct?

1. Research refers to a series of systematic activity or activities undertaken to find out the solution to a problem.
2. It is a systematic, logical, and unbiased process wherein verification of hypothesis, data analysis, interpretation, and formation of principles can be done.
3. It is an intellectual inquiry or quest towards truth.
4. It leads to the enhancement of knowledge.

Select the correct answer from the codes given below:

A. 1, 2 and 3 **B.** 2, 3 and 4
C. 1, 3 and 4 **D.** 1, 2, 3 and 4

Q.38 Which of the following statements defines the main objectives of Research?

A. Research should be highly focused and feasible.
B. Research makes accurate use of concepts.
C. Research is done to find out the hidden truth.
D. All of these

Q.39 The process of copying files to a CD-ROM is known as:

A. Burning **B.** Zipping
C. Digitizing **D.** Ripping

Q.40 IP addresses are converted to:

A. A hierarchy of domain names
B. Alpha numeric string
C. A binary string
D. A hexadecimal string

Q.41 Which of the following is the appropriate definition of Information Technology?

A. Information Technology refers to the use of hardware and software for processing information
B. Information Technology refers to the use of hardware and software for the distribution of useful information
C. Information Technology refers to the use of principles of Physical sciences and Social sciences for processing of information of many kinds.
D. Information Technology refers to the use of hardware and software for storage, retrieval, processing and distributing information of many kinds.

Q.42 Virtual memory is:

A. An extremely large main memory.
B. An extremely large secondary memory.
C. An illusion of extremely large main memory.
D. A type of memory used in super computers.

Q.43 Which network topology requires a central controller or hub?

A. Star **B.** Mesh **C.** Ring **D.** Bus

Q.44 The statement of purpose in a research study should:

A. Identify the design of the study
B. Identify the intent or objective of the study
C. Specify the type of people to be used in the study
D. Describe the study

Q.45 Division of the entire population into different groups and then selection of sample on the basis of proportion of each group in the entire population is called as _______.

A. Judgement sampling
B. Sequential sampling
C. Cluster sampling
D. Quota sampling

Q.46 Which of the following is not an element of communication?

A. Mode of communication
B. Chain of communication
C. Purpose of communication
D. Communication planning

Q.47 Which type of evaluation focuses on the identification of deficiencies and difficulties of the learner?

A. Summative evaluation
B. Follow up evaluation
C. Diagnostic evaluation
D. Criterion-referenced evaluation

Q.48 Choose the right code :

A deductive argument claims that:

1. The conclusion does not claim something more than that which is contained in the premises.
2. The conclusion is supported by the premise/premises conclusively.
3. If the conclusion is false, then premise/premises may be either true or false.
4. If premise/combination of premises is true, then conclusion must be true.

A. 1 and 2 **B.** 1 and 3
C. 2 and 3 **D.** All the above

Q.49 "If a large diamond is cut up into little bits, it will lose its value just as an army is divided up into small units of soldiers, it loses its strength." The argument put above may be called as:

A. Analogical **B.** Deductive
C. Statistical **D.** Causal

Q.50 When does the receiver take the message of the sender seriously?

A. No credibility
B. High credibility
C. Low credibility
D. Uncertain credibility

// Smart Answer Sheet //

Correct — Indicates percentage of students who answered questions correctly.

Skipped — Indicates percentage of students who skipped questions.

Q.	Ans.	Correct	Skipped
1	A	67.46 %	1.95 %
2	A	57.38 %	1.09 %
3	B	62.36 %	1.83 %
4	C	46.97 %	1.38 %
5	D	65.91 %	1.27 %
6	A	49.73 %	1.82 %
7	B	57.46 %	1.2 %
8	B	56.26 %	1.86 %
9	D	46.49 %	1.83 %
10	C	67.38 %	1.43 %
11	B	59.49 %	1.42 %
12	B	43.7 %	1.31 %
13	C	46.12 %	1.4 %
14	A	88.57 %	0.0 %
15	C	41.13 %	1.35 %
16	C	52.65 %	1.01 %
17	D	46.81 %	1.1 %
18	C	44.76 %	1.96 %
19	D	56.71 %	1.87 %
20	A	84.45 %	0.0 %
21	C	78.76 %	0.0 %
22	D	58.36 %	1.73 %
23	C	44.24 %	1.28 %
24	B	53.76 %	1.26 %
25	A	19.33 %	3.59 %
26	A	59.84 %	1.16 %
27	A	50.62 %	1.47 %
28	C	40.08 %	1.52 %
29	B	57.85 %	1.44 %
30	C	80.14 %	0.0 %
31	C	54.87 %	1.52 %
32	B	23.59 %	4.81 %
33	C	14.03 %	4.22 %
34	D	85.04 %	0.0 %
35	A	84.43 %	0.0 %
36	D	83.39 %	0.0 %
37	D	67.77 %	1.79 %
38	D	60.54 %	1.17 %
39	A	67.64 %	1.68 %
40	A	56.77 %	1.69 %
41	D	48.06 %	1.31 %
42	B	83.62 %	0.0 %
43	A	40.56 %	1.63 %
44	B	50.51 %	1.82 %
45	D	20.85 %	3.89 %
46	D	60.95 %	1.87 %
47	C	49.68 %	1.9 %
48	A	29.87 %	3.93 %
49	A	58.22 %	1.14 %
50	B	67.84 %	1.94 %

Performance Analysis	
Avg. Score (%)	63.0%
Toppers Score (%)	73.0%
Your Score	

//Hints and Solutions//

1. "Life Insurance in its modern form came to India from England in the year 1818. The Oriental Life Insurance Company started by Europeans in Calcutta was the first life insurance company on Indian soil."

Upon perusal of the above statement, it can be concluded that the paragraph is about the Genesis of insurance in India.

Hence, the correct option is (A).

2. "All the insurance companies established during that period were brought up with the purpose of looking after the needs of the European community and Indian natives were not being insured by these companies."

Upon perusal of the above statement, it can be concluded that initially, insurance companies used to discriminate between Indian and European clients.

Hence, the correct option is (A).

3. "In the year 1912, Life Insurance Companies Act and Provident Fund Act were passed."

Upon perusal of the above statement, it can be concluded that Provident Fund grew along with insurance business in India.

Hence, the correct option is (B).

4. "The Oriental Life Insurance Company started by Europeans in Calcutta was the first life insurance company on Indian soil."

Upon perusal of the above statement, it can be concluded Europeans were the first to start the insurance business in India.

Hence, the correct option is (C).

5. "The Indian Mercantile, General Assurance and Swadeshi Life (later Bombay Life) were some of the companies established during the same period."

Upon perusal of the above statement, it can be concluded Swadeshi Life was later renamed Bombay Life.

Hence, the correct option is (D).

6. The maximum growth rate ($\%$) of the population was registered in $1961-1971$

Decade wise growth rate= $\frac{\text{Growth}}{\text{initial population}} \times 100$

$1951-1961$	$\frac{1}{20} \times 100=5\%$
$1961-1971$	$\frac{3}{21} \times 100=14.28\%$
$1971-1981$	$\frac{3}{24} \times 100=12.5\%$
$1981-1991$	$\frac{3}{27} \times 100=11.11\%$
$1991-2001$	$\frac{2}{30} \times 100=6.67\%$
$2001-2011$	$\frac{3}{32} \times 100=9.37\%$

Hence, the correct option is (A).

7. Average decadal growth rate $\%$ of population is 9.82% (approx.)

Average $=\frac{\text{sum of observations}}{\text{total no. of observations}}$

$1951-1961$	$\frac{1}{20} \times 100=5\%$
$1961-1971$	$\frac{3}{21} \times 100=14.28\%$
$1971-1981$	$\frac{3}{24} \times 100=12.5\%$
$1981-1991$	$\frac{3}{27} \times 100=11.11\%$
$1991-2001$	$\frac{2}{30} \times 100=6.67\%$
$2001-2011$	$\frac{3}{32} \times 100=9.37\%$

Total of growth
$\%=(5+14.28+12.50+11.11+6.67+9.37)\%$
$=58.93\%$

Total no. of decades $=6$

Average $=\frac{58.93\%}{6}=9.82\%$

Hence, the correct option is (B).

8. $35+\frac{35 \times 9.28}{100}=38.44$ million

The population in the year 2021 will be 38.44 million.

Hence, the correct option is (B).

9. In the year 1951, the power availability per person was 500 W.

1 GW $=1000$ million watt

10 GW $=10000$ million watt

The power availability per person $=\frac{\text{Electrical Power Production}}{\text{Population}}$

$=\frac{10000}{20}=500$ watt

Hence, the correct option is (D).

10. The average power availability per person was maximum in 2011.

The power availability per person $=\frac{\text{Electrical Power Production}}{\text{Population}}$

1951	$\frac{10000}{20}=500$ watt
1961	$\frac{20000}{21}=952.38$ watt
1971	$\frac{25000}{24}=1041.67$ watt
1981	$\frac{40000}{27}=1481.48$ watt
1991	$\frac{50000}{30}=1666.67$ watt

2001	$\frac{80000}{32} = 2500$ watt
2011	$\frac{100000}{35} = 2857$ watt

Hence, the correct option is (C).

11. The purpose of higher education is to promote critical and creative thinking abilities among students so that they can become self-dependent. These abilities will help them to think independently, develops creativity, and also ensure job placements.

So the conclusion is both (A) and (R) are true but (R) is not the correct explanation of (A).

Hence, the correct option is (B).

12. NEAT objective is to use Artificial Intelligence to make learning more personalized and customized as per the requirements of the learner for better learning outcomes in higher education.

All India Council for Technical Education (AICTE) under MHRD, the national level regulator for technical education in the country, would be the implementing agency for the NEAT program.

Hence, the correct option is (B).

13. The demerits of globalization of higher education are:

- Promotion of elitism in education
- The commodification of higher education
- Increase in the cost of education

Hence, the correct option is (C).

14. Miranda House, Delhi was ranked the best college in the country (2017) as per the National Institutional Ranking Framework (NIRF). Miranda House is a constituent college for women at the University of Delhi in India. Established in 1948, it offers degrees in the sciences and liberal arts.

Hence, the correct option is (A).

15. The teaching in the universities of ancient India was controlled by board of eminent teachers. The affairs of Nalanda University were administered by the Board of Vikramsila University. It is stated that Vikramshila University Board was also accountable for the administrative affairs of Nalanda university.

Hence, the correct option is (C).

16. In the case of over communication, the actual message is lost in the jungle of information whereas under communication the sender is blamed for sharing less information. Communication barriers are the factors that obstruct the effectiveness of communication. They result in a mismatch between understanding of the message by the sender and the receiver. These barriers can occur at any stage of the communication process—sending, encoding, transmission, decoding, or receiving.

Hence, the correct option is (C).

17. Effective teaching demands knowledge of communication in the following ways:

- Effective communication can be maintained using different audio-video techniques in the classroom.
- Effective communication demands careful use of nonverbal cues in the classroom.
- Using an honest and tactful tone will also add to effective communication in the classroom.

So the conclusion is (A) is false, but (R) is true.

Hence, the correct option is (D).

18. Poor retention is not a semantic barrier to communication.

The Semantic Barrier refers to the misunderstanding between the sender and receiver arising due to the different meanings of words, and other symbols used in the communication.

Differences in dialect, cultural differences, body language, and choice of word, pronunciation differences, and spelling errors are the main causes of a semantic barrier.

Hence, the correct option is (C).

19. Given:

3, 12, 39, 120, ?

Calculation:

3 × 3 + 3 = 12

12 × 3 + 3 = 39

39 × 3 + 3 = 120

120 × 3 + 3 = 363

∴ The missing number is 363.

Hence, the correct option is (D).

20. The pattern is:

1st term: 10

2nd term: 100 = 10 + 90

3rd term: 200 = 100 + 100

4th term: 310 = 200 + 110

Similarly,

5th Term: 430 = 310 + 120

So, the answer is 430.

Hence, the correct option is (A).

21.

Alphabets	A	B	C	D	E	F	G	H	I	J	K	L	M
Positional value	1	2	3	4	5	6	7	8	9	10	11	12	13
Positional value	26	25	24	23	22	21	20	19	18	17	16	15	14
Alphabets	Z	Y	X	W	V	U	T	S	R	Q	P	O	N

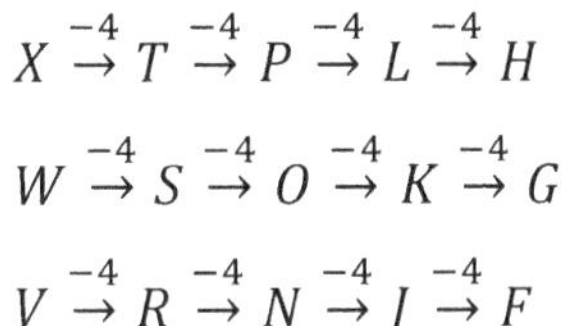

$$X \xrightarrow{-4} T \xrightarrow{-4} P \xrightarrow{-4} L \xrightarrow{-4} H$$

$$W \xrightarrow{-4} S \xrightarrow{-4} O \xrightarrow{-4} K \xrightarrow{-4} G$$

$$V \xrightarrow{-4} R \xrightarrow{-4} N \xrightarrow{-4} J \xrightarrow{-4} F$$

So, 'HGF' is the correct answer.

Hence, the correct option is (C).

22.

Alphabets	A	B	C	D	E	F	G	H	I	J	K	L	M
Positional value	1	2	3	4	5	6	7	8	9	10	11	12	13
Positional value	26	25	24	23	22	21	20	19	18	17	16	15	14
Alphabets	Z	Y	X	W	V	U	T	S	R	Q	P	O	N

The pattern followed here is:

Letter	S	U	R	E
Positional value	19	21	18	5
Code	19 + 21 + 18 + 5 = 63			

Also,

Letter	G	O	N	E
Positional value	7	15	14	5
Code	7 + 15 + 14 + 5 = 41			

Similarly,

Letter	W	I	N	D
Positional value	23	9	14	4
Code	23 + 9 + 14 + 4 = 50			

So, 50 is the right answer.

Hence, the correct option is (D).

23. According to the question,

A tree has 9 branches and on each branch, there are 9 Nests.

Total Nest = 9 × 9 = 81

Each nest have 9 birds.

Total birds = 81 × 9 = 729

Each bird needs 9 grains to be fed.

Total grains are = 729 × 9 = 6561

Hence, the correct option is (C).

24. Only conclusion 2 follows.

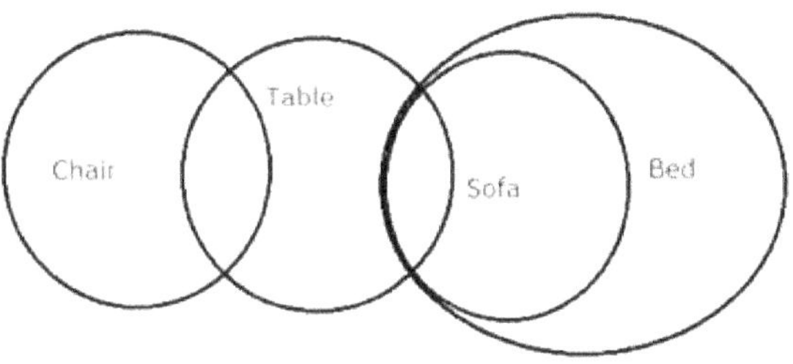

(i) Some beds are chairs does not follow as there is no direct relation between bed and chair.

(ii) Some tables are beds follows as from the diagram some part of the tables lies in bed.

(iii) Some sofas are chairs does not follow as there is no direct relation between sofa and chair.

(iv) All beds are sofas does not follow as some bed are sofa are true but not all.

Hence, the correct option is (B).

25. (i) and (ii) is correct.

A deductive argument: is an argument in which it is believed that the premises provide a guarantee of the truth of the conclusion.

A deductive argument is said to be sound if and only if the argument is both valid and all the premises are true.

Hence, the correct option is (A).

26. Both Statement I and Statement II are true.

Statement I: Paravidya means knowledge that transcends human experience

Para Vidya is defined as the intuitive vision of non-duality; it is the transcendental knowledge which is beyond all limits of knowledge, experience and reason, which is, beyond intellect, mind and sense.

Therefore, Statement I is correct.

Statement II: Aparavidya means knowledge based on the human experience.

Para Vidya is the knowledge of the Absolute whereas Apara Vidya is the knowledge of the world; the former has Reality as its content and possesses a unique quality of ultimacy which is singular and free from reason, senses, etc., but the latter has the phenomenal world as its content.

Thus, Statement II is correct.

Hence, the correct option is (A).

27. Following are the characteristics of the learner which facilitates the teaching-learning system to become effective are:

- Prior or previous experience of the learner facilitates the teaching-learning process a lot because without students' good previous knowledge or learning a good teaching-learning process does not take place.

- The aptitude of a learner, Student talent, behavior, or aptitude facilitates the teaching-learning process effectively.
- The stage of development of a learner also affects the teaching-learning process if the learners are at the preschool level. His/her physical and intellectual development takes place very rapidly in comparison to other stages of development.

Hence, the correct option is (A).

28. Although it is possible to carry out experiments in all the given fields of study, experiments in science offer organized methods for analyzing the cause and effect relationship. The science skills approach guides students to develop an understanding of the experimental skills required to perform a scientific investigation. Experiments and observation develop a sense of understanding for students.

Hence, the correct option is (C).

29. Teaching can be done in a formal as well as in an informal manner. Whereas formal learning happens in a training based organization, workplace, mobile devices, classrooms, online over the internet, and through e-learning portals, informal learning is based on practical and lifelong learning.

Hence, the correct option is (B).

30. The quality of teaching can be reflected in the best way through the quality of questions asked by the student. The quality of student's questions reflects the interest level and curiosity level of a student during the teaching-learning process.

The questions of the students give the teacher an idea about how much their student is grasping the content taught by the teacher which further allows the teacher to improve their teaching skills in order to make teaching more effective. Qualifying questions asked by the students ensures an effective teaching-learning process.

Hence, the correct option is (C).

31. Hazards can be of various kinds namely- geological, climatic, environmental, biological and industrial/chemical and so on. Out of the given options, volcanic eruption is not correctly matched. Volcanic eruption is a kind of geological hazard, not chemical hazard. Chemical hazard would include oil spills, industrial disaster etc.

Hence, the correct option is (C).

32. As society advances, we are discovering more pollutants that are contributing to negative climate change effects and global warming. Many of these pollutants come from our manufacturing and power generating industries, and no matter how much they are minimized, there are always going to be some pollutants that will enter our atmosphere. Thermal power plants are known for producing a wide range of pollutants that are released into our atmosphere.

Impact on the Atmosphere:

Thermal power plants are known to pump out a lot of greenhouse gases and ash, which are by-products of burning fossil fuels. Whilst some thermal power plants do use solar or nuclear energy, they are heavily reliant on fossil fuels.

Carbon dioxide:

- Carbon dioxide is one of the main gases that is released from the burning of fossil fuels and is known to be a greenhouse gas and a contributor to global warming.
- Out of all the gases released from a thermal power plant, carbon dioxide is the main one, and thermal power plants are one of the main contributors to the increased carbon dioxide levels throughout the world.

Sulphur dioxide:

- Sulfur dioxide is another gas that is released from power plants.
- Whilst it is technically not a greenhouse gas, it is known to have indirect effects on the atmosphere because it can affect the scattering of incoming sunlight, the formation of clouds, and precipitation patterns.
- So, in many cases, it is considered an indirect greenhouse gas. Sulfur dioxide forms sulphuric acid in the atmosphere.

Nitrogen oxides:

- Nitrogen oxides are another set of gases that are released to the atmosphere by thermal power plants.
- Thermal power plants are also one of the biggest contributors to global nitrogen oxide levels.

Particulate matter:

- The other big pollutant to the atmosphere is ash.
- Ash often contains harmful particulate matter, as well as heavy metals.
- Ash can have multiple effects; it can get into waterways and soil wherever it falls (it doesn't have to be the local environment) and change the alkalinity of the soil/water, which can render the soil unusable for agricultural purposes and the water undrinkable, and it can cause visibility issues.
- Ash and the particulate matter contained within are also a major cause of smog—which is being seen in many cities around the world on a much more frequent and hazardous scale.

Hence, the correct option is (B).

33. The Sustainable Development Goals (SDGs) were born at the United Nations Conference on Sustainable Development in Rio de Janeiro in 2012.

They were adopted by all United Nations Member States in 2015 as a universal call to action to end poverty, protect the planet, and ensure that all people enjoy peace and prosperity by 2030.

The 17 SDGs are integrated that is, they recognize that action in one area will affect outcomes in others and that development must balance social, economic, and environmental sustainability.

The SDGs replaced the Millennium Development Goals (MDGs), which started a global effort in 2000 to tackle the indignity of poverty.

Hence, the correct option is (C).

34. All of the above mentioned indoor plant helps to improve indoor air quality.
A study by NASA confirms that common houseplants are the natural air purifiers. These include aloe Vera, areca palm, lady palm, dragon tree, bamboo among others.
Hence, the correct option is (D).

35. Correct match:

List I	**List II**
Emitted Pollutants	**Environmental Impact**
A. Carbon dioxide	IV. Contribution to global warming as a Greenhouse gas
B. Carbon monoxide	III. Toxic and can cause respiratory diseases
C. Nitrogen oxides	I. Formation of acid rain
D. Benzene and hydrocarbon	II. Toxic and are carcinogenic

Hence, the correct option is (A).

36. Variable research is not a type of research.

Exploratory research is to gain familiarity with a phenomenon or achieve new insights into it. Explanatory Research is the research whose primary purpose is to explain or elaborate on how the events occur to build.

Applied research is a type of research design that seeks to solve a specific problem or provide innovative solutions to issues affecting an individual, group, or society.

Hence, the correct option is (D).

37. Research is an investigation that comprises creative work undertaken on a systematic and logical basis to increase the stock of knowledge, culture, and society. It deals with the verification of hypothesis, data analysis, interpretation, and formation of principles, and by using this stock of knowledge (research) new applications are being devised. Research is also an intellectual inquiry towards truth.

Hence, the correct option is (D).

38. The objective of Research is to make accurate use of concepts. Research can also be done to find out the hidden truth. Research's objective should be highly focused and feasible.

Hence, the correct option is (D).

39. The term burn describes the action of creating a CD or other recordable discs. Burning refers to the process of copying files to a CD-ROM. You can identify a burned or recordable disc by looking at the bottom of the disc. Any blank disc or recordable disc can be used in a burner to create a new disc or copy an existing disc.

Hence, the correct option is (A).

40. Internet Protocol(IP)

- It is a unique logical address assigned to every single computer or any device that is part of the Transmission control protocolTC(P)/IP Based network.
- The IP address is the core unit on which entire networking architecture is built in a hierarchical structure or in sequence wise steps.
- IP Address provides the network node on address such that it can communicate with other nodes/networks.

The IP address is numerically divided into 2 parts:-

- The network part mentions which network this address belongs to.
- The host part further source the exact location.

Therefore, IP addresses are converted to a hierarchy of domain names.

Hence, the correct option is (A).

41. Use and tools of scientific, technological and scientific methods and management techniques for the handling and processing of information, the interaction between human and machine in social, economic and cultural matters ".

Information technology refers to the use of hardware and software for the storage, retrieval, commercial and distribution of many types of information.

Hence, the correct option is (D).

42. In computing, virtual memory (also virtual storage) is a memory management technique that provides an "idealized abstraction of the storage resources that are actually available on a given machine" which "creates the illusion to users of a very large (main) memory".

Hence, the correct option is (B).

43. In star topology, no computer is connected to another computer directly but all the computers are connected to a central hub. Every message sent from a source computer goes through the hub and the hub then forwards the message only to the intended destination computer.

Hence, the correct option is (A).

44. The statement of purpose in a research study should identify the intent or objective of the study.

The research purpose is a statement of "why" the study is being conducted, or the goal of the study. The goal of a study might be to identify or describe a concept or to explain or predict a situation or solution to a situation that indicates the type of study to be conducted (Beckingham, 1974). Its main purpose is to help the researcher outline their sets of objectives for the study.

Hence, the correct option is (B).

45. Division of the entire population into different groups and then selection of sample on the basis of proportion of each group in the entire population is called as quota sampling.

When you conduct research about something, it's rarely possible to collect data from each one of them in that population. Instead, you select a sample. The sample is the group of individuals who will actually participate in the research. To draw valid conclusions from results, carefully selecting sample that is representative of the population as a whole is vital.

Hence, the correct option is (D).

46. Communication planning is not an element of communication.

Communication is the act of transmitting information, ideas and attitudes from one person to another person. It is a two-way process. It forms a chain as shown in the diagram below. Also, modes of communication include TV, mobiles, computer, etc.

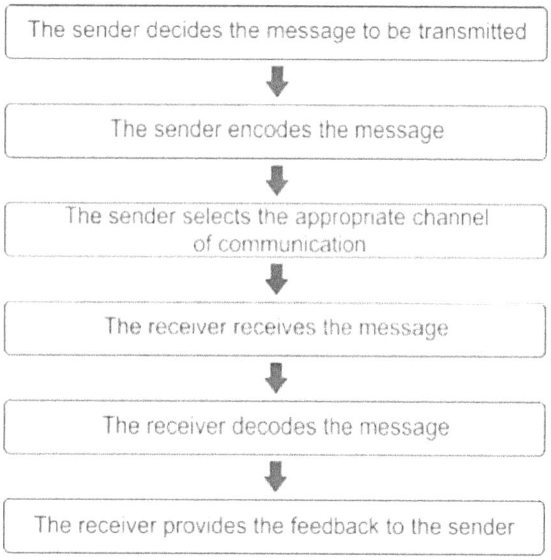

The sender decides the message to be transmitted

↓

The sender encodes the message

↓

The sender selects the appropriate channel of communication

↓

The receiver receives the message

↓

The receiver decodes the message

↓

The receiver provides the feedback to the sender

Hence, communication planning is not an element of the communication process.

Hence, the correct option is (D).

47. Diagnostic evaluation focuses on the identification of deficiencies and difficulties of the learner.

Evaluation is integral to the teaching-learning process which helps in facilitating student learning and improving instruction. a systematic process of collecting and analyzing data in order to determine whether and to what degree, objectives have been achieved.

It is conducted along with the formative assessment. It attempts to find the deficiencies or underlying causes for the problems in learning. The keyword in this evaluation is identifying 'learning difficulties'.This assessment is done through a diagnostic remedial test.

Hence, considering the given points it can be said that diagnostic evaluation focuses on the identification of deficiencies and difficulties of the learner.

Hence, the correct option is (C).

48. Statement 1 and 2 are correct.

A deductive argument is the presentation of statements that are assumed or known to be true as premises for a conclusion that necessarily follows from those statements. The argument may be valid or invalid, independent of whether they are sound. The argument's validity depends on whether the conclusion naturally follows from the premises.

A deductive argument can be invalidated by a false assumption as a starting point. Before a deductively reasoned argument can be totally proven wrong, both its supporting premises and its conclusion must be proven false.

Hence, the correct option is (A).

49. "If a large diamond is cut up into little bits, it will lose its value just as an army is divided up into small units of soldiers, it loses its strength." The argument put above may be called Analogical

Analogical reasoning or argument by analogy can be defined as a specific way of thinking, based on the idea that because two or more things are similar in some respects, they are probably also similar in some further respect.

Hence, the correct option is (A).

50. The receiver takes the message of the sender seriously when he has high credibility in the sender.

Sender credibility plays a major role in effective communication. If it has high credibility that means the receiver has full confidence, respect, and trust in the sender of the message.

If it has low credibility that means the receiver will thoroughly check the message and look for hidden meanings or tricks and distort the entire message. So, the sender must establish his trust in the receiver, otherwise, it will act as a barrier to communication.

Hence, the correct option is (B).

Mock Test 19

Ques (1-5):Direction: Read the passage and answer questions:

Once the decision has been made to enter an overseas market, a business must consider the extent to which it will adapt its offerings to local conditions. It is possible to market the product in almost the same way in every country which is known as a global strategy, or will the marketing have to be adjusted for each market? If a business pursues a global strategy this means it is adopting essentially the same marketing mix wherever it competes. A Pan global marketing strategy has been adopted by business in several markets, such as jeans soft drinks and luxury goods. One advantage of a global approach is that it offers marketing economies of scale. For example, the business can develop one advertising campaign and one approach to packaging worldwide. However, this type of strategy does not respond to the requirements of different national markets and so the business may lose sales to competitors who focus more on local needs. In markets such as food and drinks and the media, a business may need to adapt significantly to local requirements. On the other hand, amore local approach may meet customer needs more precisely, but may be more expensive and more complex to manage. In reality, most companies will choose a balance between the global and local approach. There are global brands that sell in many different markets. They have the same name and logo everywhere. However, some advertisements are made in the way the product is promotional to reflect local conditions.

Q.1 The assessment of global brands in the passage is that:

A. they should have a single packaging approach

B. they should advertise the product reflecting global conditions

C. the global products should have different names and logo

D. the globalization of business marketing is a reality

Q.2 If the global strategy is benefit of local conditions, the business consequence is:

A. more investment in media advertising campaigns

B. emergence of different national markets

C. change in the customer needs

D. the dominance of competitors who focus on local conditions

Q.3 The benefits from a non global approach is to opt for:

A. grand sale of non - luxury goods

B. market expansion of costly products

C. single advertising campaign worldwide

D. refreshing marketing economies of scale

Q.4 What does global strategy mean?

A. Opting for the same marketing mix in every competitive market

B. Globalize the local conditions of marketing

C. Creating product differentiation to suit different markets

D. Making overseas marketing non - competitive

Q.5 What should be the global strategy in business?

A. Sell different brands in different overseas market

B. Market the same product in every country the same way

C. Decide to enter the overseas market

D. Know the local conditions of the local market

Q.6 In a city the noise levels represented by equivalent sound pressure level over 8 years period were reported as 80 dB (A). What does 'A' refer to?

A. a type of amplifier used in the measurement

B. a type of microphone used in the measurement

C. the measurement of day time

D. a type of weighting used in the measurement

Q.7 One of the anthropogenic sources of gaseous pollutants chlorofluorocarbons (CFCs) in the air is:

A. Cement industry **B.** Fertiliser industry

C. Foam industry **D.** Pesticide industry

Q.8 Which of the following is/are the source(s) of soil pollution?

A. Solid waste

B. Pesticides and chemical fertilizers

C. Effluent and sewage

D. All of these

Q.9 Consider the following statements regarding noise pollution:

(a) Noise levels decrease as we move away from the source of noise.

(b) Materials with high surface/mass density act as good noise barriers.

(c) Sound pressure of 2 Pa corresponds to a noise of zero decibel.

Choose the correct option from those given below:

A. (a) and (b) only **B.** (b) and (c) only

C. (a) and (c) only **D.** (a), (b) and (c)

Q.10 Given below are two statements:

Statement I: Diesel Vehicles emit excessive amounts of oxides of nitrogen and fine particulate matter.

Statement II: The diesel engines run with mixtures having high air to fuel ratio.

In the light of the above statements, choose the Correct answer from the options given below:

A. Both Statement I and Statement II are correct

B. Both Statement I and Statement II are incorrect

C. Statement I is correct but Statement II is incorrect

D. Statement I is incorrect but Statement II is correct

Q.11 Expressive communication is driven by what?

A. Passive aggression

B. Encoder's personality characteristics

C. External clues
D. Encoder-decoder contract

Q.12 Using the central point of classroom communication as the beginning of a dynamic pattern of ideas is referred to as:
A. Systemisation **B.** Problem-orientation
C. Idea protocol **D.** Mind mapping

Q.13 In a classroom, use of communication technology pre-supposes:
A. Inattentive audience
B. Luxurious ambience
C. Extrapolation of contents
D. New forms of expression and applications

Q.14 The most powerful barrier of communication in classroom is:
A. noise in the classroom
B. lack of teaching aids
C. confusion on the part of teacher
D. more outside disturbance in the classroom

Q.15 In communication, attributing our own thoughts and feelings to other is called _____.
A. Stereotyping **B.** Projection
C. Halo effect **D.** Barrier

Q.16 The headquarter of Mahatma Gandhi Antarrashtriya Hindi Vishwavidyalaya is situated in:
A. Wardha **B.** Sevagram
C. New Delhi **D.** Ahmedabad

Q.17 The University Grants Commission has a scheme for "Human Rights and Values in Education". Under this scheme, which statement is incorrect among the following for 'Human Rights and Duties Education' component?
A. To establish value and wellness centers in schools.
B. To encourage research activities.
C. To develop interaction between society and educational institutions.
D. To sensitize the citizens so that the norms and values of human rights are realized.

Q.18 Which of the following are the demerits of globalization of higher education?
1. Exposure to global curriculum
2. Promotion of elitism in education
3. The commodification of higher education
4. Increase in the cost of education

Select the correct answer from the codes given below:
A. 1 and 4 **B.** 1, 3 and 4
C. 2, 3 and 4 **D.** 1, 2, 3 and 4

Q.19 Direction: Find the missing number in place of the question mark (?) in the given series.
2, 8, 18, 32, 50, ?
A. 62 **B.** 68 **C.** 72 **D.** 78

Q.20 A sum of money is lent by Mr. X to Mr. Y at simple interest amounts to Rs.1728 in 2 years and to Rs. 1792 in 3 years. Find the sum of money.
A. Rs. 1500 **B.** Rs. 1600 **C.** Rs. 1400 **D.** Rs. 1200

Q.21 A man travels a distance of 30 km in 5 hours and a distance of y km in 8 hours. Find the speed in which he will cover 2y distance in 6 hours.
A. 12 km/hr **B.** 18 km/hr **C.** 16 km/hr **D.** 8 km/hr

Q.22 Person X borrows Rs. 18000 at 20% compound interest. He pays Rs. 5000 at the end of the first year. How much is required for him to pay at end of the second year?
A. Rs. 17820 **B.** Rs. 19920
C. Rs. 18720 **D.** Rs. 16820

Q.23 Instead of dividing Rs. 468 among A, B, C in the ratio 13 : 14 : 12, by mistake it was divided in the ratio 3 : 4 : 2. Who gained from the transaction?
A. A **B.** B
C. C **D.** All of these

Q.24 Pointing to the woman in the picture, Govind said " she is the mother of my only cousin's son" How is she related to Govind's wife?
A. Wife **B.** Sister
C. Sister-in-law **D.** Cousin

Q.25 Direction: Select the related letter/number from the given alternatives.
XY : 2425 : : ? : 1213
A. LM **B.** NL **C.** ML **D.** LN

Q.26 In a certain code language, "SCARCE" is coded as "18351931". How will "REGRET" be coded in that language?
A. 185422857 **B.** 184208587
C. 185201857 **D.** 188201847

Q.27 Xe is father of Fr. Fr is married to Za. Gr is son of Za. How is Fr related to Gr?
A. Mother
B. Father
C. Either Mother or Father
D. Brother

Q.28 There are five friends in a class. P scores more marks than R but not as much as Q. S is the highest marks scorer. T scores more marks than Q. Who scores the lowest marks?
A. P **B.** Q **C.** R **D.** T

Q.29 The best method of teaching is _______.
A. impart information
B. ask students to read books
C. suggest good reference material
D. initiate a discussion and participate in it

Q.30 For a teacher, which of the following methods would be correct for writing on the blackboard?
A. Writing fast and as clearly as possible.
B. Writing the matter first and then asking students to read it.
C. Asking a question to students and then writing the answer

as stated by them.

D. Writing the important points as clearly as possible.

Q.31 For promoting international understanding a teacher should avoid:

A. developing a proper regard for the use of reason rather than force

B. being concerned with the healthy development of the child's body and mind

C. indoctrinating the mind of the pupils

D. organizing activities for developing international outlook in the students

Q.32 Nowadays the most effective mode of learning is ________.

A. self study

B. face-to-face learning

C. e-learning

D. blended learning

Q.33 Which is the most important characteristic of a good teacher?

A. Good motivator

B. Less subject knowledge

C. Strict disciplinarian

D. Giving more homework to students

Ques (34-38):Direction: Study the bar graph and answer the following question.

The Bar graph shows quantity of different types of mangoes sold (in kg) by a shop in May 2017 and May 2018.

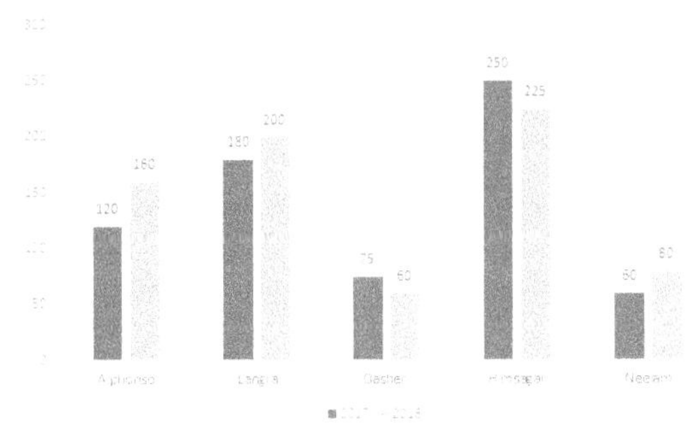

Q.34 The quantity of Langra mangoes sold in May 2017 is what percent of the quantity of Alphonso and Neelam mangoes sold in May 2018 together?

A. 33.33% **B.** 66.67% **C.** 62.5% **D.** 75%

Q.35 What is the difference between the quantity of all mangoes sold in May 2017 and 2018?

A. 36 kg **B.** 15 kg **C.** 40 kg **D.** 25 kg

Q.36 What is the percentage decrease in sales of Himsagar mango in May 2018 with respect to May 2017?

A. 15% **B.** 5% **C.** 25% **D.** 10%

Q.37 In case of Dasheri mango, the quantity sold in May 2018 was 80% of the total sales that year. What ratio between total quantity of Dasheri sold in 2018 and Himsagar sold in May 2018?

A. $2:5$ **B.** $1:3$ **C.** $3:8$ **D.** $1:4$

Q.38 What is the average quantity of Mango sold by the shop in June 2018, if average sales is increased by 20% than May 2018?

A. 174 kg **B.** 165 kg **C.** 182 kg **D.** 168 kg

Q.39 Which one of the following represents the correct order of sequence for reading skills in the context of research?

A. Read, question, recall, review, survey

B. Questions, survey, read, recall, review

C. Recall, review, survey, question, read

D. Survey, question, read, recall, review

Q.40 In a research setting, participants may act differently because they think they are getting special attention. This reaction of treatment group to the special attention rather than the treatment itself is called as:

A. Hawthorne effect **B.** Attention deficit

C. Jung effect **D.** Marlov effect

Q.41 An empiricist believes that:

A. Natural science methods should not be applied to social science research.

B. Social science methods cannot be applied in natural sciences.

C. Knowledge is acquired through our sensory perceptions.

D. None of these

Q.42 A researcher while writing his/her thesis does not give the rationale underlying use of statistical techniques. This will be best described as a case of:

A. Technical lapse

B. Ethical misconduct

C. An error of commission

D. An error of omission

Q.43 Which of the following statements regarding the meaning of research are correct?

(1) Research refers to a series of systematic activity or activities undertaken to find out the solution to a problem.

(2) It is a systematic, logical, and unbiased process wherein verification of hypothesis, data analysis, interpretation, and formation of principles can be done.

(3) It is an intellectual inquiry or quest towards truth.

(4) It leads to the enhancement of knowledge.

Select the correct answer from the codes given below:

A. 1, 2 and 3 **B.** 2, 3 and 4

C. 1, 3 and 4 **D.** 1, 2, 3 and 4

Q.44 HTML stands for:

A. Hyper Text Magic line

B. Hyper Text Markup Line

C. Hyper Text Markup Language

D. High Text Markup Language

Q.45 Which one of the following options can be considered as the Cloud?

A. Hadoop
B. Intranet
C. Web Applications
D. All of the mentioned

Q.46 Given the following email fields, which of the email addresses will Swami be able to see when he receives the message?
To... ram@test.com
Cc... raj@test.com; ravi@test.com
Bcc... swami@test.com; rama@test.com

A. ram@test.com
B. ram@test.com; raj@test.com; ravi@test.com
C. ram@test.com; rama@test.com
D. ram@test.com; rama@test.com; raj@test.com; ravi@test.com

Q.47 CDMA stands for _______.

A. Code Division Multiplexed Access
B. Code division Multiple Access
C. Code Division Mobile Access
D. Code division Mobile Adapter

Q.48 Which of the following is false? Consider the following statements.

A. Using of information and Communication Technology (ICT) for learning promotes fast communication
B. Information and Communication Technology (ICT) promotes cooperative learning for students
C. Information and Communication Technology (ICT) promotes student privacy
D. Plagiarism cannot be prevented through the use of ICT

Q.49 Which is the highest body to advise central and state governments on education?

[UGC NET Sociology, 2020]

A. UGC **B.** CABE **C.** NSDA **D.** NIEPA

Q.50 Which of the following are the main recommendations of 'Knowledge Commission' with regard to higher education in India?

(a) More regulatory institutions
(b) Closure of private universities
(c) Massive expansion of higher education.
(d) Focus on affirmative action
(e) Efforts to achieve excellence
(f) Nationalisation of higher education

Choose the correct answer from the options given below:

A. Only (a), (b) and (c)
B. Only (b), (d) and (f)
C. Only (c), (d) and (e)
D. Only (d), e) and (f)

// Smart Answer Sheet //

Correct Indicates percentage of students who answered questions correctly.

Skipped Indicates percentage of students who skipped questions.

Q.	Ans.	Correct	Skipped
1	B	54.81 %	1.44 %
2	D	65.92 %	1.24 %
3	C	59.59 %	1.6 %
4	A	69.51 %	1.9 %
5	B	65.01 %	1.46 %
6	D	69.14 %	1.77 %
7	C	87.31 %	0.0 %
8	D	43.77 %	1.47 %
9	A	19.13 %	4.05 %
10	C	65.38 %	1.97 %
11	B	46.17 %	1.81 %
12	D	76.31 %	0.0 %
13	D	82.57 %	0.0 %
14	C	54.04 %	1.6 %
15	B	50.48 %	1.51 %
16	A	83.9 %	0.0 %
17	A	40.31 %	1.62 %
18	C	68.18 %	1.73 %
19	C	79.97 %	0.0 %
20	B	65.47 %	1.45 %
21	C	50.37 %	1.19 %
22	B	60.67 %	1.47 %
23	B	53.47 %	1.14 %
24	C	48.4 %	1.53 %
25	A	40.34 %	1.38 %
26	C	60.94 %	1.74 %
27	C	81.23 %	0.0 %
28	C	51.5 %	1.54 %
29	D	46.69 %	1.87 %
30	D	51.36 %	1.48 %
31	C	46.93 %	1.93 %
32	D	13.11 %	3.44 %
33	A	59.45 %	1.54 %
34	D	53.51 %	1.03 %
35	C	49.67 %	1.54 %
36	D	62.41 %	1.35 %
37	B	63.6 %	1.37 %
38	A	58.08 %	1.61 %
39	D	12.5 %	3.18 %
40	A	15.19 %	4.18 %
41	C	67.58 %	1.14 %
42	D	21.99 %	4.88 %
43	D	44.66 %	1.09 %
44	C	54.33 %	1.88 %
45	A	53.09 %	1.08 %
46	B	62.82 %	1.49 %
47	B	51.01 %	1.43 %
48	D	45.45 %	1.29 %
49	B	86.87 %	0.0 %
50	C	30.59 %	4.59 %

Performance Analysis	
Avg. Score (%)	42.0%
Toppers Score (%)	56.0%
Your Score	

//Hints and Solutions//

1. The assessment of global brands in the passage is that they should advertise the product reflecting global conditions.

From the passage, 'In reality, most companies will choose a balance between the global and local approach' indicates the assessment of global brands, in which they have to choose the marketing strategy which reflects the global conditions.

Option (A), (C) and (D) don't reflect the assessment of global brands in a broader way. Single packaging, name, logo and globalization are the components that help global strategy.

Hence, the correct option is (B).

2. If the global strategy is benefit of local conditions, the business consequence is the dominance of competitors who focus on local conditions.

Option (A), (B) and (C) are not mentioned anywhere in the passage.

From the passage, 'the business can develop one advertising campaign and one approach to packaging worldwide. However, this type of strategy does not respond to the requirements of different national markets and so the business may lose sales to competitors who focus more on local needs.' indicates that global strategy may be beneficial to the local market however the business may face stiff competition, even lose sales to those who concentrate on local need.

Hence, the correct option is (D).

3. The benefits from a non global approach is to opt for single advertising campaign worldwide.

From the passage, 'For example, the business can develop one advertising campaign and one approach to packaging worldwide. However, this type of strategy does not respond to the requirements of different national markets and so the business may lose sales to competitors who focus more on local needs.' indicates that it is one of the strategies that may benefit the non global approach.

Option (A), (B) and (D) are out of the context, not mentioned anywhere in the passage. and not related to the non global approach.

Hence, the correct option is (C).

4. From the passage, 'If a business pursues a global strategy this means it is adopting essentially the same marketing mix wherever it competes' clearly indicates that global strategy means choosing same market mix in all competitive market.

Option (B), (C) and (D) don't reflect the meaning of global strategy.

Hence, the correct option is (A).

5. From the passage, 'It is possible to market the product in almost the same way in every country which is known as a global strategy, or will the marketing have to be adjusted for each market? If a business pursues a global strategy this means it is adopting essentially the same marketing mix wherever it competes' This clearly indicates that global strategy is marketing the same product in every country the same way.

Option (A) is out of the context, not mentioned in the passage.

Option (C), the decision to enter the overseas market is not a strategy.

Option (D) indicates the local market approach only.

Hence, the correct option is (B).

6. Decibel (dB) is a unit for expressing the ratio between two physical quantities, usually amounts of acoustic or electric power, or for measuring the relative loudness of sound. 'A' refer to a type of weighting used in the measurement.

A dB (A) measurement has been adjusted to consider the varying sensitivity of the human ear to different frequencies of sound.

Hence, the correct option is (D).

7. Chlorofluorocarbons released into the atmosphere since the 1930s in various applications like air-conditioning, refrigeration, blowing agents in foams, etc. One of the anthropogenic sources of gaseous pollutants chlorofluorocarbons (CFCs) in the air is in the Foam Industry.

Hence, the correct option is (C).

8. Solid waste, pesticides and chemical fertilizers and effluent and sewage are the sources of soil pollution.

Pollution refers to the contamination of the body which results in being harmful to lives and/or ecosystems when exposed to the environment.

Soil pollution: Soil pollution is caused due to industrial activity (electronic waste disposal), agricultural activities (use of pesticides, insecticides, fertilizers, etc on the farmland), waste disposal (seepage of leachate from the waste landfills), accidental oil spills, acid rain, etc.

Hence, the correct option is (D).

9. Noise levels decrease as we move away from the source of noise and materials with high surface/mass density act as good noise barriers are correct statements regarding noise pollution.

Noise pollution: Noise pollution is that unpleasant sound that causes uneasiness to the ear and can lead to serious health hazards. It is more prevalent in metropolitan cities compared to suburban areas. Traffic is the main noise pollution in urban areas.

Features of Sound/Noise:

- A sound is a form of energy that causes the sensation of hearing. It is the main mode of communication.
- Sounds travel in the air or any other substance in the form of longitudinal waves. These waves are produced by the vibrations of the sound-producing source.
- Sounds get louder as we move closer to the source and softer as we move away.
- In other words, noise levels decrease as we move away from the source of the noise.

- Heavyweight structures with high mass transmit less sound energy than lightweight structures.
- The high density of heavyweight materials restricts the size of the sound vibrations inside the material.
- This high-density high-mass layer acts as a good noise barrier to the transmission of energy through the material.

Hence, the correct option is (A).

10. Diesel Vehicles emit excessive amounts of oxides of nitrogen and fine particulate matter. Statement I is correct.

The diesel engines run with mixtures having high air to fuel ratio. Statement II is incorrect.

In recent years, exhaust emission from motor vehicles has been increasing. To combat this, the motor industry has been promoting the diesel car as cleaner than petrol cars due to their greater fuel economy and reduced maintenance requirements. Emissions from diesel vehicles are considered relatively less harmful to human health in comparison to petrol vehicles.

Hence, the correct option is (C).

11. Expressive communication is driven by encoder's personality characteristics. Expressive communication refers to the encoding of a message to the decoder to make something in progress.

Expressive language includes making requests, giving information or command, and so on; hence, it cannot be passive. Individuals with language disorders and those who lack expressive language skills suffer the frustration of not being able to get across and it reflects in behaviour which is one of passive aggression. This phenomenon is observed in toddlers, too. They get irritable and throw tantrums when they are unable to express what they want, or how they feel.

What one expresses flow from one's mind; so, external slues do not drive it. It does not depend on the equation between the encoder and the decoder.

Hence, the correct option is (B).

12. The central point of the classroom communication as the beginning of a dynamic pattern is known as mind mapping.

It captures information and ideas, helping us to improve our brainstorming sessions and become more organized and productive.

Hence, the correct option is (D).

13. In a classroom, use of communication technology pre-supposes new forms of expression and applications

The role of the teacher shifts from a knowledge transmitter to a facilitator. It automatically leads to more student interaction and engagement. Use of new technologies it presupposes new forms of expressions and applications. It helps in keeping the teachers and students updated and connected.

Hence, the correct option is (D).

14. The most powerful barrier of communication in classroom is confusion on the part of teacher.

Communication involves sharing of an idea, thought, feeling or information with others, which includes thinking, dreaming, speaking, arguing and so on. For communication to be complete and effective it has to achieve the desired objectives as intended by the communicator.

A barrier is a term used to express any interference in communication between source and receiver. Successful communication is the one in which the message is conveyed undiminished with kart distortion. However, it is not always possible as a number of barriers that make the process of communication complex. Barries can be of many types.

Hence, the correct option is (C).

15. In communication, attributing our own thoughts and feelings to other is called projection.

Projection:

- In projection, people attribute their own traits (thoughts and feelings) to others.
- Thus, a person who has strong aggressive tendencies may see other people as acting in an excessively aggressive way towards her/him.

Hence, the correct option is (B).

16. Mahatma Gandhi Antarrashtriya Hindi Vishwavidyalaya is a central university located in Wardha, Maharashtra, India. The university began through an Act of Parliament which received the assent of the President on 8 January 1997. The purpose of the act was to establish and incorporate a teaching university for the promotion and development of Hindi language and literature, through teaching and research, with a view to enabling Hindi to achieve greater functional efficiency and recognition as a major international language.

Hence, the correct option is (A).

17. The University Grants Commission has a scheme for "Human Rights and Values in Education". Under this scheme, to establish value and wellness centers in schools. The other guidelines listed are to develop interaction between society and educational institutions and to sensitize the citizens so that the norms and values of human rights are realized. To establish value and wellness centers in school is not a component listed in the 'Human Rights & Duties Education' scheme.

Hence, the correct option is (A).

18. Demerits of globalization of higher education are as follows:

1. Promotion of elitism in higher education.
2. The commodification of higher education (It has become a saleable commodity.
3. Increase in the cost of education (not affordable by everyone to study abroad.

Hence, the correct option is (C).

19. The series follows the following pattern:

$1^2 \times 2 = 2$

$2^2 \times 2 = 8$

$3^2 \times 2 = 18$

$4^2 \times 2 = 32$

$5^2 \times 2 = 50$

$6^2 \times 2 = 72$

So, the next number is 72.

Hence, the correct option is (C).

20. Given:

Amount in two years $=$ Rs. 1728

Amount in three years $=$ Rs. 1792

Formula used

Simple interest $= \frac{P \times r \times t}{100}$

Where P, r and t represents principal, rate of interest and time

Interest for 1 year $=$ Amount in 3 years $-$ Amount in 2 years

$=$ Rs. $1792 -$ Rs. 1728

$=$ Rs. 64

Interest for 2 years $= 64 \times 2$

$=$ Rs. 128

Principal = Amount of 2 years $-$ simple interest for 2 years

= Rs. $1728-$ Rs. 128

$=$ Rs. 1600

Hence, the correct option is (B).

21. Given:

$D_1 = 30$

$T_1 = 5$ hours

$T_2 = 8$ hours

$T_3 = 6$ hours

Formula used:

Distance $=$ Speed $\times$ Time or $D = S \times T$

Speed $= \frac{\text{Distance}}{\text{Time}}$ or $S = \frac{D}{T}$

Now, $S_1 = \frac{D_1}{T_1}$

$\Rightarrow S_1 = \frac{30}{5} = 6$ km/hr

As he travelled y km with same speed

$\Rightarrow y = S_1 \times T_2$

$\Rightarrow y = 6 \times 8 = 48$ km

Now he will travel $2y$ distance in 6 hours

Speed $(S_2) = \frac{2y}{6}$

$\Rightarrow S_2 = \frac{(2 \times 48)}{6}$

$\Rightarrow S_2 = 16$ km/hr

Hence, the correct option is (C).

22. Given:

Rate of interest = 20%

Principal amount = 18000

Formula used:

$A = P\left(1 + \left(\frac{R}{100}\right)\right)^n$

Where,

n is number of years, P is Principal amount. R is rate of Interest and A is amount.

Now,

Calculate the amount to be paid at end of the first year

$\Rightarrow 18000 \times \left(1 + \left(\frac{20}{100}\right)\right)^1$

$\Rightarrow$ Rs. 21600

Now, 5000 of this total amount was already paid

$\Rightarrow$ Remaining amount = 21600 – 5000

$\Rightarrow$ Remaining amount = 16600

Now, the final amount to be paid

$\Rightarrow 16600 \times \left(1 + \left(\frac{20}{100}\right)\right)^1$

$\Rightarrow 16600 \times 1.20$

$\Rightarrow$ Rs. 19920

Hence, the correct option is (B).

23. Let $13:14:12$

Actual amount they have to got -

$\Rightarrow A = \frac{(468 \times 13)}{39} =$ Rs. 156

$\Rightarrow B = \frac{(468 \times 14)}{39} =$ Rs. 168

$\Rightarrow C = \frac{(468 \times 12)}{39} =$ Rs. 144

But mistakenly they got the amount in the ratio $= 3:4:2$

$\Rightarrow A = \frac{(468 \times 3)}{9} =$ Rs. 156

$\Rightarrow B = \frac{(468 \times 4)}{9} = \text{Rs. } 208$

$\Rightarrow C = \frac{(468 \times 3)}{9} = \text{Rs. } 104$

$\because B$ gained in the transaction.

Hence, the correct option is (B).

24. The figure is given below:

Symbol in Diagram	Meaning
○	Female
□	Male
═	Married Couple
—	Siblings
|	Difference of a generation

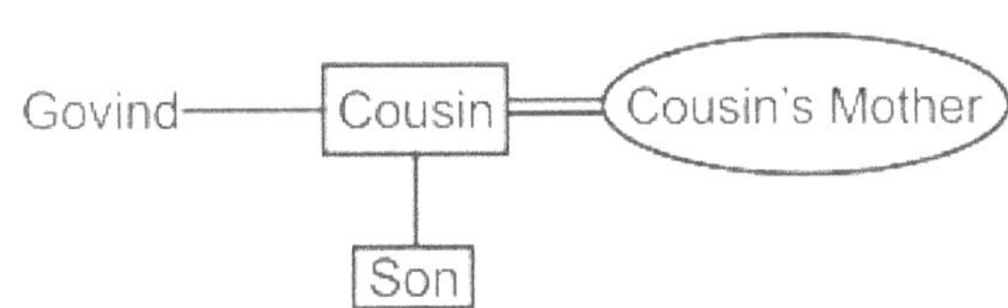

From the figure, we get to know that, the lady is the sister-in-law of Govind's wife.

So, the correct answer is sister-in-law.

Hence, the correct option is (C).

25. Given:

XY → 2425 (X → 24 and Y → 25)

Let's check the options:

(A) LM → L → 12, M → 13, LM → 1213

(B) NL → N → 14, L → 12, NL → 1412

(C) ML → M → 13, L → 12, ML → 1312

(D) LN → L → 12, N → 14, LN → 1214

Hence, the correct option is (A).

26. The positions of the letters according to the English alphabet series:

Alpha bets	A	B	C	D	E	F	G	H	I	J	K	L	M
Positi	1	2	3	4	5	6	7	8	9	1	1	1	1

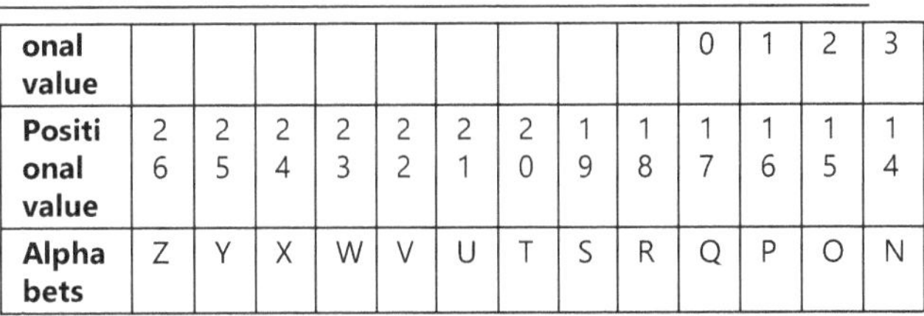

onal value										0	1	2	3
Positi onal value	2 6	2 5	2 4	2 3	2 2	2 1	2 0	1 9	1 8	1 7	1 6	1 5	1 4
Alpha bets	Z	Y	X	W	V	U	T	S	R	Q	P	O	N

The pattern followed here is:

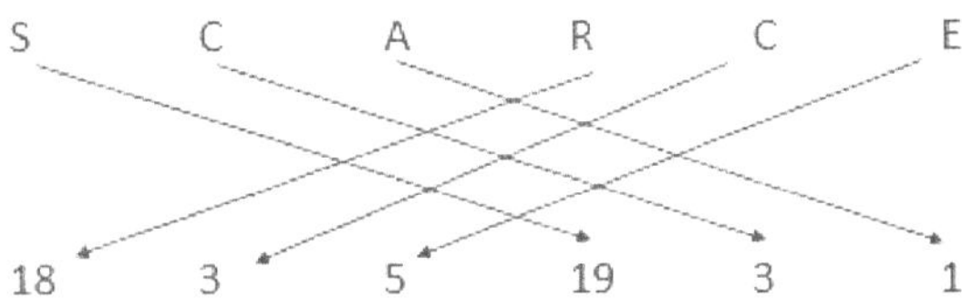

Similarly,

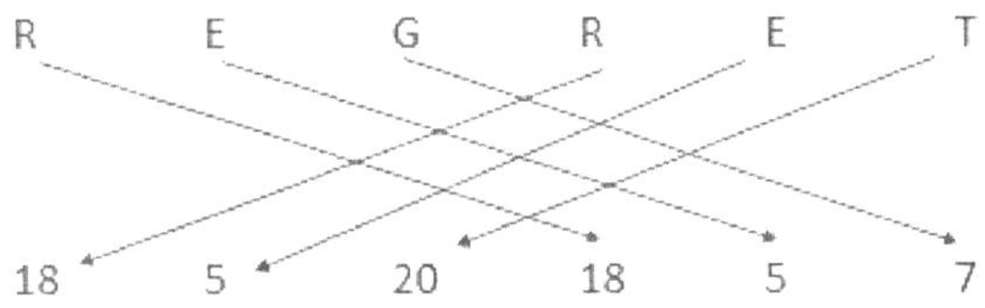

So, "185201857" is the correct answer.

Hence, the correct option is (C).

27. Preparing the family tree using the following symbols:

Symbol in Diagram	Meaning
○	Female
□	Male
═	Married Couple
—	Siblings
|	Difference of a generation

Possible tree diagram will be:

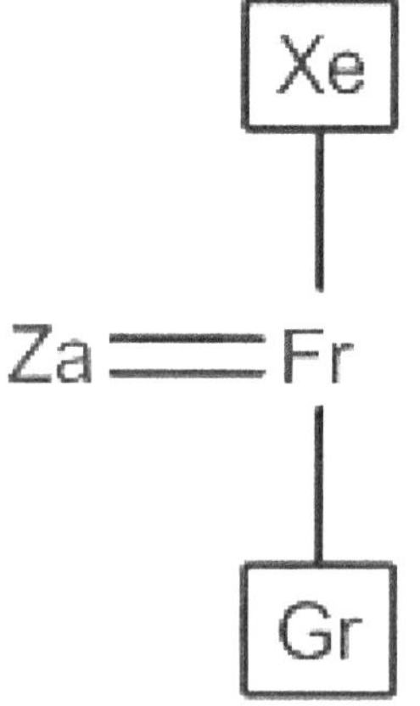

So, Fr is either mother or father of Gr.

Hence, the correct option is (C).

28. There are five friends in a class.

1) P scores more marks than R but not as much as Q.

Q > P > R

2) T scores more marks than Q.

T > Q > P > R

3) S is the highest marks scorer.

S > T > Q > P > R

Therefore, the final scores arrangement is:

S > T > Q > P > R

Therefore, from the above arrangement, it is clear that R is the lowest scorer.

So, the correct answer is R.

Hence, the correct option is (C).

29. The best method of teaching is to initiate a discussion and participate in it.

Discussion methods are a variety of forums for the open-ended, collaborative exchange of ideas among a teacher and students or among students for the purpose of furthering students thinking, learning, problem-solving, understanding, or literary appreciation.

Hence, the correct option is (D).

30. For a teacher, writing the important points as clearly as possible would be correct for writing on the blackboard.

A blackboard (also known as a chalkboard) is a reusable writing surface on which text or drawings are made with sticks of calcium sulfate or calcium carbonate, known, when used for this purpose, as chalk. Since writing the matter first, fast, just asking the students to read it is not the appropriate use of writing on the blackboard.

Hence, the correct option is (D).

31. For promoting international understanding a teacher should avoid indoctrinating the mind of the pupils.

International understanding means what we know and understanding of the people, system, and other processes of the world and learn from them. For promoting international understanding about the world a teacher should develop a proper understanding of the world. The student's understanding largely depends on the competence of the teacher, their knowledge, understanding, attitude, interest, critical thinking, and so on.

Hence, the correct option is (C).

32. Nowadays the most effective mode of learning is blended learning.

Blended learning is an approach to education that combines online educational materials and opportunities for interaction online with traditional place-based classroom methods. Blended learning (also known as hybrid learning) is a method of teaching that integrates technology and digital media with traditional instructor-led classroom activities, giving students more flexibility to customize their learning experiences.

Hence, the correct option is (D).

33. A teacher work as a role model for students. A teacher is the best source of motivation. A teacher can guide the students to the right path and can make their future brighter. Above characteristics are important for a teacher and to be a motivator is the prime role and the duty of a teacher.

Hence, the correct option is (A).

34. Quantity of Langra mangoes sold in $2017 = 180$ kg

Quantity of Alphonso mangoes sold in $2018 = 160$ kg

Quantity of Neelam mangoes sold in $2018 = 80$ kg

$\therefore$ Required percentage $= \frac{180}{(160+80)} \times 100$

$= 75\%$

Hence, the correct option is (D).

35. Total quantity of mangoes sold in May $2017 = (120 + 180 + 75 + 250 + 60) = 685$ kg

Total quantity of mangoes sold in May $2018 = (160 + 200 + 60 + 225 + 80) = 725$ kg

$\therefore$ Required difference $= (725 - 685)$ kg

$= 40$ kg

Hence, the correct option is (C).

36. Quantity of Himsagar sold in May $2017 = 250$ kg

Quantity of Himsagar sold in May $2018 = 225$ kg

$\therefore$ Percentage decrease in sales $= \frac{(250-225)}{250} \times 100$

$= 10\%$

Hence, the correct option is (D).

37. Quantity of Dasheri mango sold in May $2018 = 60$ kg

Let the total sale in the 2018 year be x.

According to the question,

$60 = 80\%$ of x

$\Rightarrow 60 = \frac{80}{100} \times x$

$\Rightarrow 60 \times \frac{100}{80} = x$

$\therefore x = 75$ kg

Total quantity of Dasheri mango sold in $2018 = 75$ kg

Quantity of Himsagar sold in May $2018 = 225$ kg

$\therefore$ Required Ratio $= 75:225$

$= 1:3$

Hence, the correct option is (B).

38. Total quantity of mangoes sold in May $2018 = (160 + 200 + 60 + 225 + 80) = 725$ kg

$\therefore$ Average quantity of mango sold in May $2018 = \frac{725}{5} = 145$ kg

$\therefore$ Average quantity of mango sold in June 2018

$= 145 + 145 \times \frac{20}{100}$

$= (145 + 29) = 174$ kg

Hence, the correct option is (A).

39. The correct order of sequence for reading skills in the context of research is survey, question, read, recall, review.

1. **Survey:** It refers to a quick glance through the chapter of the course work. For example, after receiving the study materials you tend to open the materials and give a glance to the contents. This is known as the survey.
2. **Question:** There is a purpose why you choose to read the particular content of the course material. You ask yourself certain questions regarding the content.
3. **Read:** Reading requires active participation: it is NOT just running your eyes over the contents of the book. You as a learner need to develop a critical mind so as to answer questions you have asked yourself in relation to the contents of the subject matter.
4. **Recall:** Reading a text is not the final step in learning; instead, it is the first step. Units/chapters that have been read need to be retained. Retention of what has been read will help you to improve the learning.
5. **Review:** It is a quick repeat of the other four steps: namely, Survey, question, read and recite. It is a review of what you as a learner have achieved while reading the text.

Hence, the correct option is (D).

40. In a research setting, participants may act differently because they think they are getting special attention. This reaction of treatment group to the special attention rather than the treatment itself is called as Hawthorne effect.

The Hawthorne Effect refers to the fact that people will modify their behavior simply because they are being observed.

- When individuals or groups become aware that they are being observed, they may change their behavior.
- Depending upon the situation, this change could be positive or negative – it may increase or decrease, for example, their productivity – and may occur for a number of reasons.
- When a change in the behavior of persons or groups is attributed to their being observed it is known as the Hawthorne effect.
- The use of observation in such a situation may introduce distortion: what is observed may not represent their normal behavior.

Hence, the correct option is (A).

41. An empiricist believes that knowledge is acquired through our sensory perceptions. Empiricists claim that sensing experience is the ultimate source of all our concepts and knowledge. The senses give us all our raw data about the world and without this raw material, there would be no knowledge at all. This is termed as a posterior. It is related to induction.

Hence, the correct option is (C).

42. A researcher while writing his/her thesis does not give the rationale underlying use of statistical techniques. This will be best described as a case of an error of omission. An error of omission also known as "false negative". When something is incorrectly excluded from consideration or from mentioning when it should have been included, it is an error of omission. When a researcher doesn't rationalize the use of the statistical techniques used in the research, it is a case of error of omission.

Hence, the correct option is (D).

43. The correct answer is 1, 2, 3 and 4.

Research is an investigation that comprises creative work undertaken on a systematic and logical basis to increase the stock of knowledge, culture, and society. It deals with the verification of hypothesis, data analysis, interpretation, and formation of principles, and by using this stock of knowledge (research) new applications are being devised. Research is also an intellectual inquiry towards truth.

Hence, the correct option is (D).

44. HTML (Hypertext Markup Language) is the code that is used to structure a web page and its content. For example, the content could be structured within a set of paragraphs, a list of bulleted points, or using images and data tables.

Hence, the correct option is (C).

45. Hadoop can be considered as a cloud. Whenever any intranet becomes large enough in size that a diagram is not able to differentiate the individual physical system, so at that stage intranet also becomes known as a cloud.

Hence, the correct option is (A).

46. Swami will be able to see the mail addresses which are mentioned in 'To' and 'Cc' option i.e., ram@test.com; raj@test.com; ravi@test.com.

As bcc stands for blind carbon copy and cc stands for carbon copy. So, Swami will receive all the sender's details and the persons attached in cc (carbon copy). The email ids of bcc are not visible to everyone.

Hence, the correct option is (B).

47. CDMA stands for Code Division Multiple Access.

Code-division multiple access (CDMA) is a channel access method used by various radio communication technologies. CDMA is an example of multiple access, where several transmitters can send information simultaneously over a single communication channel.

Hence, the correct option is (B).

48. 'Plagiarism cannot be prevented through the use of ICT' is the false statement.

Plagiarism is the act of copying someone else's work and publishing it as your own. This includes text, media, and even ideas. Examples of plagiarism range from small infractions such as not putting quotes around a quotation to blatant violations such as copying an entire website.

Hence, the correct option is (D).

49. CABE is the highest body to advise central and state governments on education.

The Central Advisory Board of Education, the oldest and the most important advisory body of the Government of India in education was first established in 1920 and dissolved in 1923 as a measure of the economy. It was revived in 1935 and has been in existence ever since.

The Central Advisory Board of Education or CABE is the apex advisory body responsible for advising the Central and the State Governments in the field of education.

Hence, the correct option is (B).

50. The main recommendations of 'Knowledge Commission' with regard to higher education in India are:

- Massive expansion of higher education.
- Focus on affirmative action
- Efforts to achieve excellence

Knowledge commission was also known as the "National knowledge commission", was a think-tank of policies that aimed to improve the knowledge-intensive service sectors. This commission was created on 13th June 2005 by the former Prime Minister of India, Manmohan Singh.

Hence, the correct option is (C).

Mock Test 20

Ques (1-5):Direction: Read the passage given below and answer the questions that follow by choosing the correct option.

Most of us think we know what peace is, but people often have very different definitions of this apparently simple word. And although almost everyone would agree that some form of peace—however it is defined—is desirable, there are often forceful, even violent, disagreements over how to obtain it. Frequently, there is an unstated assumption in peace discourses that peace is universal and unchanging. This premise underlies much peace talk, both Western and non-Western. But few if any peace scholars and activists provide reasons and arguments to justify this belief. And most conversations about peace prior to the past century have been among Western and East Asian men of privilege. This is gradually changing, however, as female, non-Western, and previously unempowered peace advocates and peacemakers make their voices heard.

An additional belief, especially in Occidental peace theories prior to the twentieth century, has been that peace is "the absence of war." In other words, peace has been defined "negatively," almost always in the context of inter-state political violence. This binary opposition between peace and war entails the further belief that peace and war are mutually exclusive—e.g. nations are either "at peace" or "at war"—and that there is no continuum between war and peace. It also implies that nations (at least from the 17th century on) and empires (through the end of World War I) have been the major peacemakers and belligerents.

However, since, roughly, the mid-twentieth century and the end of the Second World War, other actors, including multinational corporations, non-governmental organizations, peace and related social justice movements, spiritual and religious leaders, and groups labeled "terrorist" by states, have become important players on the global stage. Also, since 1945, intra-state conflicts and proxy wars (especially in the "developing" world) have replaced wars between great powers. Additionally, there are often significant conflict zones within nations formally "at peace" and without declared civil wars. For example, perhaps the three most powerful nation-states—the United States, Russia, and China— while officially "at peace" among themselves, are riven by internal conflicts and "terrorist" attacks, as in southern parts of Russia, some American cities, and Western parts of China. Systemic racism still lingers in the U.S.; there is a widespread lack of freedom for Christians in China and for Muslims in Russia, and all three countries have endemic and increasing inequities of income and power.

Q.1 What kind of disagreements are there about obtaining peace?

A. Negatively

B. Universal and unchanging

C. Gradually changing

D. Forceful and violent

Q.2 What entails the binary opposition between peace and war?

A. Continuum between war and peace

B. Proxy wars

C. Peace and war are mutually exclusive

D. Systematic Racism

Q.3 What is gradually changing about peace conversations?

A. They are not anymore limited to privileged men

B. Developing nations are dominating the conversations

C. Women are now primary interlocutors.

D. These conversations is only empowering the males

Q.4 Who has become important players on the global stage?

A. Multinational corporations

B. China

C. Non-governmental organizations,

D. Spiritual and religious leaders

Choose the correct answer from the options given below:

A. A, C and D **B.** A and C

C. C and D **D.** A, B and C

Q.5 What has replaced wars between great powers?

A. Inequities of income and power

B. Developing world

C. Intra-state conflicts and proxy wars

D. Peace opportunities

Ques (6-10):Direction: Study the following table to answer these question.

The number of watches of different companies sold in various shops in a year.

Shop Name	No. of watches sold		
	Titan	**Sonata**	**Fastrack**
A	750	850	680
B	920	670	960
C	1050	470	850
D	710	780	820

Q.6 What percentage of the total number of watches sold by shop A were Titan watches?

A. 29.9 **B.** 32.89 **C.** 38.15 **D.** 28.67

Q.7 The total number of watches sold by shop D is what percentage of the total number of watches sold by shop B?

A. 78.91 **B.** 81.67 **C.** 90.59 **D.** 93.48

Q.8 By what percentage is the number of Fastrack watches sold by shop C more than the number of Fastrack watches sold by shop A?

A. 15 **B.** 835 **C.** 25 **D.** 20

Q.9 In which shop the average number of watches was sold the highest?

A. A **B.** B **C.** C **D.** D

Q.10 The number of Sonata watches sold by Shop B is what percent of the total number of Sonata watches sold by all shops together?

A. 28.32 **B.** 22.69 **C.** 27.52 **D.** 24.19

Q.11 Direction: Read the statements given below and select the correct option.

Statement I: Communication is a continuous process.

Statement II: Verbal communication without non-verbal communication is the most effective for conversation between peers.

A. Both Statement I and II are true
B. Only Statement I is true
C. Only Statement II is true
D. Both Statement I and II are false

Q.12 Match Set I and Set II:

Set I	Set II
(i) Filtering	a. seeing what one wants to see.
(ii) Selective perception	b. Projecting one's own motives into other behavior.
(iii) Information overload	c. Manipulation of information by the sender to make it favorable for the receiver.
	d. exposure to or provision of too much.

Choose the correct code:

A. (i)- b, (ii)- d, (iii)- a **B.** (i)- c, (ii)- a, (iii)- d
C. (i)- c, (ii)- b, (iii)- d **D.** (i)- d, (ii)- b, (iii)- c

Q.13 Which of the following set of statements is correct for describing the human communication process?

1. Non-verbal communication can stimulate ideas.
2. Communication is a learnt ability.
3. Communication is not a universal panacea.
4. Communication cannot break-down.
5. More communication means more effective learning by students.
6. Value of what is learnt through classroom communication is not an issue for students.

Code:

A. 1, 3, 5 and 6 **B.** 2, 4, 5 and 6
C. 1, 2, 3 and 4 **D.** 1, 4, 5 and 6

Q.14 Communication will be effective if:

A. it is delivered slowly and clearly
B. it is delivered in a calm situation
C. it reaches the receiver completely
D. it reaches the receiver as intended by the sender

Q.15 In which year Education Commission under the Chairmanship of Dr. D.S. Kothari was set up?

A. 1960 **B.** 1955 **C.** 1952 **D.** 1964

Q.16 As per the latest data released by U.G.C. how many state universities are there in India?

A. 789 **B.** 123 **C.** 394 **D.** 260

Q.17 When was the University Education Commission constituted?

A. November 4, 1947 **B.** November 4, 1948
C. November 4, 1949 **D.** November 4, 1950

Q.18 Collective psychology of the whole period is a theory which -

A. Can explain all phases of historical development
B. Means the psychology of the whole society
C. Means psychological approach of the collection
D. All of the above

Q.19 Poonam told Reeta who is a girl, "Your mother's husband is my father. Poonam is a female."

Which of the following statement is not true?

A. Reeta is sister of Poonam.
B. Poonam is mother of Reeta.
C. Poonam and Reeta are siblings.
D. There is only one married couple.

Q.20 L is the mother of K and the sister of N, K is the sister of O. If P is the husband of O and N is the husband of M, then how is O related to N?

A. Cousin **B.** Niece
C. Daughter **D.** Granddaughter

Q.21 Abhishek is the father of Yogita. Ahana is the sister of Varun. Kavya is Yogita's sister and the only daughter of Ahana. How is Yogita related to Varun.

A. Niece **B.** Nephew
C. Uncle **D.** Can't be determined

Q.22 If "LAWYER" is coded as 9 and "KETTLE" is coded as 9, then how will "CALIBRI be coded?

A. 10 **B.** 11 **C.** 7 **D.** 8

Q.23 In a code language, if '568734' is coded as '20-10-32-11-12-8' then how will '312858' be coded in the same language?

A. 13-5-8-12-20-11 **B.** 15-5-8-12-30-12
C. 12-5-8-12-20-12 **D.** 12-5-9-12-20-12

Q.24 Direction: Given below are two statements (a) and (b). Four conclusions are drawn from them. Select the code that states validly drawn conclusion(s) [taking the statement individually or jointly].

Statements:

(a) All diamonds are precious stones.

(b) Some carbon compounds are diamonds.

Conclusions:

(i) All precious stones are diamonds.

(ii) Some non-carbon compounds are precious stones.

(iii) All precious stones are stones compounds.

(iv) Some carbon compounds are precious stones.

A. (i) and (iv) **B.** (ii) and (iv)
C. (iii) only **D.** (iv) only

Q.25 Which of the following statements about Choice Based Credit System (CBCS) is true?

(A) Consists of three main courses.

(B) Uses a 5 point grading system.

(C) Makes education at par with global standards.

(D) Difficult to estimate the exact marks.

(E) Introduces research component in Under-Graduate courses.

Choose the correct answer from the options given below :

A. (A), (B), (C), (D) only
B. (B), (C), (D), (E) only
C. (A), (B), (C), (E) only
D. (C), (D), (E), (A) only

Q.26 Identify the skills needed by present day teachers to make classroom teaching more efficient.

(i) Knowledge of technology

(ii) Use of technology in classroom transactions

(iii) Knowledge of students needs

(iv) Content Mastery

A. (i) and (iii) **B.** (ii) and (iii)
C. (ii), (iii), and (iv) **D.** (ii) and (iv)

Q.27 By which of the following methods the true evaluation of the students is possible?

A. Evaluation at the end of the course
B. Evaluation twice in a year
C. Continuous evaluation
D. Formative evaluation

Q.28 Which of the following are the important characteristics of an effective teacher?

(I) Knowledge of content.

(II) Effective verbal communication skills.

(III) Impressive personality.

(IV) Ability to command respect from students

A. (II) and (III) **B.** (I) and (II)
C. (III) and (IV) **D.** (I) and (IV)

Q.29 Which of the following set of statements represents acceptable propositions in respect to teaching-learning relationships? Choose the correct code to indicate your answer.

i. When students fail a test, it is the teacher who fails.

ii. Every teaching must aim at ensuring learning.

iii. There can be teaching without learning taking place.

iv. There can be no learning without teaching.

v. A teacher teaches but learns also.

vi. Real learning implies rote learning.

A. ii, iii, iv and v **B.** i, ii, iii and v
C. iii, iv, v and vi **D.** i, ii, v and vi

Q.30 Which of the following was the central aim of the Paris Agreement?

A. To reduce the CFCs emissions
B. To strengthen the global response to the threat of climate change
C. To address biological diversity issues
D. To address the problem of ozone layer depletion

Q.31 Wind energy is very sensitive to the wind velocity because wind power is directly proportional to the:

A. Wind velocity
B. square of the wind velocity
C. square root of the wind velocity
D. cube of the wind velocity

Q.32 Which of the International Agreements/Convention/Protocols are legally binding on the member countries (parties)?

(A) Convention on Biological Diversity

(B) Kyoto Protocol

(C) Montreal Protocol

(D) Paris Agreement

Choose the most appropriate answer from the options given below :

A. Only (C) **B.** (A) and (C)
C. (A), (B) and (C) **D.** (B), (C) and (D)

Q.33 Direction: Choose the correct answer from the following code:

Assertion (A): The environmental movements favor the sustainable management of natural resources.

Reason (R): They range from being local to global in nature.

A. Both (A) and (R) are true, and (R) is the correct explanation of (A)
B. Both (A) and (R) are true, and (R) is not the correct explanation of (A)
C. (A) is true, but (R) is false
D. (A) is false, but (R) is true

Q.34 Which of the sets of activities best indicate the cyclic nature of action research strategy?

[UGC NET Home Science, 2018]

A. Reflect, Observe, Plan, Act
B. Observe, Act, Reflect, Plan
C. Act, Plan, Observe, Reflect
D. Plan, Act, Observe, Reflect

Q.35 In the two sets given below, Set I provide levels of teaching while Set II gives their focus of concern:

Set I (Levels of Teaching)	Set II (Focus of concern)
(a) Autonomous development level	(i) Problems raising and problem solving
(b) Memory level	(ii)Affects and feelings
(c) Understanding level	(iii) Recall of facts and information
(d) Reflective level	(iv) Seeing of relationship among facts and their examples
	(v) Peer learning

Select correct answer from the options given below:

A. (a)-(i), (b)-(ii), (c)-(iv), (d)-(v)
B. (a)-(i), (b)-(iv), (c)-(iii), (d)-(ii)
C. (a)-(ii), (b)-(iii), (c)-(iv), (d)-(i)

D. (a)-(v), (b)-(iv), (c)-(iii), (d)-(ii)

Q.36 The principal of a school conducts an interview session of teachers and students with a view to explore the possibility of their enhanced participation in school programs. This endeavor may be related to which type of research?

A. Evaluation Research
B. Fundamental Research
C. Action Research
D. Applied Research

Q.37 The issue of 'Research ethics' may be considered pertinent at which stage of research?

A. At the stage of problem formulation and its definition
B. At the stage of defining the population of research
C. At the stage of data collection and interpretation
D. At the stage of reporting the findings

Q.38 What are the characteristics of Continuous and Comprehensive Evaluation ?

(a) It increases the workload on students by taking multiple tests.

(b) It replaces marks with grades.

(c) It evaluates every aspect of the student.

(d) It helps in reducing examination phobia.

Select the correct answer from the codes given below :

A. a, b and d **B.** b, c and d
C. a, c and d **D.** b, c and a

Q.39 Which of the following statements(s) is/are true in respect of wireless technology?

P: Bluetooth is a wireless technology that can be used to connect a headset to a mobile phone.

Q: Bluetooth is a long-range wireless technology and is a low-cost means of data transfer.

A. P only **B.** Q only
C. Both P and Q **D.** Neither P nor Q

Q.40 Read the following two statements:

I: Information and Communication Technology (ICT) is considered a subset of Information Technology (IT).

II: The 'right to use' a piece of software is termed as copyright.

Which of the above statement(s) is/are correct?

A. Both I and II **B.** Neither I nor II
C. II only **D.** I only

Q.41 The Internet Protocol generally correspond to the ___ OSI layer?

A. Network Layer **B.** Transport Layer
C. Data Link Layer **D.** Session Layer

Q.42 Which of the following shows an error in a computer program?

A. Bit **B.** Bug **C.** Spam **D.** Virus

Q.43 The output quality of a printer is measured by:

A. Digits per inch **B.** Dots per mm
C. Dots per inch **D.** Dots per cm

Q.44 Which of the following statement best describes the role of a teacher in ancient higher education system:

a. The number of students admitted to a course was not limited.

b. Teachers had complete autonomy in all aspects.

c. Lecturing was the primary method of teaching.

A. a and b only **B.** a, b, and c only
C. a and c only **D.** b and c only

Q.45 Direction: Identify the diagram which best represents the relationship among the classes given below.

Mobile, Pencil, Electronics

A.

B.

C.

D.

Q.46 Direction: On the basis of the given figure, answer the question given below:

Which letter represents the set of persons who play all three games?

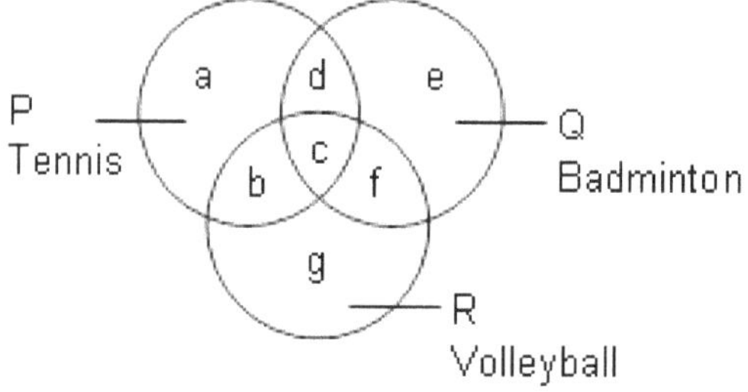

A. b **B.** c **C.** f **D.** g

Q.47 Direction: Given are statement I and Statement II. Find the correct answer from the statements.

Statement I: The Aristotalain syllogism is deductive and formal while the Nyaya is deductive-inductive and formal-material.

Statement II: There are five propositions in Nyaya syllogism and only three of them accepted in Aristotalian syllogism.

A. Both Statement I and Statement II are correct

B. Both Statement I and Statement II are false

C. Statement I is true but Statement II is false

D. Statement I is false but Statement II is true

Q.48 A deductive argument is considered invalid when:

A. Its premises are true and conclusion is to be false

B. Its premises are true and conclusion is to be true

C. The conclusion is satisfactory to the premises

D. Premises are true but conclusion is still unknown

Q.49 For which purpose circular type of communication is most suitable?

A. Member dissatisfaction

B. Effective judgement process

C. Member satisfaction

D. Effective transmission of information

Q.50 Environmental studies aims at developing:

A. Understanding local environment/environmental issues

B. Understanding global environment/environmental issues

C. To develop positive attitude towards environment

D. All of the above

// Smart Answer Sheet //

Correct Indicates percentage of students who answered questions correctly.

Skipped Indicates percentage of students who skipped questions.

Q.	Ans.	Correct	Skipped
1	D	42.64 %	1.07 %
2	C	46.23 %	1.84 %
3	A	50.84 %	1.44 %
4	A	51.59 %	1.76 %
5	C	51.77 %	1.05 %
6	B	48.81 %	1.8 %
7	C	61.94 %	1.06 %
8	C	55.85 %	1.52 %
9	B	62.89 %	1.55 %
10	D	44.63 %	1.95 %
11	B	40.01 %	1.02 %
12	B	23.87 %	4.08 %
13	C	68.13 %	1.25 %
14	D	52.05 %	1.47 %
15	D	88.39 %	0.0 %
16	C	89.12 %	0.0 %
17	B	60.6 %	1.49 %
18	A	42.37 %	1.68 %
19	B	50.18 %	1.9 %
20	B	40.08 %	1.21 %
21	B	67.56 %	1.57 %
22	A	44.27 %	1.71 %
23	C	32.7 %	4.84 %
24	D	46.6 %	1.32 %
25	D	25.95 %	4.53 %
26	C	48.34 %	1.67 %
27	C	61.08 %	1.6 %
28	B	87.55 %	0.0 %
29	B	50.65 %	1.12 %
30	B	65.72 %	1.59 %
31	D	43.43 %	1.25 %
32	B	18.93 %	4.65 %
33	B	12.31 %	4.99 %
34	D	64.31 %	1.03 %
35	C	29.98 %	3.89 %
36	C	65.76 %	1.64 %
37	D	30.73 %	3.14 %
38	D	54.61 %	1.01 %
39	A	69.21 %	1.67 %
40	B	58.83 %	1.7 %
41	A	81.08 %	0.0 %
42	B	87.25 %	0.0 %
43	C	76.42 %	0.0 %
44	A	58.0 %	1.08 %
45	C	53.31 %	1.25 %
46	B	45.85 %	1.65 %
47	A	59.55 %	1.54 %
48	A	48.5 %	1.89 %
49	C	56.71 %	1.51 %
50	D	63.25 %	1.56 %

Performance Analysis	
Avg. Score (%)	57.0%
Toppers Score (%)	73.0%
Your Score	

//Hints and Solutions//

1. The 2nd line of the first paragraph mentions, 'And although almost everyone would agree that some form of peace—however, it is defined—is desirable, there are often forceful, even violent, disagreements over how to obtain it.'

The above-given statements say that people agree that peace is desirable but how it should be obtained is ironically full of conflict.

People disagree over the means of obtaining peace so much so that those disagreements turn forceful or even violent.

Therefore it's clear from the above-given points that disagreements about obtaining peace can be forceful and violent.

Hence, the correct option is (D).

2. Let's look at the meaning of some difficult words from the question:

Entails means to involve something as a necessary consequence

Binary means something that is composed of only two things.

So, the question means what becomes the necessary consequence when we perceive war and peace as two extreme ends?

We can find the mention of war and peace as the binary opposition in 3rd line of the second paragraph, 'This binary opposition between peace and war entails the further belief that peace and war are mutually exclusive'.

The author wants to convey that peace and war are and never were mutually exclusive. they have always existed in a continuum.

Thus if we perceive peace and war as binary opposition then it will mean that 'Peace and War are mutually exclusive.'

Hence, the correct option is (C).

3. In the first paragraph of the passage, the author is trying to tell us that the earlier understanding of peace is not correct anymore since a lot has changed in the world.

He remarks that the peace conversation was earlier limited to the privileged men of West and East

The final lines of the first paragraph talk about how it's changing, 'This is gradually changing, however, as female, non-Western, and previously unempowered peace advocates and peacemakers make their voices heard.'

Now other social groups such as women, non-western as well as newly empowered peace advocates are also participating in the conversations of peace.

Thus, the peace conversations are changing because these are not limited to privileged men anymore.

Hence, the correct option is (A).

4. The passage focuses on refuting the previous beliefs about peace and how it has changed over time due to multiple social and political events.

This change is also seen in the players or the parties who effects the peace conditions globally.

The beginning of the third passage states, 'However, since, roughly, the mid-twentieth century and the end of the Second World War, other actors, including multinational corporations, non-governmental organizations, peace and related social justice movements, spiritual and religious leaders, and groups labeled "terrorist" by states, have become important players on the global stage.'

Thus, we can see from the above-given statements that there are multiple entries on the global stage which include multinational corporations, non-governmental organizations, and spiritual and religious leaders.

Hence, the correct option is (A).

5. Let's look at the mentioned line of the last passage states, 'Also, since 1945, intra-state conflicts and proxy wars (especially in the "developing" world) have replaced wars between great powers.

Let's look at the meaning of some difficult words from the above statement:

Intra means on the inside or within

Proxy means a substitute

The author wants to point out that wars have been replaced by other types of conflicts such as intrastate conflict which means conflict inside the state and proxy wars which means war between two states which is instigated by other dominant states which do not want to get involved.

Therefore, wars still take place but great powers have resorted to conducting them through intrastate conflict and proxy wars.

Hence, the correct option is (C).

6. From the table,

Total watches sold in shop A $= 750 + 850 + 680 = 2280$

Titan watches sold in shop A $= 750$

Required percentage $= \frac{750}{2280} \times 100 = 32.89\%$

$\therefore 32.89\%$ of total numbers of watches sold by shop A were Titan watches.

Hence, the correct option is (B).

7. From the table,

No. of watches sold				
Shop Name	**Titan**	**Sonata**	**Fastrack**	**Total number of watches sold**
B	920	670	960	920+670+960=2550
D	710	780	820	710+780+820=2310

Required percentage $= \frac{2310}{2550} \times 100\% = 90.588\% \approx 90.59\%$

∴ The total number of watches sold by shop D is 90.59% of total number of watches sold by shop D.

Hence, the correct option is (C).

8. From the table,

The number of Fastrack watches sold by shop $A = 680$

The number of Fastrack watches sold by shop $C = 850$

The increase in the sale of Fastrack watches

$= 850 - 680 = 170$

Required percentage $= \frac{170}{680} \times 100\% = 25$

∴ Number of Fastrack watches sold by shop C is more than the number of Fastrack watches sold by shop A by 25%.

Hence, the correct option is (C).

9. From the table,

No. of watches sold					
Shop Name	**Titan**	**Sonata**	**Fastrack**	**Total number of watches sold**	**The average number of watches sold**
A	750	850	680	750+850+680=2280	$\frac{2280}{3} = 760$
B	920	670	960	920+670+960=2550	$\frac{2550}{3} = 850$
C	1050	470	850	1050+470+850=2370	$\frac{2370}{3} = 790$
D	710	780	820	710+780+820=2310	$\frac{2310}{3} = 770$

∴ The average number of watches sold in shop B was the highest.

Hence, the correct option is (B).

10. From the table,

Total number of Sonata watches sold by all shops together $= 850 + 670 + 470 + 780 = 2770$

The number of Sonata watches sold by shop $B = 670$

Required percentage $= \frac{670}{2770} \times 100\% = 24.187\% \approx 24.19\%$

∴ The number of Sonata watches sold by Shop B is 24.19% of the total number of Sonata watches sold by all shops together.

Hence, the correct option is (D).

11. Communication tends to be an on-going process. It comprises both verbal as well as non-verbal communication. It is believed that verbal communication without the use of non-verbal communication tends to be less effective whether it is a conversation between peers, teachers, learners etc.

Thus, Only Statement I is true.

Hence, the correct option is (B).

12. Filtering refers to a sender manipulating information so, it will be seen more favorably by the receiver.

Selective perception means seeing what one wants to see. The receiver, in the communication process, generally resorts to selective perception i.e., he selectively perceives the message based on the organizational requirements, the needs and characteristics, background of the employees, etc.

Information overload is exposure to or provision of too much information or data. information overload is usually caused by the existence of multiple sources of information, over-abundance of information, difficulty in managing information.

Hence, the correct option is (B).

13. Human communication is the process of creating meaning between two or more people. Following are the statement that describes the human communication process:

Nonverbal communication: It is the transmission of messages or signals through a nonverbal platform such as eye contact, facial expressions, gestures, posture, and the distance between two individuals. In other words, it is a way of sending an idea from one person to another without the use of words.

More communication means more effective learning by students. To be precise, effective communication benefits both students and teachers. Effective communication makes learning easier, helps students achieve goals, increases opportunities for expanded learning strengthens the connection between student and teacher, and creates an overall positive experience.

Communication is not a universal panacea: Interpersonal communication is essential in establishing and sustaining relationships. it is always not to cure every problem or situation in our lives.

The value of what is learned through classroom communication is not crucial for the overall personality development of students.

Hence, the correct option is (C).

14. Communication is defined as the process of passing information and understanding from one person to another. In other words, Communication is simply the act of transferring information from one place, person, or group to another. Effective communication is the process of sending a message in such a way that the message received is as close in meaning as possible to the message intended.

Hence, the correct option is (D).

15. In 1964, an education commission was set up under the Chairmanship of Dr. DS. Kothari. This commission laid down the principles and guidelines for the development of education from the primary to a higher level.

Hence, the correct option is (D).

16. As per the latest data released by UGC, there are 892 universities comprising 394 state universities, 125 deemed universities, and 325 private universities. These Universities are competent to award degrees as specified by UGC under Section 22 of the UGC Act with the approval of the statutory councils, wherever required through their main campus. Wherever the approval of the statutory council is not a pre-requisite to start a programme, the Universities are required to maintain the minimum standards regarding academic and physical infrastructure as laid down by the concerned statutory council.

Hence, the correct option is (C).

17. University Education Commission was constituted on November 4, 1948, under the chairmanship of Dr. Sarvapali Radhakrishnan. The commission was inaugurated by Abdul Kalam Azad on Dec 6, 1948. The Commission studied the problems of University education in India and submitted its report in August 1949. The Commission gave important recommendations with regard to the aims and objectives of higher education. The main aim was to discover new knowledge for the welfare of the countrymen and to utilise that knowledge for vocational, scientific and industrial development.

Hence, the correct option is (B).

18. Collective psychology of the entire period is a theory that can explain all stages of historical development. According to Fisher - "Social psychology can be defined by defining how a person's behavior is influenced by others present in the social environment, which in turn also affects that person's behavior."

Hence, the correct option is (A).

19. From the given information,

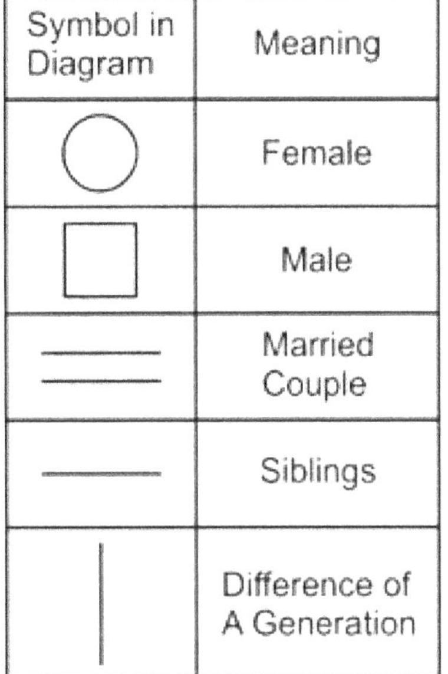

Symbol in Diagram	Meaning
○	Female
□	Male
═	Married Couple
—	Siblings
|	Difference of A Generation

Based on given data, we can draw family tree-

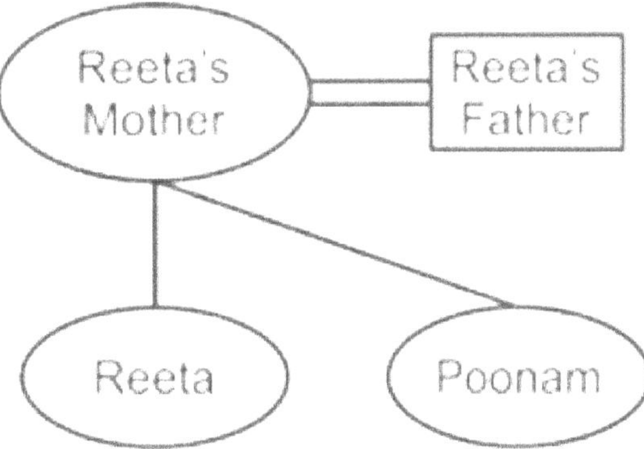

On checking each option:

1. Reeta is sister of Poonam → True
2. Poonam is mother of Reeta → False (as they are daughters of same mother and are siblings)
3. Poonam and Reeta are sibling's → True
4. There is only one married couple → True

Hence, the correct option is (B).

20. Family chart,

Symbol in Diagram	Meaning
	Female
	Male
	Married Couple
	Siblings
	Difference of A Generation

Drawing the family tree to the given information:

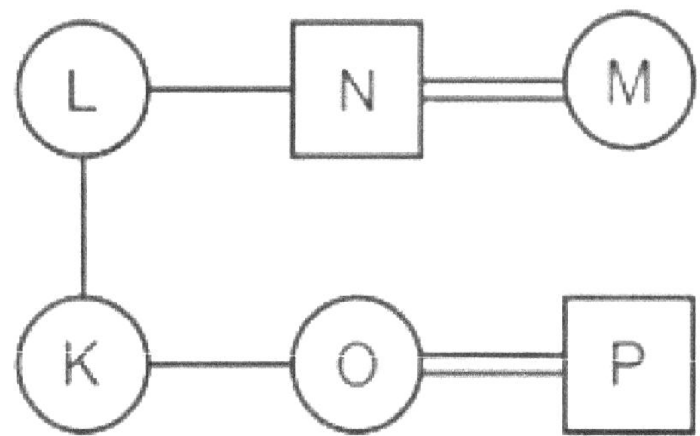

From the family tree,

O is the daughter of L and L is the sister of the N.

So, O is the niece of N.

Hence, the correct option is (B).

21.

Symbol in Diagram	Meaning
	Female
	Male
	Married Couple
	Siblings
	Difference of A Generation

(1) Abhishek is the father of Yogita.

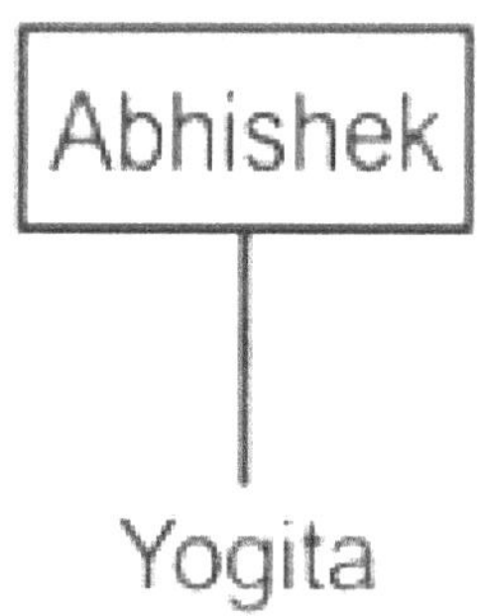

(2) Ahana is the sister of Varun.

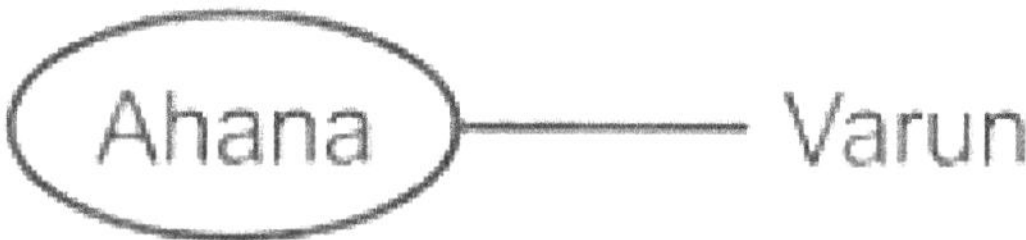

(3) Kavya is Yogita's sister and the only daughter of Ahana implies that Ahana is married to Abhishek and Yogita is a male.

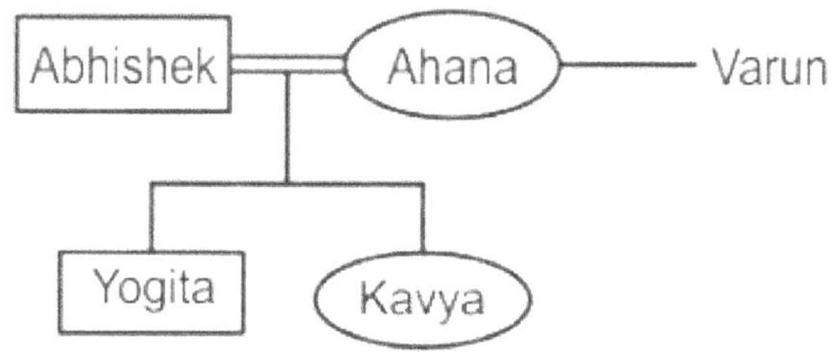

So, Yogita is the nephew of Varun.

Hence, the correct option is (B).

22.

Alph									I	J			

abets	A	B	C	D	E	F	G	H			K	L	M
Positional Value	1	2	3	4	5	6	7	8	9	10	11	12	13
Alphabets	N	O	P	Q	R	S	T	U	V	W	X	Y	Z
Positional Value	14	15	16	17	18	19	20	21	22	23	24	25	26

As, LAWYER → Number of letters + 3 → 6 + 3 = 9
KETTLE → Number of letters + 3 → 6 + 3 = 9
Therefore, CALIBRI → Number of letters + 3 → 7 + 3 = 10
Hence, the correct option is (A).

23. The logic is:

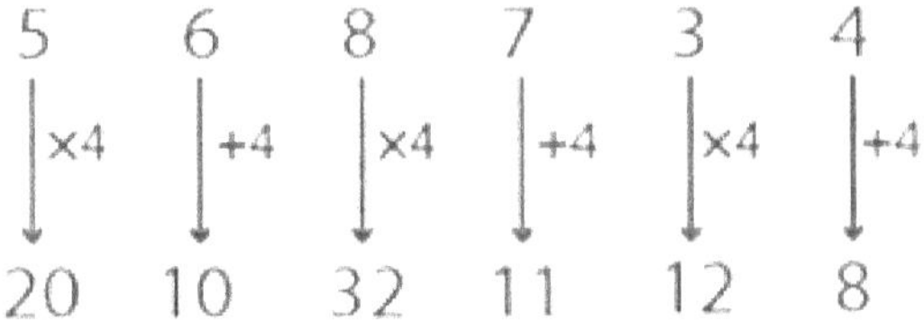

Similarly,

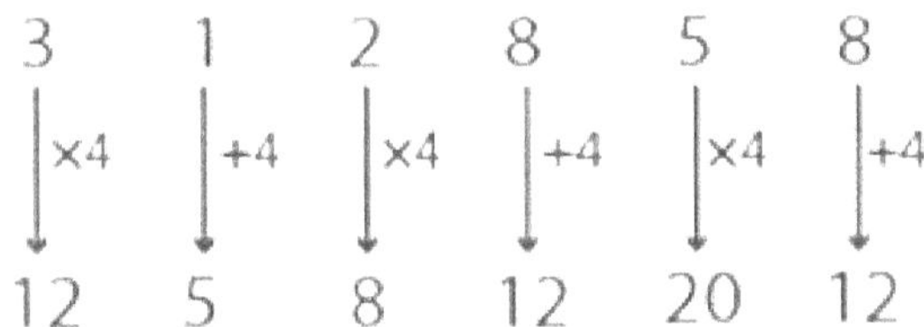

So, "12-5-8-12-20-12" is the correct answer.

Hence, the correct option is (C).

24. Minimum Possible Venn Diagram:

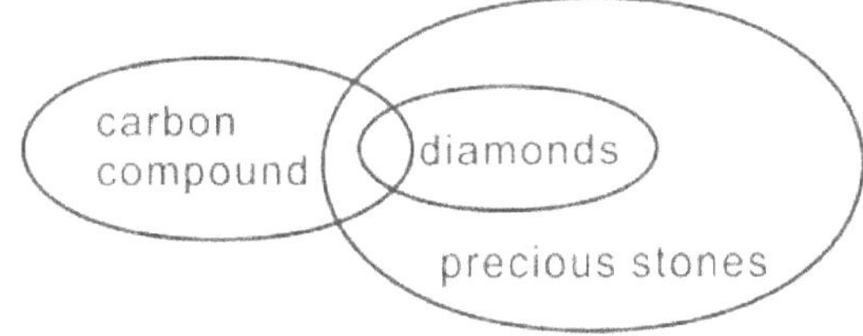

Conclusions:

(i) All precious stones are diamonds. → False (It is possible but not definite)

(ii) Some non-carbon compounds are precious stones. → False (As nothing is given about non Carbon compound)

(iii) All precious stones are stones compounds. → False (As nothing is given about stones compound)

(iv) Some carbon compounds are precious stones. → True

So, "Only iv" is the correct answer.

Hence, the correct option is (D).

25. Choice Based Credit System (CBCS):

- The Choice Based Credit System (CBCS) is a concept proposed by the University Grants Commission of India (UGC).
- It gives students an effective learning platform by moving from the conventional marks and percentage-grading system to the standard credit-based assessment method.
- The Choice Based Credit System (CBCS) provides a choice for students to select from the prescribed three main courses (core, elective and ability enhancement courses).
- The CBCS system allows and encourages students in higher education to pick a course of their own choice.
- The introduction of the systems opens the door to smart and integrated classroom learning opportunities whilst preserving the aims and objectives of education.
- It adopts a 10 point grading system.
- It has introduced a research component in Under-Graduate courses.

Hence, the correct option is (D).

26. Role of teacher in the 21st century: It is clear that the 21st-century classroom needs are very different from the 20th-century ones.

In the 21st century classroom, teachers are facilitators of student learning and creators of productive classroom environments, in which students can develop the skills they might need at present or in the future.

Hence, the correct option is (C).

27. Continuous evaluation are the methods the true evaluation of the students is possible.

Evaluation: It is a systematic process through which one can determine the extent of the achievement of the instructional objective. It is a comprehensive process and continuous in nature. Based on the phase of evaluation, it could be classified into,

- Continuous evaluation
- Formative evaluation
- Diagnostic evaluation
- Summative evaluation

All of the above evaluations had conducted at a specific phase of the instruction after its specific goal.

Hence, the correct option is (C).

28. Knowledge of content and Effective verbal communication skills are the important characteristics of an effective teacher.

Effective teaching can be defined in many ways including teacher behavior (warmth, civility, clarity), teacher knowledge (of subject matter, of students), teacher beliefs, and so forth. Here we define effective teaching as the ability to improve student achievement as shown by research.

Recent studies confirm the importance of organization and clarity. The organization is reflected in arranging concepts and content to be taught in a systematic and orderly fashion to enable students to understand it better.

Hence, the correct option is (B).

29. Teaching is a series of principles and methods through which a teacher tries to bring modification in student's behaviour. so, according to the question, various are the efforts of a teacher:

i. When students fail in a test it is the teacher who fails means it is the failure of a teacher's effort if he is unable to bring the improvement in students learning.

ii. Every teaching must ensure that learning means the aim and objective of teaching is to modify the student's behaviour and ensures learning.

iii. There can be teaching without learning taking place states that if teacher put all his/her efforts in the teaching process even if a student doesn't want to learn then no teaching can make him learn but teaching is in the process.

v. During the process of teaching and learning, it is not the students who are learning but it is the teacher also who learns a number of things like handling different types of student's behaviour, discovering new ways for making teaching more effective, etc.

Hence, the correct option is (B).

30. To strengthen the global response to the threat of climate change was the central aim of the Paris Agreement.

Aims of the Paris Agreement:

- Limit global warming to well below 2, preferably to 1.5 degrees Celsius, compared to pre-industrial levels.
- Reach global peaking of greenhouse gas emissions as soon as possible to achieve a climate-neutral world by mid-century.

Hence, the correct option is (B).

31. Wind energy is very sensitive to the wind velocity because wind power is directly proportional to the cube of the wind velocity.

Wind velocity is affected by the trees, buildings, hills and valleys around us. Wind is a diffuse energy source that cannot be contained or stored for use elsewhere or at another time.

Hence, the correct option is (D).

32. Convention on Biological Diversity and Montreal Protocol are the International Agreements/Convention/Protocols are legally binding on the member countries (parties).

A convention becomes legally binding to a particular State when that State ratifies it. Signing does not make a convention binding, but it indicates support for the principles of the convention and the country's intention to ratify it.

Hence, the correct option is (B).

33. The environmental movement has sought to protect the natural world through a number of initiatives, including reducing pollution, conserving natural resources, preventing endangered species from becoming extinct, and shielding natural areas from destruction or overdevelopment.

Both the statements are true but both the statements are unrelated.

Therefore, (R) is not the correct explanation of (A).

Hence, the correct option is (B).

34. Planning stage, Acting stage, Developing and observing an action plan, Communicating and reflection are sets of activities best indicate the cyclic nature of action research strategy.

Hence, the correct option is (D).

35. Autonomous development level concerns regulating behaviour through the self, it is enhanced by a person's capacity to reflect and evaluate his or her own actions.
At the Memory level, the teacher focuses on memorization of facts and information by learners, there is no attention on an understanding of information, procedures, and concepts.
In the understanding level, the learners are required to comprehend factual information, to know the meaning of different concepts and their relationship and to apply facts, concepts and principles.
The reflective level involves the use of a problem-centric approach.
Hence, the correct option is (C).

36. Action research is most appropriate because the Principal wants to 'improve' the participation of teachers and students. Action research is a systematic process of solving educational problems and making improvements.
Hence, the correct option is (C).

37. The issue of research ethics may be considered pertinent at the stage of reporting the findings.

Research ethics exercise control over the level of conduct for scientific researchers. They carry the values needed for collaborative work like mutual recognition and fairness.

Hence, the correct option is (D).

38. The characteristics of Continuous and Comprehensive Evaluation are:

It increases the workload on students by taking multiple tests. It replaces marks with grades. It evaluates every aspect of the student. Although it looks like 'It increases the workload on students by taking multiple tests' it actually benefits them by continuous monitoring.

Hence, the correct option is (D).

39. Bluetooth is a protocol for wireless communication over short distances. It was developed in the 1990s, to reduce the number of cables. Devices such as mobile phones, laptops, PCs, printers, digital cameras, and video game consoles can connect to each other, and exchange information. This is done using radio waves. It can be done securely. Bluetooth is only used for relatively short distances, like a few meters.

Hence, the correct option is (A).

40. Information and Communication Technology is not considered as a subset of Information Technology.

The 'right to use' a piece of software is not termed as copyright.

So, both the statements are not correct.

Hence, the correct option is (B).

41. The Internet Protocol generally corresponds to the Network Layer of the OSI layer.

The network layer is a portion of online communications that allows for the connection and transfer of data packets between different devices or networks.

Hence, the correct option is (A).

42. A software bug is an error, flaw or fault in a computer program or system that causes it to produce an incorrect or unexpected result, or to behave in unintended ways. Bugs can trigger errors that may have ripple effects. Bugs may have subtle effects or cause the program to crash or freeze the computer.

Hence, the correct option is (B).

43. The output quality of a printer is measured by DPI. DPI stands for Dots per inch, in which the quality of the printer is being measured. DPI, or dots per inch, is a measure of the resolution of a printed document or digital scan. The higher the dot density, the higher the resolution of the print or scan. Typically, DPI is the measure of the number of dots that can be placed in a line across one inch or 2.54 centimeters.

Hence, the correct option is (C).

44. In ancient India, both formal and informal ways of education system existed. Indigenous education was imparted at home, in temples, pathshalas, tols, chatuspadis and gurukuls.

Higher education in ancient India:

- In ancient India, students went to viharas and universities for higher knowledge.
- Teaching was largely oral and students remembered and meditated upon what was taught in the class.
- Gurukuls, also known as ashrams, were the residential places of learning. Many of these were named after the sages.
- During that period, the gurus and their shishyas lived together helping each other in day-to-day life.
- The main objective was to have complete learning, leading a disciplined life and realizing one's inner potential.
- Students lived away from their homes for years together till they achieved their goals.
- While pursuing their education in different disciplines like history, art of debate, law, medicine, etc., the emphasis was not only on the outer dimensions of the discipline but also on enriching inner dimensions of the personality.

Role of teacher in ancient education system:

- Teachers had complete autonomy in all aspects from selection of students to designing their syllabi.
- When the teacher was satisfied with the performance of the students, the course concluded.
- He would admit as many students as he liked and taught what his students were keen to learn.
- Debate and discussions were the primary methods of teaching.
- Teachers were assisted by their advanced level students.

Thus, the statement 'the number of students admitted to a course was not limited' and 'teachers had complete autonomy in all aspects' best describes the role of a teacher in ancient higher education system.

Hence, the correct option is (A).

45. Mobile is an electronic device. The pencil is not related to mobile or Electronics.

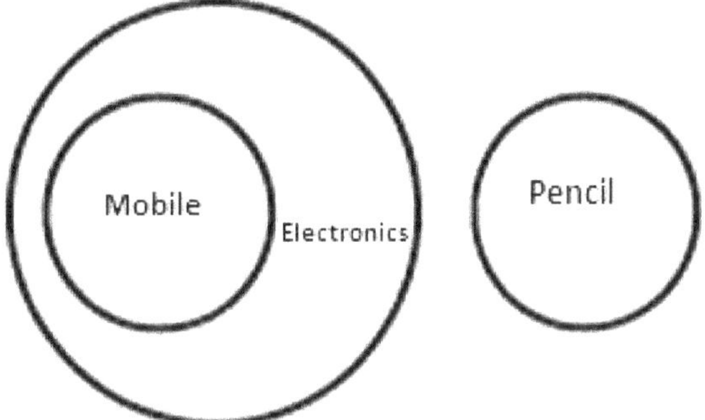

Hence, the correct option is (C).

46. It is clear from the diagram that the letter 'c' represents the set of persons who play all three games.

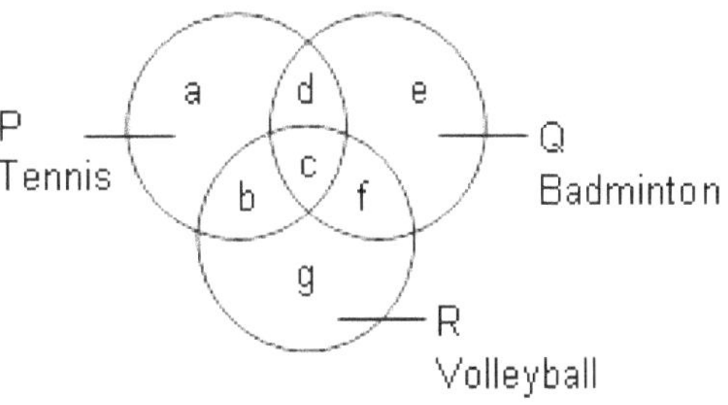

Hence, the correct option is (B).

47. Aristotle defines syllogism as "a discourse in which certain (specific) things having been supposed, something different from the things supposed results of necessity because these things is so."

Following are the features of Aristotelian syllogism:

The Aristotelian syllogism is only deductive and formal.

The Aristotelian syllogism is verbalistic.

In the Aristotelian syllogism, the major and the minor terms stand apart in the premises though they are connected by the middle term with each other.

The Aristotelian syllogism, the Indian inference has three terms:

- minor term: paksa
- middle term: linga/ hetu
- major term: sadhya

Nyaya Syllogism:

The Nyaya syllogism is deductive-inductive and formal-material.

The Nyaya syllogism recognizes the fact that verbal form is not the essence of inference and is required only to convince others.

These five propositions of the Indian syllogism are called 'members' or avayavas. the following is a typical nyaya syllogism:

- this hill has fire (pratijna).
- because it has smoke (hetu).
- whatever has smoke has fire, e.g., an oven (udaharaNa).
- this hill has smoke which is invariably associated with fire (upanaya).
- therefore this hill has fire (nigamana).

Thus, both statements are true.

Hence, the correct option is (A).

48. A deductive argument is considered invalid when its premises are true and conclusion is to be false.

Deductive arguments:

- A deductive argument asserts that the truth of the conclusion is a logical consequence of the premises.
- Based on the premises, the conclusion follows necessarily (with certainty).
- Deductive arguments are sometimes referred to as "truth-preserving" arguments.
- For example, All flowers are fragrant. Rose is a flower. So, rose is fragrant.

Validity of Deductive Arguments:

- Deductive arguments may be either valid or invalid.
- If an argument is valid, it is a valid deduction, and if its premises are true, the conclusion must be true
- A valid argument cannot have true premises and a false conclusion.
- A deductive argument, if valid, has a conclusion that is entailed by its premises.
- The truth of the conclusion is a logical consequence of the premises
- If the premises are true, the conclusion must be true.
- It would be self-contradictory to assert the premises and deny the conclusion, because negation of the conclusion is contradictory to the truth of the premises.
- A deductive argument is considered invalid when its premises are true and conclusion is to be false.

Hence, the correct option is (A).

49. 'Member satisfaction' purpose circular type of communication is most suitable.

Circular Communication:

- It is the communication that takes place in the circle.
- It is not a straight way of communication.
- It builds a network of relationships and a sense of community.
- It intersects with the uniqueness of each individual, coaching, guiding, and mentoring.
- Its main purpose is to transfer information effectively.
- It is proposed by Osgood and Schramm.

Hence, the correct option is (C).

50. Environmental studies aims at developing Understanding local environment/environmental issues, Understanding global environment/environmental issues and To develop positive attitude towards environment.

Environmental studies aim at the following:

- Creating awareness about the environment as a whole as well as its related problems.
- Gaining experiences and acquiring a basic understanding of the environment and its allied problems.
- Skill acquisition for identifying and solving environmental problems.
- Protection of the environment through participation.
- Acquiring an attitude of concern towards the environment and solving its problems.
- Developing an ability to evaluate and analyze measures to protect the environment.
- Raise consciousness about the environment.
- Creating environmental ethics and environmentally sensitive society.
- Teaching environmentally appropriate behaviour.

Hence, the correct option is (D).

// Notes //

// Notes //

www.ingramcontent.com/pod-product-compliance
Ingram Content Group UK Ltd.
Pitfield, Milton Keynes, MK11 3LW, UK
UKHW061703190726
13853UKWH00008B/2374